THE WAR ON LEBANON

A READER

Edited by Nubar Hovsepian
Foreword by Rashid Khalidi

OLIVE
BRANCH
PRESS

An imprint of Interlink Publishing Group, Inc.
www.interlinkbooks.com

First published in 2008 by

OLIVE BRANCH PRESS
An imprint of Interlink Publishing Group, Inc.
46 Crosby Street, Northampton, Massachusetts 01060
www.interlinkbooks.com

Copyright © Nubar Hovsepian, 2008
Foreword copyright © Rashid Khalidi, 2008

Library of Congress Cataloging-in-Publication Data
The war on Lebanon : a reader / edited by Nubar Hovsepian ; foreword by Rashid Khalidi.
p. cm.
Includes bibliographical references and index.
ISBN 978-1-56656-680-3 (pbk.)
1. Lebanon War, 2006. I. Hovsepian, Nubar.
DS87.65.W37 2007
956.9204'4—dc22   2007006827

Cover image © AP Photos/Oded Balilty
Printed and bound in the United States of America

Some essays in this volume were previously published or derive from previously published works. All are reprinted with the permission of the authors, translators, and, where relevant, the original publishers, as follows:
George Corm's essay, "A Cedar Ready to Fall," was originally from *Le Monde Diplomatique*, April 2005 www.mondediplo.com. It is translated by Harry Forster. "Hizballah & its Civilian Constituencies in Lebanon," by Lara Deeb, includes some material originally published in "Hizballah: A Primer," *Middle East Report* online, available at www.merip.org, and in "Deconstructing a 'Hizballah Stronghold,'" *MIT Electronic Journal of Middle East Studies* 6 (Summer 2006). "A Letter to Our Comrades in the Democratic Left Movement," by Elias Khoury and Ziad Majed, was published in the Lebanese press on Sunday, 30 July 2006. The letter was translated by Iraqi poet and writer Sinan Antoon and published in the *Middle East Report* (Fall 2006). "Meditations upon Destruction," by Elias Khoury was originally published in Arabic, in the London paper *Al-Quds al-Arabi* 19 September 2006. It is translated by Michael Scott. "You are Terrorists, We are Virtuous," by Yitzhak Laor, was originally published in the *London Review of Books* 28.16 (17 August 2006). "Travels in Israel," by Gabriel Piterberg, was originally published in the *London Review of Books* 28.18 (21 September 2006). "The Culture of Annihilation," by Azmi Bishara, was originally published in *Al-Ahram Weekly* 806 (3–9 August 2006). "Illusions of Unilateralism Dispelled in Israel," by Yoav Peled, was originally published in the *Middle East Report* online (11 October 2006). Parts of Sara Roy's "Jewish Plea," though slightly rewritten here, first appeared in the preface to her *Failing Peace: Gaza and the Palestinian-Israeli Conflict* (London: Pluto Press, 2007) xi–xxiii. "Lebanon on the Brink" includes translations of two columns by Fawwaz Traboulsi, originally published in *Al-Safir*, on 24 November and 7 December of 2006. "Peace or Perpetual War," by Azmi Bishara, was originally titled "Precarious Clarity" and published in *Al-Ahram Weekly* online 28 September–4 October 2006. An earlier version of Fred Halliday's essay "All Wars are Different..." was published on Open Democracy in August 2006. It draws from material in Chapter 5 of his *The Middle East in International Relations* (Cambridge University Press, 2005). "Remember, Palestine Is the Region's Festering Sore," by Rami G. Khouri, was originally published in the Lebanese English-language daily newspaper the *Daily Star* (21 August 2006). Parts of Nubar Hovsepian's afterword appeared in "The Palestinian Refugee Camps in Lebanon: More Than a Lebanese Problem," ZNet 24 June 2007.

To my children Lara and Rami,
who experienced their first war in July 2006

May it be the last for them and for the people of Lebanon.

CONTENTS

FOREWORD
Rashid Khalidi

Israel's war on Lebanon during the summer of 2006 marked a number of important milestones. Most obviously, it constituted the latest major Israeli incursion into Lebanon, one of a series going back to the 1968 raid on Beirut International Airport, and including the 1972 destruction from the air of the Nabatiyeh refugee camp, the 1973 assassinations of three PLO leaders in Beirut, the 1978 Litani invasion, and the 1982 invasion and siege of Beirut.

The summer 2006 conflict was also another in a series of Arab–Israeli wars, although it was not on a par with the 1948, 1956, 1967, 1968–1970 (war of attrition), 1973, and 1982 wars in terms of the number of powers involved, the size of the military forces committed, or the number of victims on either side. Nevertheless, this was another in a series of military conflicts between Israelis and Arabs going back to the founding of Israel, and like all others in Lebanon, it was related to that seminal event, however indirectly.

Finally, events in Lebanon in July and August of 2006 marked a new stage in the ongoing shadow dance proxy conflict between the United States and Iran. This conflict is mapped onto—and is only one among many other factors in—other regional conflicts, whether inside Iraq, inside Israel/Palestine and within the Palestinian polity, or in other parts of the Middle East. Israeli incursions into Lebanon have been perceived as proxy wars before, and have been part of the Arab–Israeli conflict before. But previously these were generally proxy wars linked in some sense to the cold war, and they therefore had an entirely different nature.

During the entire cold-war period, from the immediate post-World War II years until 1990, the most important series of crises involving the superpowers in the Middle East were those relating to the Arab–Israeli wars. Six of these wars directly involved the superpowers, sometimes in different configurations. The first of these were the 1948 War and the 1956 Suez conflict, in both of which the United States and Soviet Union found themselves on the same side, aligned in 1948 with Israel and in 1956 against Britain, France, and Israel. These were followed by four Arab–Israeli wars during which the superpowers were aligned against one another, with the

USSR supporting the Arab states and the United States supporting Israel: the June 1967 War, the 1968–1970 war of attrition, the 1973 War and the 1982 Israeli invasion of Lebanon. There were also many less severe Arab–Israeli confrontations, which at times involved the superpowers, some of them related to the 1975–1990 Lebanese Civil War.

In the four major wars starting with that of 1967, the superpowers came to be deeply involved with and identified with opposite sides, and these wars—the first three erupting when a major East–West confrontation was still raging in Indochina—therefore constituted major international crises, causing the eastern Mediterranean to once again become an important strategic arena. For all their severity and potential for causing a wider conflagration, however, these crises were in some measure self-contained, at least in regional terms, and were not generally linked to other crises. This may have had to do with the fact that all these crises took place within the context of a fixed and defined cold-war system, where conflict had to be rigorously limited because of the danger that an unlimited outbreak might lead to a nuclear holocaust. It may also have been a function of the fact that these Arab–Israeli wars took place in the context of a relatively stable regional system, where a certain balance had developed between differing Arab states, and between Arab and non-Arab states. Finally, it may have been because the Arab–Israeli conflict itself was essentially contained to a few states, and to one narrow, clearly defined region.

Whatever the reason, it was rarely the case that the grave international crises that developed around the periodic Arab–Israeli wars threatened to spill over into broader regional contexts,[1] although such crises were often influenced by these broader contexts—the fierce Egyptian–Saudi rivalry of the mid-1960s, for example, contributed to the slide into the June 1967 War. Thus, throughout the cold war, and indeed until its final stages, the crises involving the superpowers relating to Arab–Israeli wars were in some sense localized, and unconnected to other regional crises and conflicts. This was true even if these wars had a broader regional dimension, and even though this region was an important arena of the cold war. Through the 1980s, Arab–Israeli wars were, as it were, compartmentalized and separate from crises and wars, for example, in Libya and Chad, or in the Gulf region (including the massive Iraq–Iran War of 1980–1988), or in Afghanistan. This was true even though the United States and the Soviet Union (and occasionally other lesser powers like France and Britain) were deeply involved in all these conflicts, and these powers often saw them as linked in terms of their rivalries with one another.

But the relatively stable pattern of isolated crises that the Middle East has seen since World War II has changed with the collapse of the Soviet Union and the consequent end of the cold war in 1989–1990, and with it the relatively stable, if perilous, system of international relations that had prevailed for 45 years. The change has also to do with developments growing out of the Iranian Revolution and with the ongoing wars in Afghanistan that began with the Soviet invasion of that country in 1979. Finally, this change also appeared to be related to the connection that developed between Iraq's disastrous 1990 invasion of Kuwait, and the launching in the following year of the Madrid peace process. There may well be other linkages that go farther back and deeper than any of these.

What has changed is that lasting and close connections are developing between the longstanding unsolved crises relating to the Palestine question and the issue of Israel's borders with Syria and Lebanon, and other issues farther afield, some quite far away from Palestine, Lebanon, and Syria. The Lebanon war of the summer of 2006 provided the most striking recent example of these connections. The Israeli war on Lebanon developed directly out of the Israeli siege of Gaza that had been going on for many preceding weeks, long before the capture of the Israeli soldier Gilad Shalit on June 25, an action that only led Israel to escalate further its already vigorous attacks on the Gaza strip (nominally in response to Qassam rockets fired into southern Israel). Hizballah's leader, Sheikh Hassan Nasrallah—whether sincerely or not is irrelevant—described his organization's capture of two more Israeli soldiers in a cross-border attack on July 12 (the proximate cause of the Israeli summer 2006 war on Lebanon) as intended to reduce Israeli pressure on Gaza. This pressure had consisted of many weeks of sporadic air and artillery bombardments of the Gaza Strip, Israel's blockade of entry into and egress from Gaza, and the international financial blockade imposed on the Palestinian Authority after Hamas won a majority on the Palestinian Legislative Council in January 2006 and formed a government. Moreover, just as Israel and Israel's patrons in Washington saw Hamas and Hizballah as being connected in terms of support they both received from Iran and Syria, so did many Palestinians and Lebanese see an integral connection between Israel and the conservative Arab regimes, in terms of the support that both received from the United States and Europe.

There is nothing particularly unusual about a connection between the Arab–Israeli conflict and crises involving Lebanon. As we have seen, this linkage goes back at least to the first Israeli attacks on Lebanon in 1968, in the immediate aftermath of the 1967 War. What was unusual in this case was that this was not just a further phase of the Arab–Israeli conflict, or another crisis involving Israel and Lebanon, but rather appeared in important respects to be an indirect confrontation between the United States and Iran (and to a lesser extent Syria), via the intermediary of their respective local allies, Israel and Hizballah. Irrespective of whether in fact the important decisions in unleashing this conflict were taken in Beirut, Jerusalem, and Tel Aviv, or in Washington, DC, Tehran, and Damascus, there was a perception on the part of leaders of the local, regional, and international actors that this was in some measure a proxy war.

This represents a new element in the Middle Eastern strategic equation. Now, not only are we witnessing extensions of the Arab–Israeli conflict into the domestic politics of neighboring countries, which is a very old pattern. And not only are we witnessing great power involvement in this and other local conflicts, also a very old pattern. What we are now also seeing is a close connection, indeed an increasingly tight linkage, between conflicts involving Israel, Palestine, Lebanon, Syria, and other actors on the one hand, and on the other conflicts in the Gulf region, as well as various other arenas that are grouped together under the Bush administration's rubric of the "global war on terror." In fact, it is obvious that this war is not truly global, but is rather being fought almost entirely within lands inhabited by Muslims. Its battlefields are nevertheless described by its proponents as ranging widely, from Iraq to Afghanistan to Pakistan and Central Asia to the Horn of Africa and Darfur.

It might be argued that this "global war on terror," this war on an abstract concept, is no more than an artifact created by the powerful, almost anti-rational, ideological drive that animates George W. Bush, Dick Cheney, and their closest advisors. Alternatively, it could be argued that it is no more than a new justification for a mammoth annual defense budget, a justification that was necessary in the wake of the cold war's end and the demise of the former Soviet bogeyman, which nominally justified such prodigious and disproportionate expenditures. While the "global war on terror" may be both of those things, it is also a real war, a monumental global effort to which is devoted much of the current annual United States defense budget of nearly $450 billion, plus an expected "emergency" supplementary appropriation for 2007 of over $100 billion to fight the Iraqi and Afghan wars,[2] and huge confidential intelligence budgets, as well as other large sums buried in other parts of the US federal budget.

Whether these hundreds of billions of dollars are spent in Iraq or Afghanistan, in Israel or Somalia or elsewhere, it is all part of a larger effort by a United States administration led by individuals who appear to believe seriously that all of the entirely discrete and separate wars, conflicts, and forces that they are dealing with are integrally linked, and that the United States is therefore fighting a single enemy in all of these disparate arenas. Is this a correct or well-informed view? It is not. We know from a recent article by an editor of the *Congressional Quarterly* that many top members of the Bush administration and the congressional leadership do not know the difference between Sunnis and Shia, or between Hamas and Hizballah.[3] There is clearly much else they do not know, or are too arrogant to care about learning, as the disastrous conduct of the war in Iraq has amply demonstrated. Given this lack of basic knowledge, how can these individuals have an informed understanding of the enemy they claim to be fighting?

Nevertheless, however misguided, primitive, and ignorant their views may be, these views constitute the basis for the recent and current actions of the Bush administration. These actions for a time escaped serious public scrutiny inside the United States because of the powerful aftereffects on the American national psyche of the September 11, 2001 attacks on New York and Washington. Today, they are increasingly being called into question—particularly where Iraq is concerned—by American elite opinion, public opinion generally, and a growing segment of the US military. Nevertheless, with the US president and vice president still tightly surrounded by the same oblivious neoconservative advisors,[4] the war in Iraq nevertheless grinds on, with no end in sight, as does American policy in other areas of the Middle East where imagined and real linkages play an important role.

These linkages—specifically that between the Arab–Israeli conflict and issues related to the conflicted US–Iranian relationship since the fall of the Shah—and thus between the ongoing wars in Palestine, Lebanon,

Iraq, and Afghanistan, go back a number of years. They are the product of a number of recent phenomena.

The destruction of the Iraqi state: This process began with the suicidally stupid decisions of the Iraqi leadership to attack Iran in 1980 (encouraged and supported by the United States and its European and Arab allies and clients) and then Kuwait in 1990. The slow disintegration of the power of the Iraqi state was then compounded and completed by Iraq's defeat and expulsion from Kuwait in 1991, the ravaging of its economy by the US/UN sanctions regime for the next twelve years, and finally by the 2003 US invasion and occupation of the country and the dismantling of its state structures and army. The result has been the dissolution of one of the most powerful of Arab states, the sparking of sectarian civil strife in Iraq and possibly beyond its boundaries, and the creation of a major power vacuum in a critical region of the Middle East.

The growth in power of an independent Iran completely outside the orbit of any great power, a process that began with the Iranian Revolution: This was followed by the radicalization and entrenchment of the clerical regime that has led Iran since the revolution. These processes were accelerated by a pyrrhic Iranian victory in the war with Iraq, and then by the gradual decline of Iraq. Thereafter Iraq's Ba'ath regime and that of the Taliban in Afghanistan were defeated and dismantled, as were the remaining state structures in Iraq, much of this courtesy of the United States, which thereby relieved the Iranian regime of two of its most deadly enemies. Iran's pursuit of nuclear power, whether for civilian or military ends, and its aggressive support of its allies throughout the region have been signs of the regime's growing power and confidence.

The destruction of the Afghan state, and the creation of a power vacuum in that country: This process began with the ill-fated 1979 Soviet invasion, and the decision by the US and its clients to intervene covertly in Afghanistan to defeat the USSR, and with the equally ill-fated US decision to support the most radical Islamic factions inside Afghanistan, including fanatical volunteers recruited from all over the Arab and Islamic worlds. This was followed by the abandonment of Afghanistan by the US after the defeat of the Soviets, and eventually by the rise to power of the Taliban and the emergence of al-Qaeda from the remnants of these fanatical recruits, and thereafter by overt US intervention and the descent of the country once again into a low-grade war involving the US, NATO, and Pakistan.

The linkage established by US Secretary of State James Baker between the support of Arab governments for the American counteroffensive against the Iraqi occupation of Kuwait and the willingness of the first Bush administration to launch a comprehensive negotiation for a resolution of the conflict between Israel and the Arab parties, including the Palestinians: This resulted in the convening of the Madrid Peace Conference and later in the negotiation of Oslo Accords and the Israeli–Jordanian peace treaty. The inconclusive—indeed in many respects negative—outcome of this process has become apparent over the past six to eight years. This in turn has called into question the wisdom of those Arab governments that accepted the sincerity of the commitment of successive US administrations to a serious effort to end Israel's occupation of Arab territories and to achieve a just peace between Israel and the Palestinians in particular.

The precipitate decline in the influence and standing of the United States in the Middle East: This has in large part been a consequence of the phenomena just described, whose cumulative impact has been to lead the United States from a position of nearly unparalleled worldwide power and influence at the end of the cold war, to one of weakness and nearly universal opprobrium in the Middle East, at least in regional public opinion. This decline in American influence has not yet led other powers to attempt to fill the resulting power vacuum, although if this trend of ill-considered decisions based on radical ideology and ignoring reality continues after the expected departure of George W. Bush from the White House in January 2009, that may eventually happen.

There have been many consequences of these phenomena. Among the most important has been a rapid decline in American public support for President Bush and especially for his administration's Iraq policy, which in one recent poll enjoyed the backing of only 24 percent of Americans. The precipitate decline in the Bush administration's popularity marked by the sweeping victory of the Democrats in the 2006 elections is quite pointed. It suggests that American citizens, notoriously insulated from news about the real situation in the world by meretricious and shallow coverage in the mainstream media, have figured out that things are going very badly in the Middle East, and that the Bush administration's policy is largely to blame.

What more can be said about this new situation, where one crisis spills over into another, and where flashpoints from Central Africa to

Central Asia are increasingly linked? It is clear that this new regional configuration poses many more dangers than did the more controlled and localized crises of the cold-war period. However adventurous or dangerous were the occasional actions of the superpowers in the eastern Mediterranean, however volatile were the Middle Eastern conflicts they became involved in, there were always clear rules of the game, and there was always the sense at the end of the day of who was in charge, even if this may well have provided a false sense of security. Today, the United States, as the sole superpower, is operating in a world without rules; indeed, the scornful unilateralists of the current administration have systematically disdained and degraded the framework of international law and institutions devised at the end of World War II. Moreover, it has become apparent in Afghanistan, in the fight against al-Qaeda, in the war in Iraq, and during the summer war in Lebanon, that Bush administration policymakers are fumbling incompetents who have little or no idea what they are doing, and that to the extent that they have something that can be called a policy, it is misguided, poorly informed, and thoroughly unsuccessful.

For all the terrors of cold-war doctrines like mutual assured destruction, for all the cynical manipulation by the superpowers of their clients and allies, for all its many negative effects, once the US government decided on a policy of containment, the cold-war system provided a relatively stable international environment, certainly as far as the Mediterranean and the Middle East were concerned. Today, in a unipolar world, there are no agreed-upon rules, and there is no clear system that governs international relations, particularly since three successive post–cold-war American administrations have failed to provide a vision for the world order that emerged after the end of the cold war, and since the current Bush administration has aggressively denounced or undermined many of the existing pillars of the system, from strategic arms limitation agreements with Russia, to crucial aspects of international humanitarian law. It is the terrible misfortune of the Middle East to be at the epicenter of this new galaxy of disorder, and of wars, crises, flashpoints, and failed, failing, or precarious states, ranging from Afghanistan and Iraq to the east, to Palestine and Lebanon in the center, to the Sudan and Somalia in the south and west.

This new situation is not just a function of the failure of Presidents George H.W. Bush, Bill Clinton, and George W. Bush to define clearly a new role for the United States in the post–cold-war world, or to try to work multilaterally toward a new shape for the international system, although all three did very little in this regard. Nor is it solely a function of the growing conflict between the United States and certain forces in the Arab and Islamic worlds. It also represents the egregious failure of other international actors, from a European Union that barely has a Middle Eastern presence, to a Russia that exercises its power fitfully, clumsily, and often brutally, to India and China, great world powers of the future that still do not behave with confidence outside their immediate neighborhoods. None of these actors has succeeded in defining a new and more active role for itself in the post–cold-war world, and in the vital Middle Eastern region in particular. Two of these powers, Europe and Russia, border directly on the region, and have historically been deeply concerned with its strategic importance, and more recently with its importance in terms of world energy supplies. India and China, while located farther away, are also affected directly by Middle Eastern strategic and energy considerations. Nevertheless, none of them has yet acted in the region in a fashion commensurate with their important interests in it.

There is one final factor that defines the situation in the Mediterranean–Middle East region. This is the complete incapacity of the Arab states (or for that matter of any single Arab state), to assert themselves successfully or to respond with any cohesion to events taking place largely within the confines of the Arab world and on its peripheries—let alone to initiate events themselves. With the exception of actions by non-state actors like Hizballah and other parties and militias, the Arab peoples no longer appear to be significant actors, or to be subjects of their own history. If they play any role, it is in the wake of larger, more powerful, and more cohesive forces. The Arab region has thus been turned into the object of the actions of others, an arena where other actors—whether external powers, or strong non-Arab Middle Eastern states like Israel, Turkey, and Iran, or sub-state actors like Hizballah—take the initiative, and the Arab states respond passively.

This inert Arab response could be seen clearly during Israel's war on Lebanon, as it has been seen for nearly 40 years during Israel's oppression of the Palestinians under occupation in the West Bank, Gaza Strip, and East Jerusalem. Not only did none of the Arab states react vigorously to Israel's hugely disproportionate response to Hizballah's provocative attack on the Israel–Lebanon border; in fact, three of the most important Arab governments (Egypt, Jordan, and Saudi Arabia) made it clear at the outset of the war that their perception of regional dynamics was aligned with that of Washington and Tel Aviv, and that they were far more alarmed by the growing weight of Hamas in Palestine and Hizballah in Lebanon than by anything Israel was doing in Gaza or Lebanon. Only such a perverse analysis could explain the covert, and in some cases overt, initial support of these three regimes for Israel's war on Lebanon. This was all the more surprising given that the Lebanese infrastructure being pounded to rubble by the Israeli air force had been constructed by Lebanese governments supported, and in part financed, by Saudi Arabia, and that the Lebanese government whose legitimacy was being undermined by the Israeli offensive was ostensibly supported by all three Arab states.

But for these three Arab regimes, and perhaps for others, three factors temporarily trumped the tattered remnants of Arab solidarity. These were the new post–cold-war linkages discussed above between the Arab–Israeli conflict and others farther afield, notably those in the Gulf; the sense that the war in Lebanon was a US–Iran proxy war, in which all three leaned to the side of the US; and the susceptibility of these regimes to anti-Islamist, anti-Iranian, and anti-Shia rhetoric, whether emanating from Washington or from within the region (or produced by these regimes themselves). Indeed, for a time these factors apparently trumped even the most elemental sense of self-preservation of these autocratic and undemocratic rulers vis-a-vis their own peoples. Their unnatural and exposed position did not last. With a week or so, the failure of Israel's war to weaken Hizballah (indeed, Hizballah was progressively strengthened during the course of the war), and its huge cost in terms of the creation of a million Lebanese refugees, the killing of a thousand Lebanese civilians, and massive destruction of Lebanese homes and infrastructure, duly transmitted by a plethora of competing satellite TV channels, had their predictable inflammatory effect on Arab public opinion. Most Arabs soon came to see Hizballah as standing up alone to Israeli aggression. In Egypt, Jordan, and Saudi Arabia, this led to widespread public condemnation of the pusillanimous posture of their own governments and to a weakening of their legitimacy. All three responded belatedly by ostensibly switching sides, from support to condemnation of the Israeli offensive. They thereby ostentatiously separated themselves from both Israel and the Bush administration, as the latter continued to push for more aggressive Israeli action for weeks after the disastrous results of the war were clear to virtually the entire world, including to most perceptive Israelis.

Indeed, there was a far better comprehension of the reality of this war in the Israeli elite than among the blindly pro-Israeli ranks of the Bush administration, the US Congress, and many Washington "think tanks," and much of the US media. Thus officials, politicians, and commentators in the United States urged a continuation of the futile Israeli air campaign, and the even more futile ground offensive, long after serious Israeli observers were questioning the sense in continuing a war that was going so badly for Israel militarily and in terms of international perceptions, and that had no visible effect on Hizballah's ability to fight on the ground or to fire rockets into northern Israel. The Bush administration was egregious not only in pushing for a continuation of the Israeli offensive, but in preventing international action at the United Nations or elsewhere to halt it, well after it had become apparent to all but the most addled Washington neocons that the war was massively counterproductive for both Washington and Tel Aviv by any rational criteria. But then the Bush administration has never been particularly friendly to what "a senior adviser to Bush" once anonymously described to journalist Ron Suskind in the October 17, 2004 *New York Times* magazine as the "reality-based community." The extent to which the top figures in this administration live in a parallel ideologically driven world of their own, in self-imposed isolation from critical input, annoying facts, and unwelcome expertise, was rarely more apparent than during the war in Lebanon (with the exception of the entire duration of the Iraq war).

In Israel, things were different. It is true that the most outspoken supporters of Israel in the United States have tended to share Bush administration and neocon views on the Middle East, and that there is a habitual tendency among Israeli officials to avoid telling Americans unpleasant truths that might lead to a lessening of their support, or to alienate the Bush administration, which is rightly perceived as the most indulgent US administration in history toward Israel. Nevertheless, proximity has always afforded Israeli governments a greater appreciation than their Washington counterparts of some key realities in the Middle East. The Israeli security establishment (which as the veteran Israeli journalist Akiva Eldar recently pointed out, generally has more influence

than the elected government in policymaking on issues of war and peace[5])
is just as addicted as the Bush administration to a doctrine based almost
entirely on the use of force, and to reductionist views of the enemy. But
in Israel, even if the security establishment generally has its way, there is
a vigorous public debate on policy, where many of the real issues are aired.
Most significantly, over the course of the war in Lebanon dissension
rapidly surfaced within this establishment, and especially within the army.
Unlike in the United States, where the grave doubts of senior uniformed
military officers about the Iraq war were for three years harshly
suppressed by Bush, Cheney, Rumsfeld, and their civilian henchmen (the
latter affectionately referred to in the Pentagon as "commissars"), in Israel
similar doubts among the high brass about the Lebanon war were
immediately translated into public questioning, which brought the entire
futile exercise to a grinding halt in five weeks.

In the wake of the war, there has been coruscating criticism in Israel,
from within the political and security establishment and without, of the
prime minister, the minister of defense, the chief of staff, senior field
commanders, and of the military high command and the intelligence
community for what were perceived as their wartime failures and
shortcomings. Not only did this internal dissension help halt the war, but
in the subsequent domestic Israeli debate some fundamental issues have
been raised. Some ministers, including Foreign Minister Tzipi Livni and
Defense Minister Amir Peretz, have called for negotiations with Syria, and
a wide range of strategists, including the head of the General Security
Service (Shin Bet), have openly stated that Israel might have been
strategically better off with Saddam in power,[6] and serious doubts have
been raised in strategic circles about whether a continued aggressive
approach to Israel's neighbors is wise.[7]

These heretical views notwithstanding, the core Israeli security
doctrines of reliance on force, preemption, and exaggerated estimations of
enemy capabilities and intentions are far from being dethroned. This can be
seen from the security establishment's unchanging reliance on the use of
overpowering force against the Palestinians (whatever the weak prime
minister and defense minister say). It can be seen as well from the continued
agitation, within Israel and from Israel and its supporters directed at the
United States, for military action against Iran. Nevertheless, it is clear that
even with regard to Israel's central strategic preoccupation with Iran, the

results of the Lebanon war, and especially of the air war, have caused some within Israel's security establishment to question whether military action is feasible or wise. By contrast, even in the fourth year of a catastrophic war in Iraq, and after the Republicans' decisive 2006 electoral defeat, no such radical questioning of its basic security doctrines has as yet occurred within the top ranks of the Bush administration, as can be seen from the president's January 2007 decision to reject serious diplomacy in dealing with Syria and Iran, and to escalate the war in Iraq further.

It remains to be seen whether the five-week Israeli war on Lebanon, one of the most limited of the Arab–Israeli confrontations since 1948, but in some ways the one with the most ramifications, will break the dismal pattern of this conflict that has prevailed until this point. With the current Iraq war about to escalate, the American–Iranian confrontation becoming more explosive,[8] the Lebanese internal crisis and its external ramifications growing more serious,[9] Palestine descending into civil war, and the Palestinian–Israeli conflict still highly volatile, it does not appear that if there is change it will be in the direction of a calmer, more peaceful Middle East. Many in Israel, the Arab world, and the United States have pointed out that there was such a possibility in the immediate aftermath of the Lebanon war, had the opportunities been seized for Israeli–Syrian and Israeli–Palestinian peace negotiations, for an entirely new American approach to the war in Iraq, and for an American–Syrian and American–Iranian rapprochement. But those opportunities, if they ever existed, seem to be disappearing in the growing din of battle, from Somalia, to Gaza, to Baghdad, to Afghanistan, and in the shadow of the horrifying and lengthening specter of the conflict between the United States, Saudi Arabia, and Israel on one side and Iran on the other leading to a potential regionwide Sunni–Shia confrontation, something unprecedented in the modern history of the Middle East.[10]

We may look back one day and see that Israel's war in Lebanon, with its unexpected outcome, offered the last opportunity to prevent a descent of this entire region into an even lower circle of hell. Those in Washington, in Israel, in the Arab world, in Iran, and elsewhere who failed to seize that opportunity, and even more so those who actively obstructed it and stoked the rising flames, will bear the responsibility for their actions. All of us will have to live with their consequences.

NOTES

1 The only possible exception to this rule of these conflicts being self-contained was the 1968–1970 war of attrition, which came to involve Syria, the PLO, Jordan, and Iraq, and which appeared at one point as if it would lead to far wider regional ramifications, but in the end did not.

2 The supplemental appropriation request for Fiscal Year 2007 was estimated at $100–128 billion. That for 2006 was $66 billion; for 2005, $82 billion; for 2004, $72 billion; and for 2003, $74 billion, all on top of the regular defense budget. See Ivan Eland, "Hidden Costs," *American Conservative* 15 January 2007: 16–17.

3 Jeff Stein, "Can You Tell a Sunni from a Shiite," *New York Times* 17 October 2006; and "Democrats' New Intelligence Chairman Needs a Crash Course on al Qaeda," CQ.com 8 December 2006.

4 See Jim Lobe, "Hardliner's Hardliner Led Bush's Iraq Review," Inter Press Service 10 January 2007.

5 Akiva Eldar, "Not Peretz Alone," *Ha'aretz* 9 January 2007. Eldar wrote: "Olmert and Peretz fell victim to the same chronic illness that afflicted then-prime and defense minister Barak, as well as most of his predecessors and successors. Military experience also failed to immunize Israeli hero Ariel Sharon or his defense minister, retired brigadier general Benjamin Ben-Eliezer, against the syndrome of the military tail wagging the political dog…. We are all paying the price of this loss of control over a General Staff that decided to liquidate the Palestinian Authority. It's a mission that ended with great success: Yasser Arafat disappeared and Khaled Meshal arrived. Chief of staffs come and go, but the march of folly continues. Mofaz… merely continued in the tradition of his predecessors, who included Barak himself and his generals. Even Prime Minister Yitzhak Rabin, despite his glorious military past, could not "sear the consciousness" of the military with the understanding that the territories had ceased to be settler country. Releasing Peretz from his (lack of) control over the military and appointing him to a 'civilian' post are certainly vital steps. But transferring control over security (and peace) policy, once and for all, from the military to the government is many times more vital."

6 See Orly Halpern, "Israeli Experts Say Middle East Was Safer With Saddam in Iraq," *Jewish Daily Forward* 5 January 2007. Halpern quotes Yuval Diskin, head of the Shin Bet, as saying "I'm not sure we won't miss Saddam." Ephraim Sneh, deputy defense minister, and Amatzia Baram, perhaps Israel's top expert on Iraq express, along with several others, similar sentiments in the article.

7 See, for example Ofer Shelah, "Anti-War," Strategic Assessment 9, 3 November 2006. This is the publication of Israel's Institute for National Security Studies, formerly the Jaffee Center, at Tel Aviv University. In it Shelah argues that new rules have emerged from this war: "In the second Lebanon War, the party that had weaponry and used it lost, and the side that desisted from war gained…. force is no longer the continuation of policy by other means… [now] the side that uses forces has the greater chance of losing."

8 There are many signs that Washington is planning an escalation of this confrontation. Michael Klare writes in "Ominous Signs of a Wider War" in the *Nation* (9 January 2007) of the unusual recent lateral move of an admiral from the US Pacific Command (PACOM) to the Central Command (CENTCOM), with responsibility for the Indian Ocean and the Middle East, including Iraq, Iran, and Afghanistan: "If… you're

thinking... of using force against Iran and/or Syria, then Admiral Fallon is exactly the man you'd want at CENTCOM. Why? Because combined air and naval operations are his forte. Fallon began his combat career as a Navy combat flyer in Vietnam, and he served with carrier-based forces for twenty four years after that. He commanded a carrier battle wing during the first Gulf war in 1991 and led the naval group supporting NATO operations during the Bosnia conflict four years later. More recently, Fallon served as vice chief of naval operations before becoming the head of PACOM in 2005. All this means that he is primed to oversee an air, missile, and naval attack on Iran, should the President give the green light for such an assault—and the fact that Fallon has been moved from PACOM to CENTCOM means that such a move is very much on Bush's mind."

9 Toby Harnden, "CIA Gets the Go-Ahead to Take on Hizballah," *Telegraph* 10 January 2007, reports recent approval for "the CIA and other US intelligence agencies to fund anti-Hizballah groups in Lebanon and pay for activists who support the Seniora government... The Bush administration hopes Mr Seniora's government, severely weakened after its war with Israel last year, will become a bulwark against the growing power of the Shia sect of Islam, championed by Iran and Syria, since the fall of Saddam Hussein. Prince Bandar bin-Sultan, the former Saudi Arabian ambassador to Washington, is understood to have been closely involved in the decision to prop up Mr Seniora's administration, and the Israeli government, which views Iran as its chief enemy, has also been supportive."

10 Regarding two of the staunchest champions beating the drums on the "Sunni side" in this confrontation, it is worth pointing out, as Israeli Knesset member Azmi Bishara did to viewers on a recent Al-Jazeera broadcast (1 January 2007), the curious fact that "neither the Americans nor Olmert are Sunnis."

PREFACE AND ACKNOWLEDGMENTS
Nubar Hovsepian

In the summer of 2006 I traveled to Palestine/Israel, Jordan, and to Lebanon. During my short flight from Amman to Beirut on July 3, the flight attendant was distributing copies of state-owned Jordanian newspapers. They are all worthless, I told him. He replied: "Sir, the only page that contains truth is the obituary page." The steward's remark succinctly captures the Arab public's distrust of the pronouncements of their leaders. On July 3, the Arab public was infuriated by Israel's bombardment and lockdown of the Gaza Strip, following Palestinian militants' seizure of an Israeli soldier. The US spoke only of Israel's "right to self-defense"; Arab leaders sat idly by.

My visit to Beirut had personal and professional objectives: visiting in-laws, attending a wedding, and embarking on a research project about memories of war. Before long, I had a fresh store of such memories. My children Lara and Rami were often awakened during the night by the eerie sounds of incoming bombs. In those early morning hours they transformed the war into a mathematical game—they counted the number and frequency of the incoming shells.

When the US embassy finally organized an evacuation of American citizens, my family and I refused. I simply could not stomach the idea of being whisked out of Lebanon by the very power that had given Israel the green light to destroy Lebanon. Instead, we drove via Tarshish to the Syrian border. En route, near Zahle, we stopped to photograph trucks bombed by the Israeli air force. The trucks had borne a load of baking flour; I touched it. Had we passed along that road two days earlier, we, too, might have been hit.

While in Beirut we were spared the indignity of watching US media coverage of the war. But upon our return home, one could not avoid the media's skewed coverage. I felt quite alienated. When the war ended I felt the need to channel my anger in a constructive manner. I called Michel Moushabeck of the Interlink Publishing Group and proposed to assemble an edited book on the war. He offered to send a contract immediately. Here is the product.

My interest in Lebanon is deep as I lived in Beirut during what Charles Dickens would call the best of times and the worst of times—before and during the civil war that started in 1975. For many of my generation, Beirut is the symbol of resistance, of cultural and political revival, and of optimism in the midst of an Arab world shadowed by authoritarian rule.

From the outset this book has been a collaborative project. Michel Moushabeck and Pam Thompson of Interlink made it easy. They encouraged me, but never pushed needlessly. I am overwhelmed with the willingness of all the authors who contributed their work in a timely and expeditious manner. Almost all of the potential authors (friends and comrades) agreed to include their work in this volume. In effect, this book is the product of a collective labor of love for Lebanon and for peace.

As always one accumulates many debts in completing such projects. Irene Gendzier was my constant advisor and friend. Her ideas are reflected in many of the choices, but I did not always heed her advice. Assaf Kfoury not only contributed, but helped identify, edit, and translate Fawwaz Traboulsi's work. Elias Khoury not only contributed his work, but inspired some of the ideas contained in the introduction. As‘ad Abukhalil gave me many suggestions and secured the piece from Hanady Salman. Barbara Aswad put me in touch with Hiam Brinjikji, and I am happy to include her powerful but sad tale.

One week before the start of the semester at Chapman University, I requested a course reduction to enable the completion of this book. Lori Cox Han, my department chair, went to bat for me. She secured our Dean Roberta Lessor's and Provost Daniele Struppa's agreement. My longtime friend and Chapman colleague, Associate Dean Don Will, also worked his magic to secure the much-needed course reduction. Thanks to his suggestion I secured the entry from Bill Hartung and Frida Berrigan.

Lastly, Chris Toensing opened the pages of *Midde East Report* to publish my "Bilateralism on Trial" (Fall 2006). Parts of this essay are included in my preface and introduction. Putting this book together required my absence from home. I hid in my office while my wife Amal (*hope*) took charge of all the duties associated with family life. Without her unselfish love and devotion this book would not have been possible. Amal and I dedicate this book to our children, Lara and Rami.

INTRODUCTION
Nubar Hovsepian

The Israeli–American war on Lebanon in the summer of 2006 was unleashed in the context of a US effort to redraw the map of the Middle East (Afghanistan, Iraq) and the continued assault on the Palestinians in the occupied territories. This war was enabled and is a function of neoconservative beliefs that are enshrined in the Bush administration's "war on terror," whose salient features include:

—Any group that the US and Israel designate as terrorist must be smashed into submission.

—All Islamic militant groups (al-Qaeda, Hamas, Hizballah) are essentially the same, hence they and their accompanying ideologies must be destroyed.

—Arabs and Muslims understand only force, a belief propagated by the likes of Bernard Lewis and Fouad Ajami. Hence they must be smashed and perpetually attacked.

—The Arab–Israeli conflict is a sideshow. Instead, the real issue is the "war on terror."

When Hizballah crossed the UN-demarcated Blue Line on July 12, 2006 and took two Israeli soldiers as prisoners, Israel unleashed a two-pronged war of revenge on Lebanon. In Chapter 7, Stephen Zunes provides evidence that Israeli Prime Minister Olmert was encouraged by President Bush to launch an attack against Hizballah during their May 23 meeting. The prime minister's testimony before the inquiry commission headed by Judge Vinograd shows that Israel's war on Lebanon was not triggered by the capture of the two soldiers, but was planned long before.[1] The war sought to punish a nation to destroy not only Hizballah, but also the idea of resistance to Israeli and US dictates. What explains Hizballah's operation and the scale of Israel's retaliation? Why did the US reject an early cease-fire, instead egging on Israel as it pummeled Lebanon? Why did President George W. Bush and Secretary of State Condoleezza Rice expect the Lebanese and the Arabs to welcome the "birth pangs" of a "new Middle East" designed by the US and Israel? Rice's "new Middle East" is predicated upon the elimination of the idea of resistance to foreign occupation through collective punishment. But Hizballah, win or lose on the battlefield, has shown that while Israel's military might causes massive destruction, it is incapable of imposing a political settlement. The question is simple: Are the US and Israel ready for a just peace in Lebanon, Palestine, and the Middle East as a whole?

After the guns fell silent, the timing of the Hizballah operation has come under scrutiny. Hizballah alone made the decision to take Israeli prisoners, which has prompted Lebanese and Arab leaders to accuse Hassan Nasrallah of recklessness. In turn, Nasrallah has conceded that he misjudged the Israeli response. In a March 5, 2007 article in the *New Yorker*, Seymour Hersh quotes Nasrallah as saying, "we just wanted to capture prisoners for exchange purposes...We never wanted to drag the region into war." Whatever Nasrallah's intentions, Hizballah has demonstrated to the Arabs an alternative to the Arab governments' docility, which has led to the frittering away of national rights. Hizballah's capable and well-organized military response to Israeli power may lead many to rethink bilateral negotiations and peace treaties. Such treaties, after all, marginalized Egypt and opened the door for Israel's war on Lebanon and the Palestinians in 1982. Hizballah's actions serve as a reminder that the Arab–Israeli conflict requires a comprehensive political solution.

Liberal and leftist Lebanese writers concluded in the war's early stages that a comprehensive Middle East peace requires a unified Arab diplomatic offensive. Liberal Ghassan Tueini, writing in *Al-Nahar* on July 17, 2006, urged the Arab League to invoke the power of oil and petro-dollars (as in 1973) to modify Israeli and US behavior. Writing in *Al-Safir* two days later, Fawwaz Traboulsi, a seasoned veteran of the Lebanese left, made a similar call. He added that the Arabs should declare that there is no Israeli partner for peace; hence, Egypt and Jordan should be pressured to abandon their bilateral peace treaties with Israel. The only remaining option is to return to collective Arab bargaining to reach a just peace for all concerned—Lebanese, Palestinians, Israelis, and Syrians.

Did Hizballah reap a political victory? Nasrallah dubbed the results of the war "divine victory." During the early stages of the war, Hizballah garnered wide support from various sectors of Lebanese society, against a backdrop of violence and the forced homelessness of a quarter of the population. The support, though widespread, was not unanimous, and is less so today. For example, on July 17, I took two taxi rides downtown. One driver, tired and unshaven, told me: "Sir, my home [in the southern suburb of Harat Hreik] was destroyed yesterday. If I had the means, I would leave Lebanon today." A few hours later, another driver said his home in southern Lebanon was also destroyed. Nonetheless: "We are all with Sayyid Nasrallah." Shopowners lament the loss of their businesses. A young waitress told me she makes $14 a day. "How am I going to live now?" Lives have been disrupted, but more often than not, anger is directed at Israel, the US, and the servile Arab leaders.

Can the party continue to be a resistance movement ungoverned by the Lebanese state? This is one of many questions Lebanon is confronting after the war, as a modern, nonsectarian state is built or the confessional order becomes further entrenched. Hizballah is not the problem; rather, it is an integral part of the solution needed for re-ordering Lebanon's state–society relations. But the solution for Lebanon is intricately connected to the wider issues of the Middle East—namely the right of the Palestinians to independence, a quest thwarted by Israel's offer to the Middle East of either collaboration in or submission to the crushing of the Palestinians.

This book attempts to answer these and other questions through an examination of the relevant historical, social, and political processes affecting Lebanon. An examination of the war and other major events in Lebanon cannot be understood in isolation; they must be viewed as three concentric circles—local (internal Lebanese dynamics), regional (the role of neighboring states), and international power politics (particularly that of the United States). A corollary of this is that major events or the policies of any of the actors involved in and with Lebanon can be explained only by viewing them within the context of these three concentric circles. We should add that the political system lacks the ability to resolve internal conflicts that are endemic to Lebanon. Thus, whether it was the civil wars of the 19th century (1840–1860), 1958, or 1975–1990, external powers intervened to assist one or more of Lebanon's sects. External interventions have tended to exacerbate the internal dependence, hence requiring more reliance on external allies and sponsors. This is the dialectic of the relationship between the internal and external dimensions.

Past and Present Wars

When direct intervention became unattractive, it was replaced by the use of local proxies. Israel seems to have had the earliest and the most clearly formulated plans for this latter kind of intervention. David Ben Gurion believed that Lebanon was the weakest link in the Arab chain. On May 16, 1955, during a joint meeting of senior officials of the defense and foreign affairs ministries, Israeli leaders insisted that Israel do something about Lebanon. Moshe Sharett, then foreign minister, records the following in his diaries:

> According to him [Moshe Dayan] the only thing that's necessary is to find an officer, even just a major. We would either win his heart or buy him with money, to make him agree to declare himself the savior of the Maronite population. Then the Israeli army will enter Lebanon, will occupy the necessary territory, and will create a Christian regime which will ally itself with Israel. The territory from the Litani southward will be totally annexed to Israel and everything will be alright.[2]

Some twenty years later Major Haddad became one of Lebanon's "Christian" saviors, providing Israel with a buffer zone to facilitate its systematic attacks against southern Lebanon and many parts of the country. The attacks culminated in Operation Litani in 1978 and Israel's full-scale invasion of Lebanon in 1982, which took place in the midst of the ongoing civil war. These wars devastated the country. More than 20,000 civilians were killed by Israel, and the civil war, which ended by 1989–1990, claimed more than 150,000 lives.

Israel's wars in and against Lebanon have lasted longer than any of the formal Arab–Israeli wars. The 1982 war is the longest Arab–Israeli war (three months) and it was ostensibly fought by the IDF and Palestinian–Lebanese irregular forces. The 2006 war went on for 34 days, during which 1,200 Lebanese and 160 Israelis were killed. Since the war ended, almost 35 Lebanese, mostly children, have died from the millions of cluster bombs planted on Lebanese soil by the IDF after the negotiated cease-fire. In both wars, the Arab states were reduced to the roles of spectator or collaborator. In the summer of 2006, the leaders of Egypt, Saudi Arabia, and Jordan feared Hizballah's fierce resistance to Israel's attacks. To undermine Hizballah's appeal to the Arab imagination, these leaders tried to foment sectarian conflicts between the Shia and the Sunnis of Lebanon and the Middle East region. I witnessed this fear firsthand in Jordan. After leaving Beirut during the war I went to Amman, Jordan to visit a friend in the Shmeisani district. I found the entire district cordoned off by security services, to prevent an announced demonstration of solidarity with the people of Lebanon and Palestine after the Friday prayers. The regimes fear their people; hence, they silence them.

Israel had multiple aims and objectives in launching the 1982 war. It sought to destroy the PLO, its leadership, and the very idea of Palestinian nationalism, in order to pacify the Palestinians living under its occupation in the West Bank and Gaza. Second, it sought to pull Lebanon out of the Syrian sphere of influence and to place it conclusively within the Israeli orbit. Third, it wanted to establish a buffer state and a puppet government in Lebanon under the leadership of Bashir Gemayel, but the latter was assassinated soon after the war. Fourth, Israel wanted to improve its position in the next phase of negotiations in the Arab–Israeli conflict by establishing normal diplomatic relations with a second Arab state. Despite its military might, Israel failed to attain its primary objectives. Though it secured the removal of PLO forces from Lebanon, it failed to quell Palestinian aspirations for independence and statehood, as evidenced by the start of the first intifada in 1987 and the al-Aqsa intifada in 2000.

Israel's invasion failed to establish a puppet regime. Instead, the war sparked a multidimensional resistance against Israeli occupation. The first act of resistance against Israel took place in Beirut, when several Lebanese militants opened fire on Israeli soldiers at a café on Hamra Street in the heart of Beirut. I watched this attack from across the street. The Lebanese resistance had formally declared its existence and intentions. Out of this conjuncture emerged the likes of Hizballah, which in turn played a central role in expelling the IDF from Lebanon in 2000. The lesson is simple: Occupation breeds resistance.

The Israeli–American alliance in 1982 and 2006 sought to establish a new order in the Middle East, but such grand designs have been frustrated on the battlefield. Military might proved incapable of establishing a new political order. Wars in the past have highlighted the derivative nature of military might. Commenting on the 1982 war, William Quandt aptly notes: "Lebanon revealed in a humiliating and costly fashion the outer limits of American and Israeli power in the region."[3] Simply put, victories on the battlefield do not lead to lasting political arrangements or solutions. Indeed, this is the primary lesson of the ongoing wars in Afghanistan, Iraq, and Lebanon. The US and Israel have shown that they are capable of wreaking havoc and causing much destruction, but they have repeatedly failed to construct order and stability that serves peace and justice.

5

Lebanon: The Internal and the External

As I note in Chapter 2 of this volume, Lebanon's founding in 1920 as a modern nation-state was met with joy and scorn by the Lebanese. Since then it has experienced periods of stability and civil war. Unlike earlier civil wars, the 1975 one is well documented. Elias Khoury notes that this is the "first time in our modern history where we concede what happened. I think the end of the 1975 civil war could, theoretically, be a point of beginning for a new history in which we will not be destined to engage in civil wars; yet this depends on many factors which, unfortunately, are not taking place."[4] Indeed, after Israel's war on Lebanon in 2006 many Lebanese feared the outbreak of a new civil war. On December 1, 2006 a Hizballah-led coalition organized an open-ended sit-in in downtown Beirut. The primary objective was to force the resignation of Prime Minister Seniora and his government. The campaign was a peaceful expression of civil disobedience. However, on January 25, 2007 tensions exploded between the opposition and the pro-government forces in the cafeteria of the Beirut Arab University. By the time the unrest was quelled, 4 people were killed and more than 150 wounded. For the first time since 1996 the Lebanese army imposed a curfew on Beirut. Rumors spread rapidly, and armed gunmen set up roving checkpoints on highways connecting Beirut to southern Lebanon. Those crossing the checkpoint were asked for their identity cards. Reporting from Lebanon, Mohamad Bazzi noted that the fact that a "checkpoint was erected within the short hours of violence on January 25 illustrates how close Lebanon might be to the brink of another civil war."[5] Such fears were also apparent after the murder of Pierre Gemayel in late November 2006. Reporting from Beirut, Robert Fisk started his November 22 article in the *Independent* with: "Civil War—the words on all our lips yesterday." Later in the same article, he offered more hope, suggesting that the "Lebanese may be too mature for another civil war."

What have the Lebanese learned from their history of civil wars, and how have the regional players exacerbated the conditions of internal peace and reconciliation? Since the establishment of Israel in 1948, Lebanon has been pulled into the vortex of the Arab–Israeli conflict. Since that time the Lebanese state and the various political parties and groups had to decide on Lebanon's regional identity and the resulting alliances. They had three options: Should Lebanon be part of the Arab fold? Should

Lebanon be neutral? Or should Lebanon ally itself with the US and Israel? Lastly, which of these alliances is more conducive to the development and consolidation of internal democratic reform?

Simply put, Lebanon's reliance on Syria to bring an end to the bloody civil war restored peace. Syria formally intervened in the ongoing civil war in 1976 and its subsequent role as a "peacemaker" was welcomed by Secretary of State Henry Kissinger.[6] Under Syrian tutelage (1976–2005) the confessional system rebounded; hence the possibilities for internal reform were hampered. In about the same period of time, Israel's multiple interventions and invasions of Lebanon not only led to massive destruction, but also propelled a popular resistance to foreign occupation. This resistance was led by Hizballah, and in 2000 its steadfastness induced Israel to withdraw from Lebanon. The assassination of Prime Minister Rafiq Hariri in 2005 set the conditions for Syrian withdrawal from Lebanon, which some heralded as Lebanon's "cedar revolution." Though the investigation of this criminal act has yet to conclude, it is widely assumed that Syria and its security apparatus was behind it. But when Israel launched its war in 2006, part of its motivation was to deliver a strike at Syria and Iran, regional allies of Hizballah. Given Lebanon's precarious geopolitical location, the Lebanese have had to decide who their regional and international allies are. Their choices are limited. To either Syria and Iran, or Israel and the US.

American intervention in the affairs of other states has been justified on the grounds of promoting freedom and democracy. This is what George W. Bush claimed as his central motivation for invading and toppling the regime of Saddam Hussein. But the record of past interventions belies this claim. Instead of promoting freedom and democracy, American and Israeli interventions in the affairs of other states have contributed to the perpetuation of authoritarian rule in those very states. Research undertaken by George Downs and Bruce Bueno de Mesquita shows conclusively that despite such lofty claims, our stated efforts are "failing miserably."[7]

These questions are addressed by various entries in this book. Here, I would like to simplify the issues by exploring the implications of the finite choices that the Lebanese have. No matter which alliance is opted for, the Lebanese face a serious conundrum. The alliance with Syria retards the internal dynamic for the construction of a more democratic and post-confessional political order. In contrast, the international community led by the US "seems undeterred in its quest to consolidate the post-Syria order in Lebanon." Shortly before the 2006 war, the US and its European allies pushed the UN Security Council to adopt a new resolution on May 17, 2006 "adding to the daunting list of demands laid down in Resolution 1559 passed on September 2, 2004. To wit, all 'Lebanese and non-Lebanese militias' are to be disarmed, and Syria is to demarcate its border with Lebanon as a prelude to establishing 'full diplomatic relations' with its small neighbor."[8] In effect, the US and Israel want to disarm Hizballah without a political quid pro quo. Unable to implement these demands, the Lebanese political system is gridlocked. The state cannot impose this solution without arriving at a new national accord between the major political parties of Lebanon. The implementation of these US-backed demands is tantamount to excluding Hizballah from the Lebanese political equation.

Any attempts to resolve the Lebanese political crisis requires the foregrounding of the history of civil war as a given context. This history is filled with many unresolved questions about what constitutes political community in a post-conflict setting. After years of war, rebuilding, and more war, the Lebanese have yet to pose simple questions: Why did we fight and at what cost? Rather, most Lebanese seem to blame everyone but themselves for their misfortunes. Postwar reconciliation requires agreement on postwar power-sharing arrangements. Mahmood Mamdani, writing on a similar context in Rwanda, concludes: "Instead of using its resources and influence to bring about a political solution to the civil war, and then strengthen it, the US signaled to one of the parties that it could pursue victory with impunity."[9] Accordingly, as reported by Seymour Hersh, the US, instead of facilitating the negotiation of a Lebanese national accord, is instead working to undermine the prospects for internal cohesion. Hersh observes that in Lebanon, "the [Bush] administration has cooperated with Saudi Arabia's government, which is Sunni, in clandestine operations that are intended to weaken Hizballah…" The US government has pledged financial support to the Seniora government, including military and security aid. Some of this aid is being channeled to "emerging Sunni radical groups in northern Lebanon, the Beqaa Valley, and around Palestinian refugee camps in the south." Hersh adds, "these groups, though small, are seen as a buffer to Hizballah; at the same time, their ideological ties are with Al

Qaeda."[10] But a political settlement in Lebanon depends on a national agreement that includes Hizballah, or Lebanon risks sliding into further conflict that could serve as a tripwire for an unplanned escalation to civil war. What can be done to undo the internal gridlock?

Lebanon's Postwar Predicament: Where To?

The untimely death on Febraury 25, 2007 of Joseph Samaha, a prominent Lebanese journalist and activist, offers interesting insights about the options that the Lebanese have. Unlike his assassinated colleagues (Samir Kassir, George Hawi, Jibran Tueni), Samaha died from a sudden heart attack. Eulogies and poetic tributes followed from the pens of many of his friends and colleagues including Adonis, Elias Khoury, Fawwaz Traboulsi, and Ziad Majed (the last three are contributors to this volume). In a moving tribute in *Al-Nahar Literary Supplement* of March 4, 2007, Elias Khoury celebrates Samaha's "natural" death as an affirmation of normalcy, as contrasted with the many losses of life through war or at the hands of cowardly assassins. Now Khoury and the Lebanese can mourn death, but can also celebrate life that entails natural death.

Joseph Samaha, Elias Khoury, Fawwaz Traboulsi, among others, are longtime progressive, secular, radical thinkers whose reputations transcend Lebanese frontiers. Their visions of a Lebanese future reflect much that is unique, though little known—especially in the US—about Lebanon, namely, its trenchant critics, writers, journalists, intellectuals, and activists with a Lebanese conscience and an internationalist outlook.

After the assassination of the former Prime Minister Rafiq Hariri in February 2005, Samaha, who is thoroughly secularist, firmly supported Hizballah and rejected US and Israeli interference in Lebanon. His choice caused a rift between him and some of his former comrades. How can one reconcile two seemingly conflicting positions? The national struggle requires a coalition of national resistance to oppose US–Israeli hegemony. In contrast, the democratic struggle requires a broader coalition intent on securing independence from regional tutelage (Syria) as well as negotiating a democratic and nonsectarian pact. During the war of 2006, Elias Khoury and Ziad Majed tried to combine these positions into one platform (see Chapter 10). Why should the national struggle be divorced from the struggle for reform and democracy? This is the question that the Lebanese political forces grapple with today.

The political system in Lebanon is presently quite polarized. The Hariri bloc (March 14 movement) is pitted against the Hizballah-led coalition (March 8 movement). The internal conflict, as I've noted, has led to the precipice of another civil war. Outside powers (Saudi Arabia, Iran, and Syria) are trying to broker political deals to diffuse the tensions in Iraq and Lebanon. Other outside powers (US and Israel) seek to expand their hegemony. In the meantime, confessional and sectarian identities in Lebanon are hardening. The logic of this situation leads to a fractured polity in which different parties seek external alliances to bolster their internal agendas. Elias Khoury argues that part of the problem resides in the incredible weakness of the secular left. To paraphrase Khoury, this political vacuum transforms Lebanon into a small home in which its confessions, through their external alliances, transform it into a regional theater.[11]

Yes, there is disagreement among the contending political forces on several important issues. These disagreements, as they have in the past, will find some short-term solutions that reinvigorate the confessional distribution of power to the exclusion of a more effective national pact.[12] The details change, but the discussions exhibit some form of national amnesia. An honest discussion would require more serious probing into the unsolved and underlying tensions emanating from the history of the still recent civil war. The Taif Accord (October 22, 1989) was endorsed by all, if not most, political parties in Lebanon with the hope of restoring state sovereignty, and toward that end they favored the formation of a unified national government. This objective required the production of a revised curriculum for Lebanese schools to educate the young and to reshape a postwar identity. Teams of educators were assembled to undertake this task.[13] But twenty years later the teams of educators have yet to revamp the history and civics curricula. The failure of the state to construct a shared narrative of the civil war prevents the state from forging a unified national identity. As Ernest Renan notes, national and group identities require both common remembering and common forgetting.[14] An agreement on all details is not essential, and some forgetfulness might be useful, but complete amnesia is potentially quite dangerous. Today Lebanon hovers between the need for complete disclosure and complete amnesia.

But to end this section on a dour note would emphasize the "pessimism of the intellect" rather the "optimism of will," to paraphrase Antonio Gramsci. In his 1993 interview with Michael Young, Elias

Khoury recasts the role of Lebanon and Beirut as the place "where all democratic forces in the Arab world can congregate, debate, and plan the future of the Arab world. This is the real meaning of the country, if we want to give it any meaning." He adds, and I quote him at length:

> Lebanon's new ruling class wants to make Lebanon part of the petro-dollar system and to convert it into a small Hong Kong for the Arab–Israeli peace. This is one option. We have another: to make Lebanon part of a search for democracy, identity, and change in the Arab world. Part of the responsibility for the destruction of Beirut—I say part because, in the end, we the Lebanese destroyed it—but part of the responsibility for the destruction of Beirut, maybe even the major part of it, was held by two groups: one was the Arab regimes which did not want to see Beirut become a forum for the Arab opposition; this is why we witnessed such hate directed against the city. The other was Israel, which also wanted to destroy Beirut because it was democratic, and because it was the only place to welcome the Palestinians, give them a refuge, and provide them with a base to conduct their struggle. Only Beirut could do this, not because it was better than any other Arab city, but because it was democratic. This is why the Arab regimes and Israel both had the same objective: to destroy the spirit of the city. It was a spirit which threatened both the Arab regimes and Israeli domination of the Arab world.[15]

Outline of the Book

This book is divided into six parts. Part One contains five chapters that set the historical context for Lebanon's prewar period. Ussama Makdisi, professor of modern Middle Eastern history at Rice University and author of a book on the culture of sectarianism in 19th century Lebanon, invites us to think conceptually and comparatively. Instead of reducing sectarianism to "simply mindless violence," he insists that it can more usefully be understood as a "historically contingent moment" that orders the modern politics of representation. The relevance of his article applies not only to modern Lebanon but to Iraq as well. Building on these insights, I observe that the sectarian make-up of both state and society in Lebanon was temporarily challenged by civil war (1975–1990). The sectarian political structures proved resilient enough, however, to prevent the articulation of a more secular alternative. Georges Corm, a prolific writer and former Lebanese minister of finance, situates in its regional and international context the Lebanese internal crisis in the wake of the assassination of Prime Minister Rafiq Hariri. Rather than ushering in a new Lebanese spring, he argues that external meddling has only intensified Lebanon's precarious position in ongoing region-wide conflict.

The 1982 Israeli invasion of Lebanon is one of the factors that accelerated the emergence and growth of Hizballah. Lara Deeb, who wrote the remarkable book *An Enchanted Modern: Gender and Public Piety in Shi'i Lebanon*, uses her skills to profile the historical and social origins of Hizballah as a multidimensional movement best understood as a combination of political party and social and resistance movement, as contrasted with the rather opaque and dismissive view of Hizballah as a mere "terrorist" organization. Assaf Kfoury, a highly accomplished mathematician, adds to our understanding of Hizballah by providing a profile of its leader Sayyid Hassan Nasrallah. In May 2006, Noam and Carol Chomsky, Irene Gendzier, and Assaf Kfoury visited with Nasrallah in the southern suburbs of Beirut. Nasrallah emerges as a "logical and reflective man, not given to effusive gestures or hyperbole," a depiction that sharply differs with that available in mainstream US media.

Part Two aims to show that the 34-day war on Lebanon in 2006 can best be understood as an American–Israeli war. Noam Chomsky, the noted linguist and leading public intellectual, shows that this war is linked to the ongoing Israel–Palestine conflict. Like many of us, Chomsky was incensed by the war and all the lies that were invoked to justify it, and he interrupted his hectic schedule to write a succinct and incisive piece for this book. Stephen Zunes, Middle East editor of the Foreign Policy in Focus project, wrote several pieces during the war. I read the first while still in Beirut. Though I had never met him, I was familiar with his astute writing on US Middle East policy, as evidenced by his book *Tinderbox*, so when I embarked on this project I immediately asked him to expand his articles into a piece for the book and he accepted without hesitation.

As noted in the Preface, Irene Gendzier contributed much more to this book than the writing of her chapter, which brings the entire discussion of US policy toward the Middle East and Lebanon into sharp historical focus. Her essay builds on her important book *Notes from the Minefield: United States Intervention in Lebanon and the Middle East, 1945– 1958*. Through careful documentary analysis, Gendzier shows the extent and consistency of Washington's support for Israeli imperatives in

Lebanon since 1948. She aptly dubs America's policy toward Lebanon as "Exporting Death as Democracy."

Part Three is composed of six entries that cover the 34-day war as a lived experience. Instead of dealing with war as abstraction, our contributors highlight the human dimension. They invite us to feel and experience how normal human beings survive the ravages of war. After living almost eight years in New York, Rasha Salti moved back to Beirut on July 11, one day before the start of the war. Overnight she inadvertently became a blogger as she chronicled her experiences of the war. Parts of her diary were published in the *London Review of Books*, the *Middle East Report*, and other places. Here, she has selected parts of her diaries and framed them with an introductory note. Kirsten Scheid, an anthropologist who lives with her family in Beirut, also kept a diary of the war. We participated in special roundtable discussion on the war at the annual meeting of the Middle East Studies Association (November 2006). Her paper focused on the importance of civil resistance during the war. I asked her to amalgamate her presentation with selections from her diary for this book. In her writing, the Lebanese emerge as actors engaged in resistance, rather than victims. Hiam Brinjikji, a school counselor living in Michigan, offers yet another diary. After an absence of 32 years from her birthplace, she ventured to visit Lebanon (mostly the south) in the summer of 2006. Her visit home proved fateful. She lived to tell about it, but two weeks after her return to the US she was informed that both her grandmother and aunt had died under the rubble of their home, which was destroyed by Israeli missiles.

Hanady Salman, a Lebanese journalist, offers us glimpses of ordinary people's lives during the war. In a similar vein, novelist Elias Khoury reports on the destruction and devastation visited upon ordinary Lebanese citizens. He insists that destruction does not eliminate memory; rather, he notes that memory "is the sign of life, for it challenges death and surpasses... imagination." But wars are also occasions that require the rethinking of one's political positions. In the second week of the war, Khoury and Ziad Majed published an open letter to their comrades urging national unity against the Israeli invasion, though both of them are founding members of the Democratic Left Movement, which had been critical of Hizballah.

To analyze the importance of international law as it pertains to the war on Lebanon, I turned to a trusted friend, mentor, and prolific writer

Richard Falk. Within days of my request he provided me with drafts of articles in progress. His analysis of international law, which opens Part Four, is co-authored by Asli Bali, one of his former students from Princeton. They end their essay with a warning: "What is painfully evident is that the norms of international law are put aside by recourse to and conduct of the war by the United States and Israel, and that the lawlessness exhibited in the Lebanon war is part of a wider pattern that increasingly threatens a disastrous war of regional scope."

The United Nations has long been involved in multiple capacities in Lebanon. To cover this subject, I turned to my longtime friend Phyllis Bennis. She is a prolific writer and activist for peace and justice who has written widely on the UN. She analyzes UN resolutions and provides a context for understanding UN involvement in Lebanon from 1978 to the present. Frida Berrigan and William Hartung of the World Policy Institute demonstrate US involvement in Lebanon and the region through a policy of military assistance. They also point out that Israel's use of American-made cluster bombs is a direct violation of bilateral agreements forbidding Israel from using such weapons against civilians.

Part Five invites the reader to understand the "other" Israel—the dissenting voices who challenge official state orthodoxies. Here are voices a reader outside Israel might not readily encounter. How did the war affect Israel? How was the war justified in official discourse? Was it a simple act of self-defense? The contributors to this section of the book are all critical of formal justifications for the war. Earlier in this introduction, I noted that Prime Minister Olmert and his staff planned to go to war against Hizballah months before the capture of Israeli soldiers. In this context, Yitzhak Laor suggests that Israel's war can be understood as the logical outcome of the dominance of military thinking in Israeli society. The IDF personifies Israeli political culture, which "reveals our national psychosis, and it derives from our over-identification with the military." Gabriel Piterberg, a friend who teaches at UCLA, provides us with insights about the war. He travels during and after the war—through time and space—to various parts of Israel/Palestine. He is ashamed to recall his participation in the 1982 war, but concludes that past Israeli efforts in Lebanon and in Palestine were designed to construct new realities. But at what price?

Israel defines itself as a Jewish state, but clearly not all of its citizens are Jewish. I chose to include a piece by Azmi Bishara, a longtime friend and an advocate for equality for all citizens of Israel. He is an Arab nationalist and a former member of the Israeli Knesset at the same time. He sheds further light on Israel's military culture by dubbing it a culture of the annihilation of the "other." Yoav Peled and Virginia Tilley analyze the logic of Israeli foreign policy. Yoav published his essay in the *Middle East Report* online. I immediately asked for his permission to reprint it. Yoav Peled and I were members of study group in New York in the early 1980s. His father, the late General Matty Peled, was my friend and I admired his courage. Yoav argues that the Lebanon war has ostensibly eliminated "unilateralism" as a policy option. Rather, Israel seems to have no choice but to seek a negotiated comprehensive peace. Virginia Tilley invites us to think about Israeli foreign policy from an entirely different vantage point. She argues that "until Israel's doctrine of ethnic statehood is addressed, none of its spin-off effects, including Israel's continuing military ambitions in Lebanon, can be addressed effectively."

This part of the book concludes with a *cri de coeur* from my longtime friend Sara Roy. Sara's parents are survivors of the Holocaust, a fact that makes her ponder how and why many survivors tend to deny the fundamental humanity of the "other"—Palestinian and Lebanese. She asks: "Can we ever turn away from our power to destroy?" For her courage, Sara has been subjected to vilification by the Israel lobby. She remains undeterred, as she continues to insist on justice for all.

The book's final section offers a number of assessments of the repercussions of the war. These entries are organized to enable an understanding of the local, regional, and international dimensions of the conflict. Haneen Sayed and Zafiris Tzannatos, Beirut-based economists with the World Bank, present a stark picture of destruction and loss. Will the Lebanese government use the occasion to adopt policies and plans that eliminate difference (social, class, confessional) or perpetuate it? From divergent perspectives, Elias Khoury, Fawwaz Traboulsi, and Asʿad Abukhalil open up a debate about the internal challenges confronting Lebanon. The central issue that causes difference is the connection between the national struggle (resistance) and the quest for a less confessional and more secular Lebanon. From a regional perspective Azmi Bishara argues that Israel must choose between peace or perpetual war. Fred Halliday connects the war to the wider regional context, a Greater West Asian Crisis, which involves a multilayered conflict between Iran and its allies, the forces of radical Sunni insurgency, and the US and its regional allies. Such a condition he compares to Europe of 1914.

Richard Falk concludes that the war will not be remembered for the claim that it will produce a "new Middle East." Rather, the war is but "one of the early indications of death tremors for a system of world order," accustomed to war "as the inevitable basis for stability and change among sovereign states." To move away from war in the 21st century, we need political approaches, ethical realism, and diplomacy.

The book ends with a short entry written by Rami Khouri, a Beirut-based syndicated columnist. He returns our attention to Palestine and to the need for a comprehensive Arab–Israeli peace. Indeed the war on Lebanon in the summer of 2006 was only the latest round of the ongoing Arab–Israeli conflict, in which Lebanon has served as a regional theater for this festering conflict. One can therefore classify it simultaneously as the sixth Arab–Israeli war and the American–Israeli war on Lebanon.

NOTES

1 The British *Guardian* reports that preparations for Israel's war in Lebanon were actually drawn up more than four months prior to Hizballah's taking of two Israeli soldiers as prisoners on July 12, 2006. The report is based on Prime Minister Olmert's submission to a commission of inquiry which has been leaked to the press. See Conal Urquhart, "Israel Planned for Lebanon War Months in Advance, PM Says," *Guardian* 9 March 2007. This fact has been pointed out on numerous occasions by Uri Avnery. In particular see his article, "Olmert's Truth," of 10 March 2007, published by Gush Shalom at http://zope.gush-shalom.org/home/en/channels/avnery/1173578966/.

2 Quoted from Livia Rokah's *Israel's Sacred Terrorism*, (Belmont, MA: AAUG, 1980).

3 William B. Quandt, ed., *The Middle East: Ten Years After Camp David* (Washington, DC: The Brookings Institution, 1998) 9.

4 "Politics and Culture in Lebanon," 24 March 1993 interview with Elias Khoury by Michael Bacos Young, published in *Beirut Review* 5 (Spring 2003); www.lcps-lebanon.org/pub/breview/br5/khourybr5.html.

5 Mohamad Bazzi, *Nation* online 31 January 2006. The article is located at www.thenation.com/doc/20070212/bazzi.

6 Elizabeth Picard, *Lebanon: A Shattered Country* (New York: Holmes and Meier, 2002) 116–117.

7 George Downs and Bruce Bueno de Mesquita, "Gun-Barrel Democracy Has Failed Time and Again," *Los Angeles Times* 4 February 2004. Downs and de Mesquita add: "Between World War II and the present, the United States intervened more than 35 times in developing countries around the world. But our research shows that in only

one case—Colombia after the American decision in 1989 to engage in the war on drugs—did a full-fledged, stable democracy with limits on executive power, clear rules for the transition to power, universal suffrage and competitive elections emerge within 10 years. That's a success rate of less than 3 percent."

8 Reinoud Leenders, "How US Pressure on Hizballah Impedes Lebanese Reform," *Middle East Report* online 23 May 2006.

9 Mahmood Mamdani, "The Politics of Naming: Genocide, Civil War, Insurgency," *London Review of Books* 29.5 (8 March 2007).

10 Seymour M. Hersh, "The Redirection: Is the Administration's New Policy Benefiting Our Enemies in the War on Terrorism?" *New Yorker* 5 March 2007.

11 Elias Khoury, "When Mistakes Recur," *Al-Nahar Literary Supplement* 25 February 2006.

12 The Lebanese and the American press have been reporting on meetings between parliamentary majority leader MP Saad Hariri and the speaker of parliament Nabih Berri. At issue is whether the parliament will approve the international tribunal that is investigating the assassination of former PM Rafiq Hariri. In addition the discussions focus on the possibility of expanding the current cabinet to include more opposition (Hizballah-affiliated) ministers. See the reports in *Al-Safir*, *Al-Nahar*, and the *Daily Star*, as well as the *New York Times* 9–10 March 2007.

13 Around the same time a similar undertaking was started in Palestine, under the auspices of the newly formed Palestinian Center for Curriculum Development. They produced new textbooks covering a myriad of topics, including history and national (civic) education. The history and civic texts were the most difficult and contested tasks undertaken by the PA and its education ministry. My forthcoming book on the politics of Palestinian education focuses on these issues. For a short coverage of these educational challenges in Lebanon see, Hassan M. Fattah, "A Nation with a Long Memory, but a Truncated History," *New York Times* 10 January 2007.

14 Ernest Renan [1882], "What is a Nation?" in Homi Bhabha, ed., *Nation and Narration* (London: Routledge, 1990) 8–22.

15 See note 4.

Part One

THE LEBANESE STATE,
THE CONFESSIONAL SYSTEM,
AND HIZBALLAH

1.UNDERSTANDING SECTARIANISM

Ussama Makdisi

In the archetypal Lebanese sectarian system, religious affiliation defines and limits political participation and representation. It is expected that a Shiite must therefore represent the Shia; a Maronite, the Maronites (or the "Christians," as the term is often used in Lebanon); a Sunni, the Sunnis. The system is equitable but not equal: it is equitable in the sense that all the major players in Lebanon have bought into it, but not equal in the sense that the political shares of the respective sects are not equally distributed; nor do they reflect their true proportional weight among the population of the country. Furthermore, secularists are totally excluded from the political process, making it impossible for their demand for a transcendent one citizen–one vote kind of equality to exist.

For as long as anyone can remember, this is the way it has been in Lebanon, and as long as popular discourse continues to conflate religious and political communities, this is the way it shall always be. But memories are short and political expediency is not commensurable with historical facts. In Lebanon as in India, in Indonesia, in the Philippines, in the Balkans, and, of course, in Iraq, religious violence and sectarian political discourse are very much products of the modern world, and not inevitable products of ancient history.

The dominant explanation for sectarianism has long been that sectarianism and modernity—invariably defined as secular and of Western origin—are opposites, mutually exclusive. This eurocentric paradigm insists that religious feelings, beliefs, culture, passions are persistent and immutable. Sectarianism, therefore, is almost always identified as a problem affecting less-developed countries, or those peripheral regions of Europe such as the Balkans or Northern Ireland. The destruction by Hindus of a mosque in late 20th-century India, for instance, is often explained as the inevitable outcome of a long history of antagonism between Hindus and Muslims in South Asia. Similarly, Maronite conflict with Druze in Lebanon is placed in the context of what is described as an age-old civilizational clash in the eastern Mediterranean. Sunni attacks on Shiites in Iraq are regarded as simply the latest example of a primordial schism within Islam.

The power of this paradigm can be explained by a simple observation: The discourse accompanying and justifying sectarian violence is itself expressed in language that leaves little room for historical nuance. More often than not, this language implies that Muslims (Sunni or Shia), Hindus, Jews, and Christians of the eastern world are irreconcilably different, inherently violent, and incorrigibly hostile to a collective transcendent identity, and therefore in a constant and immutable state of antagonism and hostility. The notion of age-old hostility, which is reinforced by every act of violence between religious communities and which ignores specific historical context, provides a reassuringly simple explanation for the otherwise bewildering nature of a complex modern world.

The Exemplary Case of Lebanon

For many observers, the case of Lebanese sectarianism is exemplary. Because the recent civil war (which ostensibly ended in 1990) mimicked many of the aspects of an earlier 19th-century conflict between Druze and Maronites that devastated the region in 1860 and culminated in unprecedented massacres of Christians in Dayr al-Qamar and Hasbayya, Lebanon has been written about as if its religious antagonisms stemmed from ancient grievances that have forever robbed it of an opportunity to "become" modern. The Balkans in the 1990s were "Lebanonized," it was said; now Iraq is said to have caught the Lebanese sectarian disease.

Bernard Lewis and other Orientalists such as the Israeli Moshe Maoz have suggested time and again that sectarianism represents a Muslim reaction, indeed a rage, against the modernization policies advanced by the Ottoman reform movement, which declared the equality of Muslim and non-Muslim and began a wholesale administrative, cultural, and military transformation of the Ottoman Empire. The implication of this polemical argument is that the Muslim majority could not really be modern; that is to say, Muslims could never accept Jews or Christians as equals, but had to be cajoled into a Western and presumably alien modernity by authoritarian regimes. Invariably the only evidence presented to support Lewis's interpretation is the testimony of contemporary European sources or the fact of the violence itself, as if the outbreak of religious hostilities in 1860 in and of itself was sufficient to prove a thesis of age-old sectarianism.

In trying to explain sectarianism, other historians have stressed social and economic pressures and the dislocations caused by the impact of European industrialization on the Syrian textile industry, which consequently declined. And still others have claimed that European rivalries played a decisive role in fomenting sectarian divisions. Historians, in short, have sought to explain the secular context of sectarianism; few have ever seriously grappled with sectarianism itself except to treat it as an easily grasped phenomenon, a cultural essence, a tribal will, a primordial religiosity that is antithetical to a liberal, egalitarian, and secular Western modernity.

To the extent that sectarianism in modern Lebanon is religious in articulation, it is indeed antithetical to an idealized secularism that totally separates religion from politics. However, since sectarianism emerged out of a 19th-century intersection of Ottoman reformation and Western intervention, it clearly should not be classified as antithetical to modernity. Before the 1860 massacres, social status—not religious affiliation—defined politics in Mount Lebanon. While in the Ottoman Empire as a whole, and in urban areas in particular, Muslims enjoyed political and cultural primacy over non-Muslims, the operative social and political distinction in rural Mount Lebanon was between knowledgeable elites on the one hand and ignorant commoners on the other, regardless of their respective religious affiliation. Both Christian and Druze religious authorities legitimized the traditional political and social order. It was the Europeans who, insisting on saving the "subjugated" Christians of the Orient, singled out religion in Mount Lebanon as the subject that required modern reform, and then became a sign of its achievement. In the mid-19th century, European powers intervened in the region on an explicitly sectarian basis, with the French championing the Maronites and the British protecting the Druze. The European powers also insisted, despite Ottoman protests, on a religious partition of Mount Lebanon along separate Christian and Druze lines in 1842. They downplayed the fact that in many areas Druze and Maronites either lived in the same villages or in the same districts.

In an effort to resist European encroachment and to construct a notion of a secularized Ottoman subject-citizen in the 1840s, the Ottomans in Mount Lebanon guaranteed equal political representation and taxation to Muslim (and Druze) and non-Muslim (Maronite) communities. The problem facing European powers, Ottoman authorities, and local elites alike was how to transform religious communities into political communities, while also preserving a hierarchical social order that discriminated between "knowledgeable" elites and "ignorant" commoners. The inability of foreign powers and local elites to manage this transformation, the squabbles over the meaning of Ottoman reform, and the battles that began between Druze notables and their erstwhile Christian subjects (who rejected "Druze" rule as incompatible with Ottoman reform) in Dayr al-Qamar opened the door to non-elite political participation and violence. Communal relations inadvertently democratized politics as non-elites forced themselves to the forefront of sectarian mobilizations which, in turn, often violated traditional hierarchies. Maronite commoners not only challenged Druze notables, but they also interpreted Ottoman reform to mean social as well as religious equality. The Maronite church in turn interpreted Ottoman reform to mean a "restoration" of an imagined Maronite Christian emirate in Mount Lebanon, though in fact such had never existed.

Ultimately, conflicting interpretations over the meaning of Ottoman reform rather than age-old religious antagonisms led directly to the sectarian violence in Mount Lebanon in the 1840s and culminated in the massacres of 1860. The war of 1860 and the massacres of Christian villagers by Druze forces, which were quickly followed by French and Ottoman military intervention in Syria, constituted the culmination of this formative period of sectarianism in Lebanon. These events marked the advent of a new culture of sectarianism, not a regression to an atavistic state. A post-1860 Administrative Council that was divided along religious lines and assisted the non-native Christian governor of Mount Lebanon built on earlier arrangements from the 1840s. This sectarian administrative "balance" was in turn elaborated by French mandatory power of the 1920s and 1930s, which clearly privileged the Maronite community in Lebanon. This imbalance was supposedly rectified by the 1943 National Pact, which legitimated the sectarian politics at the heart of post-independence Lebanon. Sectarianism, as a result, reached its most exaggerated form in the modern Lebanese state, which divides power on a supposedly proportional basis among the various religious communities in Lebanon. In this respect, the Taif Accord of 1989 is simply the latest in a series of sectarian arrangements that have defined Lebanese modernity.

The violence of this new culture should not obscure its revolutionary nature: European "humanitarian" intervention, Ottoman reform, and local aspirations combined to make the religious synonymous with the communal, and the communal parallel to the individual in the mid-19th century. In the social context of Mount Lebanon, sectarianism allowed non-elites to participate in politics to an unprecedented degree precisely because politics was defined along communal rather than exclusively elite lines. In the context of the Ottoman Empire as a whole, and against the backdrop of several hundred years of Muslim rule over Christian minorities, sectarianism represented a no less profound change: the state no longer had a single majority and several minorities, all defined in exclusionary religious terms, but a series of interdependent religious communities whose members were granted equal social and political status before the law.

That this sectarian revolution was radically distorted to favor the Maronites because of French colonialism in Lebanon during the post-Ottoman era (and which ultimately led to two civil wars to redress the imbalance) should not obscure its crucial break with an Ottoman history that privileged Muslim over non-Muslim and elite over commoner. Nor should it obscure the fact that by singling out religious community as the basis of modern political representation the sectarian revolution reified the idea of the sect, and therefore negated the possibility of any overarching secular citizenship.

The Components of Sectarian Culture

Sectarianism as a culture, therefore, is more than simply mindless religious violence: it is the historically contingent moment when religious difference becomes accepted and imagined as the bedrock of a modern politics of equal representation. Rather than stress individual equality, or a national citizenship that can and should aspire to transcend religious affiliation, the diversity of religious identity becomes the basis of national citizenship. The foundation of coexistence in modern Lebanon, therefore, depends on a notion that religious communities must be represented as political communities. Diversity makes Lebanon possible; it also immediately and effectively impedes any sense of a secular Lebanese citizenship.

Sectarianism as a culture is therefore not a "plot" concocted by foreign powers past and present. Rather it reflects the deliberate choices made by various groups at particular historical junctures. A key ingredient to the hegemonic culture of sectarianism in Lebanon and elsewhere—it is emerging in Iraq today—is the constant availability of local actors who are willing and eager to play the part of leaders and interlocutors for their respective communities. While the overt and covert intervention of Western powers certainly hastened the emergence of modern sectarianism in the Middle East, so too did the willingness of various local groups to actively work with these Western-inspired sectarian solutions, to accommodate themselves and to shape, enliven, and justify its outlines. History, in short, while filled with plans and plots and outside interventions and domination, is not so much the story of these plots and plans, but of how power gets translated in different settings and with different results. It is rarely, if ever, simply a story of how the powerful dominate, but almost always a larger and more complex story in which the less powerful allow themselves to be dominated. There are very few utterly powerless people in history.

The intense competition among local elites and non-elites to represent various essential religious communities, however, does not mean that we should ignore the obvious: the tentative nature of their efforts, and their many failures. For all the determined work to cohere a unitary notion of a community, there almost always has been and remains a deep struggle across class and regional lines to define this community, to silence internal dissidents, and to pretend that the evident fractures within it no longer indicate, though they once did, the instability of the notion of "sect." One has only to compare the desperation of the Maronite church in the late 1850s to create a unified vision in the face of Tanyus Shahin's commoner Maronite rebellion with today's lament by the Maronite Patriarch that Christian ranks in Lebanon are divided, to appreciate the degree to which the essential representation of a sect is not the same thing as its reality.

From Lebanon to Iraq

I wish, however, to clarify my argument. I am not saying that sectarianism is good because it is modern. And I am not suggesting that sectarianism is the only kind of modernity, as sectarian ideologues would have it. Nor am I suggesting that sectarianism is an ideal system. Clearly it is not: it is chronically unstable because constant struggles between and within religious communities to define political control of, and the limits to, these communities consistently overwhelm every attempt to build a national platform. In this sense, what is occurring today in Iraq is not analogous to the current situation in Lebanon. In Iraq there is an active, multidimensional, bloody struggle for power in the vacuum produced by the toppling of Saddam Hussein's repressive Arab nationalist regime and the presence of an illegitimate and incompetent US occupation. The extraordinary sectarian violence there is indicative of the total collapse of an established order of things: its final result may well be the dissolution of Iraq. Only if and when the US occupation forces withdraw, and only if the Iraqis are able to establish a government in which posts are regularly allocated according to religious or ethnic affiliation, will Iraq join the world's chronically sectarian regimes.

More to the point, there is a profound difference in specific context between Lebanon and Iraq. The culture of Lebanese sectarianism was born during the Ottoman era, before the British and French created the modern map of the Middle East, before the establishment of Israel and the concomitant ethnic cleansing of the Palestinians, before the advent of the Arab–Israeli conflict, the rise of Arab nationalism, the Iranian Revolution, the US support for Islamist movements in Afghanistan during the 1980s, and before the age of US hegemony. Modern Iraqi sectarianism, in contrast, comes very much after all these events and forces radically reshaped the region. Moreover, the tragedy to which we are now witness in Iraq is more shattering than that in Lebanon, for in Iraq the opportunity presented by independence from the British, by the rise of a coherent Arab Iraqi nationalism, and by the abundance of oil wealth was utterly squandered by independent Iraqi governments long before the US invasion of Iraq. Decades of successive Iraqi regimes' ruthless oppression of domestic opposition, their manipulation of potential tribal and religious opponents, their schemes of ethnic cleansing, and in Saddam's era, Iraqi wars of conquest, in effect paved the way for an American invasion and the subsequent fragmentation of the country.

There are, to be sure, some similarities in the situations of Lebanon and Iraq. Just as was the case in the 19th century, and just as is the case in present-day Lebanon, the sectarian reality of Iraq today cannot be separated from outside intervention (American, rather than British and French) or from the willingness on the part of Iraqis themselves to position themselves as authentic interlocutors for their respective communities. More ominously, the divisive legacy of the violence of 1860 and 1975–1990 in Lebanon has endured despite the formal end of fighting heralded by the end of the civil war. And in Iraq, assuming that the state survives, the violence will almost certainly have a similarly negative, profoundly destabilizing legacy, because its scale is extraordinary by any calculation. Finally, in the culture of sectarianism the articulation of a broad, national, and secular citizenship will always be sacrificed on the altar of narrower communal interests. This is the case in Lebanon, because it was upon these communal interests that the Lebanese state was founded and it is these interests that continue to dominate the state. Assuming the survival of Iraq, this will likely be the case there as well.

As important as it is to reject a sectarian version of history that interprets the past only in light of what it supposes were unchanging Muslim, Christian, or Jewish communal identities, it is also important to reject the conceit that sectarianism is either an atavistic urge or simply a colonial construction. In the case of Mount Lebanon, sectarianism represented the transition from a pre-colonial and pre-reform Ottoman history to a post-reform history dominated by the West. In the final analysis, what makes sectarianism so tenacious in Lebanon today is that it is an intrinsic component of the modern nation: it is a manifestation, but at the same time a subversion, of a discourse of equality. As a political culture it promises national accord, but works against the very idea of a transcendent national identity. Without recognizing the historical, social, and political complexity of sectarianism, the secular criticism of it will continue to be little more than indignant sound and fury—as impotent as it is misdirected. It will continue to miss the point of the intensity and the proliferation of modern sectarian allegiances and antipathies.

2. STATE–SOCIETY RELATIONS AND THE REPRODUCTION OF THE LEBANESE CONFESSIONAL SYSTEM

Nubar Hovsepian

This essay was written in 1991 and revised in January 2007. No attempt is made to cover post-1991 developments, a task covered in the essays by Georges Corm and Lara Deeb. The present tense in the essay refers to 1991.

In the period prior to the outbreak of the 1975 civil war, state–society relations in Lebanon were mostly analyzed through two prisms: the consociational model or the pluralist approach to the study of state–society relations.[1] All of these writings assume the existence of a central state. It is my contention that the writ never ran in Lebanon. The first task, then, is to pose questions about the particularities of state formation in Lebanon. Did the state, as juridically constituted, exercise hegemony over the entire territory of Lebanon? A second question will focus on the corresponding structure of civil society. It will be noted that the organization of society along "confessional"[2] cleavages seems to deny the state the ability to consolidate its centralization and to develop hegemonic power.

My intention is to analyze the tension between the state and civil society that is produced within the confessional parameters of their existence. In examining these relationships, we can identify the reasons for the persistence of fragmentation and the inherent tendency of the confessional system to produce internal strife and civil war. But to limit our analysis to internal factors would produce only a partial picture. Hence it is proposed that events in Lebanon cannot be understood in isolation; they must be viewed as three concentric circles: local (internal Lebanese dynamics), regional (the role of neighboring states), and international power politics (particularly by the United States). A corollary of this is that major events or the policies of any of the actors in the Lebanese drama can be explained only by viewing them within the context of the three concentric circles.

State and Society

Joel Midgal develops a model of state–society relations applicable to Third

World societies.[3] He attempts to delineate the factors that render states "strong" or "weak." Hence, his book focuses on "how to understand state capabilities." The first part of the Migdal model "emphasizes the distribution of social control among the many organizations in society that vie to make the rules about how people should behave." This leads him to explore the reasons why in many Third World societies, the state has been unable to become the effective organization that "establishes those rules of behavior." Thirdly, Migdal delineates the salient reasons for the development of certain social patterns that "impeded the growth of state capabilities" in a variety of Third World countries.

To determine whether a state is strong or weak, he proposes to assess the capabilities of states,[4] which enable them to induce social control, defined as, "getting people to behave differently from what they would otherwise do." Conjunctionally, the failure of some Third World states to secure peoples' compliance—in the cities or even in the more remote areas—to state objectives and goals, in effect, undermines state capabilities. Migdal's central concern is, therefore, to explore the "duality of states—their unmistakable strengths in penetrating societies and their surprising weaknesses in effecting goal oriented social-changes." Finally, to explain this paradox, Migdal draws our attention to the societal forces responsible for "resistance to the designs of state leaders and of the factors that make state leaders unable or unwilling to overcome such resistance."

Though Migdal is explicitly critical of statist approaches that regard the state as an "autonomous" entity from society, he nevertheless joins them in defining the state in classical ideal-type Weberian terms.[5] Timothy Mitchell has pointed out that an inherent weakness with such a definition lies in its inability to determine the contours of the boundaries between state and society.[6] Despite the potential for confusion arising from such definitions, Migdal refutes the state-centric paradigm by focusing on the endless struggle for social control between state leaders and an assortment of "strongmen" who resist the state through their respective social organizations.[7] Through these patron-client networks, local leaders provide support and devise survival strategies for significant portions of society.[8] Ultimately, state power resides in the ability of state leaders to increase state social control. In the event of the persistence of internal weakness, the propensity for external interference or aggression increases. Migdal makes this point with a clear reference to the state of disintegration in Lebanon, which made it into a theater for intervention by official and non-official local, regional, and international armed forces.[9]

Migdal conceptualizes society "as a melange of social organizations." Thus, the mechanisms of social control in society are diverse and are exercised by "fairly autonomous groups rather than concentrated largely in the state." Therefore, a high level of authority is concentrated in society, but the exercise of this authority tends to be fragmented and marked by internal conflict.[10] In the competition for social control between the state and other social organizations, Migdal suggests that the state can prevail, and therefore increase its social control if it increases the level of "compliance," "participation," and "legitimation."[11]

Migdal analyzes the limitations of states in the context of their interaction with "weblike" societies by focusing on the historical, socio-cultural, political, and economic factors that developed during precolonial, colonial, and postcolonial eras. He observes that the persistence of, inter alia, boundary disputes, fractionalism (ethnic, linguistic, and religious), fragmented social control, and the existence of competing systems of justice, has mitigated against the emergence of state hegemony over society. As such, Migdal cautions that state capabilities cannot be understood outside of the social structures that define them. Thus, the inherent weakness of most Third World states is a by-product of both internal and external weaknesses, which undermine their ability to forge real nation building.

Some critics might argue that societal pluralism is the "exception rather than the rule throughout the Third World, and state control over society appears to be stronger than Migdal's analysis would suggest."[12] But such conclusions fail to note that centralized authority in many Third World countries is a function of the state's monopoly control over the means of violence and not a result of voluntarily bestowed legitimacy.[13] Thus, despite a high level of concentration of coercive power in state institutions, with, as Migdal puts it, "a tremendous concentration of social control," many individuals and social sectors have failed to attain citizenship through a process of enfranchisement. Instead of drawing upon their historical experience, the decolonized states pursued the inherited colonial policies leading to the perpetuation of fragmented social control.[14] To maintain their hegemony, state leaders have tried to implement policies of cooptation and accommodation, intended to curtail the development of independent organizations that are run by the "strongmen" who are in conflict with the state. Paradoxically, these measures have led to the perpetuation of the "strongmen's" influence, which is dependent on state resources. Migdal, in agreement with Chazan and Azarya, concludes that this leads to the "enfeeblement of the state." Finally, he notes that "strong states" can emerge, and indeed have emerged, as a result of wars, revolutions, massive migrations, and military threats from the outside. In such a context, Third World states can consolidate their hegemony, Migdal contends, if they develop effective and independent bureaucracies filled with capable and independent cadres, and backed by strong leadership.

Migdal's rejection of the statist analysis leads him to an equally problematic position. Do state and society become "independent" as a result of the "enfeeblement" of the former? The question of boundary is central. Though the distinction between state and society is important, it would seem that their relationship is one of perpetual intersection. I agree with Markovitz that the state remains the focal point of activity.[15] Through their activities, actions, and policies of survival, both state leaders and the "strongmen" (civil society) are targeting the state and seeking its support. The arena of conflict is best defined as a struggle between competing or conflicting interests (class, ethnic, national, or, in Lebanon's case, confessional).[16] Therefore the boundary between state and society is the effect of the constant interaction between the two. Commenting on the state–society dichotomy, Mitchell observes: "The essence of modern politics is not policies from one side of this division being applied to or shaped by the other, but the producing and reproducing of this difference."[17]

Finally, Migdal's analysis leaves me uncertain as to whether the process of democratization is best served by weak or strong states. I agree with David Held that for democracy to flourish in Third World countries, let alone in the new states of Eastern and Central Europe, a process of "double democratization" is needed.[18] This requires the interdependent transformation of both state and civil society, as they struggle to define their "interpenetrate," as Markovitz puts it, boundaries and jurisdictions.

Gramsci and the State–Society Problematique

Several centuries before Antonio Gramsci developed his concept of hegemony in the *Prison Notebooks*,[19] an almost identical meaning was given to this concept by Ibn Khaldun. Ibn Khaldun was concerned—almost obsessed—with the strength or weakness of states. For him state strength is composed of two key ingredients: The actual capabilities of the state and the recognition by others (civil society) not only of these capabilities, but also of the legitimacy of the professed ideology of the ruling *asabiyya*.[20]

Gramsci's notion of hegemony applies not only to the strategy of the proletariat but also to the practices of the ruling classes in general.[21] A class displays its supremacy in two ways: "domination" and "intellectual and moral leadership."[22] Briefly, it leads the allied classes and dominates the opposing classes. Class hegemony is not simply the result of simple political alliances, but, as Chantal Mouffe notes, it is the product of "a complete fusion of economic, political, intellectual and moral objectives which will be brought about by one fundamental group and groups allied to it through the intermediary of ideology...."[23] In other words, the power of a state does not reside in its monopoly on violence, but in securing the acceptance of the ruled to the worldview of the rulers—the hegemonic class. This, then, is the precise source of state legitimacy.

National consensus or "national will" result from a condition where the relationship between the state (political society) and civil society are not disjointed. In this context, a genuine "collective will" is the result of the fusion and interaction between the state and societal institutions such as religious institutions, political parties, trade unions, schools, and most importantly the intellectuals. The simultaneous existence and interaction between "hegemony" and "collective will" presupposes the capacity of the class or classes exercising political power to not only rule, but to also lead.

If the relations between the state and society are ruptured, a fragmented order will prevail. This means that for the state to preserve its strength it will in effect abandon the ideological claim for its legitimacy. In this context, the state neither leads nor governs; it simply rules. The rule of law, then, becomes more or less an arbitrary instrument for formalizing state rule. The result is either authoritarian rule, or a state of near anarchy, as exemplified by fragmented societies plagued by internecine conflict and civil war. Put differently, the absence of a hegemonic class and state causes a rift with civil society. This leads to the perpetuation of fractional or clannish rule in the name of a non-existing "general will" that corresponds with the narrowing of a regime's social base. For countries like Lebanon, the problem is how a genuine ideological unity might be forged between different social groups (confessions) in such a way as to induce them to unite into a single political unit. To solve this, one must grapple with the problems associated with decolonization, minorities and nationalities, the national security state, or the weak state.

One can deduce from Gramsci's formulations that a strong state is predicated on the attainment of genuine hegemony. Moreover, it is interactive and intersecting with society, which leaves the door open for the exercise and implementation of various forms of democratic rule, as a function of the presence of hegemony.

The remainder of this essay will focus on the particularities of state–society relations in Lebanon. I will cover only a select number of topics, with the intention of identifying key problematics: The impact of confessionalism on the state–society; the impact of a fragmented society on the extent of state hegemony; the absence of legitimacy for Lebanon as a state among the Lebanese and its Arab neighbors (disputed or artificial boundaries); the endemic nature of conflict and civil strife in a confessional system; the tendency and general proclivity of the confessional system to seek exogenous support in adjudicating internal conflict; and finally, the role of crises in contributing to the politicization of religion.

State Formation: Confessionalism

The outbreak of civil war in and for Lebanon in 1975 is an expression of the persistence of a fundamental disagreement among the Lebanese over the "historicity of their country: the Christians by and large affirming it, and the Muslims denying it."[24] Before the formation of the Lebanese state in 1920, its sovereignty and legitimacy were secured through Ottoman recognition. Modern Lebanese history, which can be traced to the end of the 17th century,[25] witnessed the development of a relatively secular emirate in Mount Lebanon ruled jointly by the Maronites and the Druze. Worsening relations between the Maronites and the Druze led to open and violent conflict in 1840. The Ottomans, already weakened by a rising European challenge, failed to establish direct rule in Mount Lebanon. Hence, from 1841 Mount Lebanon was divided by the European powers into two *kaymakamates* (administrative units): the northern one for the Maronites and the southern one for the Druze. One of the inherent shortcomings of this system lay in the fact that despite the demarcation of borders between the *kaymakamates*, the Druze region retained a Christian majority. Wade Goria concludes that this "bicephalous Maronite–Druze polity had, by its very nature, accented Druze–Maronite sectarianism."[26] This led to social tensions that were exacerbated by economic dislocations caused by the penetration of European products into the local markets. The Maronites sought the assistance of the French, and the Druze countered by seeking British protection.[27] Together these factors led to a full-scale civil war in 1860 between the Maronites and the Druze. French forces occupied Lebanon in 1860, which led to the adoption of the Reglement Organique, to replace the *kaymakamate*. The new system reorganized Mount Lebanon into a *mutasarrifate*: a single administrative region (sanjak) of the Ottoman Empire to be ruled by a Christian governor appointed by Istanbul with the approval of the European powers. This system remained intact until 1915. The Maronites sought the expansion of Lebanon to include the present day Beqaa Valley, the coast (Beirut), the south, and parts of northern Palestine. These ambitions, which were part of a cultural and literary revival movement, enabled the Maronites to introduce the concepts of nation and state into their political vocabulary. Their project, however, could only be realized, they argued, under French tutelage. Their vision was one of a "Grand Liban."[28]

With the defeat of the Ottomans in World War I, the French and the British divided up much of Middle Eastern territory among themselves, and through the League of Nations secured the right to rule these areas as Mandates.[29] Thus on September 1, 1920 General Gouraud, on behalf of the French and with Maronite prodding, proclaimed the formation of Greater Lebanon, with Beirut as its capital.[30] Meir Zamir correctly notes that the establishment of modern Lebanon is the product of the evolution of the centuries-old Druze *imara* (feudal state) into a Maronite-dominated entity, as well as of French colonial designs.[31] The establishment of the Lebanese nation-state was simultaneously rejoiced by the Maronites and vehemently opposed by almost 50 percent of the population—the Muslims. So from the outset, the Republic of Lebanon[32] was a fragmented society, which produced a state dominated and monopolized by the elites of only one of its fractions or confessions—the Maronites. Kamal Salibi, formerly an advocate of political Maronitism, concludes: "In Lebanon, while the Christian political establishment dominated by the Maronites was fully determined to make a success of the state, there was a Muslim opposition which was equally determined to make it a failure."[33] The Maronites were to rely on France, and the Muslims were to seek solidarity with their Arab brethren, especially in Syria.[34]

From the outset, as a political community Lebanon was divided along two not only competing, but opposing, visions and ideologies: Particularist (Lebanism) and Universalist (Arabism).[35] Salibi points out that from the beginning both of these forces "collided on every fundamental issue, impeding the normal development of state and keeping its political legitimacy and ultimate viability continuously in question."[36]

The Maronite and Sunni Muslim elites adopted an unwritten National Pact in 1943, the year Lebanon became independent. Through this pact the proportional and confessional system became the central and guiding principles of the political system. It was not until 1946 that most of the population and the leaders of the other confessions were to discover the contents and provisions of this "Pact."[37] Shortly before the outbreak of the 1975 civil war, the French political scientist Maurice Duverger noted that the confessional system serves to "consolidate the domination of the privileged classes... [which] tends to unite the ruling classes and divide the downtrodden."[38]

The confessional system (state–society relations) in Lebanon has led to the politicization of religious and sectarian differences.[39] This system produced and often required the existence of political organizations with feudal-style leaders representing various sects and vying with other such organizations for a share of Lebanon's resources. The Lebanese were recognized not as citizens or members of civil society, but as members of the officially recognized confessions. By necessity each Lebanese must belong to one of these sects—or otherwise be a non-person. Each sect has a formal leadership, promulgates laws governing marriage, inheritance and other personal matters, maintains courts and juridical procedures, elects deputies to parliament, sponsors political parties,[40] runs schools with educational orientations that are often hostile to other communities[41] and provides hospitals, health facilities, and other social agencies.

All of these factors engender clannishness within Lebanese society and promote, to a limited extent, the geographical segregation of the religious-ethnic groups. The system promotes separateness among the Lebanese on the basis of their sectarian identity; it enhances sectarian suspicions and allegiances. Therefore real power lies in the elites of the sectarian institutions, and the state's ability to govern is greatly diminished.[42]

The confessional system in addition lacks the ability to resolve internal conflicts that are endemic to it. Thus, intervention by foreign powers has always been necessary when internal conflicts rage out of control. The French served as foreign guarantor from the 19th century to the middle of the 20th. In the 1950s, the rising tide of Arab nationalism coupled with the outbreak of civil war in 1958 induced the US to intervene to maintain "stability." In other words, US intervention intended to keep the confessional system intact, and the US became the new exogenous guarantor of the Lebanese system.[43]

From the standpoint of Migdal's model of state–society relations, Lebanon could very well be viewed as a special case where both state and society are weak. The state does not possess the capabilities to induce social control. The state serves as an arena from which the elites of each confession secure resources for their respective members. The weak state is a reflection of the original structural design, and not a result of resistance emanating from the autonomous groups of the weblike society.[44] The turbulence, upheaval, deaths, and social dislocations that have plagued Lebanon since 1975, coupled with the numerous military threats from the outside, have not and cannot lead to the emergence of a strong state. Neither can the emergence of an independent bureaucracy or strong leadership secure that desired goal. Simply put, the perpetual intersection between state and society within the confines of confessionalism can only reproduce a weak state and perpetuate a fragmented society.

Confessionalism survived and thrived as long as the elites maintained a consensus on the need to maintain the confessional setup. However, this consensus was predicated on a created or constructed myth— Lebanese nationalism. The formation of Lebanon created the juridical components of sovereignty and nationality. In this context, Salibi asks: "But are administrative bureaucracies, flags and national anthems sufficient to make a true nation-state out of a given territory of people who inhabit? What about the question of nationality?"[45] Therefore, Lebanon's problems do not stem from the absence or presence of a weak state. The root of the problem stems from the social and political institutions within which "decolonized... [Lebanese] have lived and tried to survive."[46] The ideology of "nation-statism," which in Lebanon grew out of 19th-century conjunctures, has made social conflict with a propensity for full-scale civil war a central feature of the confessional system. I would agree with Migdal that the persistence of internal weakness in Lebanon has made foreign intervention not only easier, but also usually invited by one or another of the protagonists of the confessional system.

The End of Consensus: Civil War

Gramsci's notions of hegemony, hegemonic class, and collective will are most useful on the prescriptive level of analysis. Namely, could the Lebanese system become de-confessionalized—and how? Did the outbreak of the second Lebanese civil war since the institution of the National Pact open the possibilities for the formation of a democratic secular state animated by the ideals of equality of citizenship similar to those of the French Revolution of 1789?[47] Clearly, it is beyond the scope of this essay to study the details of the civil war that started in 1975 and essentially ended in 1990.[48] The civil war represents the extreme case of the inherent conflictual nature of the confessional system. What caused the breakdown? Did this breakdown offer the opportunity for the realization of a hegemonic state with its legitimacy rooted in a genuine collective will?

As mentioned before, the system lacks the ability to resolve the internal conflicts that are endemic to Lebanon, so inevitably foreign powers are called in. In the 1970s, the system began to disintegrate because of two new elements. The first was the rise of disparities between classes, whose needs and demands could neither be accommodated nor forcibly repressed. The second was the absence of foreign powers willing or able to intervene and resolve the conflict as in the past. This development came about primarily because of the basic split among regional and world powers caused by the Arab–Israeli conflict. But when intervention became unattractive, it was replaced by the use of local proxies.[49]

Accelerating economic growth and development in the late 1960s and early 1970s caused many dislocations and internal migrations,[50] resulting in severe socioeconomic inequalities that rendered Lebanon a "crisis-prone society."[51] A nascent industrial sector in the urban areas was hardly capable of absorbing the flood of landless peasants. Tourism and banking were the mainstays of the economy. In this connection, Roger Owen points out that only two of the sixteen largest banks were locally owned.[52] Moreover, the economy was essentially monopolized, causing a severe reduction in the standard of living of the disadvantaged classes. Finally, the economy was well integrated into the world market system, but only in its role as a relay station between Western capital and markets in the East. Beirut's reputed affluence presented a facade of stability to outside observers, but internally it aggravated social tension because of the system's inability to deliver the needed goods to its people (particularly in the south). The ensuing large-scale emigration and internal migration to the cities resulted in the founding of "poverty belts" in and around Beirut, Saida [Sidon], and Tripoli. These places were the center of fighting in 1975–1976.

Economic protests broke out that were national and class-based, rather than sectarian. Workers, peasants, students, and fishermen staged repeated strikes. In 1974, during the 35-day period from March 26 to April 29, there was at least a strike a day, as well as a 3-day national strike.[53] This upsurge of protest was supported and led by the nascent Lebanese National Movement (LNM), which was also allied with the Palestinian movement. The LNM was composed of 13 different organizations and the syndicalist unions, and thus posed a potential for cross-confessional alliances.[54] Such a development alarmed not only the dominant Maronite Phalangists, but also Lebanon's neighbors, Syria and Israel. The civil war erupted,[55] and the political stage was filled with two competing tendencies. The LNM, representing the secular Arabist forces (universalist), sought the overhaul of confessionalism and the establishment of a secular democratic order.[56] On the other side, the particularist and sectarian right-wing coalition known as the Lebanese Front (LF) sought the preservation of the basic provisions of the 1943 National Pact.[57]

Syria's invasion in 1976[58] and Israel's invasion of south Lebanon in 1978 contributed to the widening of the war. With these external thrusts, the internal battle for and against confessionalism was muted.[59] The interplay of inter-Arab and Arab–Israeli conflicts had by 1978 pulled Lebanon "more directly than ever into the vortex of the Arab–Isreali problem."[60] Israel's 1978 invasion proved to be a dress rehearsal for its major invasion of Lebanon four years later.[61]

All of these internal and external factors contributed to the disintegration of the Lebanese order. Yet despite the extent of this disintegration and agony,[62] Lebanese confessionalism survived—albeit with some minor reforms initially introduced in 1976 and later revised and adopted through the 1989 Taif Accord.[63] The central government is still trying to extend its authority over the entire country, in an attempt to emulate the "stability" of prewar times. But can the restoration of the status quo ante, characterized by a weak state and society, help prevent the outbreak of future crises? Government officials and other leaders have sought answers to this question in the context of a severely diminished state and a society more segregated than ever along sectarian lines. This particular outcome of the civil war has, according to Lebanese sociologist Salim Nasr, "gravely weakened the social basis of Lebanese society."[64]

The Resilience of the Confessional Order

After almost sixteen years of war and internal strife, Lebanon is at a critical juncture. Current efforts at accommodation and national reconciliation are unfolding in a Lebanon impoverished by war. Before the war, Lebanon was ranked in the top tier of the less developed countries. Today it has slipped into the bottom tier. About 40 percent of the population is unemployed and current income compared to 1974 has been reduced by at least 50 percent. At least one-third of the population is in need of assistance for education, healthcare, and shelter. Income disparities are greater today than they were in 1974. The cost of the cumulative damage sustained over the last sixteen years is conservatively estimated at $25 billion. The level of investment required for the revitalization of the economy over the next ten years exceeds $40 billion.[65]

The net effect of this rather discouraging socioeconomic picture is that Lebanon has returned to a condition resembling the dynamics of the early 1970s. Secondly, the war has for all practical purposes eliminated the salaried middle class. The upper economic class has for the most part imposed exile on itself, mostly in the major cities of Western Europe. Salim Nasr estimates that the assets of this "transnationalized" sector are estimated at $10–20 billion. He notes that this has caused a considerable shift in the sectarian composition of the economic bourgeoisie, which today is roughly equal between Christian and Muslim.[66] Plans for reconstruction assume that the Lebanese have embarked on a process of reconciliation. Can the Lebanese go beyond what Kamal Salibi described as a "house of many mansions"? Can the conflicting histories of the past be replaced with a common and unified synthesis of Lebanese history, which would also accept the legitimacy of its internationally recognized boundaries? In other words, to attain a shared collective will, Lebanon must be viewed as a public space to be shared by all of its diverse communities. Simply put, Lebanon must come to terms with its past in order to project a common basis for a new social and national contract.

In August of 1991 while on a visit to Lebanon I engaged leading Lebanese writers and intellectuals of diverse political backgrounds in serious discussions. I conducted more than a dozen interviews, and with no exception all of those interviewed agreed that the war was over. But the war ended not because a new social contract had been reached, but simply because the combatants were exhausted. Moreover, all the ambitions of individual sects (Maronite, Shiite, Druze, etc.) were defeated or frustrated. Finally there was a strong desire to preserve a "shared Lebanon." The most interesting, fruitful, free, and open discussions were held jointly with Joseph Abu-Khalil, a Maronite writer and formerly editor for 25 years of *Al-Amal* (newspaper of the Phalangist party), and Elias Khoury, a leading Arab novelist and a Greek Orthodox who fought the Phalangists not only with the written word, but with arms as well. Abu-Khalil was already ostracized by the remaining diehard advocates of political Maronitism. He was strongly against the reestablishment of a Maronite state. Instead he advocated institutional reforms, as part of a transitional approach (adoption of a civil code, civil marriage, nationality law, rule of law, etc.) to modernize and secularize the Lebanese polity. Khoury did not disagree with Abu-Khalil's prescriptive approach per se. He depicted Lebanon as "not a homeland... it is just a place where people exist." In turn Khoury posed a difficult question to Abu-Khalil: "We are talking about the future, but we have yet to discuss why we shot at each other [literally] for sixteen years. Why does the process of reconciliation deny us a platform for such a conversation? Your mistake resides in ignoring our sins!"[67]

In my reading and interpretation of Middle Eastern history since 1967, the years 1975–1976 represent a conjunctural (Braudel's term *conjoncturel*) moment where the possibility for secular democracy to prevail was great. Such a moment existed in 1975 under the leadership of the iconoclastic leader Kamal Jumblatt. Not only were sectarian cleavages being challenged, but counter-hegemonic forces were near victory on the battlefield. Confessionalism was in retreat, and the possibility for a new Lebanese republic based on democratic secularism seemed to be within reach. As result of the efforts of the counter-hegemonic forces (classes and cross-sect alliances), a hegemonic state and a reconstituted civil society were a likely outcome. The now exiled bourgeoisie was interested in securing reform to avoid the "revolution" that ensued. Clearly this outcome could not have been instituted in one fell swoop. This is precisely why the LNM under Jumblatt's leadership had proposed a Transitional Program toward the deconfessionalizing of state–society relations. This of course did not happen. Why? We need to subject this question to rigorous inquiry.

I agree with Elias Khoury that the possibilities for a secular Lebanon were buried and decimated by the Syrian intervention of 1976.[68] This intervention resulted in the historic defeat of the LNM's thesis for transitional change. I would surmise that had Jumblatt not been killed by the Syrians he would have been reduced to a Druze chieftain or opted for exile. Lebanon's situation within the various spheres of conflict—inter-Arab and Arab–Israeli—contributed to the defeat of the secularizing forces. Why did Syria, Israel, and other regional and international forces intervene? Did they agree with Jumblatt's hypothesis that a secular order in Lebanon could have triggered a regionwide political reformation? Syria's 1976 intervention[69] essentially intended to maintain an outcome similar to the 1958 equilibrium of "no vanquished and no conquerer" in Lebanon.[70] The United States, which assisted Syria and Israel to reach an entente cordiale, was then as in the 1950s interested in preserving Lebanon's precarious balance to insure its economic interests in the region through Lebanon.[71] This new conjuncture negated the previous conjunctural moment, which led to the preservation of confessionalism albeit in the context of continuing civil strife. All of these developments served to accelerate the process of political polarization, thus rendering sectarianism as the only possible basis of political cleavage. The persistence of a revitalized sectarianism paved the way for the intensification of the religious component of the conflict. Multiple and continuous political realignments occurred. Secular parties lost their membership to the rejuvenated sectarian/religious parties.[72]

Confessionalism had not only survived, but was in fact saved from extinction by the combined forces operating within our three concentric circles.

NOTES

1 See in particular, Leonard Binder, ed., *Politics in Lebanon* (New York: Wiley, 1966), especially the essay by Edward Shils, "The Prospect for Lebanese Civility" (1–11); Michael Hudson, *The Precarious Republic: Political Modernization in Lebanon* (New York: Random House, 1968); and Elie Salem, *Modernization Without Revolution: Lebanon's Experience* (Bloomington, IN: Indiana University Press, 1973).

2 The term "confessionalism" is derived from the Ottoman millet, a system of quasi-autonomous ethnic religious communities that provided a form of centralized control over decentralized religious groups. The latter paid taxes to the former. This relationship has served both to strengthen existing sects and undermine the formation of an effective state. The millet system was also helpful to the Europeans in their successful political and economic penetration of the Ottoman Empire. See Lois A. Aroian and Richard P. Mitchell, *The Modern Middle East and North Africa* (New York: Macmillan Publishing Company, 1984) 55, 93–94; and also consult Nubar Hovsepian, "The Lebanon Quagmire," *Nation* 6 June 1981: 686–689.

3 Joel S. Migdal, *Strong Societies and Weak States: State–Society Relations and State Capabilities in the Third World* (Princeton: Princeton University Press, 1988). His model was previously developed and published as "A Model of State–Society Relations," in Howard Wiarda, ed., *New Directions in Comparative Politics* (Boulder, CO: Westview Press, 1991) 45–58. Where not marked by other notes, the Migdal references are, in order, from the following pages: xx, 4n3, 9, 28, 262, 266, 270–275.

4 For Migdal, state capabilities are divided into four clusters of capacities: the penetration of society, the regulation of social relations, the extraction of resources, and the appropriation of resources for use in ways determined by the state (4–5).

5 The state is an organization that claims a monopoly within fixed boundaries over the legitimate use of violence. Moreover, it is composed of various agencies—executive authority—capable of imposing binding rules for all the people (Migdal 19).

6 See the poignant analysis in Timothy Mitchell, "The Limits of the State: Beyond Statist Approaches and Their Critics," *American Political Science Review* 85 (1991) 77–96, especially 82.

7 The category "strongmen" includes chiefs, landlords, bosses, rich peasants, clan leaders, za'im, effendis, aghas, etc. (Migdal 33).

8 Survival strategies are marshaled on two basic fronts: the struggle for internal social control, and the struggle in the international arena against external threats. The Westphalia model of nation-states seems best suited to serve the latter function. Accordingly, despite the "strongmen's" ability to devise survival strategies, these abilities tend to be diminished when confronting an external enemy. In turn, the state accrues more power over society precisely because it is better suited to mobilize armies and other institutions such as tax collecting and the expansion of a judicial system (Migdal 21–22).

9 This point will be elaborated in our specific discussion of Lebanon below. See Migdal 24.

10 The conflict could be over who has power to determine the content of national education policies, religious considerations, or ethnic conflicts over boundaries and territoriality (Migdal 30). The diminished role of the state in the realm of education in Lebanon will be discussed below. See in particular, Munir Bashur, "The Role of Education: A Mirror of a Fractured National Image," in Halim Barakat, ed., *Toward A Viable Lebanon* (Washington, DC: Center For Contemporary Arab Studies, Georgetown University, 1988) 42–67. On the state's role in education and social change, see the impressive work by Martin Carnoy and Joel Samoff, *Education and Social Transition in the Third World* (Princeton: Princeton University Press, 1990).

11 Migdal suggests that compliance most often pertains to the control of force. Participation denotes the ability to incorporate people, voluntarily, in the institutions of the state; legitimation is secured through people's "approval of the state's desired social order through their acceptance of the state's myths" (32–33).

12 See Paul Orogun's review of Migdal's work in *American Political Science Review* 85 (1991) 669–672, especially 671.

13 See Basil Davidson's book, *The Black Man's Burden: Africa and the Curse of the Nation-State* (New York: Times Books, 1992).

14 With deep insight, Basil Davidson shows that in Africa colonial rule was instrumental in eliminating the essentially native African forms of community and self-government. In turn, the nationalists who led the independence movements adopted a new European ideology of "nation-statism." According to Davidson, this new form perpetuates social fragmentation and enables the state to acquire enormous powers over society. Therefore it follows that the problem of legitimacy is a function of this dichotomy.

15 Irving Leonard Markovitz, "An Uncivil View of Civil Society in Africa," in *Civil Society and Democracy in Africa*, Nelson Kasfir, ed. (London: Frank Cass, 1998).

16 Migdal is quite dismissive of approaches that insist on the relevance, indeed the need, for identifying the class interests of the state. He goes as far as to suggest that "questions of overall class relations may be beyond the influence of the state" (19n19). Many authors have argued that state actions in the Third World do affect not only class relations, but have an impact in the restructuring of classes as well. For an example of this approach, consult Alan Richards and John Waterbury, *A Political Economy of the Middle East: State, Class, and Economic Development* (Boulder, CO: Westview Press, 1990) especially 8–51. Elsewhere Markovitz makes the same point (n15).

17 Mitchell 95.

18 See David Held, *Models of Democracy* (Stanford, CA: Stanford University Press, 1987) especially ch. 9.

19 Antonio Gramsci, *Selections From the Prison Notebooks* (New York: International Publishers, 1971).

20 Ibn Khaldun (1332–1406) wrote his Prolegomena to his *Universal History* between 1375 and 1379. Centuries before Hobbes and Locke, Ibn Khaldun sought the bases of legitimacy for kingship. Understanding that force alone could not keep states together, he made famous the Arabic terms *asabiyya* (social solidarity or the strength of

blood ties among the people), and *iltiham*, which is the "ultimate form of hegemony in its insistence on social integration by and around the ideology professed by the ruling asabiyya." Quoted from Ghassan Salame, "'Strong' and 'Weak' States: A Qualified Return to the Muqaddimah," in Giacomo Luciani, *The Arab State* (Berkeley: University of California Press, 1990) 32. For an English edition of Ibn Khaldun's work, see *The Muqaddimah: An Introduction to History*, translated by Franz Rosenthal (Princeton: Princeton University Press, Bollingen Series, 1967).

21 My treatment of Gramsci is more or less schematic, as opposed to comprehensive. I only wish to interject some of his notions to enable a comparison and possibly a critique of the Migdal approach.

22 Gramsci 57.

23 Chantal Mouffe, "Hegemony and Ideology in Gramsci," in Chantal Mouffe, ed., *Gramsci and Marxist Theory* (London: Routledge & Kegan Paul, 1979) 181.

24 Quoted from Kamal Salibi, *A House of Many Mansions: The History of Lebanon Reconsidered* (Berkeley: University of California Press, 1988) 3. Salibi is regarded as a revisionist Lebanese (Christian) historian. The outbreak of civil war forced him to reconsider the problems associated with Lebanese state formation. This book then is not a history of Lebanon, but rather it is an examination of the competing historiographies and their underlying ideologies.

25 Kamal Salibi, *The Modern History of Lebanon* (London: Weidenfeld and Nicolson, 1965) xii.

26 Wade R. Goria, *Sovereignty and Leadership in Lebanon 1943–1976* (London: Ithaca Press, 1985) 16.

27 Economic dislocations cannot be attributed only to the penetration of European capital. Struggles between feudalists and landless peasants were rampant. But this period can be viewed as the incorporation of Lebanon in the capitalist world-system. For a brief but poignant discussion of these issues, see Paul Saba, "The Creation of the Lebanese Economy: Economic Growth in the 19th & Early 20th Centuries," in Roger Owen, ed., *Essays on the Crisis in Lebanon* (London: Ithaca Press, 1976) 1–22. For a state-of-the-art synopsis of Lebanese socioeconomic history, see Claude Dubar and Salim Nasr, *Les Classes sociales au Liban* (Paris: Presses de la Fondation Nationale des Sciences Politiques, 1976) especially 1–62.

28 To say the least, this historical narrative is quite condensed and somewhat schematic. For a complete account of this important conjuncture of modern Lebanese history, one must consult the following works: Albert Hourani, "Lebanon: From Feudalism to Nation-State," in Albert Hourani, *Europe and the Middle East* (London: Macmillan, 1980) 142–88; Albert Hourani, *Syria and Lebanon: A Political Essay* (Oxford: Oxford University Press, 1947); Salibi, *The Modern History of Lebanon*; Dominique Chevalier, *La Societe du mont Liban a l'epoque de la revolution industrielle en Europe* (Paris: Geuthner, 1971); and Ahmad Beydoun, *Identite confessionnelle et temps social chez les historiens Libanais contemporains* (Beyrouth: Universite Libanaise, 1984).

29 See "The Remaking of the Near East 1918–1923" in M.E. Yapp, *The Making of The Modern Near East: 1792–1923* (London: Longman, 1987) 301–351; and Albert Hourani, *A History of the Arab Peoples* (Cambridge: Belknap/Harvard University Press, 1991) especially 315–332.

30 This feat was achieved as French troops defeated and overturned the Faisal government in Damascus in July 1920. France applied the classic divide-and-rule colonial policies to Syria. "Greater Lebanon" was pieced together by annexing Ottoman provinces previously part of "Greater Syria" to Mount Lebanon. This in effect doubled the size of Lebanon. The newly annexed areas were predominantly Muslim (now north and south Lebanon, the Beqaa Valley, and Beirut). Aroian and Mitchell (see note 2) conclude: "By attaching these territories to Lebanon, France assured that the Maronites who had dominated old Mount Lebanon would remain dependent on the French for protection against inclusion in a greater Syria where they would be overwhelmed" (201). An independent "Greater Syria" is what the Arabs believed was promised to them by the British (Husayn–McMahon correspondence, July 1915–January 1916) as a reward for joining the war effort on the side of the allies. On this point, consult Charles D. Smith, *Palestine and the Arab–Israeli Conflict*, 6th ed. (New York: Bedford/St. Martin's Press, 2007) especially 63–69.

31 See the incisive study by Meir Zamir, *The Formation of Modern Lebanon* (Ithaca, NY: Cornell University Press, 1985).

32 Greater Lebanon became the Republic of Lebanon on May 23, 1926, after the adoption of a constitution. It provided for a system of proportional and confessional representation.

33 Salibi 34. The same point is made by Goria 19.

34 The Syria–Lebanon nexus played a crucial role in advancing the pan-Arab yearning for unity. The advocates of this position rejected the fragmentation and designation of artificial boundaries between Syria and Lebanon on the grounds that such a development was contrary to the yearning and promise for unity. See George Antonius, *The Arab Awakening* (New York: Capricorn Books, 1965). For the most recent scholarly work on this subject, see Rashid Khalidi, Lisa Anderson, Muhammad Muslih, Reeva S. Simon, eds., *The Origins of Arab Nationalism* (New York: Columbia University Press, 1991).

35 By particularism I mean a form of nationalism aimed at integrating people within fixed nation-states, best represented by the Lebanese Phalangist party. On the other hand, universalism denotes the ideas of political integration that cut across state frontiers such as Islamic revivalism and Islamic modernism, pan-Arabism, and Marxism. See Nubar Hovsepian, "Competing Identities in the Arab World," in *Journal of International Affairs* 49.1 (Summer 1995) 1–24.

36 Salibi 37.

37 See Edmond, *La Formation historique du Liban politique et constitutionel* (Beyrouth: Librairie Orientale, 1973) 522–526. Some of the important principles included in the "Pact" are: 1) Lebanon is an independent republic; 2) It is integrally linked with the Arab world, but Muslims must accept its "Christian" character; thus, it is obliged to retain close ties with the West; 3) The confessional allotment of seats in parliament is on the basis of a six-to-five Christian–Muslim ratio. The offices of president, prime minister, and president of parliament would be held respectively and in perpetuity by the Maronite, Sunni, and Shia communities.

38 Quoted in Tabitha Petran, *The Struggle for Lebanon* (New York: Monthly Review Press, 1987) 34.

39 Religions and sects are viewed as social systems. Thus, sectarian conflict

connotes the existence and reproduction of social and cultural differences. For anthropologist Suad Joseph the "politicization of religious and sectarian differences refers to the process by which real or imagined religious and sectarian differences influence access to and control over jobs, favors, goods, services, and political power. When eligibility for these and other public resources is enhanced by sectarian membership, sectarian groups are politicized. Sectarianism is most advanced when societies require that individuals resort to sectarian organizations for most of their needs and provide few non-sectarian avenues for dealing with problems." See Joseph's "Muslim–Christian Conflicts: A Theoretical Perspective," in Suad Joseph and Barbara L.K. Pillsbury, eds., *Muslim–Christian Conflicts: Economic, Political, and Social Origins* (Boulder, CO: Westview, 1978). For the impact of this process on one of the Lebanese confessions, see Joseph's 1975 dissertation from Columbia University, *The Politicization of Religious Sects in Borj Hammoud, Lebanon*.

40 Sectarian political parties play a critical role in the politicization and ultimately in the reproduction and perpetuation of religious and sectarian differences. Such parties serve as the main conduit between their clientele and the state. The allocation and distribution of resources is conducted through this nexus. This transforms the party as a key power broker within the confessional system. Most political parties in Lebanon belong to or represent one of the existing sects, and are often led by key families representing specific economic and ideological interests. This does not preclude the existence of multiple parties within each sect. Among the Maronite community there are three key political parties: the Phalangists (Gemayel), the National Liberal Party (Chamoun), and the National Bloc (Edde, who is in self-imposed exile in France). The Armenians are represented by the Dashnaq, which today is also vying for political ascendance in the Republic of Armenia. The Shia community is represented by two key political tendencies: Amal and Hizballah. There are several important studies on these parties and movements: Michael W. Suleiman, *Political Parties in Lebanon: The Challenge of a Fragmented Political Culture* (Ithaca, NY: Cornell University Press, 1967); Augustus Richard Norton, *Amal and the Shi'a: Struggle for the Soul of Lebanon* (Austin, TX: University of Texas Press, 1987).

41 See Bashur n17.

42 See Claude Dubar and Salim Nasr 67–334, and Salim Nasr, "The Crisis of Lebanese Capitalism," *Middle East Report* 73.8/10 (December 1978) 3–13.

43 See Irene L. Gendzier "The Declassified Lebanon, 1948–1958: Elements of Continuity and Contrast in US Policy Toward Lebanon," in Barakat 187–209. See also her most recent work on the subject, *Notes from the Minefield: United States Intervention in Lebanon and the Middle East* (New York: Columbia University Press, 2007).

44 The only challenge to the system emanated from sectors of civil society who wished to eliminate the confessional basis of state–society relations. This point will be discussed below.

45 Salibi 27.

46 This statement is adapted from Basil Davidson's observations on the current African condition in his *Black Man's Burden* (10).

47 This idea was advanced by Kamal Jumblatt, the Lebanese Druze leader who presided over the leadership council of the Lebanese National Movement (LNM). At the

outset of 1975 the LNM sought the secularization and democratization of the confessional system. (This movement was superficially depicted as either leftist or Muslim by the Western correspondents who covered Lebanon.) Jumblatt was assassinated by Syrian intelligence units in 1976. See Kamal Jumblatt, *I Speak For Lebanon* (London: Zed Press, 1982).

48 The war's ending is not indicative of the resolution of the primary causes of the conflict. Military stalemate, the collapse of Lebanon's economy, and increasing war-weariness paved the way for the adoption of the Taif Accord in October 1989. This agreement was reached by the surviving members of the Lebanese parliament, who were essentially summoned to a summit held in Saudi Arabia and sponsored by Syria, Saudi Arabia, and the US. This agreement amended the National Pact by giving Muslims equal parliamentary representation and by strengthening the powers of the prime minister. The confessional system, however, remained intact. For an analysis of the Taif Accord, see Augustus Richard Norton, "Lebanon after Taif: Is the Civil War Over?" *Middle East Journal* 45 (Summer 1991) 455–473.

49 The idea of using proxy forces was articulated as early as 1955 by Israel's Ben Gurion and Moshe Dayan. See Livia Rokach, *Israel's Sacred Terrorism* (Belmont, MA: AAUG, 1980). For a general overview of foreign intervention, see Rashid Khalidi, "External Intervention in Lebanon: The Historical Dynamics," in S. Seikaly, R. Baabalki, P. Dodd, *Quest For Understanding: Arabic and Islamic Studies in Memory of Malcolm H. Kerr* (Beirut: American University of Beirut, 1991) 99–118.

50 By 1975, 50 percent of the entire population was displaced through internal migrations caused by structural economic changes and aggravated by Israeli bombardment of southern Lebanon. See Nasr, "The Crisis of Lebanese Capitalism," 10.

51 See Carolyn Gates, *The Historical Role of Political Economy in the Development of Lebanon* (Oxford: Centre for Lebanese Studies, 1989) 34.

52 Roger Owen, "The Economic History of Lebanon 1943–1974: Its Salient Features," in Barakat 37.

53 See Tabitah Petran, *The Struggle over Lebanon* (New York: Monthly Review, 1987) 130–133.

54 Kamal Jumblatt, the leader of this movement, was a paradoxical man. As a feudal landowner he distributed his land to the tenant farmers. He was an iconoclast steeped in Indian and Eastern mysticism, as well as a student of Rousseau and Marx. He was a humanist who genuinely believed that he had a calling to deliver Lebanon from the throes of confessionalism into secular democracy. Jumblatt believed that the secularization of Lebanon would cause or prompt a regionwide political reformation. Though his initial base was drawn from the Druze community, his appeal went beyond those confines. Secular-minded Lebanese gravitated toward him. His staunch secularism can also be seen as a function of his status as a member of a minority sect—equality for him could only be attained through democratic secularism rather than confessionalism. As early as 1958, he was keenly aware that political reform in Lebanon could not take place without Syrian approval. In 1976, he forgot that geopolitical fact as he pushed for the establishment of a second Lebanese Republic that would animate the ideas of 1789. The Syrians killed him.

55 See Kamal S. Salibi, *Crossroads to Civil War* (Delmar, NY: Caravan Books, 1976); Marius Deeb, *The Lebanese Civil War* (New York: Praeger, 1980); Ghassan Tueini, *Une guerre pour les autres* (Paris: JC Lattes, 1985); Elizabeth Picard, *Liban, etat de discorde: Des fondations aux guerres fatricides* (Paris: Flammarion, 1988).

56 The LNM produced two key documents through which they articulated a vision for a secular polity based on equality, social integration, and democracy. See in particular Sami Zubyan, "The Transitional Program of the Lebanese National Movement," in *Al-Haraka al-Wataniyya al-Lubnaniyya* [The Lebanese National Movement] (Beirut: Dar al-Massira, 1977) Appendix 1, 369–381; See also Documents of the Lebanese National Movement, "Charter of the Politico-Organizational Front," Beirut, 3 April 1981.

57 Some of the points in this section are elaborated in my article, "The Lebanon Quagmire." See also Nubar Hovsepian, "The Lebanese Opposition: Who's Against Gemayel—And Why," *Nation* 17 March 1984: 318–321. On the role and ideology of the Lebanese Front, see Lewis W. Snider, "The Lebanese Forces: Their Origins and Role in Lebanon's Politics," in *Middle East Journal* 38 (Winter 1984) 1–33; Elizabeth Picard, "Role et evolution du front Libanais dans la guerre civile," in *Maghreb Machrek* 90 (1980) 16–39; and see the Document of the Lebanese Front, *The Lebanon We Want to Build* (Deir Aoukar, Lebanon: 13 December 1980).

58 There are two important studies on the role of Syria in Lebanon. See Adeed I. Dawisha, *Syria and the Lebanese Crisis* (London: Macmillan, 1980) and Naomi Joy Weinberger, *Syrian Intervention in Lebanon* (New York: Oxford University Press, 1986).

59 For the geopolitical dimensions of the Lebanese civil war, consult Georges Corm, *Geopolitique du conflit Libanais* (Paris: La Découverte, 1987). For a study that situates the geopolitical dimensions of the conflict in the context of the struggle for modernity, see Georges Corm, *L'Europe et l'Orient de la Balkanisation a la Libanisation: Histoire d'une modernite inaccomplie* (Paris: La Découverte, 1989).

60 See Walid Khalidi, *Conflict and Violence in Lebanon: Confrontation in the Middle East* (Cambridge: Harvard Center for International Affairs, 1979) especially 123.

61 The literature on this subject is vast, so I will only cite a small sample: Itamar Rabinovich, *The War for Lebanon: 1970–1983* (Ithaca, NY: Cornell University Press, 1984); Ze'ev Schiff and Ehud Ya'ri, *Israel's Lebanon War* (New York: Simon and Schuster, 1984); Rashid Khalidi, *Under Seige: PLO Decisionmaking During the 1982 War* (New York: Columbia University Press, 1986); Robert Fisk, *Pity the Nation: Lebanon at War* (New York: Simon and Schuster, 1990); and, finally, Ibrahim Abu-Lughod and Eqbal Ahmad, "The Invasion of Lebanon," special double issue of *Race & Class* 24.4 (Spring 1983).

62 The human, social, and economic (including the destruction of buildings and infrastructure) toll resulting from the 16 years of strife is enormous: The number of deaths exceeds 150,000; the wounded are estimated at 200,000; the number of missing persons is more than 17,000; in addition almost 14,000 were kidnapped or held hostage. These figures are derived from official Lebanese police statistics and were cited by the *New York Times* 10 March 1992 and *Al-Sharq al-Awsat* (London Arabic daily) 30 January 1992. To assess the socioeconomic, infrastructural, and institutional needs to enable Lebanese development, see "Postwar Institutional Development in Lebanon: Assessment for Foreign Assistance," a report prepared for the Near East Bureau of the United States Agency for International Development, February 1992. Also consult "Special Economic

and Disaster Relief Assistance: Special Programmes of Economic Assistance," *Report of the Secretary General* A/46/557/Add. 2, 21 November 1991; and A/46/557, 22 October 1991.

63 In 1976 President Suleiman Franjieh offered what is known as the "Constitutional Document of 14 February 1976." See Khalidi, *Conflict and Violence*, Appendix II, 189–191. This document and the Taif Accord proposed some minor reforms, but kept the basis of the confessional system intact. Today the Taif reforms serve as the basis for the reconstitution of Lebanese confessionalism, after the ending of the internecine fighting has been secured.

64 Quoted from Salim Nasr, "Lebanon: New Social Realities and Issues of Reconstruction," paper presented to the conference of the MIT Lebanon Reconstruction Project, 1991. An excerpt is published in *Precis*, newsletter of the MIT Center for International Studies 3.1 (Winter 1991–1992) especially 14.

65 These figures are extracted from UN reports cited above and from presentations to the American Task Force for Lebanon Conference in Washington, DC, 26–30 June 1991. Some of the figures are quoted in APBA NEWS 5:4 (1991).

66 Salim Nasr, "Lebanon: New Social Realities and Issues of Reconstruction," unpublished paper, 1991: 8.

67 All of these interviews were conducted in Beirut in August 1991 and recorded in my daily journal.

68 Discussion with Elias Khoury in Beirut, 11 August 1991.

69 This intervention was supported by Saudi Arabia and the rest of the Arab League. Israel did not fear Syria's intervention because of assurances they received from the US. See Weinberger 291–294. Rabinovich adds: "Syria's implicit recognition of Israeli interests in Lebanon was the quid pro quo for Israel's conditional acceptance of Syria's intervention in Lebanon." See Rabinovich 59. Competing and not necessarily conflicting Israeli–Syrian interests brought Lebanon under two zones of influence.

70 I make this point in "The Lebanon Quagmire," 688. The current Phalangist party leader, and former advisor to Lebanese President Elias Sarkis (1976–1982), Karim Pakradouni, has written one of the most insightful accounts of Syria's Lebanon policy, *Al-Salam al-Mafqoud* [The missing peace] (Beirut: Abr al-Sharaf Printing, 1984).

71 Gendzier makes this point as pertaining to the 1940s and 1950s. This suggests that in addition to studying Lebanon's predicament in the context of regional interventionism, we might be well served to study it from the standpoint of a world-system perspective as well. In particular, see Liisa Laakso, "Ethnicity in World-System Perspective: The Case of Lebanon," in *Current Research on Peace and Violence* 12 (1989) 176–190, published by the Tampere Peace Research Institute, Finland.

72 External events also contributed to this process. For example, the Islamic revolution in Iran contributed to the ascendance of a Shiite political discourse in Lebanon as well. In the period between 1976 and 1980 and especially after 1982, secular parties like the Lebanese Communist Party lost a large number of their Shiite members to Shia-based organizations like Amal and Hizballah.

3. A CEDAR READY TO FALL

Georges Corm

From Le Monde Diplomatique, *April 2005. Translated by Harry Forster.*

President George Bush and his secretary of state, Condoleezza Rice, have made statements about Lebanon almost every day since the murder of the former prime minister, Rafiq Hariri, on February 14. European governments, led by the French, have joined the accusations, prompting sudden interest by international media.

Resolution 1559 adopted by the United Nations Security Council on September 3, 2004 went almost unnoticed—except in Lebanon. But the murder of a political leader who was respected in the Middle East and internationally, along with French and US agitation and a flurry of Israeli statements, caused turmoil in Lebanon and threatened its future.

The UN resolution had an impressive list of provisions questioning the status of Lebanon since its reorganization under the Taif Accord[1] of 1989 and subsequent transfer to Syrian control as reward for Damascus's cooperation with the US-led coalition in the 1991 Gulf War. The resolution called on the Lebanese parliament to drop plans to amend the constitution to enable President Emile Lahoud's mandate to be extended from six to nine years. In 1995, neither Washington nor Paris reacted when the same privilege was granted to the previous incumbent, Elias Hrawi, a close friend of both Damascus and Hariri.

This UN demand was surprising, given that its charter forbids any interference in the internal affairs of a member state. But the resolution went much further, calling for withdrawal of the Syrian army from Lebanon, deployment of the Lebanese army along the border with Israel, and disarmament of the Lebanese Hizballah militia and Palestinian groups in refugee camps. The demands undermined Lebanon's stability, restoring it to the unhappy position of a buffer zone between opposing outside forces contending for control of the Middle East and manipulating Lebanon's communities and political leaders for their own ends.[2]

From 1975 to 1990 the main conflicts affecting the region—the cold war, the conflict between Israel and the Arab world, the conflict between Arab states, and the Iran–Iraq War with its local and international repercussions—played out on a smaller scale in Lebanon. Rather than developing into a full confrontation, they were shadow-played on Lebanese territory: local politicians agreed to act as pawns, funded and armed by regional and international powers. The religious communities they claimed to represent provided the pretext as well as a source of cannon fodder for foreign causes. They also acted as a smokescreen for the Arab and international media, which remained hungry as always for stories to substantiate their claims of enduring hatred between the communities.

In 1988–1990, during the last act of this awful play, General Michel Aoun, then commander in chief of the army, started a war of liberation against Syrian occupation forces. In doing so he yielded to pressure from the Arab League committee tasked with finding a way out of the crisis. But Iraq was supplying arms and France providing massive political and moral support (apparently backed by limited military assistance). The consequences were disastrous, particularly for Christian communities caught in the crossfire between Aoun and his powerful rival, Samir Geagea, the leader of the (Christian) Lebanese Forces militia. Fighting between the militia and Aoun's troops, combined with attacks by the Syrian army, undermined the status of the Christian community, leaving it only a marginal role in the emerging new order.

Pax Syriana

The Pax Syriana in October 1990, with the blessing of the US, prompted widespread relief, and silence from the Israeli government. For fourteen years Lebanon enjoyed unusual stability. The only major upsets were massive Israeli attacks in the south in 1993 and 1996, attempts to tame Hizballah, which had been waging an effective guerrilla war against the Israeli occupation of southern Lebanon since 1978. In May 2000 the Israeli army gave up the struggle and withdrew. Working closely with the Lebanese army and intelligence service, Hizballah managed to prevent Israel from fomenting further conflict between Christians and Muslims, as it had done after its invasion in 1982 and during its withdrawal from Chouf in 1983 and the Saida area in 1985.

In 1991 and 1992 the successive governments of Salim al-Hoss and Omar Karami managed to disarm active militia units and bring them into the army. They restored the unity of Beirut and Lebanon as a whole, and restored the apparatus of state. A third government, led by Rashid al-Solh, organized the first elections since 1972, although unfortunately they were boycotted by many people, especially Christians. The governments included representatives of all the factions (except the supporters of Aoun, who had been forcibly exiled to Paris) and there was a plan to ask Syria to redeploy its troops in the plain of Beqaa, in compliance with the Taif Accord.[3]

Hariri then appeared on the scene, boasting the image of a benefactor capable of rebuilding Lebanon, particularly Beirut's historic center and business district, which had been so severely damaged during the fifteen years of fighting. Public euphoria greeted his appointment as prime minister. He became the focus of a remarkable personality cult fueled partly by his legendary generosity. He could count on devoted, tightly controlled media, growing friendship with President Jacques Chirac of France, and Saudi Arabia's unfailing support. There was no further talk of redeploying Syrian troops, or of their departure, subject to agreement between the governments of Lebanon and Syria.

After being ousted by Lahoud at the end of 1998, Hariri made a triumphant comeback, winning another term as prime minister in the October 2000 election. At the time no one complained that the elections had been rigged or that Syria had pulled any strings.

Reconstruction, despite its exorbitant cost and patchy results, greatly impressed visitors to Beirut from home and abroad.

Two years ago, with the end of the Israeli occupation of southern Lebanon, Beirut regained its former place in Middle Eastern politics, culture, and tourism. Who could have imagined that it would witness such spectacular, dangerous events as we have just seen? In 2000 it hosted a meeting of the Arab League's foreign ministers. In 2001 it welcomed a summit of the same organization for the first time in several decades. In 2002 it was the venue for the summit of French-speaking nations.

To mark the occasion, Chirac made a speech to parliament in which he implicitly confirmed Lebanon's status as a Syrian protectorate until the Israeli–Arab conflict was settled. "Of course a lasting, just, and comprehensive peace [in the Middle East] can only be achieved if it includes Lebanon and Syria and if it brings a fair solution to the question of Palestinian refugees, taking into account Lebanese interests," he said. "France has constantly defended this position. At the same time progress toward long-desired peace will enable Lebanon and Syria to harmonize their relations and complete full withdrawal of Syrian forces from your country, in conformity with the Taif Accord."[4] The speech was in tune with the policy statement made by Hariri on return to office in 2000, in which he confirmed the need for Syrian troops to remain in Lebanon.[5]

All this happened before the US invasion of Iraq and its greater Middle East initiative to establish order and democracy and eradicate terrorist violence—just a rehash of themes and slogans produced by US diplomacy in the early 1990s: The first President Bush had promised a new world order with the winning of the 1991 Gulf War. Two years later Shimon Peres published *The New Middle East* (Holt, 1993), announcing a new era of peace, prosperity, and economic cooperation between the peoples of the region. Only the irrational forces of Islamic fundamentalism might upset the happy prospect. The process gained further credibility with the Oslo Accords in 1993 and big economic conferences (Casablanca, Amman, Cairo, Doha) attended by officials and business people from Israel, the US, Europe, and the Arab world.

Failure of Oslo

But the spread of Israeli settlements on the West Bank and in Gaza made a mockery of the Oslo peace process. After the failure of the Camp David summit in July 2000, Ariel Sharon's provocative visit to al-Haram al-Sharif in Jerusalem, the third most sacred place in the Muslim world, sparked an explosion. The second intifada and its military escalation in response to violent Israeli incursions were of little concern to the second President Bush, who appeared in no hurry to settle the Palestinian question. His attention was once more focused on Iraq. As early as 1998, the Clinton administration had said that since UN inspections had failed to achieve their goals, the Baghdad regime represented a major threat to world peace.

After 9/11 Bush implicated Saddam Hussein in the attacks, and found, against the evidence, that he was again developing weapons of mass destruction. The stage was set for the invasion of Iraq, a country of vital importance to the balance of the Middle East.[6] After the arguments justifying the invasion lost all credibility, the US administration set about convincing the world that it intended to bring freedom and democracy to the Middle East; to liberate the people of Iraq from Saddam's dictatorship was the first step toward widespread democratic reform.

When armed resistance grew in Iraq, the US accused Syria—another Ba'athist regime dating from an era that everyone wanted to forget—of meddling. Bashar Assad, the young president of Syria who had succeeded his father, Hafez, on his death in June 2000, promised reforms. But the new regime had difficulty finding the impetus to liberalize politics and encourage free-market economics along the same lines as the countries of central Europe. Only minor political changes actually happened in Damascus, and in some cases they were short-lived. Market deregulation opened the way for private banking in which Lebanese banks had a key role. But reform of the public sector and measures to halt steeply rising unemployment have had to wait.

In fairness, the Syrian regime is no longer a repressive, dissidence-crushing machine. But the US invasion of Iraq and Washington's accusations have put the regime on the defensive and made it difficult for it to continue reforms. On December 12, 2003 the US Congress passed the Syrian Accountability and Lebanese Sovereignty Restoration Act. The act, a powerful tool to put pressure on Damascus, called on Syria to restore full independence to Lebanon. The next spring, on May 11, 2004, Bush issued instructions, based on the act, to tighten the economic blockade. The sanctions and UN Resolution 1559 delighted Aoun and his Lebanese lobby in Washington and Paris, who preach Christian secession or transformation of the country into a federal republic. His supporters now take credit for having rekindled US enthusiasm for restoring Lebanese sovereignty.[7]

In Lebanon, Walid Jumblatt, the leader of the Druze Muslim community and a longstanding ally of the Syrian regime, used the election campaign in 2000 to open hostilities, denouncing Syrian control. Some commentators assumed this was merely an electoral maneuver to pick up Christian votes, particularly as he became quiet once the elections were over. But in September the bishops of the Christian Maronite community issued an outspoken statement blaming Damascus for all Lebanon's ills: widespread corruption, national debt, social unrest, and disregard for political forces.

For the first time in the history of the Christian community, a bishop was appointed to take part in meetings of the Kornet Chehwan, a motley collection of public figures, including representatives of Aoun and the disbanded Lebanese Forces, several Maronite MPs and Amin Gemayel, the Phalangist leader and former president. The group presented itself as an opposition force, not directed against the Hariri government but against Lahoud and Syria. It advocated sending the army to southern Lebanon to replace Hizballah forces. It also called for the release of Samir Geagea, who was arrested in 1993 and sentenced for several attacks. It demanded withdrawal of the Syrian army under the terms of the Taif Accord.

After Israel pulled out of southern Lebanon in 2000, the US and many European countries pressed the Lebanese government to deploy its army along the southern border, suggesting that Hizballah forces should occupy less strategic positions and perhaps even be disarmed. But the funds promised by the West to rebuild the area, which had been occupied for 22 years, never materialized. With the war on Iraq, this sensitive issue was forgotten. US threats against Syria and Hizballah prompted a wave of protest in Lebanon, even attracting the support of the Maronite patriarch. This helped to reduce the tension.

Again a Pawn

Hariri's murder has triggered a major crisis, at a time when both regimes, in Lebanon and Syria, are in difficulty. Lebanon is once again a pawn in Middle East politics; its worst nightmares have surfaced. Only a few months after the attack on Marwan Hamade, a member of parliament close to Hariri and Jumblatt, Hariri's death reopens wounds that have never had a chance to properly heal. Many Lebanese feel they have lost a key symbol of stability and prosperity.

Hariri was the target of much criticism because of the close links he had with the Syrian ruling class. Yet at the same time he embodied hopes of a return to normality and an end to involvement in the Israeli–Arab conflict, which has caused so much suffering.

That is why Bush and Chirac's repeated calls for Syrian withdrawal and full, prompt application of Resolution 1559 resonated. They coalesced around Jumblatt, now the undisputed opposition leader, and Hariri's "family." This group includes all the members of parliament faithful to Hariri, several political groups, NGOs, and students, many—though not all—from the Christian middle classes.

Bush and some European leaders want to turn Lebanon into a

laboratory for democracy. They are convinced that, with elections in occupied Iraq and Palestine, a local council poll in Saudi Arabia, and the prospect of a multiparty presidential election in Egypt, a vote in Lebanon would give impetus to the "tide of freedom" sweeping the Middle East.

But their optimism makes no allowance for the complexity of Lebanon, or for the importance Arab public opinion still attaches to Damascus, despite its distaste for the regime. Syria is one of the last remaining obstacles to US domination of the Middle East and to a resolution of the Israeli–Palestinian conflict detrimental to the interests of the Palestinians (and, it must be noted, also to the Syrians, since the Golan Heights have been occupied by Israel since 1967 and annexed in 1981).

Jumblatt's opposition may be representative of central Lebanon, but in the north, south, and east it must compete with "loyalist" parties keen to maintain close links with Syria. Several opposition leaders were steadfast supporters of Syrian control until recently, or were responsible for massacres and forced movements of population from 1975 to 1990. The opposition is deeply divided, with widely differing political agendas. Some are determined to overthrow the existing regime. Others advocate a more moderate approach.

The loyalists include several pro-government, pro-Syrian parties regrouped around Hizballah, which is still regarded by the US as a terrorist organization, and its charismatic leader, Hassan Nasrallah. It has suddenly become the pivotal unifying force in a movement rooted in the traditions of anti-imperialism and Arab nationalism, which are shared by many others in the Middle East. A third force, led by the respected former prime minister, Salim al-Hoss, is trying hard to restore peace and calm. It is a struggle, since feelings run high.

Demonstrations and counter-demonstrations have paralyzed Lebanon since Hariri's death. How long can it survive a crisis on this scale, inflicted by Washington and Paris, before its fragile economy collapses or professional agitators spark an explosion? In practice, UN Resolution 1559 has restored Lebanon to its former status as a buffer zone. The political arena once more reflects all the tensions in the Middle East, played out without restraint by Lebanese factions.

NOTES

1 The Taif Accord is an agreement that was reached by Lebanese MPs in the town

of Taif in Saudi Arabia, encouraged by their host, other Arab countries, and the US. It provided for the redistribution of power between civilian leaders of the main religious communities and redeployment of Syrian troops in the Beqaa valley after two years.

2 See Georges Corm, *Le Liban contemporain: Histoire et société* (Paris: La Découverte, 2003).

3 For a discussion of the reasons preventing redeployment of Syrian troops and application of the constitutional provisions of the Taif Accord, see the book by Albert Mansour, former minister of defense and then minister of information under the governments in power at reunification and the end of the war (1989–1992): *Al-Inqilab ala al-Taif* (Beirut: Dar al-Jadid, 1992). This book highlights the overwhelming responsibility of former President Hrawi, who paved the way for Hariri to take office in 1992, after an artificial run on the Lebanese pound brought down the Karami government. The other decisive factor was the lack of any regional power to counterbalance Syria.

4 *L'Orient-Le Jour* 18 October 2002 (Beirut).

5 In an answer to an opposition MP who objected to this statement, Hariri said that "blaming Syria for Lebanon's problems is unrealistic." He added that without Syria "it would have been impossible to achieve stability" (full text, *Al-Nahar* 3 November 2000). Hariri stuck to this position from his first period in office in 1992 until his death.

6 See Ignacio Ramonet, *Irak: Histoire d'un désastre* (Paris: Galilée, 2005).

7 See the provocative report in *Al-Nahar* (Beirut) 3 February 2005.

4. HIZBALLAH AND ITS CIVILIAN CONSTITUENCIES IN LEBANON

Lara Deeb

This article includes some material originally published in "Hizballah: A Primer,"
Middle East Report *online, available at www.merip.org, and in*
"Deconstructing a 'Hizballah Stronghold,'" MIT Electronic Journal of
Middle East Studies 6 *(Summer 2006).*

For over a month this summer, Israeli warplanes battered so-called Hizballah strongholds in Lebanon, unleashing an assault on Lebanon's cities and villages of a scale unseen since the 1982 Israeli invasion of the country.[1] By the time a tenuous cease-fire went into effect on August 14, approximately 1,300 Lebanese had been killed, mostly civilians, including many children.[2] Thousands were wounded, and nearly a million displaced from their homes—one-quarter of the country's population. Entire villages in the south of Lebanon were flattened during the attack, as were whole neighborhoods in the southern suburbs of Beirut.[3] Humanitarian and environmental crises continue, not least due to unexploded "bomblets" remaining from Israeli-dropped (and US-manufactured) cluster munitions.[4]

While Lebanon suffered tremendously during this attack and continues to bear the burdens of environmental hazards and rebuilding (a UNDP spokesperson noted in Agence France Press a setback of fifteen years of rebuilding after the civil war [23 August 2006]), the brunt of civilian deaths and infrastructural destruction took place in the south of the country, the Beqaa Valley, and the southern suburbs of Beirut.[5] The purported reasoning behind this selective wreckage was that these regions were considered Hizballah strongholds. Grocery stores and dairy farms destroyed were thus subsumed into "terrorist targets" and civilians killed assumed to have been "harboring terrorists"—if they were not terrorists themselves.

Mainstream media outlets in the United States took up this reasoning, casting the Israeli attack on Lebanon as a retaliatory attack for Hizballah's July 12 capture of two Israeli soldiers and blaming Hizballah for "starting this war" and for "hiding behind civilians" or "using civilians as shields." In what follows, I will complicate these dominant portrayals by providing the historical and ethnographic context for this summer's violence. Two key points will emerge: First, that the July war is part of a much longer conflict, and that to insist that Hizballah started the war is to take a rather short-sighted view of events. And second, that the assertion that Hizballah "hid behind civilians" is both incorrect and ignorant of the complex relationship between the party and its constituents in Lebanon.

Hizballah's Origins in the Lebanese Context

Historically, Shiite Muslims have been politically and economically marginalized in Lebanon. The country's stagnant confessional state–society relationship contributed to disproportionate poverty among Shiite Lebanese because belonging to a sect was a key means of gaining access to state resources.[6] Shiite under-representation in government meant that they could channel fewer resources into their communities, an effect aggravated by the fact that Shiite seats in parliament were usually filled by feudal landowners and other insulated elites.

Until the 1960s, most of the Shiite population lived in rural areas, mainly in the south and in the Beqaa Valley, where living conditions did not approach the standards of the rest of the nation. Following a modernization program that established road networks and introduced cash-crop policies in the rural areas, many of these rural residents migrated to Beirut, settling in a ring of impoverished suburbs around the capital. The rapid urbanization that came with incorporation into the capitalist world economy further widened existing economic disparities within Lebanon.

Initially, this growing urban population of mostly Shiite poor in Lebanon was not mobilized along sectarian lines. In the 1960s and early 1970s, they made up much of the rank and file of the Lebanese Communist Party and the Syrian Socialist Nationalist Party. Later, in the 1970s, a charismatic cleric, Sayyid Musa al-Sadr, began to challenge the leftist parties for the loyalty of Shiite youth. Al-Sadr offered instead the "Movement of the Deprived," dedicated to attaining political rights for Lebanon's dispossessed within the Lebanese polity. A militia branch of this movement, Amal, was founded at the start of the Lebanese civil war in 1975. Alongside al-Sadr's mobilizations in the 1970s, there were also other activist Lebanese Shiite religious leaders, many of whom had studied in Najaf, working to establish grassroots social and religious networks in the Shiite neighborhoods of Beirut. Among them were Sayyid Mohammad Hussein Fadlallah, who is today one of the most popular and respected "sources of emulation" among Shiite Muslims in Lebanon and beyond, and Sayyid Hassan Nasrallah, current secretary general of Hizballah.[7]

Between 1978 and 1982 a number of events propelled the nascent Shiite mobilization forward and further divorced it from the leftist parties. First, the mysterious disappearance of Musa al-Sadr in 1978 while on a visit to Libya. This immediately initiated a surge in his popularity at the same time that it opened up a leadership vacuum in his movement and the Amal militia. That same year, to push back PLO fighters then based in Lebanon, Israel invaded the south, displacing 250,000 people. This contributed to increasing Shiite perceptions that the Lebanese left had failed, both in securing greater rights for the poor and in protecting the south from the fighting between the PLO and Israel. The following year, the Islamic Revolution in Iran set a new sort of example for Shiite Muslims around the world, and provided an alternative worldview to Western liberal capitalism different from that espoused by the left.

The final, and doubtless the most important, ingredient in this cauldron of events was the second Israeli invasion of Lebanon in June 1982. This time Israeli troops, aiming to expel the PLO from Lebanon entirely, marched north and laid siege to West Beirut. Tens of thousands of Lebanese were killed and injured during the invasion, and another 450,000 people were displaced. The importance of the 1982 Israeli invasion of Lebanon to the formation of Hizballah cannot be underestimated.

Following the events of 1982, many prominent members of Amal left the party, which had become increasingly involved in patronage politics and detached from the larger struggles against poverty and Israeli occupation. In these years, a number of small, armed groups of young men organized under the banner of Islam emerged in the south, the Beqaa Valley, and the suburbs of Beirut. These groups were dedicated to fighting the Israeli occupation troops, and also participated occasionally in the Lebanese civil war, which by this time had engaged over fifteen militias and armies. Initial military training and equipment for these Shiite militias was provided by Iran. Over time, these groups coalesced into Hizballah, with a key foundational meeting taking place in 1984, though the formal existence of the group and its armed wing, the Islamic Resistance, was not announced until February 16, 1985, in an "Open Letter to the Downtrodden in Lebanon and the World."[8] The next sections of this article address the three interrelated areas of Hizballah's activities: the Resistance, politics, and the social sphere.

Resistance and the Rules of the Game

In 1985, Israel withdrew from most of Lebanon, but continued to occupy the southern zone of the country, controlling approximately ten percent of Lebanon using both Israeli soldiers and a proxy Lebanese militia, the South Lebanon Army (SLA). Hizballah's Islamic Resistance took the lead in fighting that occupation, in conjunction with other, less organized resistance contingents. Levels of national support for the activities of the Islamic Resistance in the south fluctuated over the years, with Israeli attacks on Lebanese civilians and infrastructure—including the destruction of power plants in Beirut in 1996, 1999, and 2000—generally contributing to increases in national support. This was especially true after Israel bombed a UN bunker where civilians had taken refuge in Qana on April 18, 1996, killing more than 100 people.

The occupation of southern Lebanon was costly for Israel, and Israeli Prime Minister Ehud Barak made withdrawal a campaign promise in 1999, later announcing that it would take place by July 2000. A month and a half before this deadline, after the collapse of potential talks with Syria and SLA desertions, Barak ordered a chaotic withdrawal from Lebanon, taking many by surprise. At three in the morning on May 24, 2000, the last Israeli soldier stepped off Lebanese soil and locked the gate at the Fatima border crossing behind him. Many predicted that lawlessness, sectarian violence, and chaos would fill the void left by the Israeli occupation forces and the SLA, which rapidly collapsed in Israel's wake. Those predictions proved false as Hizballah maintained order in the border region.

This is especially poignant in places like Khiam, a village along the border where there was a notorious detention center. Lebanese civilians and resistance fighters were held, interrogated, and tortured in this center, by both Israeli troops and members of the South Lebanon Army. Today in Khiam, it is possible for a former SLA member who was a guard at this detention center and a former prisoner to live in close proximity, encountering one another while going about their daily activities. One could imagine scenarios of revenge violence, but Hizballah has explicitly forbidden this and enforces that prohibition in cooperation with the Lebanese state.

Despite the 2000 Israeli withdrawal, a territorial dispute continues over a fifteen-square mile border region called Shebaa Farms, which remains under Israeli occupation. Lebanon and Syria assert that the mountainside is Lebanese land, while Israel and the UN have declared it part of the Golan Heights—therefore, Syrian territory that is occupied by Israel. Since 2000, Lebanon has also been awaiting the delivery from Israel of the map of the locations of the over 300,000 landmines the Israeli army planted in southern Lebanon. In addition, Israel continues to hold Lebanese detainees.

Until July 2006, this continuing conflict was governed by a set of rules of the game—based on an agreement not to target civilians that was written after the Qana massacres in 1996.[9] According to these "rules," a Hizballah attack on an Israeli army post in the occupied Shebaa Farms, for example, would be answered by limited Israeli shelling of Hizballah outposts and sonic booms over Beirut. Both sides, on occasion, have broken these rules, though UNIFIL observer reports of border violations find that Israel has violated the Blue Line border between the countries ten times more frequently than Hizballah has, in part because violations of Lebanese airspace count, and Israeli planes continued to break the sound barrier over Beirut on an almost daily basis.

Also recorded in these reports are abductions by both sides. Israeli forces have kidnapped Lebanese shepherds and fishermen. Hizballah abducted an Israeli who they believed to be a spy (Israel claimed he was a businessman). And in January 2004, through German mediators, Hizballah and Israel concluded a deal whereby Israel released most of the Lebanese and Arab detainees in exchange for the abducted Israeli and the bodies of three Israeli soldiers. The Israeli Supreme Court had ruled that all the Lebanese detainees were to be released in this prisoner exchange, including Samir al-Qantar, who has been in Israeli detention for 27 years now for killing three Israelis after infiltrating the border. At the last minute, Israeli officials ignored that ruling and held on to Samir al-Qantar, as well as several other known Lebanese prisoners.

The 2004 prisoner exchange—not the first—set the stage, in terms of both precedent and reasoning, for Hizballah's July 12, 2006 capture of

Israeli soldiers. Nasrallah had announced earlier in the year that 2006 would be the year that new prisoner negotiations would take place. He also noted, in a July 20 interview on Al-Jazeera, that other leaders in Lebanon were aware of this, though no one knew the details of when a capture operation would take place. Hizballah fighters made at least two earlier attempts to capture Israeli soldiers before succeeding on July 12.

This capture must be understood in the broader context of the ongoing low-grade conflict along and over the Lebanese-Israeli border, rather than as an out-of-the-blue operation meant to instigate a war. Much has been written about why the July 12 operation led to a massive Israeli assault on Lebanon rather than the limited response suggested by the rules both sides had long played by. Most analysts point to a combination of internal political dynamics in Israel and the relationship of the attack to the US "war on terror" and designs on Iran.[10] In this regard, a few paragraphs on the relationship between Hizballah and the United States are in order.

In the United States, Hizballah is generally associated with the 1983 bombings of the US embassy, the Marine barracks, and the French-led multinational force headquarters in Beirut. The second bombing led directly to the US military's departure from Lebanon. The movement is also cited by the State Department in connection with the kidnappings of Westerners in Lebanon and the hostage crisis that led to the Iran–Contra affair and the 1985 hijacking of a TWA flight. These associations are the stated reasons for the presence of Hizballah's name on the State Department's list of terrorist organizations. In 2002, then Deputy Secretary of State Richard Armitage famously described Hizballah as the "A-Team of terrorists," possessing a "global reach," and suggested that "maybe al-Qaeda is actually the B-Team." But Hizballah's involvement in these attacks remains a matter of contention. Even if their involvement is accepted, for several major reasons, it is both inaccurate and unwise to dismiss Hizballah as "terrorists." To characterize the group as a terrorist organization is problematic because of the vagaries of the label itself, which has become a catch-all term used to justify US and allied rhetoric and violence. Since it is only applied to non-state actors, this general usage of the word leaves the terror committed by Israeli (or US) military forces legitimate. Hizballah's military activity has generally been committed to the goal of ending the Israeli occupation of southern Lebanon. As already noted, they have largely operated within tacit, mutually understood, rules of the game in ongoing, low-level border skirmishes with Israel that avoid civilian casualties. Also, Hizballah is an organization that has changed and grown significantly since its inception in the mid-1980s from a militia dedicated to resisting the Israeli invasions and occupation of Lebanon to a multifaceted organization that is both a legitimate Lebanese political party and an umbrella organization for myriad social welfare institutions, both of which will be detailed further. Another aspect of the US listing of Hizballah on the terrorist list is related to the group's reputation as undertaking numerous "suicide attacks" or "martyrdom operations." In fact, of the hundreds of military operations undertaken by the group during the Israeli invasion and occupation of Lebanon, only twelve involved the intentional death of a Hizballah fighter. At least half of the suicide attacks against Israeli occupying forces in Lebanon were carried out by members of secular and leftist parties.

The US insistence on labeling Hizballah a terrorist group is also related to the notion that Hizballah's raison d'etre is the destruction of Israel. Yet one might question the feasibility of such a project, particularly given the great asymmetry in military might and destructive power between Israel and Hizballah, evidenced in the 30:1 ration of Lebanese to Israeli civilians killed this summer. There is also reason to question Hizballah's intent, since even prior to May 2000, almost all of Hizballah's military activity took place within Israeli-occupied Lebanon. Hizballah's founding document—drafted at the time when the Israeli invasion of Lebanon had just given rise to the Hizballah militia—states that they "recognize no treaty with [Israel], no cease-fire and no peace agreements, whether separate or consolidated." But, as Augustus R. Norton notes, "While Hizballah's enmity for Israel is not to be dismissed, the simple fact is that it has been tacitly negotiating with Israel for years." Hizballah's indirect talks with Israel in 1996 and 2004 and their stated willingness to arrange a prisoner exchange today all indicate realism on the part of party leadership. That realism is also evident in the development of Hizballah into a legitimate political party in Lebanon.

Structure, Leadership, Politics

Since its founding in 1985, Hizballah has developed a complex internal structure. In the 1980s, a religious council of prominent leaders, called the *majlis al-shura*, was formed. This seven-member council included branches for various aspects of the group's functioning, including financial, judicial, social, political, and military committees. There were also local regional councils in Beirut, the Beqaa, and the south. When the Lebanese civil war came to a tired end in 1990, after the signing of the Taif Accord, Hizballah made a key decision to participate in Lebanese state politics. This decision was marked in part by the establishment of two other decision-making bodies within the party: an executive council and a politburo.

The other major marker of this transition into politics was Hizballah's decision to participate in Lebanese elections. There was a great deal of debate about this within Hizballah between leaders who wanted to maintain a more revolutionary stance outside the state and those who wanted to work within it. The current secretary general of the party, Nasrallah, had just taken that position after Israel assassinated his predecessor, Sayyid Abbas Musawi. It was under his leadership that Hizballah committed itself to working within the state and began participating in elections.

In the first postwar parliamentary elections, held in 1992, Hizballah won eight seats, giving them the largest single bloc in the 128-member parliament, and its allies won an additional four seats.[11] From that point on, the party developed a reputation for being a clean and capable political party on both the national and local levels. This reputation is especially important in Lebanon, where government corruption is assumed, clientelism is the norm, and political positions are often inherited.

In its politics, there is no doubt that Hizballah is a nationalist party. Its view of nationalism differs from that of many Lebanese, especially from the nationalism based on the Phoenician origins myth espoused by Lebanon's Christian right, and from the neoliberal US-backed nationalism of Hariri's party. Hizballah offers instead a nationalism that views Lebanon as an Arab state that cannot distance itself from Arab causes like that of Palestine. Its political ideology maintains an Islamic outlook, and the 1985 open letter that is often read as the party's "manifesto" does note the desire to establish an Islamic state, but only through the will of the people, stating "We don't want Islam to reign in Lebanon by force." The party's decision to participate in elections in 1992 not only underscored its commitment to working through the existing (sectarian) structure of the

Lebanese state, but it also indicated a shift in the party's focus toward internal Lebanese issues. Furthermore, since 1992, Hizballah leaders have frequently acknowledged the contingencies of Lebanon's multi-confessional society and the importance of sectarian coexistence and pluralism within the country. It should also be noted that many of Hizballah's constituents do not want to live in an Islamic state; rather, they want the party to represent their interests within a pluralist Lebanon.

While Hizballah is often accused of being a puppet of either Iran or Syria, the group's decisions and actions have generally focused on maintaining its position and the support of its constituents within the Lebanese polity. Hizballah officially follows Ayatollah Ali Khamenei as the party's *marja' al-taqlid*, or source of emulation in religious matters, consults with Iranian leaders, and receives an indeterminate amount of economic aid from Iran.[12] This relationship does not, however, mean that Iran dictates Hizballah's policies or decision-making, or can necessarily control the actions of the party. Meanwhile, Iranian efforts to infuse the Lebanese Shia with a pan-Shiite identity centered on Iran have run up against the Arab identity and increasing Lebanese nationalism of Hizballah itself. Similarly, while the party keeps good relations with the Syrian government, Syria does not control or dictate Hizballah decisions or actions.[13] Party decisions are made in accordance with Hizballah's view of Lebanon's interests and the party's own interests within Lebanese politics.

After the Syrian withdrawal of 2005, it became evident that Hizballah would play a larger role in the Lebanese government. Indeed, in the 2005 elections, Hizballah increased their parliamentary seats to 14, in a voting bloc with other parties that took 35. Also in 2005, for the first time, the party chose to participate in the cabinet, and currently holds the Ministry of Energy. Hizballah also plays the political game in Lebanon, where candidates run as multi-confessional district slates rather than as individuals, which means that alliances are constantly being renegotiated with other politicians who may or may not back one another's various programs and ideologies. For example, in the 2005 parliamentary contests, the Sunni Muslim on Hizballah's slate in Saida was Bahia Hariri, sister of the assassinated prime minister. Since the elections, the strongest ally of the Shiite movement has been former General Michel Aoun, who used to be the quintessentially "anti-Syrian" figure in Lebanese politics. Aoun's movement, along with Hizballah, was an important component of enormous demonstrations on May 10 in Beirut against the government's privatization plans, which would have cost jobs in Lebanon's public sector. The anti-privatization demonstrations also point to the third aspect of Hizballah's sphere of activity: its social platforms, where it views itself as representing not only Shiite Lebanese, but also the poor more generally.

Welfare and Social Platforms

One of the elements that sets Hizballah apart from other Lebanese groups is the professional level of organization that exists within the party and its institutions. It is no doubt the political party in Lebanon that best responds to its constituents' needs and desires in the country, both politically and economically. Among the consequences of the Lebanese civil war were economic stagnation, government corruption, and a widening gap between the ever-shrinking middle class and the ever-expanding ranks of the poor. Shiite areas of Beirut—namely, the densely populated southern suburbs of Beirut, known as "al-Dahiyeh" (literally, the suburb)—also had to cope with hundreds of thousands of displaced people who settled there from the south and the Beqaa.[14]

To alleviate poverty in this area, as well as the south and the Beqaa Valley, a social welfare network developed alongside the Shiite political mobilization in the 1970s and 1980s, with key actors including al-Sadr, Fadlallah, and Hizballah. Today, Hizballah functions as an umbrella organization under which many social institutions are run. Some of these institutions provide monthly support and supplemental nutritional, educational, housing, and health assistance for the poor; others focus on supporting orphans; still others are devoted to reconstruction of war-damaged areas. There are also Hizballah-affiliated schools, clinics, and low-cost hospitals, including a school for children with Down's syndrome. Hizballah is not the only major actor in the social welfare arena. Another large network of organizations is affiliated with Fadlallah. There are also a number of smaller independent welfare-provision organizations founded and run by pious Shiite women,[15] as well as family associations that serve as gathering spaces or links for the various branches of a large extended family.

These social welfare institutions are located around Lebanon and serve the local people regardless of sect, though they are concentrated in the mainly Shiite Muslim areas of the country. They are run almost entirely through volunteer labor, mostly that of women, and much of their funding stems from individual donations, orphan sponsorships, and religious taxes. Practicing Shiite Muslims pay an annual tithe called the *khums*, which is one-fifth of the income they do not need for their own family's upkeep. Half of this tithe is given to the care of the *marja'* they recognize. Since 1995, when Khamenei appointed Nasrallah and another Hizballah leader as his religious deputies in Lebanon, the *khums* revenues of Lebanese Shia who follow Khamenei have gone directly into Hizballah's coffers. People who follow Fadlallah as *marja'* similarly contribute to his institutions or independent institutions that have his permission to collect donations on his behalf. Much of this financial support comes from Lebanese Shia living abroad.

It is the social welfare aspect of the party's activities that sometimes leads to accusations that Hizballah is a "state within a state." A more apt phrasing may be that it is a "state within a non-state." The party's welfare provision network is commensurate with the sectarian relationship between state and society in Lebanon, and fills a lacuna left by the state in poor Shiite areas of the country. When the state steps up, Hizballah has thus far demonstrated that it will step back. For example, when Sukleen, the private company to which the Lebanese government contracted garbage collection, began servicing the southern suburbs of Beirut, Hizballah promptly discontinued its own garbage collection services.

In addition to its social welfare networks, Hizballah contributes to the promotion of Islamic values through cultural and leisure sites in Shiite-majority areas of Beirut and Lebanon. These cultural sites range from exhibitions devoted to the memorialization of Resistance martyrs to restaurant complexes that do not serve alcohol, to single-sex youth summer camps and recreational centers. Party-sponsored media—a newspaper and television and radio stations—can also be viewed as part of this public sphere apparatus. This is a relatively recent aspect of the party's activities, and is an arena in which the party is only one among many different agents, some of which are market-driven as much as ideology-driven.[16] To date, such cultural sphere activities have been limited to areas where a pious Shiite constituency—and a demand for pious entertainment— already exists.

Such a demand itself underscores the diverse class base from which Hizballah draws its support and highlights the fact that the party's social welfare organizations do not function as "bribes" for their constituents (a common accusation). In fact, neither socioeconomic status nor religious background nor faith determines political allegiance in this case. Not all Shiite Muslims support Hizballah and not all Hizballah supporters are Shiite Muslim, though many are. Similarly, the party's constituents are not only poor, but increasingly come from the middle classes and include many upwardly mobile, highly educated Lebanese.

Civilian Constituencies

Hizballah's popularity in Lebanon is multifaceted, based on a combination of its resistance (crucially, *successful* resistance) to Israeli occupation and violations of Lebanon's sovereignty; its Islamic ideology, political platforms, and record in Lebanon; and an approach to political-economic development that includes an efficient welfare-provision network. Different Lebanese find different aspects of the party appealing for different reasons. As with political affiliation and allegiance anywhere, these are not simple equations.

For some, Hizballah is viewed as providing a viable alternative to a US-supported government and its neoliberal economic project in Lebanon, and as an active opponent to the neoimperialism of the US in the Middle East more broadly. For others, including many Christians and Druze from the south, Hizballah is seen as the only viable possibility for protecting their villages and homes and livelihoods from Israeli attack. For some, the ability to send their children to schools that teach Islamic values along with the Lebanese state curriculum, or to visit single-sex beaches or restaurants that do not serve alcohol, is appealing. For others, the financial support provided by the party's organizations was invaluable in helping them rebuild their lives after the civil war. Various of these views may coexist. There are people who vehemently oppose the party's Islamic outlook, while supporting the Hizballah Resistance and their defense of the south. Even many of those Lebanese who believe that Hizballah's July 12 capture of Israeli soldiers was a mistake simultaneously support the Resistance and view Israel as their enemy. These are not mutually exclusive positions.

"Hizballah supporter" itself is a vague phrase. There are official members of the party; there are fighters with the Resistance; there are volunteers in party-affiliated social welfare organizations; there are recipients of aid from those organizations; there are those who voted for the party in the last election; there are those who support the Resistance in the current conflict without supporting other aspects of the party's political platform; among many others. The best way to think of the relationship among these various ideologies, positions, and activities, and the Lebanese who support or align themselves with them, is to think of imperfectly overlapping circles and ideas that are constantly shifting. Individuals traverse this terrain of institutions and ideologies in complex ways, as they do in any society. Given this complexity, asserting that Lebanese civilian casualties during the July war were the result of Hizballah "hiding behind civilians" is absurd.

An Amnesty International (AI) press release of August 23, 2006, reports that the Israeli government's position is that "they were targeting Hizballah positions and support facilities and that other damage done to civilian infrastructure was a result of Hizballah using the civilian population as a 'human shield.'"[17] AI rightly notes that this claim is "simply not credible," based on "the pattern, scope and scale of the attacks." The executive director of Human Rights Watch (HRW) similarly notes that the Israeli assertion that Hizballah was hiding among civilians "doesn't stand up to the facts," citing as an example HRW's on-the-ground investigators' findings that there had been no Hizballah presence in Qana at the time of the Israeli attack there, and stating, "[The IDF] has yet to show that Hizballah was in a civilian building or vehicle at the time of an Israeli attack that killed civilians."[18]

Both of these reports are using the term "Hizballah" to mean only armed fighters, which is only one reading in the context of this military conflict, and they importantly point out that there were no armed combatants in or near the investigated civilian sites when they were destroyed by Israeli bombardment. Either the technologically advanced Israeli military was consistently mistaken in its efforts to target armed combatants, or it was targeting something else. The latter is the conclusion drawn by the AI report, as it points to Israel's "*deliberate* destruction of civilian infrastructure" (emphasis added). Destroying civilian infrastructure entails attacking a civilian population. And indeed, given the complex relationship of Hizballah to its Lebanese constituencies—a relationship that traverses the Resistance, political, and social spheres—Israeli rhetoric stating that the purpose of this summer's attack was to "remove" Hizballah from Lebanon treads dangerously close to ideas of depopulation.[19]

Who is this Hizballah that the Israeli military so desperately wished to remove? What if one member of a family is a party member and others are not? What if the daughter of the family attends a school funded by Hizballah—does that make that family a legitimate target by Israeli reasoning? Or Fatima, a volunteer who cooks for the poor during Ramadan at a Hizballah welfare organization? Is she a target? Or Wafaa Hoteit, official party spokesperson and liaison to the press and researchers? What about the democratically elected Hizballah members of parliament? Mohammad Fneish, the minister of energy?

"Hizballah strongholds" are places where people live and work. The southern suburbs of Beirut, for example, are in fact a vibrant conglomeration of urban neighborhoods where residents have varying political perspectives, religious beliefs and identities, and lifestyles. Elaborate homes exist alongside run-down buildings, as do shops selling European fashions alongside those selling Islamic dress, all interspersed with internet cafés, vegetable stands, salons, charity organization offices, and corner markets. One of the buildings in the now entirely destroyed "Hizballah security zone" contained the party's media relations office, where reporters and researchers were granted interviews. That office was on the second floor of a block that included apartments, stores selling everything from spices to toys, and a fantastic bakery and juice bar—a far cry from the trappings of "terrorist targets."

The deliberate targeting of civilian infrastructure and strikes on civilian convoys and residences indicate the Israeli government's understanding that Hizballah is much more than an armed militia. And indeed, as we have seen, in addition to its Resistance militia, Hizballah is a political party and a social welfare network. It has to do with economic interests as well as religious ideologies, local politics, and anti-imperialist stances. This does not, however, legitimate the deliberate targeting of civilians. Israeli claims that Hizballah was "hiding behind civilians" are efforts to counter the storm of accusations of deliberate targeting by reasserting the separation between people who were and were not carrying arms and placing the blame for the conflation on Hizballah. Yet both the AI and the HRW reports found that those claims did not hold up under investigation. To remove Hizballah from Lebanon would require the "removal" of its civilian constituencies. Playing devil's advocate, one could say that the enmeshment of Hizballah with civilian life in Lebanon legitimates strikes against civilian targets because the water is as hostile as the fish swimming in it. The obvious problem with this logic is that draining the pond would be tantamount to ethnic cleansing.

Conclusion

A historical and more nuanced view of Hizballah in Lebanon highlights the group's multifaceted aspects and appeal. The support of its constituents has—despite major divisions in Lebanese public opinion in general on the party—been consolidated in the aftermath of this summer's war. On August 13, the day before the cease-fire went into effect, Nasrallah gave a televised address marking the end of the violence and devoted one-third of his airtime to discussing plans to rebuild homes and house the displaced. The very next morning, party volunteers with clipboards were assessing damage, prioritizing repairs, handing out rent money and school supplies for students, and actually beginning the work of reconstruction. It remains to be seen whether that level of efficiency and response can be maintained, as the time it will take to rebuild cannot be underestimated. Nonetheless, the immediacy of the initial response has bolstered support for the party.

Another factor adding to the increase in the party's popularity and significance, not only in Lebanon but more broadly in the region, is the perception of the July war as a victory for Hizballah—in the sense that they managed to thwart Israel's goals for the conflict. As the rebuilding process continues, against a backdrop of continued political demonstrations, assassinations, and standoffs in Lebanon, it remains to be seen how the political landscape will shift. One thing, however, is clear: Hizballah—and its constituencies—will remain major players in Lebanese politics in the years to come.

NOTES

Thanks to Lori Allen, Laleh Khalili, Nadya Sbaiti, and Chris Toensing for their comments. All this article's shortcomings remain, of course, my own.

1 Much of the best coverage of this war was available through online sources, including www.electroniclebanon.net, www.aljazeera.net, and the numerous blogs that documented and commented on events, including those of political anthropologist Augustus Richard Norton (www.bostonuniversity.blogspot.com) and political scientist

Asʿad Abukhalil (www.angryarab.blogspot.com).

2 During this time, Hizballah killed 118 Israeli soldiers and 41 civilians. Hizballah has held funerals for 184 fighters. The ratio of Lebanese to Israeli civilian casualties is 30:1.

3 Analysts estimate infrastructural damage to the country at $3 billion. This includes the destruction of runways and fuel tanks at Beirut international airport, roads, ports, power plants, bridges, gas stations, TV transmitters, cell phone towers, a dairy and other factories, wheat silos, and grocery stores.

4 Most of these were dropped during the final three days of the conflict. See "Israeli Cluster Munitions Hit Civilians in Lebanon" (Human Rights Watch, Beirut, 24 July 2006). Available at www.hrw.org/english/docs/2006/07/24/isrlpa13798.htm (accessed 26 August 2006). It is unknown whether these cluster bombs contained depleted uranium, as they have when the US drops them in Iraq, but Lebanese scientists have documented high levels of radiation around certain bomb sites. "Scientists Suspect Israeli Arms Used in South Contain Radioactive Matter" (*Daily Star* [Beirut] 21 August 2006).

5 For an excellent discussion of the southern suburbs in all their complexity, see Mona Harb el-Kak, *Politiques urbaines dans la banlieue-sud de Beyrouth* (Beirut: Centre d'etudes et de recherches sur le Moyen-Orient contemporain, 1996) and Mona Harb, "Postwar Beirut: Resources, Negotiations, and Contestations in the Elyssar Project," *Arab World Geographer* 3 (2000) 272–289.

6 All government and parliamentary positions are allocated on the basis of religious background among the eighteen officially recognized confessional communities. The original allocations, supposedly based on the 1932 census' population ratios, gave the most power to a Maronite Christian president and a Sunni Muslim prime minister, with the relatively powerless position of speaker of parliament granted to a Shiite Muslim. The system did not take into consideration demographic changes, so that the under-representation of Shiite Muslims has been exacerbated over time.

7 A "source of emulation" (*marja' al-taqlid*) is a religious scholar of such widely recognized erudition that individual Shiite Muslims seek and follow his advice on religious matters. Fadlallah is often described as "the spiritual leader" of Hizballah, a relationship that both he and the party have consistently denied. In fact, for a time there was a rift between them over the nature of the Shiite Islamic institution of the *marja'iyya* (the practice/institution of following a *marja' al-taqlid*). Fadlallah believes that religious scholars should work through multiple institutions and should not affiliate with a single political party or be involved in affairs of worldly government. In these beliefs, he is close to traditional Shiite jurisprudence, and distant from the concept of *Vilayat-al-faqih* (rule of the clerics) promulgated by Ayatollah Ruhollah Khomeini of Iran.

8 On Hizballah, see especially Augustus Richard Norton, *Hizballah of Lebanon: Extremist Ideals vs. Mundane Politics* (New York: Council on Foreign Relations, 1999). See also Dalal el-Bizri, *Islamistes, parlementaires et Libanais: Les interventions a l'Assemblee des elus de la Jama'a Islamiyya et du Hizb Allah (1992–1996)* (Beirut: Centre d'etudes et de recherches sur le Moyen-Orient contemporain, 1999); Nizar Hamzeh, *In the Path of Hizballah* (Syracuse: Syracuse University Press, 2004); Judith Harik, *Hizballah: The Changing Face of Terrorism* (London: I.B. Tauris, 1996); and Amal Saad-Ghorayeb, *Hizb'ullah: Politics and Religion* (London: Pluto Press, 2002).

9 For more on Hizballah's military activity and the "rules of the game" governing cross-border conflict, see Augustus Richard Norton, "Hizballah and the Israeli Withdrawal from Southern Lebanon," *Journal of Palestine Studies* 30 (2000) 22–35 and Daniel Sobelman, "Still Playing by the Rules," *Bitterlemons International* 36.2 (2004), available at www.bitterlemons-international.org.

10 For example, Seymour Hersh has documented a longstanding Israeli plan for the offensive along with US advance collusion, and its relationship as a potential "test ground" for or precursor to a US strike against Iran ("Watching Lebanon: Washington's Interests in Israel's War," *New Yorker* 21 August 2006).

11 The Amal militia formed by Sayyid Musa al-Sadr also developed into a political party after the civil war ended, and has been Hizballah's main political rival among Shiite Lebanese, though they are now working in tandem.

12 Party members, however, are free to follow any *marja' al-taqlid* they choose, and many follow Fadlallah instead.

13 After the assassination of former Lebanese Prime Minister Rafiq Hariri in February 2005, and the subsequent Syrian withdrawal from Lebanon, Hizballah's position was often described as "pro-Syrian." The party's rhetoric was carefully chosen not to oppose Syrian withdrawal, but to recast it as a withdrawal that would not sever all ties with Lebanon, and that would take place under an umbrella of "gratitude."

14 It is estimated that about 80 percent of the population of the southern suburbs today are Shiite Muslim Lebanese.

15 For more on these organizations and the volunteerism that maintains them, see Lara Deeb, *An Enchanted Modern: Gender and Public Piety in Shi'i Lebanon* (Princeton: Princeton University Press, 2006).

16 Mona Harb, of the American University of Beirut, has spoken about the market-driven versus ideology-driven aspects of the development of "pious entertainment" in Shiite-majority areas of Lebanon.

17 Available at: http://news.amnesty.org/mavp/news.nsf/print/ENGMDE020182006 (accessed 23 August 2006).

18 Kenneth Roth (executive director of Human Rights Watch), "Indiscriminate Bombardment," *Jerusalem Post* 17 August 2006. See also Jonathan Cook, "Hypocrisy and the Clamor against Hizballah" (*Electronic Lebanon* 9 August 2006). Available at http://electronicintifada.net/v2/article5465.shtml (accessed 27 August 2006). Cook writes, "While there has been little convincing evidence that Hizballah is firing its rocket from towns and villages in southern Lebanon, or that its fighters are hiding there among civilians, it can be known beyond a shadow of a doubt that Israeli army camps and military installations are based in northern Israeli communities."

19 "Removing" Hizballah is in fact a recycled goal, one that emerged in Israeli rhetoric and strategy during the attacks on Lebanon in 1993 and 1996 as well. Depopulation of certain areas has long been an Israeli strategy; it is a euphemism for the ethnic cleansing of territory. See, for example, Gabriel Piterberg, "Erasures," *New Left Review* 10 (July/August 2001) 31–46; and Walid Khalidi, *All That Remains: The Palestinian Villages Occupied and Depopulated by Israel in 1948* (Washington, DC: Institute for Palestine Studies, 1992).

5. MEETING SAYYID HASSAN NASRALLAH: ENCOUNTER WITH A FIGHTER

Assaf Kfoury

A decade ago, in the wake of "Operation Grapes of Wrath," the 17-day Israeli military assault on southern Lebanon in April 1996, there was a spate of articles in the Western press on Hizballah and its secretary general, Sayyid Hassan Nasrallah.[1] The Israeli operation stopped under pressure from the US government, which was wary of the political repercussions of the mounting toll among Lebanese civilians, including the massacre of more than 100 refugees in the village of Qana on April 18, 1996. Humanitarian sympathy for the Lebanese victims did not translate into a less biased image of Hizballah, which is typically presented by Western media as a shadowy and rabidly anti-Western terrorist organization.

There were very few exceptions. In the British press, Robert Fisk in the *Independent* and David Gardner in the *Financial Times* wrote honest and factual articles, including interviews they conducted with Nasrallah in May and July of 1996, respectively.[2] The most remarkable article was Eqbal Ahmad's "Encounter with a Fighter," in *Al-Ahram Weekly* (30 July–5 August 1998), in which he gave a particularly sensitive and fair account of his meeting with Nasrallah. Although it is in English, the appearance of Ahmad's article in an Egyptian weekly kept it a relatively safe distance from the censorship (and self-censorship) of the mainstream media in the West. But these remained all too few and in sharp contrast to the relentless demonization by other journalists and political commentators.

In the US press, occasional more objective views of Hizballah only appeared after the year 2000. This was probably elicited by several developments that occasionally drew some attention and respect in the West. In the 1990s, in addition to pursuing its guerrilla activities against Israeli forces in southern Lebanon, Hizballah gradually emerged as a powerful political and social movement, promoting dialogue with other Lebanese parties and winning seats for its candidates in the Lebanese parliament. Just as important was the surge in popular support among all Lebanese for the dominant role Hizballah played in the successful resistance to Israeli occupation, which came (mostly) to an end in May 2000.

In the July 28, 2003 *New Yorker*, Seymour Hersh wrote an article called "The Syrian Bet" on Syria's situation and the surrounding turmoil—the American occupation of Iraq, the bloody intifada in the Palestinian territories, and simmering discontent in Lebanon. Hersh's article included an account of a meeting with Nasrallah, informative and free of the deeply ingrained racism of others. There was a lengthy review of several books on Hizballah in the *New York Review of Books* by Adam Shatz; he also interviewed Nasrallah for the article, on a October 2003 trip to Lebanon (29 April 2004). Although too prone to pass judgment reflecting his own biases, Shatz nonetheless quoted Nasrallah on several issues on which Hizballah had been persistently misrepresented.[3]

Of all the public statements on Nasrallah, perhaps the most startling—given who the source is—came from Edward Peck. Peck is a former American diplomat and former deputy director of the Reagan White House Task Force on Terrorism, and was part of an American delegation that met Nasrallah in February 2006. Peck's assessment of Nasrallah was unusually respectful for an American official, even sympathetic, and contrasted with his earlier impressions of Hamas and Fatah leaders:

> It was interesting to meet with [Nasrallah], because we had already met with leaders of Hamas and Fatah before and after the election was over in Palestine [in January 2006], and his point was a fairly simple one, I think. Talking to us, retired diplomats, Americans, his key concerns were essentially how to free his country from the domination [...] and how to go about building the nation up again, despite all of the things that had happened to it over the years.
>
> So it was a logical, reasonable presentation. No screaming, no shrieking. You know, just an educated intelligent man talking about serious issues that he perceived. It was interesting in the sense that the projection of people like that in [the US] is of, you know, blood-soaked wackos, and there are some of those out there on all sides, but that certainly was not the case with him.[4]

In May 2006, I went to meet Nasrallah in a group of four—Noam and Carol Chomsky, Irene Gendzier, and myself. Peck's impressions were also ours: Nasrallah seemed a logical and reflective man, not given to effusive gestures or hyperboles, perhaps at his best when explaining and defending Hizballah's local politics and role in Lebanon. We met him in his heavily guarded compound in the Dahiyeh, the southern suburb of Beirut, which would be reduced to a heap of rubble by the Israeli air force a month later. Security at the entrance of the building where Nasrallah's office was located, and around it, was extremely high, in sharp contrast with the lacking or half-hearted security measures in the rest of the city.

Nasrallah greeted us warmly, shaking hands with the men, nodding and smiling toward the women. He wore the usual attire of a Shia cleric—turban and tunic. Later, he pointed to the black of his turban, a sign that he is considered a descendant of the Prophet. He mentioned the role in Shia culture the black turban enjoins of its wearer, with the smile of someone glad to introduce friendly foreigners to something they may not know.

Our meeting with Nasrallah lasted about two and a half hours. The conversation went from broad and sometimes trite generalities at the start to specific and nuanced positions on local matters at the end.

The conversation started slowly, with events in Iraq and Palestine, then covered Iran and regional events, and became more focused as it shifted to the situation in southern Lebanon and Lebanon in general.

We did not expect any criticism of Iran from Nasrallah, and we did not hear any, however veiled. On Iraq, he avoided taking sides in the rift between Shiite factions. "The difference between Ayatollah Sistani and Muqtada al-Sadr is the difference between a wise man in his seventies and an impulsive man in his thirties," he said.

But what of the prospects for secessionist movements in Khuzestan, Azerbaijan, and other oil-rich areas in Iran? we asked. We mentioned that according to some reports (real or not) there is an "Ahwazi liberation movement" in Khuzestan. Nasrallah was dismissive of such prospects, maintaining that Ahwazis as well as other minorities in Iran are well integrated, and well represented in the army and the government.

What of the possibility of a US attack on Iran or campaign to force a regime change in Iran? Nasrallah thought it would be a grave miscalculation. "We all see the chaos and destruction created by the American invasion of Iraq, even though it was relatively easy to destroy Saddam's government. It will be far more difficult to bring down Iran's government, let alone invade Iran. Iran's situation is totally different from Iraq's. Saddam's government and army were instruments against the Iraqi people. The Islamic republic in Iran enjoys the support of the Iranian people."

Nasrallah acknowledged Hizballah's good relations with Iran and Syria, but also insisted on Hizballah's independence with respect to decision-making. We did not press him on the degree of this independence, which is often questioned by outsiders because of Iran's financial support. But already in 1996, David Gardner wrote that "donations from Lebanese Shia in West Africa, from Shiites in the Gulf, and in the form of Islamic tithes have made the organization largely self-sustained." Gardner noted, for example, that a $100 million complex in the Dahiyeh with a mosque, hospitals, schools, and research centers, was paid for by a wealthy Kuwaiti Shiite, while money from Iran was estimated to be $60 million per year according to Western intelligence sources, but never exceeded $40 million per year according to Hizballah insiders.

The charge of subservience to Iran persists, chiefly by US government officials still in pursuit of reckless plans to create a "New Middle East." And Hizballah's leaders keep denying the charge. A few days after our own meeting with Nasrallah, his deputy Naim Kassem restated in an interview that his group "has no decision to enter any battle [outside Lebanon] and has said repeatedly that its position is one of defence against aggression." And again, as reported by Lin Noueihed in the *Scotsman*: "Hizballah is not a tool of Iran; it is a Lebanese project that implements the demands of Lebanese" (22 May 2006).

More to the point, however, longtime observers have dismissed attempts to portray Hizballah as an Iranian proxy. According to Amal Saad-Ghorayeb, a Beirut-based political scientist who has studied Hizballah over many years, Hizballah "has never allowed any foreign power to dictate its military strategy" (*Guardian* 15 July 2006). Saad-Ghorayeb's assessment is supported by several specialists on Middle Eastern affairs, including longtime opponents of the Iranian government, and even by officials in Washington with a better grip on reality.[5] The State Department's coordinator for counterterrorism said, "Syria can stop the flow of weapons, materiel and people into Lebanon. Yes, they can take a lot of action that they haven't. In terms of them controlling Hizballah, no, they cannot put Hizballah out of business." The same official estimated that Iran wielded more influence, but "even there, Iran does not completely own Hizballah."[6]

An uncertain battle in Iran has for years pitted reformists against conservatives, with the latter now back in power. In our meeting with

Nasrallah, this issue did not come up. He referred several times to Iran, but did not compare specific individuals or factions in the Iranian government or its opposition. Another issue left aside in our meeting was Nasrallah's views on al-Qaeda and the Taliban. But in a 1998 interview in the *Financial Times* with David Gardner, he expressed his strong opposition to these movements and presented the Islamic republic in Iran as an alternative model sketching out a path for the region toward modernity and democracy. "There are a lot of models. Some of them are very dangerous like the Taliban," he said then (8 September 1998).

In an interview with David Ignatius in the *Washington Post*, Nasrallah categorically set his group apart from al-Qaeda and its action that is fanning Sunni–Shiite tensions in Iraq. "I believe the most dangerous thing we confront is the so-called Zarqawi phenomenon," he said (3 February 2006). "This is a creed of killing without any responsibility—to kill women, children, to attack mosques, churches, schools, restaurants." Nasrallah has often pointed out the contrast between that and the Hizballah resistance, which is a Shiite organization that operates in solidarity with Sunni Hamas and Palestinians. Thus, for example, the prisoner exchange Hizballah negotiated with Israel in January 2004 involved both Lebanese and Palestinian detainees. And again, when its fighters attacked an Israeli army unit on July 12, 2006 and captured two soldiers, Hizballah announced it would exchange them for both Lebanese and Palestinian prisoners in Israel.

Turning to Palestinian matters, we asked: What of the events in Gaza and the West Bank? And the standoff between Hamas and Israel? "The Palestinians' situation is intolerable, we will help inasmuch as we can, and inasmuch as the Palestinians will ask for our help," Nasrallah said, and then in no uncertain terms: "But our own battle stops at the Lebanese border. Whatever the agreement reached by our Palestinian brothers with the Israeli government, it is their responsibility and we will abide by it, even if it is not the agreement that we prefer."

This has been Hizballah's stated position for years, both to its audience in Lebanon and to the outside world. In 2003, for example, in answer to Seymour Hersh, who asked his view on Israeli–Palestinian negotiations, Nasrallah said, "I, like any other person, may consider what is happening to be right or wrong... I may have a different assessment, but at the end of the road no one can go to war on behalf of the Palestinians, even if that one is not in agreement with what the Palestinians agreed on." And again in his interview with Adam Shatz, when asked whether he was prepared to live with a two-state settlement between Israel and Palestine, Nasrallah said he would not sabotage what is finally a "Palestinian matter."

Earlier on the day we met Nasrallah, we spent several hours in the Sabra-Shatila camp, on the southern outskirts of Beirut. We visited the site of the September 1982 massacre. It was difficult contemplating the dismal conditions of the camp—poor, dusty, overcrowded—in spite of the warm welcome from everyone we met. The contrast with the glitter and wealth in downtown Beirut was jarring. So, what about the Palestinians in Lebanon and the camps? we asked Nasrallah. "The Palestinian refugee camps are a disgrace. A Lebanese man will not even allow his dog to live in the miserable conditions of the camps," he said. "Palestinians in Lebanon should be given the same rights as other Arabs in Lebanon—the right to work, to get social benefits, to own property." As for the option of absorbing the Palestinian refugees into Lebanese society, "Lebanon in its present [confessional] configuration cannot absorb the Palestinian refugees. They cannot be given Lebanese citizenship, and they should be allowed to retain their identity as Palestinians." So, how shall the refugees be helped until the Israeli–Palestinian conflict is resolved? "Other Arab states should help out—Lebanon cannot alone carry the burden of the Palestinian refugees."

We finally turned to internal Lebanese matters. Nasrallah described Hizballah's political work and the support it enjoys among Lebanese in general. He mentioned "nearly three-quarters of all Lebanese, both Christians and Muslims, support us and our role in defending Lebanon," and made a point to stress that this popularity extends beyond the Shia community. (There was a surge of solidarity during the Israeli onslaught of July–August 2006. A poll conducted at the end of July 2006 reported that 87 percent of all Lebanese supported Hizballah's resistance to Israeli aggression—this is support for Hizballah's resistance to external aggression, not necessarily for Hizballah's policies on which the Lebanese generally remain divided. A similar survey conducted five months earlier showed only 58 percent of all Lebanese supported Hizballah's right to keep its arms and, hence, continue its resistance activity.[7]) Nasrallah referred to the success of Hizballah as an armed resistance against Israeli occupation as a byproduct of its deep roots in the local civilian population.

Yitzhak Rabin and other Israeli military men, he claimed, wrote about the difficulty of controlling southern Lebanon—"a land that can be invaded but not occupied," he said. (We did not check the authenticity of the Israeli writings Nasrallah referred to, but he is said to be a voracious reader of biographies of Israeli politicians.[8] His frequent interviews with Lebanese journalists, when discussing the conflict with Israel, are laced with references to the Israeli press.)

Though there was no explicit comparison during our conversation between Hizballah and the PLO as popular organizations, we couldn't fail noting Nasrallah's comments were implicit criticism of past attempts to organize armed resistance along the lines of a standing army. In his interview with Robert Fisk in 1996, Nasrallah was explicit: He explained the success of Hizballah guerrillas by the fact that "when they come back from an attack, they will not go to military bases and barracks like the Palestinians did in Lebanon; they will go back to their homes." The contrast with the PLO, which had projected a pervasive military presence in the 1970s and early 1980s in Lebanon, was also noted by Eqbal Ahmad, who had closely followed the development of the Palestinian movement. When he first entered the Hizballah compound in the Dahiyeh, Ahmad mentioned his surprise that

> Unlike the erstwhile PLO compounds and offices in Beirut, there were but few uniformed and armed men visibly around. The stronghold of the most effective armed organization in the Middle East had a completely civilian look, a fact that normally implies intelligent and efficient security arrangements.

Eqbal Ahmad's impression was later echoed by Edward Said, who met Nasrallah in June 2000. Said described Nasrallah as:

> A man who adopted a strategy toward Israel quite similar to that of the Vietnamese against the Americans. We cannot fight them because they have an army, a navy and a nuclear option, so the only way we can do it is to make them feel it in body bags. And that's exactly what [Nasrallah] did. In the one conversation that we had, I was impressed by the fact that among all the political leaders I met in the Middle East, he alone was precisely on time, and there were no people around him waving Kalashnikovs.[9]

The difference with the PLO was borne out during the war on Lebanon of July and August 2006. In the Israeli invasion of Lebanon in

1982, PLO forces were routed in a few days. In 2006, Hizballah fighters stood their ground for 34 days. In 1982 Israeli troops began their offensive on June 6, reached the Litani River as fast as they could drive their armored vehicles, and quickly went beyond all the way to Beirut, encircling the Lebanese presidential palace in the suburb of Baabda on June 20. In 2006 Israeli troops became bogged down against entrenched guerillas and never reached any point along the Litani River, despite a massive ground offensive of some 30,000 troops in the last two days of the war, in which 33 soldiers were killed (out of a total of 119 soldiers during the whole 34-day war).[10] There were other forces involved in resisting the advance of Israeli troops, both in 1982 and 2006. But the PLO was the backbone of this resistance in 1982, just as Hizballah was in 2006. In 2006, though the majority of Lebanese fighters killed in battle belonged to Hizballah, other parties such as the Amal movement, the Lebanese Communist Party, and the Syrian Social Nationalist Party participated in the combat and announced the deaths of some of their fighters.[11]

We asked Nasrallah how he saw the internal situation in Lebanon evolving. In answer, he talked about reforming the electoral system and state institutions so that all Lebanese citizens, both Christians and Muslims, have their fair share in the benefits and services provided by the government. Nasrallah and others in the Hizballah leadership have been often accused by their detractors of seeking to establish an Islamic republic in Lebanon. These accusations have been unrelenting and typically based on statements and writings from the early years of Hizballah, in the 1980s, when it did openly embrace the goal of an Islamic republic. Since the early 1990s the Hizballah leadership has been just as persistent in deflecting these accusations. In his 2003 interview with Adam Shatz, Nasrallah's denial could not be any more categorical: "We believe the requirement for an Islamic state is to have an overwhelming popular desire [for it], and we're not talking about fifty percent plus one, but a large majority. And this is not available in Lebanon and probably never will be." Without ever shedding its Islamist character and conservative moral code, Hizballah has in fact built alliances with other parties, secular and non-Shiite, in order to get a larger representation in the government. When it put up candidates in the last parliamentary elections, some of those on its electoral list were Christians.

Charles Glass, another veteran observer of Middle East affairs, noted in the *London Review of Books* that a hallmark of Hizballah under Nasrallah's leadership has been its flexibility to change and adapt (17 August 2006). Glass recounted several events that have shaped Hizballah's increased involvement in Lebanon's domestic politics. A revealing episode occurred in May 2000 after Israeli troops withdrew from Lebanon suddenly and without advance notice: Hizballah issued a strict warning forbidding reprisals against collaborators of the South Lebanon Army, which Israel had set up as a particularly ruthless auxiliary force to enforce its occupation. Instead, Hizballah turned over SLA militiamen to the Lebanese government without murdering any of them. Glass contrasted Hizballah's lack of retribution to the French Resistance's lust for revenge on Nazi collaborators after World War II, often enacted in barbarous public displays. As Glass noted, "What [Hizballah] sought in south Lebanon was not revenge, but votes."

Our last question to Nasrallah was about his party's weapons, an issue that had been debated among Lebanese for many months before, and about conditions under which Hizballah would relinquish its arms. He immediately put the question in a context wider than that of the Israeli-occupied Shebaa Farms, which many of his Lebanese detractors had accused him of using as an excuse to justify Hizballah's retaining its arms. "The bigger issue, the fundamental one, is how to defend our land against Israeli aggression," according to Nasrallah. He mentioned several issues, all reflecting Israeli aggressive policies: near-daily aerial and naval Israeli incursions into Lebanese airspace and territorial waters, assassination of Palestinian militants in Lebanon, refusal to release Lebanese detained in Israeli prisons, refusal to turn in maps of landmine locations in southern Lebanon, the continued occupation of the Shebaa Farms. "Resolving the problem of any of these issues separately will not resolve the bigger fundamental issue. And it is not a matter of defending only southern Lebanon—it concerns all of Lebanon," he maintained. He mentioned the need for a "national defense strategy," which

> we have raised in the National Dialogue conference, and the others
> agree there is a need for it. Some are asking the Lebanese resistance
> [i.e. the military wing of Hizballah] to dissolve itself or be merged with
> the Lebanese army. But the Lebanese army is small and weak, and given
> its present organization, from the moment the Lebanese resistance is

merged into the army, everything about the resistance will be known
by the American government, which means by the Israeli government
too—this will put us at the total mercy of Israeli military might.

Toward the end, we asked Nasrallah if we could quote him on things
he said in the meeting. He seemed eager to have all of his views
transmitted: "Yes, you can quote me on anything, absolutely." As time
was running short, we asked him whether he had questions of his own for
us. Yes, he had one question: "How can we have our point of view heard
in the US?" he asked. Addressing himself to Noam, "You know better
than us the situation in the US. If there is anything we can do, any way
of explaining our situation so that we can hope for a more equitable US
policy, then we need to hear it from you."

Noam got to finish the conversation:

> You need to reach the American public before American politicians.
> The public in the US is generally ahead of the politicians. Often public
> opinion conflicts with policies set in Washington. US politicians are
> usually elected by a minority of the population and represent two
> parties that are virtually indistinguishable on fundamental issues. If you
> can inform the public and get them to understand your position, they
> will put pressure on the politicians and hopefully prevent them from
> conducting their most destructive policies. Without internal public
> pressure, US policy is not likely to change significantly.

NOTES

1 Sayyid Hassan Nasrallah was elected secretary general of Hizballah a few years
earlier, in 1992, after his predecessor Abbas Musawi was killed in a targeted assassination
raid carried out by Israeli helicopter gunships (which also killed Musawi's wife and
daughter and four others nearby).

2 See Robert Fisk, "Hizbollah Leader Claims 'Sad Victory,'" *Independent* 5 May
1996, and David Gardner, "Lebanon: A Forceful National Party," *Financial Times* 16 July
1996.

3 Shatz's biases clearly come through in a later article, "Nasrallah's Game," *Nation*
online 20 July 2006 (www.thenation.com/doc/20060731/nasrallah_game). In this later
article, Nasrallah is depicted as an adventurist, ready to engage in high-risk gamble to
preserve Hizballah's weapons and prestige. Shatz's concluding statement is that Nasrallah
is "someone who has no fear of death" and that Hizballah's followers have a "passion
for martyrdom." Exactly the stuff peddled by most of the mainstream media, in perfect
harmony with the party line from Washington.

4 Amy Goodman and Juan Gonzalez, "Hizballah Leader Hassan Nasrallah Talks
with Former US Diplomats," *DemocracyNow!* 28 July 2006. From a former official of

the US government, Peck's pronouncements were startling in more than one way. For example, he made clear that the US government, by its own definition of terrorism, is a terrorist organization: "In 1985, when I was the deputy director of the Reagan White House Task Force on Terrorism, they asked us—this is a Cabinet Task Force on Terrorism; I was the deputy director of the working group—they asked us to come up with a definition of terrorism that could be used throughout the government. We produced about six, and in each and every case, they were rejected, because careful reading would indicate that our own country had been involved in some of those activities."

5 Guy Dinmore, "Experts Challenge White House Line on Iran's Influence," *Financial Times* 18 July 2006.

6 Caroline Drees, "Syria, Iran Lack Full Hizballah Control," Reuters, *Washington Post* 25 July 2006.

7 Amal Saad-Ghorayeb, "People Say No: Public Opinion in Lebanon Overwhelmingly Rejects US–Israeli Plans for Cleansing Lebanon of Hizballah," *Al-Ahram Weekly* 3–9 August 2006.

8 Ehud Ya'ari, "It is Not So Bad," *Jerusalem Post* 23 February 2004. Nasrallah is reported to have "invested years in studying Israel, and has read the autobiographies of Sharon and Netanyahu, Rabin, Peres, Begin and Barak."

9 Avi Shavit, "My Right of Return," *Ha'aretz* 18 August 2000.

10 Jonathan Finer and Molly Moore, "Israel Moves Thousands of Soldiers into Lebanon," *Washington Post* 2 August 2006. See also Jonathan Lis, Eli Ashkenazi, and Ari Shavit, "Former IDF Chief Says Soldiers were Sacrificed for Spin," *Ha'aretz* 14 September 2006.

11 Anthony Shadid, "Fleeing Lebanese Christians See Town Forever Changed," *Washington Post* 13 August 2006. In an earlier article, "Lebanon, My Lebanon," *Washington Post* 16 April 2006, Shadid pointed out that, historically, "virtually everyone was a leftist, either communist or an adherent of a pan-Syrian group known as the Syrian Social Nationalist Party," in the town of Marjeyoun.

Part Two

ISRAELI AND AMERICAN COLLUSION

6. THE WAR ON LEBANON IS A WAR ON PALESTINE

Noam Chomsky

Though there are many interacting factors, the immediate issue that lies behind the latest US–Israeli invasion of Lebanon remains, I believe, what it was in the four preceding invasions: the Israel–Palestine conflict. In the most important case, the devastating US-backed 1982 Israeli invasion was openly described in Israel as a war for the West Bank, undertaken to put an end to annoying PLO calls for a diplomatic settlement (with the secondary goal of imposing a client regime in Lebanon). There are numerous other illustrations. Despite the many differences in circumstances, the July 2006 invasion falls generally into the same pattern.

Among mainstream American critics of Bush administration policies, the favored version is that, as Middle East specialist and former diplomat Edward Walker, a leading moderate, puts it: "We had always approached [conflict between Israel and its neighbors] in a balanced way, assuming that we could be the catalyst for an agreement," but this Bush administration regrettably abandoned that neutral stance, causing great problems for the United States. The actual record is quite different: For over 30 years, Washington has unilaterally barred a peaceful political settlement, with only slight and brief deviations.

The consistent rejectionism can be traced back to the February 1971 Egyptian offer of a full peace treaty with Israel, in the terms of official US policy, offering nothing for the Palestinians. Israel understood that this peace offer would put an end to any security threat, but the government decided to reject security in favor of expansion, then mostly into northeastern Sinai. Washington supported Israel's stand, adhering to Kissinger's principle of "stalemate": force, not diplomacy. It was only eight years later, after a terrible war and great suffering, that Washington agreed to Egypt's demand for withdrawal from its territory.

Meanwhile the Palestinian issue had entered the international agenda, and a broad international consensus had crystallized in favor of a two-state settlement on the pre-June 1967 border, perhaps with minor and mutual adjustments. In December 1975, the UN Security Council agreed to consider a resolution proposed by the Arab "confrontation states" with these provisions, also incorporating the basic wording of UN 242. The US vetoed the resolution. Israel's reaction was to bomb Lebanon, killing over 50 people in Nabatiyeh, calling the attack "preventive"—presumably to "prevent" the UN session, which Israel boycotted.

The only significant exception to consistent US–Israeli rejectionism was in January 2001, when Israeli and Palestinian negotiators came close to agreement in Taba. But the negotiations were called off by Israeli Prime Minister Barak four days early, ending that promising effort. Unofficial but high-level negotiations continued, leading to the Geneva Accord of December 2002, with similar proposals. It was welcomed by most of the world, but rejected by Israel and dismissed by Washington (and, reflexively, the US media and intellectual classes).

Meanwhile US-backed Israeli settlement and infrastructure programs have been "creating facts on the ground" in order to undermine potential realization of Palestinian national rights. Throughout the Oslo years, these programs continued steadily, with a sharp peak in 2000: Clinton's final year, and Barak's. The current euphemism for these programs is "disengagement" from Gaza and "convergence" in the West Bank—in Western rhetoric, Ehud Olmert's courageous program of withdrawal from the occupied territories. The reality, as usual, is quite different.

The Gaza "disengagement" was openly announced as a West Bank expansion plan. Having turned Gaza into a disaster area, sane Israeli hawks realized that there was no point leaving a few thousand settlers taking the best land and scarce resources, protected by a large part of the IDF. It made more sense to send them to the West Bank and Golan Heights, where new settlement programs were announced, while turning Gaza into "the world's largest prison," as Israeli human rights groups accurately call it. West Bank "convergence" formalizes these programs of annexation, cantonization, and imprisonment. With decisive US support, Israel is annexing valuable lands and the most important resources of the West Bank (primarily water), while carrying out settlement and infrastructure projects that divide the shrinking Palestinian territories into unviable cantons, virtually separated from one another and from whatever pitiful corner of Jerusalem will be left to Palestinians. All are to be imprisoned as Israel takes over the Jordan Valley, and of course any other access to the outside world.

All of these programs are recognized to be illegal, in violation of numerous Security Council resolutions and the unanimous decision of the World Court that any part of the "separation wall" that is built to "defend" the settlements is "ipso facto" illegal (US Justice Buergenthal, in a separate declaration). Hence about 80 to 85 percent of the Wall is illegal, as is the entire "convergence" program. But for a self-designated outlaw state and its clients, such facts are minor irrelevancies.

Currently, the US and Israel demand that Hamas accept the 2002 Arab League Beirut proposal for full normalization of relations with Israel after withdrawal in accord with the international consensus. The proposal has long been accepted by the PLO, and it has also been formally accepted by the "supreme leader" of Iran, Ayatollah Khamenei. Sayyid Hassan Nasrallah has made it clear that Hizballah would not disrupt such an agreement if it is accepted by Palestinians. Hamas has repeatedly indicated its willingness to negotiate in these terms.

The facts are doctrinally unacceptable, hence mostly suppressed. What we see, instead, is the stern warning to Hamas by the editors of the *New York Times* that their formal agreement to the Beirut peace plan is "an admission ticket to the real world, a necessary rite of passage in the progression from a lawless opposition to a lawful government." Like others, the *New York Times* editors fail to mention that the US and Israel forcefully reject this proposal, and are alone in doing so among relevant actors. Furthermore, they reject it not merely in rhetoric, but far more importantly, in deeds. We see at once who constitutes the "lawless opposition" and who speaks for them. But that conclusion cannot be expressed, even entertained, in respectable circles.

The only meaningful support for Palestinians facing national destruction is from Hizballah. For this reason alone it follows that Hizballah must be severely weakened or destroyed, just as the PLO had to be evicted from Lebanon in 1982. But Hizballah is too deeply embedded within Lebanese society to be eradicated, so Lebanon too must be largely destroyed. An expected benefit for the US and Israel was to enhance the credibility of threats against Iran by eliminating a Lebanese-based deterrent to a possible attack. But none of this turned out as planned. Much as in Iraq, and elsewhere, Bush administration planners have created catastrophes, even for the interests they represent. That is the primary reason for the unprecedented criticism of the administration among the foreign policy elite, even before the invasion of Iraq.

In the background lie more far-reaching and lasting concerns: to ensure what is called "stability" in the reigning ideology. "Stability," in simple words, means obedience. "Stability" is undermined by states that do not strictly follow orders, secular nationalists, Islamists who are not under control (in contrast, the Saudi monarchy, the oldest and most valuable US ally, is fine), etc. Such "destabilizing" forces are particularly dangerous when their programs are attractive to others, in which case they are called "viruses" that must be destroyed. "Stability" is enhanced by loyal client states. Since 1967, it has been assumed that Israel can play this role, along with other "peripheral" states. Israel has become virtually an offshore US military base and high-tech center, the natural consequence of its rejection of security in favor of expansion in 1971, and repeatedly since. These policies are subject to little internal debate, whoever holds state power. The policies extend worldwide, and in the Middle East, their significance is enhanced by one of the leading principles of foreign policy since World War II (and for Britain before that): to ensure control over Middle East energy resources, recognized for 60 years to be "a stupendous source of strategic power" and "one of the greatest material prizes in world history."

The standard Western version is that the July 2006 invasion was justified by legitimate outrage over capture of two Israeli soldiers at the border. The posture is cynical fraud. The US and Israel, and the West generally, have little objection to capture of soldiers, or even to the far more severe crime of kidnapping civilians (or of course to killing civilians). That had been Israeli practice in Lebanon for many years, and no one ever suggested that Israel should therefore be invaded and largely destroyed. Western cynicism was revealed with even more dramatic clarity as the current upsurge of violence erupted after Palestinian militants captured an Israeli soldier, Gilad Shalit, on June 25. That too elicited huge outrage, and support for Israel's sharp escalation of its murderous assault on Gaza. The scale is reflected in casualties: in June, 36 Palestinian civilians were killed in Gaza; in July, the numbers more than quadrupled to over 170, dozens of them children. The posture of outrage was, again, cynical fraud, as demonstrated dramatically, and conclusively, by the reaction to Israel's kidnapping of two Gaza civilians, the Muamar brothers, one day before, on June 24. They disappeared into Israel's prison system, joining the hundreds of others imprisoned without charge—hence kidnapped, as are many of those sentenced on dubious charges. There was some brief and dismissive mention of the kidnapping of the Muamar brothers, but no reaction, because such crimes are considered legitimate when carried out by "our side." The idea that this crime would justify a murderous assault on Israel would have been regarded as a reversion to Nazism.

The distinction is clear, and familiar throughout history: to paraphrase Thucydides, the powerful are entitled to do as they wish, while the weak suffer as they must.

We should not overlook the progress that has been made in undermining the imperial mentality that is so deeply rooted in Western moral and intellectual culture as to be beyond awareness. Nor should we forget the scale of what remains to be achieved, tasks that must be undertaken in solidarity and cooperation by people in North and South who hope to see a more decent and civilized world.

7. WASHINGTON'S PROXY WAR

Stephen Zunes

Israel's war on Lebanon during the summer of 2006 was done largely at the behest of Washington as part of an expanded effort to utilize Israel as a proxy to assert American hegemony in the Middle East. In the months leading up to the outbreak of fighting through the cease-fire, actions by the US government appear to have been designed more to advance the Bush administration's geopolitical designs on the Middle East than to defend Israel's legitimate security interests. While the Israeli government was certainly quite willing to launch the attacks for its own reasons, there is little question that the United States played a critical role in Israel's initial decision to go to war, the length of the conflict, and the level of devastation inflicted upon the Lebanese. As many analysts predicted at the outset,[1] the war was a disaster for the Israelis, given their large numbers of military and civilian casualties and the negative strategic impact from Hizballah's dramatically strengthened political standing that resulted. Indeed, many Israeli officials, including some top military officials, are furious at President George W. Bush for pushing Israeli Prime Minister Ehud Olmert to war.[2] America's motivation in backing the Israeli attacks appears to have been primarily to undercut radical movements challenging US hegemonic designs, further weaken international legal institutions, discredit the human rights community, and lay the foundation for future US military intervention in the region, particularly against Iran.

The United States had hoped that Israel would be able to cripple Hizballah, Lebanon's radical Shiite political movement that, taking advantage of the country's democratic opening with the forced departure of Syrian troops in 2005, was able to win a sizable block of seats in the Lebanese parliament. Though the Lebanese government was dominated by traditional pro-Western elites, the fact that an anti-American Islamist group like Hizballah was even allowed to hold a minor cabinet post and sit in parliament was clearly unacceptable to Washington. Furthermore, Hizballah's unwillingness to disarm their militia as required in the Taif Accord and a subsequent UN Security Council resolution, and the inability of the Lebanese government to force them to do so, led the Bush administration to push Israel to take military action to crush the populist party, which had defied US efforts to democratize the region on American terms. As Ze'ev Schiff, dean of Israel's military correspondents, put it, "US Secretary of State Condoleezza Rice is the figure leading the strategy of changing the situation in Lebanon, not Prime Minister Ehud Olmert or Defense Minister Amir Peretz" (30 July 2006). In an interview with the Israeli newspaper *Ha'aretz*, Martin Indyk—who served in the Clinton administration as assistant secretary of state for Near Eastern affairs and US ambassador to Israel—noted that the United States had no leverage on Hizballah except "through Israel's use of force" (18 July 2006). As *Ha'aretz* analyst Shmuel Rosner wrote during the fighting, "the way has been found for Israel to recompense the administration for its supportive attitudes during the six years of the Bush administration," illustrating "the regional power's importance for the great power" (20 July 2006).

Seven weeks before the start of the war, in his May 23 summit with Olmert, Bush strongly encouraged the Israeli prime minister to launch an attack on Lebanon soon, offering the United States' full support for the massive military operation. Just three days later, Israeli agents assassinated two Islamic militants in Saida, leading to a series of tit-for-tat assassinations and abductions, which eventually led to the July 12 seizure of two Israeli soldiers by Hizballah, the excuse for a war that had been planned for many months.[3]

Investigative reporter Seymour Hersh quoted in the *New Yorker* a consultant with the US Department of Defense soon after the outbreak of the fighting as describing how the Bush administration "has been agitating for some time to find a reason for a preemptive blow against Hizballah." He added, "It was our intent to have Hizballah diminished, and now we have someone else doing it" (21 August 2006).

Israel had been planning the war since at least 2004 and had briefed US officials with the plans, in PowerPoint presentations, in what the *San Francisco Chronicle* described as "revealing detail." It also cited political science professor Gerald Steinberg of Bar-Ilan University as saying, "Of all of Israel's wars since 1948, this was the one for which Israel was most prepared. In a sense, the preparation began in May 2000, immediately after the Israeli withdrawal…"[4] Despite this, the Bush administration and congressional leaders of both parties tried to present the Israeli military assaults as a spontaneous reaction to Hizballah's provocative July 12 attack on an Israeli border post and its seizure of two Israeli soldiers.

According to Hersh, "several Israeli officials visited Washington, separately, 'to get a green light for the bombing operation and to find out how much the United States would bear,'" soon getting the final approval from Vice President Dick Cheney, Secretary of State Condoleezza Rice, and soon thereafter President Bush. Some reports indicated that Secretary of Defense Donald Rumsfeld was less sanguine about the proposed Israeli military offensive, believing that Israel should focus less on bombing and more on ground operations, despite the dramatically higher Israeli casualties that would result. Still, Hersh quotes a former senior intelligence official as saying that Rumsfeld was "delighted that Israel is our stalking horse."

The American Obsession with Hizballah

Since the early 1990s, Hizballah had been placing increasing energy into its electoral campaigns and social service networks and less into its militia. Rather than welcoming Hizballah's important shift away from the use of violence and terrorism to advance its political agenda, however, the Bush administration and Congress instead became increasingly alarmist about the supposed threat posed by this Lebanese political party. Investigations prior to the 2006 war by the Congressional Research Service, the State Department, and independent think tanks noted how there had not been any major act of terrorism by Hizballah since 1994.[5] Not wanting to let this fact get in the way of a possible US-backed Israeli war on Lebanon, however, the Bush administration still insisted that Hizballah be classified as a terrorist group and the US House of Representatives, by an overwhelming 380–3 vote, passed House Resolution 101 in 2005 condemning "the continuous terrorist attacks perpetrated by Hizballah."

Just as Washington's concerns about the alleged threat from Iraq grew in inverse correlation to its military capability—culminating in the 2003 invasion long after that country had disarmed and dismantled its chemical, biological, and nuclear weapons programs—the US focus on Hizballah grew as that party had largely put its terrorist past behind it. In apparent anticipation of the long-planned US-backed Israeli assault, Washington began to become more and more obsessed with Hizballah. For example, not a single congressional resolution mentioned Hizballah during the 1980s when they were kidnapping and murdering American citizens and engaging in other terrorist activities. In fact, no congressional resolution mentioned Hizballah by name until 1998, years after the group's last act of terrorism noted by the State Department. By contrast, during the session of Congress prior to the 2006 war, there were more than two dozen resolutions condemning Hizballah.

Given the number of dangerous movements in the Middle East and elsewhere that really have been involved in ongoing terrorist activities in recent years, why was Washington so obsessed with a minority Lebanese party that had—prior to rocket attacks on Israeli cities in July and August of 2006 in retaliation for Israeli attacks on Lebanese cities—largely left terrorism behind?

A key component of the Bush doctrine holds that states supporting groups that the US government designates as "terrorist" are as guilty as the terrorists themselves and are therefore legitimate targets for the United States to attack in the name of self-defense. This doctrine applies not just to Lebanon, but to Syria and Iran as well, the two countries that the neoconservative architects of the US invasion of Iraq have proposed as the next targets for attack. Though outside support for Hizballah has declined dramatically from previous years, Syria and Iran have traditionally been Hizballah's primary backers. By formally designating Hizballah as a "terrorist organization" and exaggerating the degree of Syrian and Iranian support, the Bush administration and Congress are paving the way for possible US military action against one or both countries some time in the future.

During the cold war, nationalist movements that coalesced under a Marxist–Leninist framework, such as the National Liberation Front in South Vietnam, were depicted not as the manifestation of a longstanding national liberation struggle against foreign domination, but part of the global expansionist agenda of international communism. As such, sending more than a half a million American troops into South Vietnam and engaging in the heaviest bombing campaign in world history was depicted as an act of self-defense—"If we do not fight them over there, we will have to fight them here." Once American forces withdrew, however, Vietnamese stopped killing Americans. Similarly, Hizballah stopped attacking French and American interests when they withdrew from Lebanon in 1984 and they largely stopped attacking Israelis when they withdrew from Lebanon in 2000 (with the exception of the Shebaa Farms, which they claim is part of Lebanon).

Therefore, a second reason for the US government's disproportionate hostility toward Hizballah may be to convince Americans that radical Islamist groups with a nationalist base will not stop attacking even after troop withdrawal. The Bush administration has insisted that the United States must destroy the terrorists in Iraq or they will attack the United States—even though the rise of Islamic extremist groups and terrorist attacks in Iraq came only after the United States invaded that country in 2003. If Americans recognized that attacks against Americans by Iraqis would stop if US forces withdrew, it would be harder to justify the ongoing US war. Similarly, if Americans recognized that terrorist attacks by Hamas and Islamic Jihad would likely cease if Israel fully withdrew its occupation forces from the West Bank (including East Jerusalem) and the Gaza Strip and allowed for the emergence of a viable independent Palestinian state, they would no longer be able to defend their financial, military, and diplomatic support for the ongoing occupation, repression, and colonization of those occupied Palestinian territories by the right-wing Israeli government. (As with Hizballah, Hamas and Islamic Jihad did not come into existence until after years of Israeli occupation and the failure of both secular nationalist groups and international diplomacy to end the occupation.)

This, of course, is not what the Bush administration or congressional leaders want Americans to think, however, since it would make it far more difficult to defend the wars in Iraq, Palestine, and Lebanon. Therefore, it is politically important to convince Americans that Hizballah is a terrorist group engaged in "continuous terrorist attacks" that constitute an ongoing threat to the national security interests of the United States and its allies. And, by encouraging Israel to attack Lebanon, knowing that it would provoke Hizballah attacks on Israeli civilians, Washington could then further justify continued military intervention in the Middle East—either directly or through its Israeli proxies—in the name of "the war on terrorism."

Israel Serving American Regional Objectives

In addition, with the US forces showing little signs of success in its ongoing counter-insurgency war in Iraq, the Bush administration hoped that a decisive US-backed Israeli attack on Hizballah would intimidate the governments of Syria and Iran, which have been Hizballah's principal foreign backers and which have strongly opposed US policy in the Middle East.

The *Jerusalem Post* reported on July 30 that President Bush pushed Israel to expand the war beyond Lebanon, with Israeli military officials "receiving indications from the US that America would be interested in seeing Israel attack Syria."[6] In the early days of the fighting, US Deputy National Security Advisor Elliot Abrams reportedly met with a very senior Israeli official to underscore Washington's support for extending the war to Syria, but that Israeli officials described the idea as "nuts" and decided to limit their military operations to Lebanon.[7] Shmuel Rosner noted in *Ha'aretz* that there were those in Washington who were "disappointed by Israel's decision not to attack Syria at the same time" (20 July 2006). Meyrav Wurmser, head of the Center for Middle East Policy at the conservative Hudson Institute and wife of the principal Middle East advisor for Vice President Cheney, went further, declaring that there was "a lot of anger" in Washington that Israel did not attack Syria, which she argued would have served "US objectives."[8] There was also a hope on the part of US officials that an Israeli invasion of Lebanon might lead Syrian troops to re-enter Lebanon to defend the country from the Israeli invasion, which could then be used as an excuse to expand the war to Syria itself.[9]

In support for US policy backing the Israeli offensive, the office of the White House Press Secretary released a list of talking points that included reference to a guest editorial by Max Boot, a senior fellow for national security studies at the Council on Foreign Relations, in the *Los Angeles Times*, highlighting a quote that claimed that "Our best response is exactly what Bush has done so far—reject premature calls for a cease-fire and let Israel finish the job." The article, entitled "Let the Israelis Take Off the Gloves," noted "Iran may be too far away for much Israeli retaliation beyond a single strike on its nuclear weapons complex. (Now wouldn't be a bad time.) But Syria is weak and next door." Boot, who has close ties to the Bush White House, went on to insist that "Israel needs to hit the Assad regime. Hard. If it does, it will be doing Washington's dirty work" (19 July 2006).

The primary target for the Bush administration insistence on goading Israel into war, however, appears to have been Iran. According to Hersh, the Israeli attack on Lebanon was to "serve as a prelude to a potential American preemptive attack to destroy Iran's nuclear installations," citing a Pentagon consultant as describing how the Israelis would be able "to hunt down and bomb missiles, tunnels, and bunkers from the air. It would be a demo for Iran." Similarly, Hersh noted a former senior intelligence official as describing the Israeli attacks on Lebanon as "the mirror image of what the United States has been planning for Iran."

While Hizballah had largely demobilized its militia since the Israeli withdrawal six years earlier, fears of a US–Israeli strike against Iran had resulted in Iran sending hundreds of rockets to Hizballah to place in southern Lebanon to serve as a deterrent. Indeed, it is probably no accident that Iran began the large-scale transfer of these dangerous weapons to Hizballah only after the Bush administration started making threats to attack their country. Hersh quotes a senior analyst with close ties to the Bush administration as saying, "The White House was more focused on stripping Hizballah of its missiles, because, if there was to be a military option against Iran's nuclear facilities, it had to get rid of the weapons that Hizballah could use in a potential retaliation at Israel." Without that threat, Israel might be less willing to assist in a US war against Iran.

During the spring of 2006, the White House ordered top planners from the US air force to consult with their Israeli counterparts regarding war plans against Iran in which an Israeli preemptive strike against Hizballah would be part of the process. Israeli Air Force Lieutenant-General Dan Halutz, the chief of staff of the Israeli military and principal architect of the war on Lebanon, had worked on contingency planning for an air war with Iran and consulted with US officials. Hersh reported that the Bush administration pressured the Israelis to "move quickly in its air war against Hizballah," citing a former intelligence officer who insisted that "we think it should be sooner rather than later—the longer you wait, the less time we have to evaluate and plan for Iran before Bush gets out of office." Hersh goes on to note that Vice President Dick Cheney had hoped "We can learn what to do in Iran by watching what the Israelis do in Lebanon."

Apparently, this was part of a broader effort by the Bush administration to form an alliance of pro-Western Sunni Arab dictatorships—primarily Egypt, Saudi Arabia, and Jordan—against a growing Shiite militancy exemplified by Hizballah and Iran and, to a lesser extent, post-Saddam Iraq. Though these Sunni regimes initially spoke out against Hizballah's provocative abduction of the two Israeli soldiers, popular opposition within these countries to the ferocity of the Israeli assault led them to rally solidly against the US-backed war on Lebanon.

Support for Israel's proxy war on Lebanon did not come solely from neoconservatives and other right-wing Republicans in the Bush administration, but from an overwhelming bipartisan majority in Congress as well. The Senate, in a unanimous resolution on a voice vote, passed a resolution within days of Israeli launching its assault on Lebanon unconditionally endorsing Israel's ongoing attacks. Early the following week, the US House of Representatives followed suit, passing Resolution 921 by an overwhelming 410–8 vote, and praising President George W. Bush for "fully supporting Israel," in the face of opposition from virtually the entire international community.

While the lack of success from Israel's military campaign might seemingly give pause to the idea that the United States could achieve a quick and easy victory against Iran in the event of a US-led bombing campaign, the propensity of the Bush administration to ignore historical lessons should not be underestimated. Hersh cites a former senior intelligence official as saying that "There is no way that Rumsfeld and Cheney will draw the right conclusion about this. When the smoke clears, they'll say it was a success, and they'll draw reinforcement for their plan to attack Iran." Indeed, on August 14, President Bush declared that Hizballah had "suffered a defeat" in its fight with Israel.

Rewriting History as It Was Played Out

Given that most Americans are broadly supportive of international humanitarian law and related principles, it was extraordinarily difficult for the Bush administration and congressional leaders to justify their role in Israel's proxy war, given the devastating humanitarian consequences of the massive military onslaught. As a result, there was a calculated attempt in Washington to present to the public a very different picture from what was actually transpiring, as a means of justifying the US–Israeli war on Lebanon.

For example, in a July 16 news conference, President Bush declared that the war had started because Hizballah decided to "fire hundreds of rockets into Israel from southern Lebanon." In reality, Hizballah did not fire rockets into Israel until after Israel began bombing Lebanese civilian areas on July 12 and did not extend the rocket attacks beyond border regions into Haifa until well after Israel launched attacks on Beirut.

Similarly, despite repeated claims from Washington that, as House Resolution 921 put it, Israel was "in full compliance with Security Council Resolution 425," requiring Israel to withdraw its occupation forces from Lebanon, Israel's re-conquest of Lebanese territory had placed Israel once again in violation of that resolution and nine subsequent resolutions demanding the withdrawal of foreign forces from that country. Furthermore, Israel had never fully complied with UNSC 425 due to repeated violations of Lebanese airspace well prior to the outbreak of fighting in July 2006, which Secretary-General Kofi Annan described as "provocative" and "at variance" with Israel's fulfillment of the resolution's demands for a withdrawal of ground troops from Lebanon.

Related were the claims in Washington that the Hizballah attack on the Israeli border post and capture of two soldiers was "completely unprovoked." While clearly an illegal and provocative act, it was apparently in reaction to Israel's ongoing detention of three Lebanese citizens seized by Israeli forces from within Lebanon. Hizballah had apparently hoped to work out some kind of swap, as both sides have successfully negotiated previously on several occasions. UN reports had documented numerous Israeli violations of the Israeli border in the years and months leading up to the Hizballah border raid.[10] The seizure of the Israeli soldiers on the Lebanese border was also apparently done in retaliation for the ongoing Israeli assaults on civilian population centers in the Gaza Strip.

The most difficult political issue facing Washington was the high level of civilian casualties from the Israeli assault, which took the lives of over 1,000 noncombatants by the time the cease-fire went into effect. To help cover up for the ongoing atrocities by the Israeli Defense Force (IDF), the House version of the resolution supporting the war recognized "Israel's longstanding commitment to minimizing civilian loss and welcomes Israel's continued efforts to prevent civilian casualties." Such a claim, however, runs directly counter to reports by international journalists, human rights organizations, and the United Nations that indicate that Israel had not been committed to "minimizing civilian loss" or preventing civilian casualties in its previous attacks on Lebanon or in the ongoing fighting. For example, Human Rights Watch (HRW) documented

... a systematic failure by the IDF to distinguish between combatants and civilians. Since the start of the conflict, Israeli forces have consistently launched artillery and air attacks with limited or dubious military gain but excessive civilian cost. In dozens of attacks, Israeli forces struck an area with no apparent military target. In some cases, the timing and intensity of the attack, the absence of a military target, as well as return strikes on rescuers, suggest that Israeli forces deliberately targeted civilians.[11]

Similarly, Amnesty International reported that Israeli forces "carried out indiscriminate and disproportionate attacks on a large scale," including "those on civilian infrastructure" and "direct attacks on civilian objects." Furthermore, the Nobel Peace Prize–winning human rights group issued a report that came to the conclusion that the "attacks seem to have been aimed at inflicting a form of collective punishment on Lebanon's people" (21 November 2006).

As such widespread accounts of high civilian casualties and destruction of Lebanon's civilian infrastructure increased, the Bush administration and Congress attempted to make the case that it was the Lebanese armed forces, not the Israeli, who were responsible. For example, President Bush claimed that "Hizballah terrorists used Lebanese civilians as human shields, sacrificing the innocent in an effort to protect themselves from Israeli response" (16 July 2006). Similarly, the congressional resolution condemned Hizballah "for cynically exploiting civilian populations as shields." Yet investigations by independent human rights groups such as HRW found no cases in which Hizballah deliberately used civilians as shields to protect them from Israeli attacks. Human rights groups did note that the Hizballah militia—which, like most militias, is a volunteer force whose members live with their families—did occasionally store weapons in or near homes and had placed rocket launchers within populated areas, which are indeed violations of international humanitarian law because such practices put civilians at risk. However, as HRW noted, "that does not release Israel from its obligations to take all feasible precautions to minimize harm to civilians and civilian property during military operations."

Another dilemma facing Washington was to try to justify Israeli attacks on Lebanon as a whole, including air strikes in the northern part of the country many miles from Hizballah activity, as well as on airports, sea ports, power stations, communications centers, fuel depots, Lebanese army posts, and other government facilities unrelated to the Hizballah militia. As a result, there was a concerted effort in Washington to link the moderate pro-Western Lebanese government—which just months earlier Bush had referred to as a beacon of democracy in the Middle East—with Hizballah, as a means of defending Israel's war against the nation as a whole.

For example, the congressional resolution criticized the Lebanese government for not forcibly disarming the militia but "allowing Hizballah instead to amass 13,000 rockets." Yet at a January 2006 UN Security Council meeting in which a report was presented on the implementation of Resolution 1559, the United States and the other members approved a statement that "notes with concern the report's suggestion that there have been movements of arms... into Lebanese territory and, in this context, commends the Government of Lebanon for undertaking measures against such movements."[12] In other words, the Lebanese government did not "allow" Hizballah to amass new weaponry; the problem is that their small and weak security forces—weakened further by Israeli attacks—were simply unable to prevent it.

Similarly, Congress went on record declaring that Lebanon was in violation of UN Security Council Resolution 1559 because of its failure to "disband" Hizballah and allowing the party to be "integrated...into the Lebanese government." In reality, UN Security Council Resolution 1559 does not call for Hizballah or any other Lebanese political party to be disbanded, only for their armed militias to be disbanded, which the weak Lebanese armed forces were unable to do. The only degree to which Hizballah had been "integrated... into the Lebanese government" was in naming Hizballah member Mohammed Fneish to the power and hydraulic resources ministry, one of 24 cabinet posts. Representatives of all Lebanese parties that receive more than a handful of seats in parliamentary elections traditionally get at least one seat in the cabinet.

Since most Americans are uncomfortable with their government supporting wars of aggression, the Bush administration and Congress repeatedly tried to present Israel's war on Lebanon as a legitimate act of self-defense. For example, dismissing the broad consensus of international legal scholars to the contrary, the congressional resolution insisted that the war was a manifestation of "Israel's right to take appropriate action to defend itself, including to conduct operations both in Israel and in the territory of nations which pose a threat to it, which is in accordance with international law, including Article 51 of the United Nations Charter."

A reading of the UN Charter reveals that Article 33 requires all parties to "first of all, seek a solution by negotiation, enquiry, mediation, conciliation, arbitration, judicial settlement, resort to regional agencies or arrangements, or other peaceful means of their own choice," which Israel had refused to do. More critically, Article 51 does allow countries the right to resist an armed attack and, arguably, to engage in hot pursuit in the case of the seizure of hostages, but it does not give a country the right to use a relatively minor border incident provoked by a non-state actor as an excuse to launch a full-scale war against an entire country. Article 51 also states that self-defense against such attacks is justified only "until the Security Council has taken measures necessary to maintain international peace and security," which may explain why the Bush administration blocked the UN Security Council from imposing a cease-fire or taking any other action.

Furthermore, the insistence of Congress that Israel's actions were "in accordance to international law" are countered by widespread accounts of illegal Israeli actions in the course of the conflict. For example, Amnesty International concluded, after extensive research and analysis that included a review of Israeli interpretations of the laws of war, that "Israeli forces committed serious violations of international human rights and humanitarian law, including war crimes." The International Red Cross, long recognized as the guardian of the Geneva Conventions on the conduct of war, declared that Israel had violated the principle of proportionality in the conventions as well as the prohibition against collective punishment. Similarly, UN High Commissioner for Human Rights Louise Arbour—a former Canadian Supreme Court justice who served as chief prosecutor in the international war crimes tribunals on Rwanda and the former Yugoslavia—noted how the armed forces of both Hizballah and the Israeli government have been engaging in war crimes.[13] And Jan Egeland, head of United Nations relief operations, referred to the "disproportional response" by Israel to Hizballah's provocations as "a violation of international humanitarian law."[14]

Blaming Iran and Syria

As with US-backed military interventions in Vietnam, El Salvador, and elsewhere, there was also a concerted effort by the American government to depict the intervention not as an act of foreign aggression but as a defense of a nation's sovereignty against a non-governmental armed force that, rather than being a manifestation of a popular indigenous movement against perceived injustices, was actually the proxy of a foreign power. For example, with the outbreak of the fighting, President Bush declared—in a statement reaffirmed in the congressional resolution—that the welfare of the Lebanese people and the sovereignty of the Lebanese state were being "held hostage to the interests of the Syrian and Iranian regimes."[15]

In order to gain support for its efforts to isolate and eventually overthrow the Syrian and Iranian governments, the US government needed to convince the American public and the international community that Syria and Iran were not just Hizballah allies that had over time provided arms and logistical support, but actually controlled the movement outright. For example, the congressional resolution attempted to exaggerate the foreign influence by claiming that "Hizballah's strength derives significantly from the direct financial, military, and political support it receives from Syria and Iran" and that "Iranian Revolutionary Guards continue to operate in southern Lebanon," not only "providing support to Hizballah," but even "controlling its operational activities."

If this was indeed the case, the United States and international community could then argue that the solution to the crisis was for Syria and Iran to force Hizballah to give in to American and Israeli demands. For example, the congressional resolution "demands the Governments of Iran and Syria to direct... Hizballah to immediately and unconditionally release Israeli soldiers which they hold captive." Similarly, at the G8 summit in Russia five days after the start of the war, Bush angrily rejected the idea of sending in United Nations peacekeepers, telling British Prime Minister Tony Blair "what they need to do is get Syria to get Hizballah to stop doing this shit and it's over."[16]

If Hizballah did not give in to American and Israeli demands, it would therefore follow that Syria and Iran were responsible for what has been depicted as unprovoked terrorist attacks against a beleaguered democratic ally of the West and would thereby provide the justification for possible future US military action against those countries, which have been long threatened by the Bush administration and leading members of Congress from both parties. Indeed, both statements by the Bush administration and resolutions adopted by Congress have put the United States on record that governments which "have provided continued support" for Hizballah "share responsibility for the hostage-taking and attacks against Israel and, as such, should be held accountable for their actions."

In reality, as the pro-Western government of Lebanese Prime Minster Fouad Seniora has insisted and as events of that summer confirmed, the major threat to Lebanon's security and the most serious affront to its sovereignty has been the US-backed Israeli government, not Hizballah. And Hizballah's political and military activities, like that of other Lebanese political parties, have been based primarily upon what the movement's leadership—however wrongly and cynically—have believed is in the best interest of advancing their political agenda and not that of the Syrian and Iranian governments (whose interests in Lebanon are often at variance with each other as well). For example, it is illogical to assume that a populist political party with such an ambitious electoral and social agenda as Hizballah would instruct its militia to provoke a devastating war simply to please a foreign backer.

While some Iranian Revolutionary Guards played a critical role in the initial setup of Hizballah's armed militia in the early to mid-1980s following Israel's invasion and occupation of southern Lebanon, they returned to Iran years ago and were certainly not "controlling Hizballah's operational activities" during the summer of 2006. Similarly, Syrian forces withdrew from Lebanon more than a year before the outbreak of fighting. The report to the UN Security Council on the implementation of UNSC 1559 in January 2006 noted that Syria had complied with provisions for the withdrawal of its forces from Lebanon and did not note the ongoing presence of Iranian Revolutionary Guard.[17] Syria's tactical alliance with Hizballah never amounted to outright control and Damascus ideologically has been closer to Amal, a rival Shiite movement. In short, neither the Iranian nor Syrian governments had the power to "direct" or to "get" Hizballah to do anything. The decision by Congress and the administration to overstate the leverage that Iran and Syria have over these movements—like similar exaggerations of Soviet and Cuban leverage over leftist revolutionaries in Central America during the 1980s—appears to be based less on a realistic assessment of the situation on the ground and more on helping to promote broader US policies of isolating and eventually ousting these regimes and replacing them with more compliant governments.

There has been little acknowledgment within the United States that Hizballah's strength derives primarily from popular support within Lebanon's Shiite Muslim minority, which has suffered from heightened poverty and physical displacement as a result of the US-backed Israeli occupation of southern Lebanon between 1978 and 2000, the US-backed Israeli bombardment of the largely populated areas of the country since the 1970s, and the US-backed neoliberal economic policies of the Lebanese government, which have decimated the traditional economy. As a result of the violence and misguided economic policies, hundreds of thousands of Shiites were forced to leave their rural villages in southern Lebanon and live in vast shantytowns on the southern outskirts of Beirut, where many found support through a broad network of Hizballah-sponsored social services. As a result of gratitude for such assistance and anger at Israel and the United States for their situation, many became backers of Hizballah's populist, albeit extremist, political organization. In the wake of the forced departure of the Palestine Liberation Organization and the destruction of the secular leftist Lebanese National Movement by successive interventions from Syria, Israel, and the United States during the 1980s, the radical Islamist Hizballah rose to fill the vacuum. In other words, "Hizballah's strength" was very much an outgrowth of US and Israeli policy. Indeed, the group did not even exist until a full four years after Israel began its US-backed occupation of southern Lebanon.

The outspoken endorsement by such an overwhelming bipartisan majority of Congress of such an exaggerated view of Syria and Iran's role in the conflict, of Bush's Middle East policies, and of Israel's war on Lebanon portends the likelihood of similar broad support should the United States actually decide to attack Iran or Syria.[18] In particular, given that leading Republican and Democratic members of Congress were presumably consulted, or were at least aware, of the links between the Israeli attacks on Lebanon and a possible future US attack on Iran, the broad bipartisan support given to these resolutions can be seen essentially as a green light from both parties in Congress for the Bush administration to go to war.

Indeed, given that a consensus of Republican and Democratic lawmakers agree that Israel's wanton destruction of a small democratic country's civilian infrastructure because of a minor border incident instigated by members of a militia of a minority party is a legitimate act of self-defense, surely a similar US attack against Iran—a much larger country with a sizable armed force whose government (controlled by those of a similar hardline ideological orientation as Hizballah) might be developing nuclear weapons—could also be seen as a legitimate act of self-defense.

Similarly, such a radical reinterpretation of Article 51 put forward by the Bush administration and contained in the congressional resolutions makes it easier for President Bush and future presidents to justify massive military strikes against foreign countries in reaction to relatively minor incidents provoked by irregular forces within that country.

The overwhelming bipartisan support for Israel's war on Lebanon, then, was not as much a reflection of the power of the pro-Israel lobby or fear that opposing the war could damage one's political career. Indeed, virtually all of the fifteen House members who voted against or abstained in the resolution supporting the war were reelected that November by a larger percentage than they were reelected in the previous election in 2004.[19] The actual motivation for the bipartisan support for Israel's war, then, appears to have been to further undermine the post–World War II international legal norms that restrict American unilateralism in the region. Similarly, by radically reinterpreting Article 51 of the UN Charter and discrediting reports by human rights groups and UN agencies of systematic war crimes—as was done in the congressional resolutions passed by such overwhelming majorities—has made it easier for the United States to engage in wars of aggression and violations of international humanitarian law in the future.

The US Role in Blocking a Cease-Fire

From the outbreak of the fighting on July 12, the broad international consensus was that, however reprehensible the actions of Hizballah may have been in failing to disarm and attacking the Israeli border post, Israel's actions were excessive, in violation of international legal norms, were resulting in a humanitarian disaster, and an immediate cease-fire was imperative. UN Secretary General Kofi Annan called for an "immediate cessation of hostilities and a far greater and more credible effort by Israel to protect civilians and infrastructure." The United States rejected such calls, however, with US Ambassador to the United Nations John Bolton declaring that calls for a cease-fire were "simplistic," expressing doubts as to "how you get a cease-fire from a terrorist organization."[20] Secretary of State Rice insisted that "a cease-fire would be a false promise if it simply returns us to the status quo," in which the Lebanese–Israeli border was largely quiet but an anti-American group, supported by Syria and Iran, was a major actor in Lebanese politics. A high-ranking Bush administration official told the *Washington Post*, in response to a reporter's question as to how long Israel would continue its war on Lebanon, "There's a natural dynamic to these things. When the military starts, it may be that it has to run its course."

Rice insisted that the enormous death and destruction resulting from the US-Israel war were the "birth pangs of a new Middle East," presumably one in which the United States had consolidated its control.[21] Just prior to a meeting with Israeli officials, in apparent reference to Hizballah and its supporters, Rice said that it was time to show "those who do not want a different kind of Middle East that we will prevail—they will not."

At the G8 summit in Russia, which took place during the first days of the fighting, the United States was able to prevent the leaders of the world's major industrial democracies—who issue public statements based on consensus—from declaring anything more than a call for Hizballah to release the two captured Israeli soldiers and stop firing rockets into Israel and for Israel to cease its military operations against Lebanon and withdraw its forces. The United States, however, insisted that the intent of the statement was that Hizballah had to fulfill its obligations first, only after which Israel would halt its operations, an interpretation with which none of the other summit participants (with the partial exception of Great Britain) concurred.

Meanwhile, the European Union, consisting of 25 pro Western democracies, also condemned the seizure of the Israeli soldiers but noted that Israel's military retaliation against Lebanon is "grossly disproportionate." Secretary of State Rice found herself "under siege" at meetings in Rome with world leaders due to her support for Israel to continue its offensive until Hizballah was disarmed.[22] Indeed, the United States remained virtually alone in the international community in its defense of Israel's action. As the international outcry grew as civilian casualties increased, the

Bush administration expedited the delivery of precision-guided bombs to Israel.[23]

As international and domestic pressure increased on Israel to stop the onslaught, Rice went on to Israel to push the government to continue prosecuting the war. As veteran Israeli journalist Uri Avnery put it, "Condoleezza Rice was back and forth, dictating when to start, when to stop, what to do, what not to do. America is fully complicit..."

Well into the fourth week of the conflict, the United States blocked efforts at the United Nations Security Council to stop the fighting by threatening to veto a series of draft resolutions. In an August 7 press conference with President Bush, Rice, in reference to the delays in establishing a cease-fire in the face of the mounting civilian death toll and damage to Lebanon's civilian infrastructure, declared that "this has been time that's been well spent over the last couple of weeks."[24]

By the first week of August, domestic pressure was forcing the Israelis to rethink continuing the war indefinitely. Fearing the Israelis might seek a cease-fire, President Bush reportedly told them, "You can't stop now; you're acting for all of us."[25] Israel indicated its willingness to accept a 10,000-member NATO force in southern Lebanon as a condition for a cease-fire; the Bush administration demanded that Hizballah accept a 30,000-member force or be defeated militarily first.

But by the beginning of the second week of August it was becoming apparent to US officials that Israel would be unable to inflict a decisive blow against the Hizballah militia and that Israelis were becoming increasingly resentful of their role as an American proxy. While the worsening humanitarian crisis and international outcry was not enough for the Bush administration to cause a shift in US policy, a senior administration official reported that "it increasingly seemed that Israel would not be able to achieve a military victory, a reality that led the Americans to get behind a cease-fire."[26]

The initial draft resolution proposed by the United States would have required Hizballah to "cease all attacks" but for Israel only to cease "all offensive military operations." Given that Israel and the United States had justified Israel's entire war as legitimate acts of "self-defense," such language could have given Israel license to continue fighting. No peacekeeping force would have been able to enter the area under such conditions. Eventually yielding to pressure by the other fourteen members of the Security Council, the United States accepted including a call for "a full cessation of hostilities," but insisted on including the words "based upon, in particular, the immediate cessation of attacks by Hizballah and the immediate cessation by Israel of all offensive military operations." Though Israel—both during the summer of 2006 and historically—has launched far more attacks against Lebanon than any Lebanese party has against Israel, the United States successfully demanded that the peacekeeping force only be deployed on the Lebanese side of the border, not on the Israeli side of the border.

The original US draft of this resolution (UNSC Res. 1701) condemned violations of international humanitarian law by Hizballah, but not by Israel. As a compromise, the adopted resolution failed to mention the war crimes by either side. Similarly, though Israel was responsible for at least twenty times more civilian deaths than was Hizballah and an incalculable greater degree of injuries, damage, and internal refugees, the United States insisted that the resolution refer to the deaths, injuries, displaced persons, and damage inflicted upon the civilian infrastructure as being on "both sides," implying a symmetry in the two countries' suffering.

The original US draft referred to the seizure of the Israeli soldiers as the single "root cause" of the crisis. The compromise language in the final resolution speaks of "the need to address urgently the causes that have given rise to the current crisis, including the unconditional release of the abducted Israeli soldiers." The United States rejected calls to include mention of the repeated violations of Lebanese airspace and other border violations by Israel in the months and years leading up to the July 12 attack by Hizballah on the Israeli border post. Similarly, and also at the insistence of the United States, the resolution calls for the "unconditional release of the abducted Israeli soldiers," abducted by Hizballah commandoes inside Israel, but only for "encouraging" efforts aimed at "settling the issue of Lebanese prisoners detained in Israel" who were abducted by Israeli commandoes inside Lebanon. That the resolution would essentially blame Hizballah for initiating the conflict while not criticizing Israel's widespread violations of international humanitarian law shows the heavy hand of the United States in shaping the final version of the resolution.

As with previous UN Security Council resolutions regarding Lebanon, the United States has been highly selective regarding enforcement. For example, House Resolution 1071 passed in September 2006 demanded that Hizballah, Iran, and Syria strictly abide by the provisions of Resolution 1701, but not Israel (even though, unlike Israel, Iran and Syria were not even named in the resolution). Washington has also placed great emphasis on the implementation of UN Security Council Resolution 1559, passed in 2004, which calls for the respect of the sovereignty, territorial integrity, and unity of Lebanon "under the sole and exclusive authority of the Government of Lebanon throughout Lebanon," the withdrawal of foreign forces from Lebanon, the extension of Lebanese government control over all Lebanese territory, and the disbanding and disarmament of all militias. Statements from the Bush administration and a series of congressional resolutions only mentioned the disbanding and disarmament of Hizballah, even though Israel's reoccupation of parts of southern Lebanon during the summer of 2006 were also in violation of 1559.[27]

The most unfortunate result of the US role at the United Nations showed during the crisis when it stopped the UN from brokering a cease-fire. When the combination of the strategic failures of the US-backed Israeli assault and the desperateness of other Security Council members to stop the carnage finally forced a compromise, the resulting resolution was quite weak and once again demonstrated how, with the power the United States wields in the Security Council, the United Nations is severely hampered in fulfilling its principal mandate to prevent aggression by one state against another. If a UN member state can get away with launching a full-scale attack on the civilian infrastructure of a neighboring member state following a minor border incident with a non-state actor, it is indicative of a serious breakdown in the international legal order. As with the US invasion of Iraq, the US–Israeli war on Lebanon has shown that the United States and its allies can get away with breaking the most fundamental of international laws, which have provided at least some semblance of global order since World War II.

And if the United States—the most dominant military and economic power the world has ever known—believes that it and its allies do not have to play by the rules, why should Hizballah or anyone else?

The Damage Done to Israel by US Policy

That the war on Lebanon was fought primarily as an effort to advance America's hegemonic objectives in the Middle East rather than as a defense of Israel's legitimate security interests is made more apparent by how damaging the war was to Israel's political and strategic interests.

In the years prior to Israel's July 12 air strikes on Lebanese cities, which prompted Hizballah's retaliatory rocket attacks on Israel cities, the militia had become less and less of a threat. No Israeli civilian had been killed by Hizballah for more than a decade (with the exception of one accidental fatality in 2003 caused by a Hizballah anti-aircraft missile fired at an Israeli plane illegally violating Lebanese airspace landing on the Israeli side of the border) and there had been no Hizballah deliberate attacks against civilian targets since the Israeli withdrawal in May 2000.[28] Virtually all of Hizballah's military actions between May 2000 and July 2006 had been against Israeli occupation forces in a disputed border region between Lebanon and the Israel-occupied portion of southwestern Syria. Hizballah's longstanding policy had been that they would fire into Israel only in response to Israeli attacks on their political leadership or on Lebanese civilians. When the Israeli government, in preparation for the US-backed assault on Lebanon, advised residents in northern Israel to participate in a drill in May 2006, a number of communities reported they could not locate the keys to the bomb shelters since they had been out of use for so long.[29]

Hizballah was down to about 500 full-time fighters prior to the Israeli assault and a national dialogue was going on between Hizballah and the Lebanese government regarding disarmament.[30] Hizballah was not such a serious threat to Israel's security that it demanded such a massive strike against it, much less a strike against the civilian infrastructure of Lebanon as a whole. Though Hizballah had hardly renounced their extremist ideology, major acts of terrorism were largely things of the past. The majority of Lebanese had opposed Hizballah, both its reactionary fundamentalist social agenda as well as its insistence on maintaining an armed presence independent of the country's elected government. Thanks to the US-backed Israeli attacks on Lebanon's civilian infrastructure, however, support for Hizballah grew to more than 80 percent, even within the Sunni Muslim and Christian communities, and within four months after Hizballah successfully held back the Israeli invasion, they were in a strong enough position to launch a civil rebellion to oust Siniora's moderate pro-Western government.

Even Richard Armitage, deputy secretary of state under President Bush during his first term and a leading hawk, acknowledged to Seymour

Hersh that in the third week of conflict, "the only thing that the bombing has achieved so far is to unite the population against the Israelis."

Despite US encouragement that Israel continue with the war, Israel's right-wing prime minister found himself under increasing criticism at home by early August, with polls indicating that only 39 percent of Israelis would support the planned expanded ground offensive. Meretz Party Knesset member Ran Cohen, writing in the *Jerusalem Post*, called earlier moves to expand the ground offensive "a wretched decision." Yariv Oppenheimer, general director of Peace Now, which had earlier muted its criticism of Israel's initial attacks on Lebanon, noted that "the war has spiraled out of control and the government is ignoring the political options available" and that "the government has fallen into the trap that Hassan Nasrallah has laid for it... We are ploughing back into the Lebanese quagmire."

As growing numbers of Israelis began to recognize how deleterious the war was to Israel's legitimate security interests, a growing awareness emerged of the American role in getting them into the mess. A July 23, 2006 article by Lily Galili in *Ha'aretz* on an antiwar demonstration in Tel Aviv noted that it "was a distinctly anti-American protest," including chants of "We will not die and kill in the service of the United States" and "slogans condemning President George W. Bush." Shmuel Rosner, also writing in *Ha'aretz*, referred to Israel as "America's deadly messenger." Uri Avnery of Gush Shalom described Israel as "America's rottweiler" and asked, "What interest do we have in being regarded—accurately— as the servants of the greatest enemy of the Muslim world in general and the Arab world in particular?"[31]

Indeed, *Ha'aretz* columnist David Levy argued that Israel's war was part of "an agenda invented elsewhere" and that, "as hostilities intensified, the phrase 'proxy war' gained resonance." He went on to observe:

> Disentangling Israeli interests from the rubble of neocon "creative destruction" in the Middle East has become an urgent challenge for Israeli policymakers. An America that seeks to reshape the region through an unsophisticated mixture of bombs and ballots, devoid of local contextual understanding, alliance-building or redressing of grievances, ultimately undermines both itself and Israel... Israel does have enemies, interests and security imperatives, but there is no logic in the country volunteering itself for the frontline of an ideologically misguided an avoidable war of civilizations. (4 August 2006)

Meanwhile, in the United States, progressive and moderate Jewish groups were demanding that the Bush administration—for the sake of Israel—make an effort to end the violence. For example, the liberal Zionist group Friends of Peace Now issued a statement on July 20, 2006, which declared, "The United States has an obligation—to its own citizens, to its ally Israel, and to the world in which it represents the last superpower—to intervene with the full force of American influence to stop this escalation."

A number of the otherwise liberal members of Congress who supported a nearly unanimous July 20 House resolution supporting Bush's policy of unconditional backing for Israel's attacks on Lebanon and denying Israeli culpability in civilian deaths and violations of the laws of war responded to constituents outraged at their vote by claiming they were simply defending Israel's legitimate interests.[32] In reality, however, in supporting administration policy, they were defending policies that cynically use Israel, to the detriment of the Jewish state, to advance the Bush administration's militarist agenda.

As American journalist Robert Sheer wrote,

> Long after Bush is gone from office, Israel will be threatened by a new generation of enemies whose political memory was decisively shaped by these horrible images emerging from Lebanon. At that point, Israelis attempting to make peace with those they must coexist with will recognize that with friends such as Bush and his neoconservative mentors, they would not lack for enemies.[33]

One of the more unsettling aspects of the broad support in Washington for the use of Israel as US proxy in the Middle East is how closely it corresponds with historic anti-Semitism. Throughout Europe in past centuries, the ruling class of a given country would, in return for granting limited religious and cultural autonomy, set up certain individuals in the Jewish community as the visible agents of the oppressive social order, such as tax collectors and money lenders. When the population would threaten to rise up against the ruling class, the rulers could then blame the Jews, sending the wrath of an exploited people against convenient scapegoats, resulting in the pogroms and other notorious waves of repression that have taken place throughout the Jewish Diaspora. The idea behind Zionism was to break this cycle through the creation of a Jewish nation-state, where Jews would no longer be dependent on the ruling class of a given country. The tragic irony is that, by using Israel to wage a proxy war to promote US hegemony in the region, this cycle is being perpetuated on a global scale. That the White House press office would promote an article that explicitly advocates Israel's "doing Washington's dirty work" is indicative that this notorious anti-Semitic tradition is alive and well in the nation's capital.

If this is indeed the case, the orgy of American-inspired Israeli violence during the summer of 2006 has led to a dangerous upsurge in anti-Semitism in the Middle East and throughout the world. In the United States, many critics of US policy are blaming "the Jewish lobby" for US support for Israel's attacks on Lebanon, rather than the Bush administration and its bipartisan congressional allies who encouraged Israel to wage war on Lebanon in the first place.

At the same time, Israel is not a banana republic. Even those who recognize the key role the Bush administration had in goading Israel on to attack Lebanon emphasize that rightist elements within Israel had their own reasons independent from Washington to pursue the conflict. And yet, while Israeli leaders who agreed to serve as American surrogates should be held accountable for their actions, it should also be recognized that while the Lebanese were the most immediate victims of this round of American militarism and imperial ambitions, Israel is in many respects a victim of US policy as well.

Indeed, given the enormous dependence Israel has on the United States militarily, economically, and diplomatically, this latest war on Lebanon could not have taken place without a green light from Washington. (President Jimmy Carter, for example, was able to put a halt to Israel's 1978 invasion of Lebanon within days and force Israeli forces to withdraw from the south bank of the Litani River to a narrow strip just north of the Israeli border.) By contrast, the Bush administration and an overwhelming bipartisan majority of Congress clearly believed it was in the US interest for Israel to pursue Washington's "dirty work" regardless of its negative implications to Israel's legitimate security interests, essentially showing America's willingness—in its quest for hegemony in the Middle East—to fight the Muslims to the last Jew.

NOTES

1 See, for example, my article "Israel Will Create More Terrorists Than It Kills," *South Florida Sun-Sentinel* 22 July 2006.

2 Robert Parry, "Israeli Leaders Fault Bush on War," Consortiumnews.com, 13 August 2006.

3 Robert Perry, "A Pretext War in Lebanon," Consortiumnews.com, 9 August 2006.

4 Matthew Kalman, "Israel Set War Plan More Than a Year Ago," *San Francisco Chronicle* 21 July 2006.

5 See the 2002 CRS Report for Congress, *Terrorism: Near Eastern Groups and State Sponsors* 13 February 2002: 5; the US Department of State's 2005 *Patterns of Global Terrorism*; and the International Crisis Group, "Hizballah: Rebels Without a Cause?" 30 July 2003.

6 Yaacov Katz, "IDF Prepared for Attack by Syria," *Jerusalem Post* 30 July 2006.

7 Tom Regan, "US Neocons Hoped Israel Would Attack Syria," *Christian Science Monitor* 9 August 2006.

8 Jim Lobe, "Neocons Wanted Israel to Attack Syria," Inter Press Service, 19 December 2006. This is the source of the Elliot Abrams quote as well.

9 Robert Perry, "A Pretext War."

10 Cited in Anders Strindberg, "Hizballah's Attacks Stem from Israeli Incursions into Lebanon," *Christian Science Monitor* 1 August 2006; George Monbiot, "Israel Responded to an Unprovoked Attack by Hizballah, Right? Wrong," *Guardian* 8 August 2006.

11 Human Rights Watch, "Fatal Strikes: Israel's Indiscriminate Attacks against Civilians in Lebanon," 18.3E (August 2006). HRW also documented violations of international humanitarian law by Hizballah in its indiscriminate rocket attacks against civilian areas in Israel.

12 Department of Public Information, News and Media Division, United Nations (New York), 5352nd Meeting of the Security Council, "Security Council Notes Significant Progress in Lebanon, Including Withdrawal of Foreign Forces, Holding of Parliamentary Elections in 2005," SC/8616, 23 January 2006.

13 Warren Hoge, "Attacks Qualify as War Crimes, Officials Say," *New York Times* 20 July 2006.

14 "UN Appalled by Beirut Devastation," BBC News, 23 July 2006.

15 Office of the White House Press Secretary, "Statement on Condemnation of Hizballah Kidnapping of Two Israeli Soldiers," 12 July 2006.

16 "Bush Caught Off-Guard in Chat with Blair," CNN.com, 17 July 2006.

17 Department of Public Information, News and Media Division, United Nations (New York), 5352nd Meeting of the Security Council, "Security Council Notes Significant Progress in Lebanon, Including Withdrawal of Foreign Forces, Holding of Parliamentary Elections in 2005," SC/8616, 23 January 2006

18 Ironically, liberal political action committees continued to support the election or reelection of congressional candidates who went on record supporting Washington's proxy war against Lebanon, despite massive Israeli violations of international humanitarian law and its serving as a trial run for a US war against Iran.

19 The partial exceptions were Rep. Ron Paul of Texas, the lone Republican to not support the resolution, who was unopposed in his reelection bid in 2004 but had a Democratic challenger in 2006, and Rep. Jim McDermott of Washington, who had a third-party challenger in 2006 who was not on the ballot two years earlier. In both cases, they won with more than three-quarters of the popular vote.

20 Hoge.

21 Department of State, "Special Briefing by Secretary Condoleezza Rice on Travel to the Middle East and Europe," Washington, DC, 21 July 2006.

22 "Mideast Talks 'Fail to Reach Agreement,'" CNN, 26 July 2006.

23 David S. Cloud and Helene Cooper, "US Speeds Up Bomb Delivery for the Israelis," *New York Times* 22 July 2006.

24 Office of the White House Press Secretary, "President Bush and Secretary of State Rice Discuss the Middle East Crisis," Prairie Chapel Ranch, Crawford, Texas, 7 August 2006.

25 Cited in Marjorie Cohen, "Bush's Enemy du Jour," Alternet, 1 August 2006.

26 Warren Hoge and Steven Erlanger, "The Cease-Fire: UN Council Backs Measure to Halt War in Lebanon, *New York Times* 12 August 2006.

27 Typical was President Bush's August 7 statement to the press: "Had the parties involved fully implemented 1559, which called for the disarmament of Hizballah, we would not be in the situation we're in today."

28 Compiled from the following Security Council documents: S/2000/718, 20 July 2000; S/2000/1049, 31 Oct. 2000; S/2001/66, 22 Jan. 2001; S/2001/423, 30 Apr. 2001; S/2001/714, 20 July 2001; S/2002/55, 16 Jan. 2002; S/2002/746, 12 July 2002; S/2003/38, 14 Jan. 2003; S/2003/728, 23 July 2003; S/2004/50, 20 Jan. 2004; S/2004/572, 21 July 2004; S/2004/572.Add.1, 21 July 2004; S/2005/36, 20 Jan. 2005; S/2005/460, 21 July 2005; S/2006/26, 18 Jan. 2006; and S/2006/560, 21 July 2006.

29 Liat Collins, "Not So Quiet on the Northern Front," *Jerusalem Post* 1 June 2006: 1.

30 John Pike of GlobalSecurity.org, cited in Anna Badkhen, "Civilian Toll Raises Questions," *San Francisco Chronicle* 20 July 2006.

31 Uri Avnery, "America's Rottweiler," Gush Shalom, 26 August 2006.

32 Based on a series of letters from members of Congress and interviews with peace activists in California and Massachusetts during July and August 2006.

33 Robert Scheer, "Israel's Dependency on the Drug of Militarism," TruthDig.org, 1 August 2006.

8. EXPORTING DEATH AS DEMOCRACY: US FOREIGN POLICY IN LEBANON

Irene L. Gendzier

This essay is a revised version of one originally written for the special issue on Lebanon of the MIT Electronic Journal of Middle East Studies *(2006).*

"Public Diplomacy": A History of Public Deception

In 1983, a memorandum entitled, "Public Affairs and Public Diplomacy Strategies for Lebanon and the Middle East," was prepared for the chair of the International Political Committee. It was signed by Robert C. McFarlane, as chairman of the Special Planning Group of the National Security Council. Its purpose was to mobilize public opinion in support of US policy in Lebanon. Its premise was that such support was lacking because "many Americans have difficulty relating the complicated politics of Lebanon to US vital interests. Appealing to our regional interests, i.e., Israeli security or our hope for democracy in Lebanon, is not likely by itself to convince the American people the costs are worth it."[1]

To overcome such limitations, the same memorandum argued for "an effective short-term strategy which coherently argues why Lebanon is of strategic importance to the United States, not merely because of its relationship to the Soviet and Syrian threat in the eastern Mediterranean, but also because of the linkage between what happens in Syria and Lebanon and the future stability of the Persian Gulf." Conveying this information properly required another kind of strategy, one that would "penetrate the twelve media centers in the US" in addition to reaching out to business, labor, special interest groups, as well as educational and religious institutions with the assistance of reliable "heavy hitters."

The above memo was as applicable in 2006 as when it was issued in 1983. Both periods followed US-supported Israeli invasions of Lebanon that were justified by the Reagan and, later, by the G.W. Bush administrations, in similar terms. Then as now, the administration claimed that its policies were critical to the protection of vital US national interests, including Israel and Lebanon. In both instances, developments in Lebanon were linked to those in Damascus and the Gulf; radical Lebanese Shiites were suspected of harboring Iranian connections. And then as now, public diplomacy was an instrument of public deception designed to effectively mask Washington's policies and those of its allies in the region.

The above memorandum nonetheless remains useful as it identifies elements of continuity in US policy that remain relevant nearly a quarter of a century after it was issued. The authors of the memorandum conveyed Washington's assessment of Beirut's place in its broader Middle East design, recognizing that Lebanon is inextricably linked to the Israel/Palestine struggle and to the conflicting currents of the Arab world and the Gulf.

From the outset, US policymakers were well aware of Lebanon's regional predicament and its impact on local Lebanese politics. They did not fail to recognize that over 100,000 Palestinian refugees had entered Lebanon as a result of the 1948 war, and that the number had roughly doubled by 1982.[2] But Washington's focus on Beirut was primarily a product of its commercial and strategic interests in the eastern Mediterranean country. Hence its concern to identify the members of the Lebanese elite on whom it could safely rely to promote common interests in a regional environment increasingly open to nationalist and radical forces.

On this basis, Washington sympathized with Israel's Lebanon policy, which predated 1948. US officials understood Israel's courtship of Lebanon's Christians as premised on the collaboration of like-minded minorities with a common political outlook, one that identified Arab nationalism and Palestinian resistance as antagonistic forces. Those Lebanese Christians who qualified included the Phalangists and their militias, which Tel Aviv supported in its 1982 invasion of Lebanon. The role played by the US in that invasion and what followed, when US Marines were sent to Beirut as part of the multinational peacekeeping force in Lebanon, was directly relevant to the timing of the October 23, 1983 memorandum identified above. Three days earlier a truck bomb exploded at the headquarters of the US Marines in Beirut, leaving 241 dead.

Washington had supported Israel's policies in Lebanon prior to the 1982 invasion. It supported Syrian intervention in 1976, as did Israel, at a time when Syrian policy was directed against the Lebanese left and the PLO. Further, Washington supported Israel's tactical alliance with right-wing Lebanese parties and militias bent on destroying the PLO.

Accounts of the 1982 Israeli invasion, images of devastation, reports of prison camps, testimony of foreign doctors working with Palestinians, evidence of the scale of destruction of Beirut, the agony of the Lebanese Guernica were on record, even if that record was woefully incomplete in terms of US coverage.[3] It was in this context that Israel's use of US-made cluster bombs and phosphorus bombs in densely populated civilian areas led then President Reagan, who fully supported the invasion, to call for an indefinite "suspension of shipments of such weapons to Israel." In practice, the suspension "applied only to a single shipment then ready for transport."[4] Nonetheless, in a calculated effort to salvage US interests, Washington called for an end to violence, the withdrawal of Israeli forces from Beirut, and support for US initiatives to deal with the Israeli–Palestinian conflict. The invitation excluded the Palestinians, an omission that exposed the fraudulence of Washington's claim to be an honest broker.

The authors of the 1983 memo were no doubt correct in assuming that many Americans were not supporting US policy in this period. Public opinion polls in the United States in early 1984 demonstrated that there was increasing "discontent with President Reagan's policy in Lebanon," and the desire to "extricate marines from a country where 250 Americans have already died."[5] By then, the estimated casualty toll of the Israeli invasion in Lebanon was between 17,000 and 20,000. How informed the US public was about the effects of past US policy in Lebanon was another matter altogether.

US Policy in the 1950s

In the period following World War II, US presidential doctrines consistently reiterated their support for a unified Lebanese state—that is, a state governed by a regime in harmony with US interests. These, as indicated earlier, were defined primarily in commercial terms whose strategic importance was clearly understood by US policymakers and oil executives alike. Lebanon was valued for its role as a transit state, one whose indispensable function was to carry Aramco's oil through the related US-built tapline, from Saudi Arabia to the Lebanese port of Saida [Sidon]. Beirut oil-related enterprises, in short, were part of the vast complex that was under the control of the petroleum cartel. Lebanon's history is inseparable from that of US oil and political interests in the decades following World War II.

In 1958, at the time of the first Lebanese civil war and the Iraqi revolution, US officials in Lebanon were responsible for the protection of both the US and UK pipelines, the latter connecting the Iraq Petroleum Company's oil (which did not belong to Iraq) to the Lebanese port of Tripoli.[6]

Long before 1958, US officials in Beirut identified those members of the Lebanese financial, commercial, and political elite whom they regarded as indispensable to US policies. While there was a clear understanding of the impediments to Lebanese domestic politics, the widespread corruption, and the role of the confessional system in promoting long-term stalemate, support for Lebanese reform was considered an unacceptable risk. Hence, while US officials in the early postwar years expressed sympathy for the young Kamal Jumblatt, by 1958 this leader of the opposition was regarded as a political danger by US officials. Washington identified Jumblatt and the forces of the opposition with pro-Nasserist policies, and Egyptian President Nasser as the embodiment of a radicalization that Washington considered anathema. In practice, the Egyptian leader was consistently courted and undermined by US officials who suspected his role in every regional crisis, including that which gripped Lebanon in the year of its first civil war.

On July 14, 1958, the British-supported Iraqi monarchy collapsed before the forces of the Iraqi revolution. The news arrived as the US was preparing for military intervention in Beirut, a move designed to shore up its Lebanese allies. In London, however, British Prime Minister Harold Macmillan urged US President Eisenhower to drop the idea of intervening in Lebanon and to turn, instead, to a joint intervention in Baghdad. The idea had no appeal in Washington, where the prospect of a diminished British presence in the Gulf was hardly a threat. Eisenhower therefore rejected the invitation and added the following clarification in his response to Macmillan:

> Whatever happens in Iraq and other parts of the area, we must, I think, not only try to bolster up both the loyalties and the military and economic strength of Lebanon and Jordan, we must also, and this seems to me even more important, see that the Persian Gulf area stays within the Western orbit. The Kuwait-Dhahran-Abadan areas become extremely important and Turkey and Iran have become more important. We shall seek ways to help them be sturdy allies, first in

quality and second in quantity, insofar as that quantity can be usefully provided and maintained.[7]

The members of the US Senate were not consulted on these questions, as their complaints made clear. Members of the US Senate Foreign Relations Committee that met over the course of the summer of 1958 to consider the "situation in the Middle East," with briefings on US policy by administration officials, were privy to little of what was actually going on in the region. Their prime concern was with US intervention in Lebanon, though they had numerous questions about Iraq and the failure of US intelligence to anticipate the revolution. At the outset, Senate critics demanded to know the legal basis for US intervention in Lebanon, obviously irritated by the evident disdain for congressional opinion. Such questions led beyond Lebanon to Iraq, and the more general question of US oil interests in the region.[8]

Concerning Lebanon, senators were told that US intervention was a necessary and just response to the predicament facing the Lebanese president. They were made to understand that its broader implications were justified by Washington's firm stance against radical currents in a region open to Soviet penetration and local subversion. Questions pertaining to Lebanon's civil war and the precise source of external danger to which the Lebanese president and his US ally consistently pointed went unanswered, save for repetitive accusations against Egypt, Syria, and radio propaganda that was considered a form of "aggressive indirect aggression."

As to Iraq, senators were told that US officials, including those in the intelligence community, were unaware and unprepared for news of the Iraqi revolution. Some senators, however, took issue with the derogatory descriptions of the event, suggesting that Iraqis might have exercised their legitimate rights in revolting against a corrupt and unrepresentative government. Questions concerning US oil interests in the Gulf, including Kuwait, indicated more than a passing knowledge, but they were categorically set aside. Indeed, the juxtaposition of Senate hearings with what the record shows of parallel US communiqués with Britain on the subject offers striking evidence of the profound disconnect between public talk and inside policy.

At the same time, as the Senate welcomed administration officials with the illusory hope of clarifying US policy, the US president assured

Prime Minister Macmillan of the US commitment to the defense of Anglo-American interests in the Gulf. As Senate hearings continued, US officials offered their versions of the Iraqi "coup," while Senate critics disputed a policy of intervention at the will of the executive, repeatedly raising the question of congressional authorization. Again, in virtually parallel though secret exchanges, the US secretary of state assured British officials that "we can put up sand bags around positions we must protect—the first group being Israel and Lebanon and the second being the oil positions around the Persian Gulf."[9]

The New Disorder in the Middle East

That was in 1958. In the long decades that followed, the Middle East was subjected to unprecedented turmoil as civil wars, regional wars, and revolutions fundamentally altered the political contours of the region. For the vast majority whose interests were routinely ignored, the results involved loss and displacement and a chronic political discontent. There was Israel's 1967 war and that of October 1973, the first of which enhanced Israeli territorial acquisitions at the expense of Palestinians, as well as of Egypt and Syria, leading to renewed conflict, while the second led to the imposition of an oil embargo with other repercussions. In 1975 the Lebanese civil war exploded, a toxic mix of inseparable factors whose origins were to be found in Lebanese as well as regional politics. In the same year, Washington debated the possibilities of intervention to assure its control over oil, a preoccupation that was dramatically magnified several years later by the Iranian Revolution (1979) and the Soviet invasion of Afghanistan.[10] On July 18, 1979, the *Guardian* (UK) reported: "On 16 July 1979 Saddam Hussein came to power in Iraq."

Washington's response to these developments involved two distinct though related policies, one centered on Israel–Lebanon, in which Washington backed its special ally's invasion of southern Lebanon in 1978 as well as its total frontal attack against Lebanon four years later; the second focused on developments in and around Iran and involved attempts to foment a military coup, to get arms to the Iranian military, and with the Iraq–Iran War, to assure Iran's defeat. The introduction of the rapid deployment force into the Gulf by President Carter reaffirmed US claims there, and the capacity to intervene was significantly expanded by President Reagan in 1988.

In the overlapping struggles mapped out above, Washington and Tel Aviv moved to neutralize Egypt in the Camp David Accords of 1978, which gave Israel cover for its invasion of southern Lebanon in the same year. According to one report, "an Israeli official who participated in the Blair House military talks with Egypt and the US in 1979 described those sessions as outlining not formal alliances 'but a loose division of labor,' in which the US would supply the military assistance for Egypt to police the Arab world and Israel to protect the Sadat regime against retaliation."[11] According to a 1980 *Newsweek* account of this development, Washington was reported to have been opposed to a "security partnership among Israel, Egypt and the United States," favored by Israel. But Israel's role was far more extensive in the Middle East, where— with US support—it supplied arms to opponents of the Iranian regime, and outside of that region, where it was active in parts of Africa and Latin America and later extending to Asia.[12]

As Mordechai Gur reported on the Litani Operation of 1978, its objective was for Israel to effectively reach the Litani River in southern Lebanon and, from that position, to obtain an acceptable accord with the Lebanese government, without which Israeli occupation would be extended.[13] Israeli allies in the Lebanese south, including the South Lebanon Army, were described by a former Israeli conscript who had served in southern Lebanon as "Israeli-paid gunmen [who] acted as informants, interrogators, and enforcers. Israel's strategy was to disrupt Palestinian guerrillas by punishing the surrounding Lebanese population; the result was deeply felt Lebanese anger."[14]

On the ground in southern Lebanon, "Operation Peace for Galilee," the 1982 Israeli invasion, continued until 2000. As General Gur had predicted, Israel remained in place. It expanded the "security zone" it had defined for its operations in 1978, in spite of UN Security Council Resolution 425 of March 1978 that, in addition to calling for respect for Lebanon's sovereignty and integrity, called on Israel "immediately to cease its military action against Lebanese territorial integrity and withdraw forthwith its forces from all Lebanese territory." Instead, incursions, abductions, and attacks followed, such as those of 1993 and 1996 in Qana, the latter involving an Israeli attack on a UN post in which an estimated 100 were killed and roughly the same number injured. Israeli forces were involved in abductions of Sheikh Obeid on July 28, 1988 and Mustafa Dirani on May 21, 1994.

As Zeev Maoz recalled in "The War of Double Standards," in *Ha'aretz* (24 July 2006):

> During operations "Accountability" [in 1993] and "Grapes of Wrath" [in 1996], Israel's mass bombardments of civilian targets caused mass evacuations of Southern Lebanon, the estimated number of refugees in each case exceeded 500,000 Lebanese. We do not have a good estimate of the number of civilian fatalities in each of these incidents, but during the "Grapes of Wrath" operation, Israeli shells hit a civilian shelter killing 103 civilians including many women and children.

For Lebanon, then, its long civil war was inseparable from regional developments of which it was a victim. Israel's invasion of Lebanon in 1982 was a search-and-destroy mission that targeted the PLO and its supporters of the Lebanese left. The presence of the PLO in Beirut was itself the result of the 1970 civil war in Jordan, which resulted in the expulsion of the resistance movement that resettled in Lebanon, to the consternation of Lebanon's right-wing forces. The latter, in turn, welcomed and exploited Israeli support, as in the case of the Phalangists, to enhance their military capacity and with US backing of Israeli policy, to inflict the maximum defeat on its domestic foes. These were represented by the coalition of Lebanese opposition forces that constituted the Lebanese National Movement. They constituted the link with another ongoing struggle in Lebanon, one whose class roots were to be found in the aggravated consequences of the country's uneven socioeconomic development and its transformation into an unproductive service economy. The Lebanese south was arguably the most impoverished part of the country, with its predominantly Shiite population increasingly radicalized as a result. But Lebanon's Shiite population was neither exclusively southern, rural, nor monolithic in its socioeconomic and political status. It was the disenfranchised of the south, however, who formed the supportive base of the "Movement of the Deprived" and its military arm, Amal. And it was the forces of Amal that, at a later stage, were locked in conflict with the Palestinian resistance and the left, in the mid-1980s.

The separate but interrelated factors that animated Lebanon's second civil war were exploited by regional and international forces, including Israel, Syria, and the US. For Washington, declarations in support of reconstruction and the integrity of the Lebanese state meant support for those Lebanese forces perceived as amenable to US and Israeli regional policy. Thus, in 1976, the US State Department issued a statement reaffirming its opposition to partition and its support of measures "which will insure security and opportunity for all individuals and communities in the country."[15] The Defense Department, in turn, justified its security assistance program for Lebanon, for 1978 and 1979, in terms of US support for Lebanon's national integrity and the urgency of reconstruction, with special attention to the role of the central government in restoring a moderate and a democratic state amenable to Lebanon's reintegration into the international economy. But Washington's conception of Lebanon excluded the opposition, not merely because of its support for the Palestinian resistance but because its platform risked upsetting the existing status quo on which US policy rested.

While the Lebanese civil war ended with the Taif Accord of 1989, Israel remained in control of parts of the Lebanese south until 2000, at which time the combined forces of the Lebanese resistance, including the forces of the left and, primarily, Hizballah, succeeded in forcing their ouster. In spite of this, as of 2006, Maoz reported in the same piece in *Ha'aretz* that Israel continued to violate "Lebanese airspace by carrying out aerial reconnaissance missions virtually every day since its withdrawal from Southern Lebanon six years ago."

And Now for the Past Present

Considered in historical perspective, the latest example of US–Israeli collaboration in the invasion of Lebanon in 2006 offers a perverted echo of past policies whose impact was deepened by the transformations that have occurred in the region and at the international level since 1982. Among the results were those catalogued in the reports of Amnesty International and Human Rights Watch that addressed the scale of destruction and the evidence of war crimes in Lebanon, as well as UN reports that bore witness to the dire conditions affecting Gaza as a result of Israel's systematic dismantling of its social, political, and economic infrastructure.

The collapse of the former Soviet Union in 1989 and the subsequent advances of the US in Central Asia and the Caucasus, in addition to the first US invasion of Iraq in 1991, radically changed the environment in which the US operated under its favored cover of exporting democracy and the values of Western civilization. Unprecedented oil profits in the hands of well-protected pro-American regimes in the oil-producing states of the Arab world minimized the risks to US policy from this source. The new "axis of evil" was represented by Tehran, Damascus, and the so-called non-state actor, the Lebanese Hizballah.

By contrast, the US–Israeli relationship has been eminently strengthened since the 1982 war and the 1988 US–Israeli memorandum of understanding, which basically confirmed past agreements while describing Israel as "a major non-NATO ally." Neither Israel's subsequent invasions of Lebanon in 1993 and 1996, nor its steady denial of Palestinian rights in Gaza and the West Bank, undermined this relationship.

Preparations for the latest war began, it appears, after the 2000 withdrawal. Discussions of such prospects with US diplomats, journalists, and various lobbying groups in Washington additionally provide evidence of collaboration, which was later denied. Those less reticent to confirm US–Israeli consultations, if not collaboration, indicated that "Israel had devised a plan for attacking Hizballah—and shared it with Bush Administration officials—well before the July 12th kidnappings."[16]

Washington justified its support of the Israeli invasion of 2006 in terms of Israel's right of self-defense, and its role in the "war against terror" in the Middle East, a war waged in Lebanon against what the Bush administration claimed was Iran's proxy, Hizballah. Both the US and Israel claimed to be supporters of Lebanon, a state whose near destruction, according to this logic, was to be considered a step on the path of democratization.

Washington justified its policies not only in terms of protecting the security of its special ally, but as firmly eliminating the threat from "extremists" in the region and bringing about the transformation of the "new Middle East." Examples of the latter included what was, in effect, an entente cordiale among states such as Saudi Arabia, Egypt, and Jordan, along with the states of the Gulf and Israel, to which Washington hoped to eventually add a newly reconstituted Lebanon, provided an appropriate regime was in place.

The symbol of US–Israeli collaboration in 2006, as in 1982, was the evidence of US-made and -supplied cluster bombs. In 2006, as earlier, Israel was charged with using such weapons in violation of prior agreements.[17] This time, the UN joined in the denunciation of Israel's use of these bombs, revealing that clearance experts had found 100,000 unexploded cluster bomblets at 359 separate sites. In this connection, it is worth noting that Hizballah had previously demanded that Israel supply it with a map of Israeli landmines in Lebanon, without success.

At the end of July 2006, Washington had, in fact, accelerated delivery of high-technology bombs to the Israeli military. The target was ostensibly Hizballah. As Robert Fisk reported in late October 2006,

> we know that the Israelis used American 'bunker-buster' bombs on Hizballah's Beirut headquarters. We know that they drenched southern Lebanon with cluster bombs in the last 72 hours of the war, leaving tens of thousands of bomblets which are still killing Lebanese civilians every week.[18]

In addition, according to Fisk, there was evidence of the Israeli use of "phosphorus bombs, weapons which are supposed to be restricted under the third protocol of the Geneva Conventions, which neither Israel non the United States have signed." And as Fisk and others reported, evidence implying the use of "uranium-based munitions" in Lebanon was under investigation, as well.

In mid-November 2006, the Israeli press offered additional information on the nature of the cluster bombs used by its defense force. According to the account written by Meron Rapoport—"Israel Opted for Cheaper, Unsafe Cluster Bombs in Lebanon War," published in Ha'aretz on November 14—the Israeli Defense Force used US-made bombs that were inferior to those produced by Israeli Military Industries (IMI) for budgetary reasons. "The main reason for the use of the US-made weapons: Israel uses military aid funds to purchase cluster bombs from the US and in order to buy IMI-made bombs, the Israel Defense Forces would have to dip into its own budget."

Arrangements for financing US military assistance to Israel had always been a lucrative business for US corporations such as Raytheon, Lockheed Martin, and Boeing, since according to US law, 74 percent of such assistance had to be spent on US military materiel.[19] It may be useful to recall that earlier, in 2004, according to a US congressional Research Service report, Washington increased military aid to Israel to $2.4 billion annually, from about $1.8 billion. Estimates of US arms exports to Israel between 1994 and 2003 were approximately $6.9 billion, with Israel in possession of "more F-16s than any other country besides the US."[20] Washington did not entirely ignore its favored Arab partners. Suffice it to recall the recent sale of more than $6 billion worth of military equipment to Saudi Arabia.

After the Israeli/US–Lebanon war of July 2006, another dimension of US policy played itself out. Weeks after the devastating Israeli invasion of Lebanon that was backed by Washington, the Office of the Spokesman of the Department of State issued a statement on the subject of "United States Emergency Aid to Lebanon to Clear Explosive Remnants of War." In its first paragraph it revealed that

> The Office of Weapons Removal and Abatement in the US Department of State's Bureau of Political-Military Affairs is quickly expanding its nearly decade-long landmine and unexploded ordnance (UXO) humanitarian clearance program in Lebanon in order to help remove the newest explosive remnants of war that endanger the Lebanese who are returning to their homes in the southern part of the country.[21]

In the Senate, on the other hand, other voices dominated. According to the Associated Press, on September 6, 2006, an amendment calling on the Pentagon to halt the transfer or sale of cluster bombs to those using them near civilian targets was defeated by a margin of 70–30.

In conjunction with the catastrophic results of its policies in Afghanistan and Iraq, the US-supported Israeli invasion of Lebanon merits high-level inquiry and investigation as well as official denunciation and mourning. The increasing attention paid to the consequences of official deception in the manufacture of the rationale for war on Iraq deserves to be applied to the US–Israeli war on Lebanon and Gaza. In early September 2006 no such plans were in evidence, but internal opposition to Washington's claims had long been heard from the minority of well-informed intellectuals, critics, and scholars prepared to challenge official claims, and it later became audible from defense analysts who challenged the official view of Hizballah and generals who took issue with the notion that that organization was nothing more than an Iranian dependency.

It remains for the non-generals, the non-politicians, the vast majority of others, the non-important people, the rest of us, in sum, to ask, as did journalist Amira Hass in her eloquent address in *Ha'aretz* to Israelis about their studied indifference to the decimation of Palestinian society and to the incarceration of Gaza, "Can you really not see?" (30 August 2006)

The question is ours, as well.

NOTES

1 Memorandum for the Honorable Lawrence S. Eagleburger, chairman, International Political Committee. Prepared for the Honorable Robert C. McFarlane, chairman, Special Planning Group, US Department of State, 26 October 1983. Obtained through the Office of FOI, Privacy and Classification Review, US Propaganda Action in the Middle East, National Security Archive.

2 Precise figures on the number of Palestinian refugees in Lebanon have been difficult to assess. UNRWA cited a figure of 106,800 in its 1951 assessment. But as Bayan Nuwayhed al-Hout explains, this did not include those Palestinians who were not registered with the UN organization. The total figure generally accepted was approximately 200,000. For additional discussion, see Bayan Nuwayhed al-Hout, *Sabra and Shatila: September 1982* (London: Pluto Press, 2004) 21.

3 Fawwaz Traboulsi, "Beirut-Guernica: A City and a Painting," *Middle East Report* (September–October 1988).

4 Eleanor Randolph, "Reagan Suspends Indefinitely Sale of Cluster Bombs to Israel," *Boston Globe* 28 July 1982: 8.

5 Steven V. Roberts, "Support Waning for Beirut Role," *New York Times* 4 January 1984: A10.

6 In discussion with President Eisenhower, Vice President Nixon, and defense officials, Secretary of State J.F. Dulles was reported to have argued that if Iraqi pipelines were destroyed, the US "should of course help them [the British] meet their shortages." Cited in I.L. Gendzier, *Notes from the Minefield: United States Intervention in Lebanon and the Middle East, 1945–1958,* 2nd ed. (New York: Columbia University Press, 2006) 300.

7 Cited in Gendzier preface, xxv–xxvi.

8 Gendzier xxvi–xxvii. Further discussion of US Senate hearings on the 1958 crisis can be found in ch. 13 of the same work.

9 Gendzier 355.

10 "Oil Fields as Military Objectives: A Feasibility Study," prepared for the Special Subcommittee on Investigations of the Committee on International Relations by the Congressional Research Service, Library of Congress, 21 August 1975 (Washington, DC: US Government Printing Office, 1975).

11 "We Have Problems," Steven Strasser with Kim Willenson, Fred Coleman and David Martin, William E. Schmidt and Martin Kasindorf, *Newsweek* 14 July 1980, cited in Joe Stork, "The Carter Doctrine and US Bases in the Middle East," *Middle East Report* (September 1980) 10.

12 In Noam Chomsky, *Pirates and Emperors*, new ed. (Cambridge, MA: South End Press, 2002), see Israeli sources cited; also Chomsky, *The Fateful Triangle* (Cambridge, MA: South End Press, 1999) 23–27; 457.

13 Interview by Alex Fishman with General Mordechai Gur, *Al Hamishmar* 10 May 1978, trans. by I. Shahak.

14 James Ron, "The Next Step for Israel," *Boston Globe* 25 May 2000: A25.

15 Department of State bulletin, "United States Reaffirms Commitment to Integrity and Unity of Lebanon," 11 October 1976: 459.

16 Seymour M. Hersh, "Watching Lebanon," *New Yorker* 21 August 2006.

17 Julian Borger, "US Investigations Whether Israel Violated Deal on Cluster

Bombs," *Guardian* 26 August 2006.

18 Robert Fisk, "Mystery of Israel's Secret Uranium Bomb," *Independent* 28 October 2006; see also Meron Rapoport, "Italian TV: Israel Used New Weapon Prototype in Gaza Strip," *Ha'aretz* 10 October 2006.

19 As cited in Thalif Deen, "Israel Violates US Law with Attack on Lebanon," Antiwar.com, 18 July 2006. Note that the information in this paragraph is taken from my article, "The Secretary of State Prefers Brahms," ZNet, 31 July 2006.

20 Frida Berrigan and William D. Hartung, with Leslie Heffel, *US Weapons at War, 2005: Promoting Freedom or Fueling Conflict: US Military Aid and Arms Transfers Since September 11*. Arms Trade Resource Center, June 2005: 34.

21 "United States Emergency Aid to Lebanon to Clear Explosive Remnants of War," media notes, Office of the Spokesman, US Department of State, Washington, DC. Released 23 August 2006.

Part Three

ISRAEL'S WAR ON LEBANON

9. NOTES FROM THE SIEGE
Rasha Salti

After living in New York for nearly eight years, I decided to move back to Beirut, my adopted hometown. The date of my return seemed entirely arbitrary. I booked a seat on a flight leaving New York's JFK airport on July 10, arriving late in Beirut the next evening. It was supposed to be the new chapter in my life—my divorce was concluded, apartment in the East Village on the market for sale, and eight years' accumulated belongings packed in a container for sea freight, due to arrive to Beirut's port 40 days after the ship set sail. All seemed in order. I bid farewell to New York at the end of the World Cup, with Zizou's head-butt still buzzing in the media worldwide.

On the morning of July 12, I woke up late, reeling from jet lag. I packed my laptop swiftly and rushed to the closest café with WiFi to tend to pressing professional commitments. As I negotiated the gentle upward slope of Abdel-Aziz Street, a friend hurled my name from across the street, a comrade-veteran from the civil war. I crossed the street, and he asked me if it was true that I'd moved back for good. I nodded affirmatively with a big smile. He smiled back and repressing an all-out laugh but not irony, he said: "Welcome back. The war's just started." To my puzzled look, he replied, "You clearly did not hear the news— Hizballah just kidnapped two Israeli soldiers. Israel will wage a war." I wondered out loud why that would be the cause for a war, and he patted me on the shoulder and said that he would be willing to place a bet. I walked away, shooing the entire conversation from my mind, redirecting my focus to the tasks at hand.

The moment I walked into the café, everyone was busy text-messaging and exchanging information, reports, speculation. I decided I would allow myself a lull and be in denial for the space of a few hours. Eventually, I wrote a telegraphic message to friends I had just bid farewell to in New York, just to quell their worry. My state of denial was explicit in that first e-mail. The next day, I began to resign myself to the reality that the Israeli government would wage a full-scale war. I wrote a second dispatch, longer this time, to the same list of friends, where I reneged on my initial reaction and gave full expression to dread, anger, and ambivalence. I did not have the energy to face war; I did not know where to draw strength to face another war. I resisted thinking about the implications of an imminent war on this new chapter in my life. It was too traumatizing on the one hand, too self-centered and egocentric on the other. I was embarrassed to worry about my own fate because I was only too aware that my social and class privileges would shelter me from most ills. And I had the option to leave. This war was like a radical rupture in my plans for the immediate future, the only continuity that seemed to survive was a metaphor—Zizou's head-butt. The chattering class of Beirut as well as commentators in the media could not help seeing a parallel between Zizou's head-butt and Hassan Nasrallah's maneuver.

The list of friends who received that second dispatch asked for permission to forward it to their own friends or listservs. Some of their recipients contacted me directly and asked to be listed on my own list of recipients. Thus I became a blogger in spite of myself. I was not really geared to engage in a conversation with that virtual blogosphere, nor to comply with the rules of alternative news. Very quickly, I bored of writing about myself, my emotions, and thoughts, and began to seek other people's stories. I realized that using the tone of the first-person singular was among the motifs that rendered my dispatches accessible and attractive to that obscure readership in the blogosphere, and that I would have to maintain it. Psychologically, however, I needed to lend my self (consciousness and body) and vehicle (or mediate) the subjectivity, pain, and suffering of those whose stories were not being told, or could not find space to be told.

I know that guilt claims a significant role in the experience of surviving the collective tragedy of war and organized killing. I was not aware of being animated by guilt, but I gradually became obsessed with having the deaths of everyday folks acknowledged as a first step to redressing injustice. Dead bodies remained trapped under ravaged buildings for days, weeks, and rescue workers were unable to pull them out, identify them, and deliver them to surviving kin for proper burial. The images of blood-drenched rigor mortis impressed me to the point that I internalized them and carried them within for weeks after the cease-fire. Gradually, the sensation of extinction had became palpable; it too lingered for weeks after the cease-fire.

My dispatches, which I have come to refer to as "Siege Notes," became increasingly difficult to write as the shelling became more intense, as the displaced became more and more discomforted, but also, and perhaps most remarkably, as the threat of a sectarian implosion within the Lebanese polity loomed. In a desperate attempt to fight ineptitude and helplessness, I became involved with a group of people to organize what became known as the "Civilian Resistance Campaign." Our first action, planned on August 12 (two days before the cease-fire was implemented), was a citizens' convoy to south Lebanon, intended to defy the Israeli siege on the south and to express nationwide support for the populations stranded in shelters all over the country, and for those who remained in the war zone. The initiative consumed the better part of my days and nights. I labored hard at rallying the largest possible number of people from across the political spectrum. The citizen convoy was ultimately a political success—we were able to mobilize 200 people and 55 cars, in less than 7 days of campaigning and organizing. We were unfortunately stopped in our defiant drive by the Lebanese minister of the interior and the Lebanese army in Naameh, at the entrance of the south, under the guise of our own security. The minister claimed he had received information from the Israeli military command that we would be shelled and, if we were irresponsible enough to expose our lives to such danger, he undertook the responsibility of protecting us.

The cease-fire was implemented two days after our convoy headed south. The Civil Resistance Campaign disbanded into disparate efforts to aid in reconstruction and relief to the displaced returning to their homes. I promised myself I would write a conclusion to the "Siege Notes." I have collected notes, but I am unable to conjure closure.

Ten days after the cease-fire came into effect I left the country. I went to visit dear friends to recover from the personal toll of the war that I was yet ashamed to come to terms with. Being with these beloved friends brought me back to life. I slowly regained my sense of self and of things around me.

Months later (as I draft this prefatory note and the Hizballah-led front is staging a massive mobilization in downtown Beirut demanding the resignation of the present cabinet), I can state that I have recovered. I have not been able to draw closure yet, however. With the present political tension reigning over the country, it seems as if the schisms etched by Israeli military strategy have grown deeper, namely the rift between Sunnis and Shiites, more generally the grumbling (sinister) specters of sectarian tension erupting into civil conflict. The logic of the massive displacement of the Shiite community into the delicately laced sectarian demographic mapping of the country was part of Israel's strategy to instigate disruption and instability. Two weeks before the cease-fire was implemented, "incidents" began to erupt and the Lebanese army was called to restore order. Within the last week preceding the cease-fire, tension was palpable to the extent that Hassan Nasrallah invoked his constituency, in a poignant televised speech, to remain calm, keep a very low profile, and not fall prey to sectarian or political provocation.

As I write, things are at an eerie standstill. The mobilization led by the "opposition" (a front led by Hizballah, in alliance with General Aoun's Free Movement, and a constellation of pro-Syrian and anti-American-imperialism political groups) has reached a dead end and negotiations for a truce have thus far failed. The opposition has promised to up the ante. There is unspoken, or whispered, consensus that blood will have to be spilled for either faction to cave in and agree to some sort of a deal. Everyone can smell blood.

The sorrows we live.

Siege Note 2: July 14

I am writing now from a café, in West Beirut's Hamra district. It is filled with people who are trying to escape the pull of 24-hour news reporting. Like me. The electricity has been cut off for a while now, and the city has been surviving on generators. The old system, so familiar at the time of the war, where generators were allowed a lull to rest, is back. The café is dark, hot, and humid. Espresso machines and blenders are silenced. Conversations, rumors, frustrations waft through the room.

I am better off here than at home, following the news, live, on-the-spot documentation of our plight in sound bites.

The sound of Israeli warplanes overwhelms the air on occasion. They drop leaflets to conduct a "psychological" war. Yesterday, their sensitivity training urged them to advise inhabitants of the southern suburbs to flee because the night promised to be "hot." Today, the leaflets warn that they plan to bomb all other bridges and tunnels in Beirut. People are flocking to supermarkets to stock up on food.

[…]

The night was harrowing. The southern suburbs and the airport were bombed from air and sea. The apartment where I am living has a magnificent view of the bay of Beirut. I could see the Israeli warships firing at their leisure. It is astounding how comfortable they are in our skies, in our waters; they just travel around, deliver their violence and congratulate themselves.

[...]

This is all bringing back echoes of 1982, the Israeli siege of Beirut. My living nightmare—well, one of my living nightmares. It was summer then as well. The Israeli army marched through the south and besieged Beirut. For three months, the US administration kept urging the Israeli military to act with restraint. And the Israelis assured them they were acting appropriately. We had the PLO command in West Beirut then. I felt safe with the handsome fighters. How I miss them. Between Hizballah and the Lebanese army I don't feel safe. We are exposed, defenseless, pathetic. And I am older, more aware of danger. I am 37 years old and actually scared. The sound of the warplanes scares me. I am not defiant; there is no more fight left in me. And there is no solidarity, no real cause.

I am furthermore pissed because no one knows how hard the postwar reconstruction was on all of us. Hariri did not make miracles. People worked hard and sacrificed a lot and things got done. No one, except us, knows how expensive, how arduous that reconstruction was. Every single bridge and tunnel and highway, the runways of that airport, all of these things were built from our sweat and brow, at three times the real cost of construction because every member of government, because every character in the ruling Syrian junta, because the big players in the Hariri administration and beyond, were all thieves. We accepted the thievery and banditry just to get things done and get it over with. Everyone one of us had two jobs (I am not referring to the ruling elite, obviously), paid backbreaking taxes and wages to feed the "social covenant." We fought and fought that neoliberal onslaught, the arrogance of economic consultants and the greed of creditors just to have a nice country that functioned at a minimum, where things got done, that stood on its feet, more or less. A thriving Arab civil society. Public schools were sacrificed for roads to service neglected rural areas and for a couple Syrian officers to get richer, and we accepted that; the road was desperately needed and there was the "precarious national consensus" to protect. Social safety nets were given up, healthcare for all, unions were broken and co-opted, public spaces taken over, and we bowed our heads and agreed. Palestinian refugees were pushed deeper and deeper into forgetting, hidden from sight and consciousness, "for the preservation of their identity," we were told, and we accepted. In exchange we had a secular country where the Hizballah and the Lebanese forces could coexist and fight their fights in parliament not with bullets. We bit hard on our tongues and stiffened our upper lip, we protested and were defeated, we took to the streets, defied army-imposed curfews, time after time, to protect that modicum of civil rights, that modicum of a semblance of democracy, and it takes one air raid for all our sacrifices to be blown to smithereens. It's not about the airport, it's what we built during that postwar time.

Siege Note 3: July 15

I was the only one who seemed to have experienced the weariness, to be genuinely frustrated with having to face another round of the Arab–Israeli conflict. Everyone at the gathering seemed resigned to endure this dark and sinister moment. Everyone was busying themselves with analysis and speculation. Mind games, fictions, chimeras. I regretted expressing my weariness with the fight, with having to summon the energy to face Israel and defy the destruction of Lebanon. I felt as if I had betrayed a principle, a value, disrespected people's pain and suffering. I know a great number in the country shared my sentiments—the political debates on TV returned to the question tirelessly. Still, I felt "smaller" than the historical moment demanded.

[...]

Foreign diplomatic missions are making plans to evacuate their nationals. They had planned to evacuate people by sea, but after today's shelling of the ports, they may have to rethink their strategy. Should I evacuate? Does one turn their back on a "historic" station in the Arab–Israeli conflict? If there is no cause that animates me, how do I endure this? (I could not give a damn about the Iranian nuclear bomb or Hizballah's negotiating power.) I was shamed this morning for having these thoughts... And now, at 1:30AM, as Israeli airplanes fill up my sky, I am writing them again.

[...]

Israel's strategy is not only to dismember this country and cripple communication, but also to challenge internal support for Hizballah.

People like me, for example, complaining about how my life is a small hell and I can't take it anymore, yesterday and maybe a little bit today—well, I was an agent of Israel. I was executing the Israeli strategy to break the spirit of the valiant Arabs. In fact the Israeli ambassador to the UN quoted two Lebanese MPs citing how little support for Hizballah there is in Lebanon. This is the rhetoric. But in point of fact it is true, that Israel has not spared an area at this stage, whether Hizballah stronghold or not, and they want to make us pay for housing Hizballah in our parliament. Maybe they prefer an Iraqi scenario?

Siege Note 4: July 16

Ehud Olmert promised scorched earth in southern Lebanon after missiles hit Haifa. Warnings have been sent to inhabitants of the south to evacuate their villages because the Israeli response to Hizballah will be "scorched earth." As major roads are destroyed and the south has been remapped into enclaves, it is not clear how these people are supposed to evacuate. And where to. It seems the "sensitivity training" that the IDF went through for evacuating the settlers from Gaza is really paying off, even on the "civilians," because Ehud Olmert offered the hapless inhabitants of the south shelter in Israel. Now that's leadership! Will they be sprayed by DDT as were the Jewish populations shuttled from Iraq, Morocco, and Egypt in the 1950s and 1960s? Will there be *maabarot* [transit camps] ready for them? They want the 20-kilometer buffer zone and they will burn, destroy, and maim to get it. Maybe they should build another wall?

[...]

So Hizballah dragged us without asking our opinion into this hell. We are in this hell, caught in this crossfire together. We need to survive and save as many lives as possible. The Israelis are now betting on the implosion of Lebanon. It will not happen. There is UNANIMITY that Israel's response is entirely, entirely, UNJUSTIFIED. We will show the Arab leadership that it is possible to have internal dissent and national unity, pluralism, divergence of opinion and face this new sinister chapter of the Arab–Israeli conflict.

Siege Note 5: July 17

I started writing these siege notes to friends outside Lebanon to remain sane and give them my news. I was candid and transparent with my emotions. The ones I had and the ones I did not have. They were more intended to fight dementia at home, in my home and in my mind, to bridge the isolation in this siege, than to fight the media black-out, racism, prejudice, and break the seal of silence. Friends began to circulate them (with my approval). By the third siege note, I was receiving replies, applause, and rebuke from people I did not know. It's great to converse with the world at large, but I realize now that candor and transparency come with a price. A price I am more than happy to pay. However, these siege notes are becoming something else, and I realize now that I am no longer writing to the intimate society of people I love and cherish, but to an opaque blogosphere of people who want "alternative" news. I am more than ever conscious of a sense of responsibility in drafting them. They have a public life, an echo that I was not aware of, and that I experience now as some sort of a burden. I have been tortured about the implications of that public echo. Should I remain candid, critical, spiteful, cowardly, or should I transform into an activist and write in a wholly different idiom? There is of course a happy medium between both positions, but I don't have the mental wherewithal to find it now. And I don't want to sacrifice candor, transparency, and skepticism at the risk of having my notes distorted to serve some ill-intentioned purpose, or in the vocabulary of official rhetoric, "give aid and comfort to the enemy." The enemy does well without the aid of my ranting (they have a nuclear bomb, a hero soccer player from Ghana, the gift of democracy, fantabulous drag queens, and a right-wing freak whose first name is Bibi). Notes from a hapless stranded thirty-something caged in Ras Beirut (i.e., the privileged of the privileged), I believe, will not really make a difference.

[...]

My Palestinian friends are protesting that the Israeli campaign in Gaza has been eclipsed by Beirut. Don't look away from Gaza. The same cannons are firing. The same children are orphaned, the same people are being displaced, shoved outside history and the attributes of humanity, rendered to integers in the logs of NGOs for donations of bags of flour and sugar. The same.

By Day 5 of the siege, a new routine has set in. "Breaking news" becomes the clock that marks the passage of time. You find yourself engaging in the strangest of activities: you catch a piece of breaking news, you leap to another room to announce it to family although they heard it too, and then you text-message it to others. At some point in the line-up, you become yourself the messenger of "breaking news." Along the way you collect other pieces of "breaking news," which you deliver back. Between two sets of breaking news, you gather up facts and try to add them up to fit a scenario. Then you recall previously mapped scenarios. Then you realize none works. Then you exhale. And zap. Until the next piece of breaking news comes. It just gets uglier. You fear nighttime. For some reason, you believe the shelling will get worse at night. When vision is impaired, when darkness envelops everything. But it's not true. Shelling is as intense during the day as it is during the night.

Siege Note 6: July 18

I had the opportunity to leave tomorrow by car to Syria, then to Jordan, and from there by plane to wherever I am supposed to be right now. For days I have been itching to leave because I want to pursue my professional commitments, meet deadlines, and continue with my life. For days I have been battling ambivalence toward this war, estranged from the passions it has roused around me and from engagement in a cause. And yet when the phone call came informing me that I had to be ready at 7AM the next morning, I asked for a pause to think. I was torn. The landscape of the human and physical ravages of Israel's genial strategy at implementing UN Resolution 1559, the depth of destruction, the toll of nearly 250 deaths, more than 800 injured and 400,000 displaced, had bound me to a sense of duty. It was not even patriotism— it was actually the will to defy Israel. They cannot do this and drive me away. They will not drive me away.

[…]

I decided to stay. I don't know when I will have another opportunity to leave.

[…]

Imagine our horror, our sad, sad horror: we are now on borrowed time, the only reason our lives are not under grave threat is because passport holders from G8 countries are being evacuated safely to safer harbors. Even with this relative calm, a sense of impending doom feels almost palpable. Time, space, light, and movement are subsumed in an eerie stillness. It fills the air of the city. As it wafts from room to room, from apartment to apartment, as it turns a corner and travels to another neighborhood, every gesture is a little slowed, surreptitiously lethargic, every thought lingers too long in the inchoate or unfinished state. This eerie stillness numbs the perception of the passage of time and things material. Objects seem both familiar and unfamiliar. They are familiar because they were there the day before and seem not to have moved from their place. They are unfamiliar because they seem to belong to another time, another life. There was another life, I had another life, it seems distant and foreign now. The morning is different, noon is different, sunset is different. Another Beirut has emerged. Wartime Beirut. Wartime Lebanon. Wartime mornings, wartime noons. Siege-time Beirut, siege-time morning, siege-time sunsets. Everyone else in the world is going about their day as they had planned it or as it was planned for them. The shakers and movers of this world, the fledgling middle classes of the developing world, the 11 million child-workers in India, the good-doers and the evil-doers. We are in a different geography of time, of agency, we are besieged, captive, hostage. No chance of the Stockholm syndrome this time. Our every move is monitored: every moving vehicle delivering food, fuel, or medicines is monitored, every phone call is listened to, every e-mail read, every dream snarled at, every desire crushed. Israel has the right to explode it to smithereens.

[…]

Because I am a staunch secular democrat, I have never endorsed Hizballah, but I do not question their legitimacy as a political agent on the Lebanese scene. I believe they are just as much a product of Lebanon's contemporary history, war and postwar, as are all other agents. If one were to evaluate the situation in vulgar sectarian terms, when it comes to representing the interests of their constituency they certainly do a better job than all the other political representatives today and in the past.

It would be utter folly (in fact it would be murderous folly) to regard Hizballah as another radical Islamist terrorist organization, at least in the ideological and idiomatic vein of the American intelligentsia and punditry. (There is something about a stubbornness to misunderstand that betrays intent to see a crisis linger or even escalate in the US. If Americans feel better being misguided idiots, at least Israelis should know better. If the Israeli intelligentsia wants to play deaf like Americans, the only outcome will be an Iraq scenario, although I reiterate that Lebanon is not Iraq and the Lebanese are not and will not be Iraqi, and will not be manipulated into the barbaric sectarian horror. We've tried that before and it does not work, and we are tired of fighting each other.)

Hizballah is a mature political organization that, with its Islamist ideology, has grown organically within the evolution of Lebanese politics and learned (very quickly) to coexist with other political agents in this country, as well as other sects. If Lebanese politics has been a representation of shortsighted petty sectarian calculations, the lived social experience of postwar Lebanon has been different. Sectarian segregation is extremely difficult to implement in the conduct of everyday social transactions, in the conduct of business, employment, and all other avenues of commonplace life. There are exceptional moments when the country came together willingly and spontaneously (as with the Israeli attacks in 1993 and 1996), but there are also other smaller, less spectacular moments punctuating lived experience after the war that every single Lebanese can recall, in which sectarian prejudice was utterly meaningless, and experienced as meaningless.

[...]

If Israel plans to annihilate Hizballah, it will annihilate Lebanon. Hizballah and its constituency are not only Lebanese in the perception of all, they are also a key, essential element of contemporary Lebanon. Moreover the specifics of UN Resolution 1559 may have regional implications, but at heart and in essence these issues can only be resolved within the Lebanese consensus. Israel *cannot* take it upon itself to implement that UN resolution. The idea that Israel should implement any UN resolution is, of course, sinister folly, considering its stellar record of snarling, snickering, and shrugging at every single UN resolution that does not suit its sensibilities.

Hizballah is not al-Qaeda, though Israeli and US propaganda will portray it as such, and that is the downfall of public opinion; that is the tragedy at the root of the consensus that agrees to watch Lebanon burn. In more ways than can be counted they are different political ideologies, groups, and movements. First, they are not suicidal. Second, they are not anti-historical. Third, they are a full-fledged political agent at the center of a dynamic polity. Their ideology is not an ideology of doom—they represent as much the petty interests of their constituency. They are imbricated in the fabric of regional politics.

Siege Note 7: July 22

"Cruise beyond your dreams" read posters pasted on the walls of the huge air-conditioned tent that functions as the final stage in processing the evacuees before they board the ship. The ship, as if someone wanted to amuse Edward Said for a brief minute, is called the *Orient Queen*. It is part of a Lebanese-owned fleet of commercial cruises, Abu Merhi Cruises, and is contracted by the US embassy to schlep American passport holders to Cyprus. Holders of American passports stranded in the south were shuttled by buses earlier that day to the port of Beirut. They were greeted by US embassy personnel, a small contingent of US Marines, and the *Orient Queen* crew. The buses were parked on the dock and passengers waited long hours for their turn to be searched, their stuff searched, their papers processed, and then onto the ship.

The platoon or brigade (whatever the appropriate word) of US Marines landed in Beirut some twenty years after the bombing of their base in 1983. In fact, to a renowned American journalist, they revealed that they were known as "the Beirut platoon" (or contingent or company). This twenty-some years' "return" of the marines was presented as a big to-do—everybody had high emotions about it. Its significance escaped me. So what? They were going to be here for two days to evacuate American passport holders and then they went back to their lives. Their lives? As it turns out they were to return to Jordan, where they were training the Jordanian army. (Oops—that was not supposed to be said. Delete from the record.)

The marines were courteous in the manner army personnel is trained to be courteous. Their coordination with the *Orient Queen* staff would have made sense only if it were a Monty Python film script. Some very, very funny movie with prophetic visions of social and political horror to come. The *Orient Queen* has apparently a special brigade of Rio Brazil Dancers.

[…]

The moment you come across a member of the US embassy personnel they correct you: "It's assisted departure, not evacuation." This is how they manage the feeling of the Lebanese, they explain. "No one is forcing anyone to leave," they add. Evacuation seems too terminal, too definitive and only those who choose to leave do. True. But evacuees are almost all in a state of shock. Those who were trapped in the south particularly, they testify that the Israeli weaponry is entirely new, unfamiliar, a lot more frightening.

[...]

One of my closest friends, really my beloved sister, Maria, left two days ago. Up until a few hours before she was supposed to follow instructions from the British embassy for evacuation, she could not get herself to leave. She has two boys, aged nine and five. Maria and her husband lived in London for a long while and earned citizenship there. Everyone who matters in her life called and urged her to evacuate with the Britons. By the second day of the siege, she had moved to the mountains.

She and I had remained in contact by phone. Maria is so close to my heart, she is a foundational element of my bare consciousness of the world. From the moment this horror had started, our sentences had shortened, the tone of our conversations become contemplative, inconclusive, incapable of circling to some sort of closure. We could not even say "goodbye"—invariably we ended conversations with "I will call you back." It felt better to say that, to claim the exchange of information and emotion not yet complete, rather than the opposite. We called one another to exchange pointless information, we repeated headlines, "breaking news" that we had heard and had no hope of breaking as new to the other. We repeated news of other friends, so and so moved to there, so and so left, so and so went nuts... Although admittedly absurd, our phone conversations had the rare virtue of being constitutional—that is, they charged our respective systems and reminded us of the people we once were, the lives we once lived. We asked one another the same question over and over: "Should I leave?" "Should you leave?" She did not want to but felt she should, for the boys. The eldest of the two was seized with anxiety and panic at the escalating horror of Israel's retaliation.

She caved in two days ago. I called as she waited on the docks with her two sons. Her husband did not want to leave. "It's awful, it's awful," she kept saying. "It's awful, it's awful," I echoed. "Have I done the right thing?" she pleaded. "Absolutely," I replied, crushing the slightest hint of hesitation. I could not help telling her that I would miss her. It felt selfish, needy, in the way children can be self-centered and demanding. In truth I was terrified of living through the siege without her. I felt like a good part of my heart, at least a good part of what I love about being in Beirut, was standing at the docks waiting with her two sons. We spoke on the phone three times. Three times my tears flowed uncontrollably; three times I did not want her to feel anything in my voice; three times I said, "I will call you back."

Evacuations are not "assisted departures"—they are uprootings, they are borne from decisions made under duress so sinister, they feel nothing like decisions. Standing on the dock of Beirut's port two days later, watching American passport holders who were shuttled from the south in buses, I got a full sense of what evacuation means when you're the one staying behind. Whether reasoned or reasonable or not, there is an ineffable foreboding of extinction, of perishing. These people may very well remember us one day, all of us they have seen and interacted with before they boarded the ship. I just don't know where we will be when they remember us.

Siege Note 8: July 23

Writing is becoming increasingly difficult. Putting words together to make sentences to convey meaning, like the small gestures and rituals that make up the commonplace acts of everyday life, has begun to lose its meaning and its cathartic power. I am consumed with grief. Another me trapped inside cries all the time. And crying over the death of someone is a very particular cry. It has a different sound, a different music, and a different feel. I dare not cry in the open. Tears have flowed, time and time again, but I have repressed the release of pain and grief. My body feels like a container of tears and grief. I am sure it shows in the way I walk.

Writing is not pointless per se, but it is no longer an activity that gives me relief. The world outside this siege seems increasingly far away, as if it was evacuated with the binational passport holders and foreigners.

The death toll has been increasing in a horrific exponential invigorated with the White House giving the green light for the military assault to persist. Beirut has been spared so far, but not the southern suburbs. Today is Day 12 of the war. The Israeli military has conducted 3,000 air raids on Lebanon in twelve days. Out of the total deaths so far, which range close to 400 (numbers are not definitive), almost 170 are children. The numbers of the displaced increase by the hour. Have you seen the pictures of the deaths? The mourners in Tyre? Have you seen the coffins lined up? And the grieving mothers.

It is impossible not to grieve with them. It is impossible to shut one's ears to their wailing. It haunts me, echoes from the walls of the city, bounces off the concrete of destroyed bridges and buildings. In trying to explain what drove Mohammad Atta to fly an airplane into one of the towers of the World Trade Center, someone (I forget who it was, sorry fact-checkers) once said to me that Atta must have felt that "his scream was bigger than his chest." That description stayed with me. I don't know if I agree with it, or if that's how Atta felt in reality, but it comes back to me now because I feel that my grief is bigger than my chest and I have no idea how to dissipate it.

[…]

The displaced have been dispersed in the country. They have been placed in schools, universities, government-owned buildings. Aid is arriving, but still in chaotic manner. Volunteers are beginning to get weary. Nothing, however, compares to the distress of the displaced. They are in a state of complete emotional upheaval. Their presence has already changed the habits and rituals of the neighborhoods where they have been placed.

As the sun begins to set and the harshness of its rays begins to dim, you see families strolling on Hamra Street [a main commercial thoroughfare in west Beirut]. Boutiques and sandwich shops are closed, cafés open only hesitantly, but the sidewalk provides an escape from the confinement of the makeshift shelters where they have been relocated. You can see it in their stroll, their gait. Their pace seeks peace of mind not destination, their lungs expand, drawing in oxygen to conjure quietude, not to relieve cardiovascular pressure. They exude a deep, mournful, sorrowful gaze. They left behind their entire lives, maybe even their beloveds.

In Ras Beirut, modest and usually slothful back streets have come to life. To escape the heat of indoor confinement, displaced families have begun to put plastic chairs and *nargileh* on front porches or in the entrance halls of buildings. Two nights ago, when I walked home after a long day of working with journalists, as I zigzagged through these back streets, I was comforted by their gentle presence. Shrouded in the thick of night, they chatted softly, huddled together to ward off the brunt of their respective tragedies, in muffled anxious watch for the sound of Israeli warplanes, for the next round of twenty-some-ton shells raining from the sky. An endless radio newscast sounded softly, its flow comforting. It too seemed heartened by the weight of the tragedies it reported. Eerily gentle was that summer night, and uprooted, dispersed families surrendered to its gentleness.

On the next block, three young women stood in line, queuing for access to a public payphone. That too has become a familiar sight in Beirut. People lining up at public payphones. They stood clearly weary but resilient. My *good evening* was returned with kind smiles and another round of *good evenings*. I was relieved to note that they felt safe, that they roamed the city at night without qualms. How long would they be able to afford to pay for these phone calls is another question.

On the next block, a Mercedes packed with people was parked at a corner, in front of the entrance of a building. The car's doors were flung open and the flow of the newscast from the radio sounded softly. It was a visit. Two displaced families on a nightly visit. They huddled together gently, heartened by one another's small tragedy, and a soft breeze blew with clemency.

Siege Notes 9 & 10: July 26

My day started today with news from Bint Jbeil. (In effect it is Day 13 of the war, but just another morning under siege for me.) Ghassan Ben Jeddo, director of Al-Jazeera's Beirut bureau was analyzing the situation on the southern front in that bordering town. He announced flatly that Hizballah had conceded the military surrender of the southern town, that the IDF had besieged it, and that it had been almost entirely flattened to rubble. My breathing became tight. I knew well, and had been told for days, that military defeats and victories were very tricky to determine in this type of unusual warfare, that a conventional army registers clear retreats and advances whereas a band of guerrillas does not. The military defeat in itself did not really matter enough to cause tightness in my chest, although I was a little worried about the IDF becoming emboldened to proceed with scorched-earth plans or some other nightmarish fancy of theirs. My breathing became tight because I immediately thought about some 1,500 people, making up some 400 families, who were trapped in Bint Jbeil. Some were displaced from villages around Bint Jbeil and had taken refuge in the town. They were trapped there in two buildings, one of which was a government school. I could not imagine what they were living. As Al-Jazeera showed footage around Bint Jbeil, there was a continuous soundtrack of pounding from Israeli tanks. I could only see them and hear that pounding: were they huddled together? Were they laying down on the floor, their hands over their heads? How does one survive two days of continuous shelling like that? Had they any hope of fleeing?

They stayed with me, those 1,500 souls in Bint Jbeil. I went to the public garden where displaced people were now living, I went to the cooperative supermarket in Sabra, I went to an air-conditioned café with WiFi, and the 1,500 were with me. I had lunch, tried to write—still with me. After sunset, a journalist friend told me he had interviewed the mayor of Bint Jbeil in the afternoon. The man had suffered a stroke last Sunday and had been evacuated for treatment. By today he had recovered and was struggling to find a way to rescue the remaining Lebanese-Americans trapped in Bint Jbeil. My friend allowed me to sigh with some relief: the trapped souls were 400, not 1,500 today. (Most of the residents of Bint Jbeil are Lebanese-Americans from Dearborn and Detroit, Michigan.)

[...]

I am haunted by the nameless and faceless caught under rubble. Underneath destroyed buildings. Awaiting proper burial.

Siege Note 11: July 28

We live from day to day. The scenarios for the conclusion of this war seem very difficult to articulate, even to imagine. The US is intent on the continuation of the war, Israel has suffered a defeat and the goals it has set to determine some sort of victory don't seem fathomable. The Israeli press was beginning to ask a few intelligent questions until the Israeli army suffered losses in an ambush set up by Hizballah. One damn ambush, a handful of soldiers, and the entire press corps went ballistic overnight. They were all about flattening Lebanon, hurting the government, bringing out the big guns, more troops. One damn ambush where a mere handful of soldiers were faced with a reality they were not prepared to contend with: that Hizballah guerrillas are well trained and will fight without blinking to defend the land from a ground invasion. What a funny army! What a funny society! What do they expect when they go to war with guerrillas?

[...]

I spent the afternoon yesterday in Karm al-Zeytoon, a neighborhood in Ashrafieh (literally, "olive grove") where some schools have been opened to house some of the displaced from the south and from Beirut's southern suburb. I went to visit friends who were in charge of the

Nazareth Nuns school [a public school]. A band of dashing young men and women, not yet thirty years of age, who have taken upon themselves the task of ensuring the well-being and safety of some 120 or so men, women, children, and elderly. Some in that band of volunteers belong to the Democratic Left movement, and the school, as are two neighboring other schools, are under the charge of the Samir Kassir Foundation. Although they have established a schedule of shifts so as not to have their entire lives taken over by their volunteering, still, their entire lives are on hold and all they do in effect is tend to the displaced. The atmosphere inside the school was convivial, slow-paced, but a low-grade tension is impossible to ignore. All throughout my visit I was smitten by their grace. They have had to organize every single aspect of everyday survival in that school: spaces where people sleep, the use of bathrooms, the overall hygiene and cleaning of the place, the collection of garbage, the preparation of meals, the keeping stock of supplies, medicines, medical needs of the group, fun and games for the kids, security of the site, etc. That night they were going to have the first attempt at screening a DVD (*Finding Nemo*) in the school's open-air courtyard. They are not yet thirty years old and yet they have to sort through the everyday problems that arise between adults their parents' age.

A nine-year-old boy came nagging to T, one of the main volunteers, as he and I chatted in the makeshift "salon" (a broken table and school bench at the side of the gateway to the school). He wanted T's permission to go to a printer's shop where he had heard he could find work on a day-to-day basis. He implored him. T promised he would talk to the boy's father that night and they would see. The boy told him that some man in the group assured him that he would find him work. T did not have the heart to lecture him about the ills of child labor. The boy was in turmoil over the humiliating state of his family and was eager to share the burden with his father (a taxi driver whose earnings have gone extremely low).

Siege Note 12: August 2

This siege note I wish to dedicate to Maher

Coming into consciousness of, or bearing witness to, a massacre only a few kilometers removed from one's being (or home), feels very much like the experience of being in the proximity of a very powerful explosion, only at an extremely, extremely slowed motion. Taking stock of the information on time, place, and the toll of victims, watching televised transmission of rescue workers piling a kindergarten in rigor mortis, is identical to the astounding sensation of the air being sucked from all around that typically precedes a huge explosion. And at some point, it all sinks in, the information processes into information, and the images breakdown into their compositional elements (rescue worker carrying four-year-old with hand stretched to the sky and fingers widespread), and you explode, or implode, with some sort of a system shutdown. For a split second your heart does not beat the way it is used to, and your lungs don't quite inhale or exhale according to the book.

[…]

Maher called. I woke up. He said he was leaving with a team of journalists for Tyre. Did I want to come? I did not know. I should be ready in ten minutes if I wanted to go. I said no, and regretted it for the rest of the day. Now when I write, I regret it.

Maher is a filmmaker. When this war started he was in Paris. He went nuts after a few days and decided to return. He wanted to be here for the war. He came on one of the ships that the French sent to evacuate French passport holders. His voyage was surreal, but that's another story.

He has a project to establish a website to collect and disseminate the record of the lived experience of this war, lest it should lapse from the collective record again. He has started to distribute cameras to young filmmakers, artists, even volunteers, to record, film, transcribe the mundane and the non-sensational everyday of surviving this war.

Maher had been itching to go to Tyre, closest to one of the sites of battle. He went with the convoy of journalists and humanitarian aid workers. If my rage took me to the street and the mob scene, his drove him to the front, to the site where the hurt is most poignant. He told me he was going to Qana, and I was not surprised.

I called him the next day in the afternoon. He had indeed been to Qana, and visited the site, and smelled death. From his voice, I felt that something had happened, something that still impressed him greatly. His locution was more sullen than lazy, I could barely make out what he said, and I kept asking him to repeat what he said. He did not get exasperated; his voice was detached. He was speaking to me from a netherworld.

My heart sank. He said Qana was exactly what I saw on TV. He kept referring to going through Srifa as being very difficult. "Very difficult" he kept saying. Nearly all of Srifa is destroyed. Limbs covered in powdered concrete emerge from between the ravages of collapsed buildings. No one has had the energy or courage to pull out the dead. The Red Cross and Civil Defense ambulances have been targeted relentlessly by Israel. When the guns quiet, we will discover that Qana is small-time compared to Srifa. There is a pattern emerging now: Marwaheen, Srifa, Blida, and Qana: terror to induce forced displacement (or pardon my French, "deportation"). Scorched earth and mass graves—this is how we achieve the New Middle East.

Maher said nearly 60 percent of Bint Jbeil has become flat rubble. Most of its central area. There, too, limbs stick out of collapsed buildings and the smell of death is everywhere. While rescue workers pulled the dead from that shelter in Qana, the IDF was shelling the only functioning hospital in Bint Jbeil, the day before Maher's visit. That's how battered Bint Jbeil was—even its hospital the IDF had decided was a Hizballah stronghold and posed a grave security threat for the well-being of the children of Kiryat Shmona who to go to school, who not dwell in shelters, who kiss the shells that their army will shower on Lebanon to implement UN Resolution 1559 and eradicate terror.

In the convoy to Bint Jbeil, journalists outnumbered rescue workers, and they found a group of elderly men and women who were trapped in a shelter. They could not walk without assistance and had not eaten for four or five days. They were carried out and given some water and driven to places where they could receive the care they needed.

The BBC produced a number of excellent reports from Bint Jbeil, and in the background, I saw Maher's face. His demeanor confirmed the impression I had after speaking to him on the phone. He had seen the face of death. Not death as in the sorrowful but inevitable expiring of everyday life, and not the death of a soldier on the battlefield. He had seen the face of organized, carefully orchestrated, mass-scale death, the planned death of hundreds and thousands as a solution to restoring regional hegemony.

You never leave a mass grave unscathed. Maher had seen several that day. Even if helping survivors seems like a life-affirming release, it does not alleviate the burden, the imprint, of the face of death. I know he has been branded forever now and there is not anything that can be done about it. My forever beloved Marwan worked collecting the bodies of victims in Sabra and Shatila after the massacre. Seeing the face of death was so overwhelming he left the country shortly thereafter. He moved to London and did not return to Lebanon for decades. You can still feel the brand of that mass grave in the lining of the timbre of his voice, in the lining to his gaze, a mute inconsolable sorrow.

I don't know if Maher will leave Lebanon, but I know he will return to Beirut markedly changed. For the time being the pull of the mass graves, of the people trapped in shelters, of bodies surging through rubble is too powerful—he wants to be near them. While the journalists he drove down with have left Tyre, he called last night to say he is tempted to stay. His voice came from a netherworld. Israel is now engaged in a massive ground offensive in the south.

This siege note took a couple of days to write. I could not find my words or sense of self after news of the massacre on Sunday.

Siege Note 13: August 5

Throughout the war, shelling, siege, grief, and sorrow, the bougainvilleas have been in full, glorious bloom. Their colors are dizzying in their intensity: purplish red, garish fuchsia, glaring white, and sometimes canary yellow. Most of the time, their bloom, which is the objective outcome of natural factors, namely, access to water, sun, heat, and even perhaps wind, has irritated me. Everything has changed in this time of war, except the full glorious bloom of the bougainvilleas. Other flowering trees have wilted or shied as their franchised gardeners or patrons no longer operate on the same schedule or have evacuated on the ships of the binationals. On the road to Saida [Sidon], I was struck, irked, even upset by the bougainvilleas' full bloom. From between their abundant leaves and flowers, vignettes of the ravages appeared. Bridges broken framed by the purple and fuchsia bloom of the bougainvilleas.

[. . .]

As we drove out of Beirut, the road was increasingly empty, but there were a few trucks carrying boxes of supplies labeled Médecins sans Frontières and Hammoud Hospital. The last available bit of Hariri's proud highway from Beirut to the south was the tunnel. I noted the graffiti *W R = Love forever* and smiled. There was something comforting about that marking. Or the absence of other markings.

We drove along the old road. It had not survived unscathed. There were small holes in its middle, and pieces of rocks, cement, and debris. From within the winding inner roads, the new highway was visible and the big craters from the shelling.

[...]

The coastal road would have been bustling at this time in the summer. Expats, binationals, students on summer vacation, tourists. This is the stretch of the south's most visited beaches. They range from the very fancy to the modest. At this time in the summer, the roads would have been busy with the town's handsome beach boys, tanned, strutting in swim trunks and a claim to some local fame. Everything was eerily deserted. Even army soldiers, posted in spots with seemingly no rhyme or reason, walked cautiously, expecting to duck for cover at any moment. Life all around had folded and packed. What remained was suspended in terror from the Israeli barges lounging with arrogance and too far from eyesight in the sea. The eye could not see them, but every muscle stretched stiff with anxiety under their watch. Life was at the mercy of the Israeli army's whims. They had shelled the entire coast repeatedly, as if only to satiate their cruelty, to assert their might.

We drove on the small roads inside Jiyyeh and inside Rmeileh and the small towns in between. We drove by closed homes, doors locked, windows shut, shutters sealed. The last gaze of their dwellers still lingering on the front porches, the gaze of a hesitant farewell that quickly ran a checklist to make sure all was safely tucked and hoped for the best, maybe even whispered a prayer or invoked God or Christ's clemency and then hurried into the car and sped away for a temporarily safer haven. Under the cruel watch of the Israeli warships, lounging with arrogance and too far from eyesight in the sea.

[...]

Maher's instructions were delivered during our abbreviated phone conversations when he was in Tyre. They were brief because he could not really say much, and I did not feel I could pressure him to say much either. I call them instructions for kicks, to pretend I was on some sort of a mission. Maher wanted me to collect stories and footage or images for his project. Abdel-Karim and Dalal, his wife, are his lifelong comrades. Abdel-Karim runs a center in Saida that provides training for people with disabilities so that they may integrate fully in the social economy of everyday life. They receive local funding as well as funding from Europe.

With the outbreak of the war, the center's life and role has been turned wholly upside down. Abdel-Karim and Dalal have themselves become displaced and Dalal, who has another job, has now become involved in the center's relief work. They now reside in Saida, in a house shared by several other families. Abdel-Karim and Dalal don't have any disabilities, but the wheelchair-bound vice president, who resides in Zrarieh, a village further south, had to be evacuated and relocated to Saida with his family.

In the space of a few days, the center's administration realized they had to set up an emergency plan. The center opened its fully equipped bathroom to all the women and children who needed to take a shower. The center's kitchen, also fully operational, offered meals to all those who needed them. Two large pots with stuffed eggplant and squash were cooking in tomato sauce when I visited. A ceaseless clothes collection drive was provisioning people with clean garb. One of their ateliers was transformed to a storage area for diapers, food rations, and medicines. The computer classroom was transformed to a sleep area, as was their exercise and recreation room.

Teams of volunteers were called and assigned tasks. By the time I visited they counted more than fifteen teams comprising four or five people each, some with disabilities, others not. Their emergency plan began with tending to their "own" people, namely the community of people with disabilities they knew. They visited them in their homes and made sure they had everything they needed. As streams of displaced people were guided to the municipality, volunteers from the center contacted the teams who were receiving families to inform them they had the know-how and expertise to handle people with all forms of disabilities and special needs and could be entrusted with their care. Two weeks into the war, the "census" according to the municipality's paperwork showed there were only 20 people with disabilities with special care. Abdel-Karim and Dalal were very skeptical. So Dalal assigned a team of volunteers that toured every single site where the displaced were resettled: schools, hospitals, public buildings. Wherever they went, they spread word that they would be able to answer the needs of the disabled. They found 250. They noted the needs of each and assigned volunteers to visit them every day and meet their needs. A simple example: bathrooms. Public and private schools are not outfitted for people with disabilities, so the center ordered special devices from a local carpentry shop to facilitate bathroom use (more than 20 of these devices were purchased from the center's budget).

People with physical and mental disabilities are severely marginalized in everyday life in Lebanon even under normal conditions. During war their marginalization becomes heart-wrenching. As people were evacuating under duress, in haste and panic, families were separated, the disabled were sometimes entrusted to the care of others more able or left behind. Their special needs were disregarded (wheelchairs, crutches, supplies of medication left behind, etc.)... Abdel-Karim was relaying horrific stories, and his voice became hoarse. He choked and repressed his tears as he told me the fatal ones: a woman had died because her vital doses of insulin were not administered and one of their volunteers died as he drove under shelling to rescue and evacuate three disabled persons left behind in the village of Qasmiyeh just above Tyre. The three were eventually brought into safety and they did not know someone had died on his way to their rescue.

I sat in the main office across from Abdel-Karim's small desk cluttered with paperwork and a large computer monitor. Dalal buzzed around us with missives and missions. The office was bustling with activity. It felt like the headquarters of a major operation. People walked in and out, reporting on their "missions," delivering things, taking things. The phone did not stop ringing and yet there was not a hint of tension, anywhere. It was the first time since the outbreak of this war that I found myself in a place where love was palpable. Love as in the spontaneous convivial filiation that binds a community overpowered by a dark circumstance.

Abdel-Karim ended every transaction or exchange with a joke or a very affectionate note. I was mesmerized by his ability to smile as often as he did. He is a tall, thin man, dark-skinned, handsome, finely chiseled features. He exuded so much tenderness and amiability that the fine angular chisel of his features melted to roundness. Dalal, on the other hand, is of short stature, but she exudes so much energy, you cannot fit her being in the size she actually occupies. She is fair-skinned, with colored eyes and a killer laugh. She is a straight-to-the-point, no-bullshit gal, who cannot sit down for more than fifteen minutes. Theirs is a great love story, but that's a whole other story.

They are both former fighters from the Communist Party who retired from the front decades ago. In the political landscape of power-wrangling in Saida, they are caught in the stampede of competition between the two "ruling" poles of Saida: the Hariri family and the Saad family. Sadly— actually the right epithet ought to be "sinisterly" but I don't know if that exists in the Queen's English—relief for the displaced (in all its aspects) has been severely politicized. Abdel-Karim's gentle disposition turned to unforgiving rancor when he assured me that once the war is over, he will not let anyone get away with the corruption, the thievery, and the banditry he has witnessed. To the best of his abilities he was compiling a daily log (too brief to become a journal) precisely to make sure he did not forget the crimes he was seeing. "This is our political class," he said, "when it's time to do politics, they do emergency relief, and when it's time to do emergency relief, they do politics." Dalal had not shied from fighting in public with officials who withheld medicines for people she knew needed them badly. She has resorted to every imaginable stratagem: She faked her voice and affiliation to secure beds for badly injured people in private hospitals that only open their doors to the wealthy and the well connected (eight cases that I went to visit). They found her out after the eighth case. She caused a minor uproar in the press during an interview on Al-Jazeera and revealed a corruption scheme regarding one of the medicines needed for people with mental disabilities. Abdel-Karim and Dalal both exploded in laughter as they recounted her exploits. (A couple of days prior to my visit, the Ministry of Health caught one of their employees stealing medicines and selling them to pharmacies in Beirut. The minister of health had made a big brouhaha about the "scandal" to show he was in control of the situation.)

A young woman stepped into the office, shyly. She needed to use the phone. She asked Abdel-Karim for permission. She called her family, who had relocated to some other town. She reminded me of the people I see lining up at public payphones in Beirut. In their gait you can read the long list of questions they are burning to ask. She spoke hurriedly, so as not to distract the office's phone line for too long. Her conversation was like a telegraphic ledger of who's where and how they were doing. She reported her information and information was reported back to her. She hung up, smiled from within a veil of anxiety and thanked Abdel-Karim, shyly. He gave her a compliment about her dress. She giggled a little but walked out hunched from the weight of the information freshly delivered to her, her mind processing facts, recalling each one, nailing each one so none would slip her memory.

The center was now also helping people find their kin. They gave shelter to people who were sleeping on the street, totally stranded. Among these, a Sri Lankan woman who worked as a housemaid and whom the household that employed her had left behind.

I was ready to receive instructions from Abdel-Karim and mostly Dalal (she had more of a bent for instructions) as to where to go. Ziad called. He was ready to meet me. I gave him directions to the center and went down to the street to fetch him. Ziad is in his twenties and walks with a slight enough strut that you know his street smarts still run deeper than his engagement with video art. He is tall, charming, ties his hair in a ponytail, wears a goatee, and has an unforgettable, fatal, killer smile. And smiles almost as often as Abdel-Karim. He came accompanied by a friend of his, Hussein. A Pentax dangled from Ziad's neck and Hussein carried the video camera.

[...]

The Dar es-Salam building stood on a hill overlooking old Saida and the fort. There was a soft gentle breeze and all was quieter up on that hill. We went through the charade of introductions, and finally, it was Ziad's family name (his father) and my own (my father) that allowed us entry. We requested to visit only those new patients who had come as a result of the war, those with "special needs."

We were guided by one of the administrators in charge of the institution. The floor was inundated with natural light. Even the corridor was well lit. The rooms were spacious and fit with four beds. The floor was not at full capacity.

In the first room, Amal and her two brothers. The brothers are not able to walk, she has only a slight physical disability but stayed with them. A round soft face, amiable, gorgeous black eyes. When we walked in she was adjusting her coif. One of her brothers leaned by the window that gave onto the garden, and the other lay on the bed, not engaged with us. Their family was relocated to a school and came to visit them. They had been at the hospital for eleven days.

In the next room lay a man on a bed with severe mental and physical disabilities. "He was packed in the trunk of a car," the administrator said, "and driven from Aitaroun (now practically destroyed) to Saida. His brother drove him here, left Mahmoud, his son, to take care of his uncle, and drove with the rest of the family somewhere else." Mahmoud was a fifteen-year-old boy who seemed a little too short for fifteen in my opinion. He had a bright, bright, radiant, gorgeous face. Wide hazel eyes. Mahmoud struck Ziad's heart. He walked up close to him. "I wanted to take care of my uncle," replied Mahmoud to someone's question. That implied changing diapers, feeding and bathing, explained the administrator. My heart dropped to my knees with sorrow. Mahmoud and his uncle had been there for eleven days. When his father dropped him off with his uncle, Mahmoud had no idea where his family would end up. He was without news for days. Mahmoud thought they would stay in one of the schools in Saida. Somebody reported seeing them in one of the schools, but it turned out to be false news. His father called one day from Syria. Unfortunately, Mahmoud had gone to the mosque to pray. One of the patients in the neighboring room answered the phone call and took down the information. Mahmoud was deeply saddened to have missed the call.

The administrator praised him a lot and the extent to which his spirits were positive, but reported catching the boy standing by the window looking sorrowful and mournful into the horizon.

In the next room, there were two men who had both sustained serious injuries and were recovering at Dar es-Salam to alleviate pressure on the hospitals. The first man did not speak. At least not when we were there. He is from Aynata (the village received a pretty dramatic pounding). He had two injuries in his legs. He asked the administrator for crutches. In the second bed lay an elderly man with an injury to his leg as well. He had been rescued from the same village by the Red Cross, and driven to Tyre, from where he was transferred to Labib Hospital in Saida, and from there to Dar es-Salam. He was in good spirits. His family was relocated to a school next door.

In the next room, lay two women. One was of an advanced age. Her son sat next to her and was caring for her. Across from her was an elderly woman with physical disabilities who could not walk. She was from Abbasiyyeh. She had been left behind. The mayor of that village had dropped her off and left. She did not speak. No one knew anything about her. She carried no identity papers. She lay in bed and stared into the garden. Her gaze was not unfocused. In fact it was intent. I have rarely seen such sharp, pure, focused sorrow. We moved around her room and she did not budge. The hospital administrator greeted her, to no reply.

In the next room four elderly women were lodged. One, from Zrarieh, was a diabetic on dialysis, whose legs were amputated. She had piercing green eyes. Ziad, with his killer smile, got the old ladies to talk. He walked in and asked each one where they were from. He asked the old lady from Zrarieh if she knew the Kojok family. She said she was born a Kojok. "I recognized the green eyes," he replied knowingly. Her neighbor was from Adloun. She needed cataract surgery and had been there for 20 days. One of the women nudged me to ask, and so I found out that she was from Srifa. "You will hear about the massacre of Srifa, you will hear," she said to me. She had driven with her family to Tyre, then to Saida, but her mother, who shared the room with the other elderly ladies, had walked a week later from Srifa. "Walked for three days, without respite," she kept repeating. "An old lady like me, walking for three days. We saw death and we could do nothing but walk."

[...]

As they drove me back to meet Ahmad, Ziad was playful again: "The crucial question in this war is, where are the women of Saida? How could they have disappeared?" Hussein replied that they all moved to Broumana [in the mountains] or evacuated with the foreigners. "Damn our luck, all the women of Saida are binationals!" "They're all gone? There must be some left, we must find them," Hussein chuckled.

Ahmad and I drove back the same way. I looked forward to the fragrance of orange blossoms and could forgive the bougainvilleas their full glorious bloom. My heart had never felt as heavy. There was a lot to hang on to. I mean for hope or strength or whatever it is that keeps people going. But there was so much wretchedness.

The sorrows I have seen.

10. A LETTER TO OUR COMRADES IN THE DEMOCRATIC LEFT MOVEMENT

Elias Khoury and Ziad Majed

Novelist Elias Khoury and political writer Ziad Majed issued this letter to their comrades in the Democratic Left Movement. The DLM played an important role in organizing the "independence uprising" in the spring of 2005, following the assassination of Lebanese Prime Minister Rafiq Hariri. The uprising culminated with the one-million-strong march and the eventual departure of Syrian forces from Lebanon. The broader movement is referred to as the March 14 coalition, which since its inception has been at odds with Hizballah. As the war raged, Khoury and Majed issued a call (published in the Lebanese press on Sunday, 30 July 2006) urging national unity against the Israeli invasion. The letter was translated by Iraqi poet and writer Sinan Antoon and initially published in the Middle East Report *(Fall 2006).*

For more than two weeks now, our country has been subjected to a ferocious Israeli war, for which the United States is providing the cover. Using an operation carried out by Hizballah as a pretext, Israel is inflicting its crimes against Lebanese civilians and infrastructure in violence whose scale shows the depth of Zionist antipathy for Lebanon and its people.

The war on Lebanon follows weeks of open war waged against the Gaza Strip, which commenced before the operation that captured the Israeli soldier there. All of this takes place amid Israeli and US calls for uprooting "extremism" and establishing a "new Middle East."

Our national, ethical, and leftist responsibilities compel us to reiterate some first principles, which some comrades, friends, and allies have, alas, forgotten.

We have disagreed with Hizballah and still do—over ideas, politics, and regional alliances.

We disagreed with its unilateral decisions about war and peace in Lebanon, when to escalate the battle with the Israeli enemy and when to de-escalate it.

We have disagreed with Hizballah and still do—over its relationship with the oppressive regime in Syria, a regime whose hegemony over Lebanon we helped to resist, and then defeat, in Beirut's spring.

We have disagreed with Hizballah and other sectarian movements and still do— —over how to carry out the project of building a democratic, secular state of social justice and Arab renaissance.

But we were never neutral vis-à-vis the battle with the Israeli enemy and we never relinquished our commitment to the demands of that struggle, as determined by Lebanon's interests and capabilities.

It pains us to hear what is said nowadays among some of our comrades and friends in the March 14 forces: that Lebanon has nothing to do with the ongoing war; that Hizballah is solely responsible for its continuation; that one should avoid discussing the US role in providing cover for the aggression and allowing it to continue; that one should hesitate in demanding an immediate cease-fire or link the cease-fire to demands internal to Lebanese politics—the very demands that some forces had ceased calling for since the 2005 elections, when we warned against overlooking the importance of building a new state that transcends sect and has sovereignty over all its territory; that Lebanon is not involved in regional political axes, on the one hand, but on the other hand adopting a discourse identical to that of the Saudi–Egyptian–Jordanian axis—the wrong choice, in our view, for confronting the Syrian–Iranian axis.

All this pain us, as it pains many Lebanese who confronted Syrian hegemony in Lebanon in years past and fought to build a society that will learn from its mistakes, from the experiences of sectarian confrontation, from the history of betting on external patrons.

Accordingly, we are here compelled to state the following:

The national priority today is to confront Israeli aggression against our country and people. When the homeland is under attack, citizens must rise to its defense and resist occupation through various means. We must recall that Hizballah, despite our deep and fundamental disagreement with it, is made up of Lebanese citizens who are part of our society and are resisting the enemy with competence and valor in the south of our country. They deserve our full support and respect.

We should reject the suppression of debate about the reasons for the status quo and the preconditions for a way out, as servile and oppressive Arab regimes do, and instead acknowledge disagreement as a sign of vibrancy and diversity in our society. Such debate does not and should not preclude making the demand for an unconditional halt to this savage aggression a national priority.

The Lebanese government must be the sole party delegated to negotiate internationally in order to find a solution that preserves Lebanon, safeguards its sovereignty and protects those who engage in resistance within Lebanon.

All forms of popular action in Lebanon and the Lebanese diaspora must be organized to demand an end to the aggression, support its victims, and stress the importance of embracing the displaced, as is now taking place in Beirut, the mountains, and all regions.

We stress that building a modern state requires abandoning sectarian calculations and refashioning a Lebanese and Arab identity that is consonant with liberation and progress, according to Lebanese interests defined by the Lebanese people alone, free from the influence of retrograde and totalitarian regimes.

There will be no peace or stability in the region as long as Israel continues its policies of aggression in Palestine, and as long as Arab lands are occupied with the aid of US backing and Arab impotence—the product of decades of regimes of militarism, oppression, and oil.

An Arab, democratic, sovereign, and independent Lebanon cannot be a battleground for outsiders, of course, but neither can it be an island, isolated from the causes of our region and the battles for freedom, progress, development, and justice being fought therein.

11. MEDITATIONS UPON DESTRUCTION
Elias Khoury

This essay was originally published in Arabic, in Al-Quds Al-Arabi *(London) on September 19, 2006. It is translated by Michael Scott.*

It is devastation. It is a pure devastation that is like nothing you have ever seen—apart from devastation. Ruins stretching to the horizon, challenging the sky. Stars trembling, and so also are people's eyes. Everything is tremulous and shimmering, everything is in suspension.

Destruction alone propels you beyond time and place, and sketches the faintest of outlines for a recollection, a memory of scattered particulate floating into oblivion.

Only destruction transforms imagination into allusion and simile, rudely thrusting you into a tent woven of illusory threads, to live in.

Destruction, rubble, and dust. Throughout 33 days we were here listening to the sounds of missiles raining down on the Dahiyeh, our city's southern suburbs. We would light candles in the darkness of Lebanon, and become all ears, to pick out the agonies of the collapsing edifices. We would see with the eyes of darkness itself and smell the scent of death, a rage somehow akin to sadness gushing through our arteries.

And when the electricity would arrive, like a thief with no prior appointment, we would rush to the TV sets to see what we have already heard, and choke amid the cries of the victims for help and amid the photos of children covered with the sand of death and the ashes of the end.

The darkness brings us back to the voices and sounds. We see nothing save the shudders of the light dying in the candles, and we shiver with the shivering of our homes. Our homes have become tiny ships bandied about by the waves of darkness and distantly beckoning cries for help. Who is seeking the help of whom? There is no one to help, no deliverer from distress. Who listens to whom? There is no sound but the crashing of blood through the artery walls, and the roar of the heart rising up to the temples and pounding.

Thirty-three days longer than an eternity in which we lost everything, and forgot the voices of friends who had moved away. We lived the present as if it were a memory. For in the moments of darkness nothing can convince you that you are still alive, apart from the fact that you can remember. Memory is the sign of life, for it challenges death and overwhelms imagination. This is why you travel in your memory to secret places where no foot has ever trod, other than your own. Then, with the first light of dawn, you see the city covered with something like fog. And you feel a wild, untamed yearning for this city spreading through your pores, and you scream at the invaders to move on and leave this land alone. This land now transformed into tombs.

On the 34th day at last you go on down to rediscover the suburbs and the villages of the south, and you see just how deceptive and lying the photographs have been. A picture can only convey the surface of things. There is no meaning to destruction without the experience of the sound of feet crunching on top of the rubble. There is no meaning to the rubble without the stench of gunpowder blending with the smells of decaying corpses, cement, and iron. And there is no meaning to the smell without the feeling that everything is sand, sand becoming more sand.

Those who saw the images of Lebanese devastation on their TV screens, in the Arab world, and in the rest of the world, and then cried or cursed or swore or became upset—really they did not see anything at all. Believe me, my friends, you are living in the delusion that you have seen, but you have not seen. The eye alone does not see—despite the fact that the eye is the torch of the body, as the prophets proclaimed. Human beings see with all of their limbs, organs, and senses. With all of these we confront the unknown, and when the unknown comes to us we become part of it.

I saw, though, and I became part of this horizon covered in ruin. In the Dahiyeh, I saw people wandering about looking for their places. Even more difficult to endure than losing one's home is losing the capacity to identify the road to one's home. I saw people's eyes darting from side to side, searching for a familiar place in the rubble. These were people who had lost any recognition of the features of the streets and the places they knew, people who were no longer able to determine where their home might have been, or even where the road to it might be.

It was a mix of terror and bewilderment. The place had simply abandoned the people, and it had become featureless. Without any signs or indications to go by, memory seemed about to disintegrate as well. At this moment I recalled Palestine. Harder to bear than the Israeli occupation and suffering eviction from one's home has been the aggression against the place, and the modification of its features through demolition.

The souls of the dead flee to their places and spread their shadows over the homes, their perfume mingling with the scent of flowers in the meadows. What would the souls of the dead say today, wandering amid the ruins? Do the Israelis over there in Palestine, or those who are right here, in Lebanon, know that they have been unable to win more than the curses of the dead?

But Palestine only comes to light in southern Lebanon: the ruin of the Lebanese Galilee is embraced by the ruin of the Palestinian Galilee. These are the slopes of the soul that lead you to God. In the south I discovered the fields of lemon trees that stretch from Saida to the horizon's end, and I breathed the perfume of the orange blossom, the flower that is in its transformation like nothing so much as the silkworm. The silkworm fashions its silk before it becomes a moth. But here the white moth that spreads out on the branches of the trees transforms itself into a fruit, the fruit that gave its name to the "orange" in European languages. And from the perfume of the *naranj* we come to the boisterous guffaw of history that you hear reverberating in the Beaufort crusader castle.[1]

Today nothing remains of those *franj* crusaders apart from their fortress, which has become the practically invincible fortification of the resistance. Just as we wrote our graffiti on its walls in the seventies, so they write on them today. But the dogged irony of history does not appear quite so clearly here as it does in the destroyed villages beyond the fortress. In Bint Jbeil, Aita al-Shaab, Siddiquine, and Aitaroun—there you see how closely the destruction and devastation coheres and binds with the will to resist and with the will to remain steadfast on one's land. You can see how the trembling, shimmering pulverized dust hanging in the air becomes a voice that immerses itself in silence, and then produces it. There, the sloping hills stretch out and carry you to a horizon that seems to be embracing the souls of the dead, and you feel that you have been cast into an endlessly circular path.

The roads were full of rubble, devoid of features. I was like someone who could hear the moaning of the stones. I see people setting up their tents on top of the destroyed houses. I discovered the way in which the graveyards were torn up and the remnants of the dead were burned. As if the dead were dying anew, so that they could go out to welcome the victims who were entombed in their homes.

A wizened woman, whose name I don't know, sits alone in a tent erected upon the rubble of her home. She holds in her hand a key, and she talks to it—or so it seemed to me. I approached her, to ask her about the key, but words betrayed me. She looked at me and told me it was the key to the house.

"The photographs are gone, the door is gone, everything is gone. But the key is still with me."

I remembered a displaced woman from Tel Zaatar,[2] who only carried with her one small photo of her martyred son. "This is all that I have left," she said, adding, "we have to learn how to protect the photographs." Then she pulled from her abaya a rusty key and said that she had been able to smuggle the key to her house from her village in Galilee.

"The key is more important than the photographs," she said.

A woman from Aitaroun carries a key and returns to her village, smiling to her key and looking toward the Palestinian Galilee, where destruction still awaits the keys.

Notes

1 "Of the dozen-odd Crusader castles in Lebanon none can compare in size, scenic grandeur, or close connection with Lebanese history down to modern times, with isolated Beaufort, perched on its cliff a thousand feet above the rushing Litani River...." From stronghold.heavengames.com/history/cw/cw64—Ed.

2 Palestinian refugee camp northeast of Beirut destroyed by Lebanese Christian militiamen following a three-month siege that culminated in a notorious massacre of 2,000 or more Palestinians, on August 12, 1976, a major milestone in the initial "Two-Year War" at the outset of the sixteen-year Lebanese civil war—Ed.

12. WE WILL NEVER FORGET
Hanady Salman

A war, they decided to call it. For Zahra Sh'ayto it was the summer that she and her family were buried alive under the rubble of their house in Tiri.

For Fatima Ghadboun it was the summer when her husband Ali was killed on the road from Tyre to Qana in a van loaded with bread.

Label it as you wish—frame it, too. It will never be what you decide to call it. It will only be what they know it was. *They* are the ones who lived through all of it, barely.

It's a different world, the one that unfolds south of the Litani River. A simple one. A clear one.

Between the river and the border they live. Between the river and the border they often get killed. Too often. Between the border and the river, or on the road leading there.

The border is on one side and the olive trees are on the other. The olive trees they burned and those that are still green. The tobacco plants are scattered, yellow as they went dry while their owners were away at harvest time.

What do you call these villages? The borderline villages? The villages south of the Litani River? How many have visited them after what happened between mid-July and mid-August 2006? This is a land of fire and rubble.

Silence prevails here. A deep, sad silence. A silence that is interrupted once in a while by the noise of someone rushing in to build back what was destroyed.

This land is ours, the noise says, this our home, it always has been and it will always be.

The remains of the houses pile up on what was once a life; some pile up on the remains of their owners.

If you come from Tyre, with the border to your right, devastated villages lie to your left—rubble, burned trees, damaged seasons, and dusty roads. On the other side of the border, nice brick houses, green and fruity trees, and paved roads link the colonies one to the other.

Pain. Pain is scattered everywhere. A deep pain, unspoken most of the time; only sometimes it turns into loud, angry words. Even the villages that became "famous" due to the atrocities they witnessed in the summer of the year 2006 are almost totally abandoned today. The disaster happened, photos were shot, declarations of regret issued, relief efforts requested, aid delivered to Beirut (and "mysteriously" disappeared), and that was it. End of story.

Or perhaps another story started: the "blame it on the victim" story.

This is a land of fire and rubble. A land left to its own destiny, surrounded on the south by the hills of Palestine and surrounded by poverty and neglect from all sides.

People rush toward visitors, drag them to their houses, or what's left of them. "Come and take photos here." "Please come to our house after you finish the Hajj's, we'll be waiting for you." They are soon disappointed, once they discover that those visitors are mere reporters, and not relief agency employees. It is always the same disappointment, quickly followed by a different kind of excitement: "Good, actually no one spoke about us or wrote about our town, despite all what we've been through."

And then, everybody starts talking at the same time. Each telling his or her own story. They talk as if they were silent for ages and have finally found someone who will listen. Everyone talks as though they are speaking to themselves, yet aware of the presence of a witness who gives an added value to each story. I can finally share with someone the horrifying story that happened to *me*.

From the gardens of their houses, from the rooms inside, they gather and keep the remains of bullets, rockets, and shrapnel. Do they keep them to prove that "it" really happened or do they keep them so they won't forget?

Some were killed here because they did not have the money to leave. Those who left their kids in cellars under the fire did not even have a donkey to use. Some were killed because there are no decent hospitals in the whole region. There are no adequate health organizations in the towns scattered on the fire line since 1948.

What kind of country is it that lets its children get murdered on the roads or under the rubble of shelters because their parents cannot afford to move them to a safer place? What kind of country keeps electing the same political leaders who let this happen, keeping themselves busy splitting the aid among themselves and throwing the blame in each others' faces? Who of them visits the south? Who knows what is happening there? Who visits the hospitals? Who hears what the people have to say? Who asks them to tell their stories?

This was a land for life. It is a land for life.

Between the ruins some things are still the way they were left on July 12, 2006: laundry hanging in the backyards, chairs scattered on the porches where people like to have coffee by sunset, a notebook open on a table in a garden… all is still the way it was, except that it's all deserted now.

At Fatima Khalil's house in Blida, the bag used to turn yogurt into *labneh* is still hanging on the clothesline. It stayed there long after the rockets hit the shelter's ceiling, where the family was hiding. They were all injured. The father lost both his legs. The line of blood stretches from the shelter through the little garden to the bathroom. In the bathroom, small pink eyeglasses were left behind on the shelf beneath the mirror. Blood is in the kitchen. Blood is everywhere around and inside the house. Two months after the aggression, and no one has wiped it up yet. The family members made it to a hospital in Beirut and they were taken from there to the United Arab Emirates for further treatment. Every corner of the house tells a small detail of the life that used to be. That life is gone forever now, and the yogurt bag is still hanging on the clothesline.

In the small yards of the houses people spread thyme, sumac, and sesame under the sun. Life goes on and people prepare winter provisions. On burned fields, people work their crops, and in destroyed houses, the tobacco leaves hang neatly to dry despite everything.

The people of the ruined and half-ruined houses welcome visitors with warmth and hugs. Some offer glasses of water and feel offended if you don't drink it: it's all they have to offer. They offer you bottled mineral water; the wells in their gardens were polluted by the Israelis.

Most houses are covered by jasmine and bougainvillea. Colorful butterflies spring out of the ruins. This is a land for life, the flowers, the colors, the butterflies say; this is a land for life despite the pain, oppression, and destruction. This is a land for life, says the warmth of love.

This is a land where, despite the long years of isolation during the Israeli occupation, the people never forgot who they were, never stopped being who they are. After liberation in the year 2000, these villagers would host the summer visitors and tourists three months a year, then they'd go back to being who they are: hardworking farmers who live on their land, who live thanks to their land.

In villages where everyone has left except for the elderly, you have to raise your voice when you speak to them so they can hear you. The 34 days of heavy shelling harmed their ears. And if you happen to meet a woman who is over 70, don't hesitate to hug her: no one has hugged her in a while. She will tell you her story; you don't even need to ask. She will recite it again and again, happy that she has an audience. She won't shed a tear until you hug her. Her story remains a simple tale until you hug her: hugging her means that you can see her, feel and share with her; hugging her means that she exists for real.

In those villages, some can tell their incredible stories in ten minutes. An old lady in Mhaibeb stood by the wall and said: "I was in the house with my son. We had no water, no food, and no electricity. My son got injured. We left the house at night under the fire and bombing and we walked all the way to Mays al-Jabal. He was bleeding on the way and their air fighters were in the sky. We made it to Mays and they took him to the hospital and I stayed in the mosque. Later, they moved us to Jdeidet Marjeyoun, then to the army barrack, then the Israelis bombed our convoy heading to western Beqaa." That's it. The story's over. Then what? "Nothing, this is the story, but today, who will fix my house?"

Stories are similar in each village. Some families managed to reach Beirut, others stayed, survived hunger, thirst, and fear. Some families knew about their relatives' injuries from the media and others are still looking for a grandfather or a grandmother who refused to leave the village.

In Khiyam they talk about the martyr Hajj Hassan Akar, who refused to leave his house when his son came to fetch him all the way from Beirut under fire. He held on to his front door and would not let go. Three weeks after the bombing had stopped, his body was still under the rubble of his house.

In Mhaibeb they keep telling the story of Khadija Ghenwi. When her son got killed, this 90-year-old woman left her house and went to seek help from her neighbors. The Israeli snipers killed her on the way and burned her corpse. Then they placed the helmet of a resistance fighter over her remains, so people would think they had killed a fighter. When the war stopped, the neighbors found a tiny piece of her walking stick left unburned. That was all what remained of her—a tiny piece of a walking stick.

Families sit on their balconies facing the border and the enemy's military bases, which are only a few steps away. Between laughter and the clink of coffee cups, you can hear them shout, *Ahlan, tfaddal* [hello, come in please], every time a car passes by. Life is not back to normal yet, not quite.

"Aren't you afraid to stay here, so close to them?"

Yes, they are frightened, they say, but this is their home, their land, their shelter, and their shield.

What they are really afraid of is the night.

"The night is terrible, really scary."

"Yes, we won this war—the boys pushed them out and forced them to leave, humiliated. They are cowards, they avoid confrontation and fear it... But they have tanks and air fighters; hadn't been for the planes... we can never trust them."

Trust. Who would know more than the people who live south of the Litani River? If you ask the elderly about the last war they will start the story from 1948: "We witnessed many wars, but none was similar to what happened this year. They are killing children, women, and civilians. They are chasing them on the roads, in their vaults, they are burning our trees. Fighters are supposed to have ethics too. No other war was similar, not the war of seven (1993) nor the war of sixteen (1996)..." This is how they label the wars: by how many days each lasted.

What people witnessed here during the war is similar to the stories one could only read in novels. Novels from a different time and place. Here, in the year 2006, people got hungry and could not feed their newborns. Here, they got thirsty a few steps away from their wells; here, they were murdered, barefoot in their pajamas. Here, families surveyed the rubble, not knowing who had survived and who had been killed. Here, family members walked a distance of three to four villages under fire, looking for safety. Here is a life similar to no other. Here is a land for life.

In each village, people tell about the ones who helped the survivors during the 34 days. No names were given; charity implies discretion.

The relations between the resistance fighters and the people in the villages are similar to the novels written by leftists in the 1970s. The people know everything: what has really happened, how it happened, and why. They know what they should say and what they should keep quiet. Some women stayed in the villages only to cook for the fighters. Others stayed to finish reading the Qur'an for the boys. Some old men used to stay up late at night to pray for them.

They talk about "the boys" as if they were their own sons. They tell how the boys stopped the enemies from invading the villages: "Three warriors in a house in Hula trapped the Israelis and killed eighteen of them. The Israelis said that only five were killed, but after the battle, two helicopters came to move the casualties. Isn't one helicopter enough to carry five bodies?" In Mays, the boys used to visit the families who stayed. "They'd knock on the doors around 11:30 or midnight to ask us if we needed anything. They'd bring us water and some food and they'd leave." In other villages, the fighters would ask the families to leave if they felt that the battles were getting heavy, and they'd provide someone to safely get them to another village. They'd help injured civilians if they could. Some of them even cried while they were bidding the villagers goodbye.

"The fighters were not from our town," the elderly would say with barely hidden smiles. "We didn't know them. Some of them visited us to ask for forgiveness for using our house while we were away, and some came to pay the price of whatever provisions they had "borrowed" from our shops. They wrote what they took on a piece of paper, estimated their price and paid everyone back!"

Some people laugh while they're telling their stories: they recall how and where they hid, they repeat children's sentences and laugh. They also shed tears. "What can we do?" they add after almost every sentence.

It is a mixture of pride and defeat. Both pride and defeat show in people's eyes and hearts. Pride for what has been accomplished and defeat because the other Lebanese don't admit the accomplishment. As if they alone were Israel's enemies, as if they had called for what had happened to them.

They feel lonely, estranged from the rest of the nation, which treats them as though they are victims of a natural disaster. They have become more Shiites than any time before—Shiites, not citizens. A woman in Khiyam shouts, "I want to say to the rest of the country that we Shiites are not terrorists." When a young man, who seems to be from Hizballah, looks at her with reproach, she stops and disappears.

Those people talk a lot about the hospitality they witnessed in other villages. They talk about how they met people from other religions and got the chance to know them closely. They have become friends and kept in touch. What country is it, where people thank each other for standing by each other? What country is it, where its citizens get to know each other only through disasters?

The southerners say that have learned a lot from this war: they know now that shelters are not useful, since there are rockets that can destroy them. They learned that hiding in one place should be avoided since it might only mean a massacre. They are not expecting much from the government: "In 1996, they came and gave each destroyed house a number and said they'd be back to rebuild it. We are still waiting for them."

The southerners are poor and they are used to suffering. But their land is a land for life. They rebuilt their lives every time, over and over again, ever since 1948. They gather the scattered bits of their lives: the house, the yard, the garden, the shops, the provisions, the olives, the tobacco, the figs, the wheat, everything that colors life and gives it a name. They remove the rubble and go back to their lives. "What can we do?" It is their destiny, it seems. It is the same destiny of the poor people of the rest of world—abandonment. They are left to their fates, and they are used to managing on their own. Hizballah? It's a part of them. It is them. They made it so to take care of what the others would not.

"On those hills, the enemy was defeated." "Mays the town of martyrs." "Welcome to Hula, the land of liberation, the village of the 142 martyrs." Land of liberation. Triangle of victory. Square of victory. Town of martyrs.

That is how the villages in the south decorate their streets. The villages are far from the capital and its usual business. Beirut collected itself fairly quickly and got back to "normal," leaving behind, far behind, the lives and deaths in the villages south of the Litani River.

The story is not over yet. The wounds are not healed, the martyrs are not all buried. The families are not all back yet. And Israel is still there, surrounding the villages like a grip around the neck.

We will never forget. We will never forgive.

13. NO INNOCENT VICTIMS:
POSTWAR ACTIVISM & LEBANON'S CIVIL SOCIETY
Kirsten Scheid

Thursday, July 13, 2006

This morning we hear of mobilizations by the Israelis. We drive down to Beirut at 6AM. Micheline calls to say she won't come to the publishing house today because she wants to go Saida [Sidon] to get her parents, whom she hasn't been able to call. Samah argues that is silly, because Saida isn't being targeted but roads are, and the stupidest thing would be to try to go south now. He adds that he has come down from Faraya only to work with her on the magazine. We learn from her that Israel has hit the airport runways and the bridge of Damour. It won't be safe to go to Beiteddine for the concerts, Samah warns. I say I could go from the back route, through Ain Zhalta. Samah is annoyed. He thinks I shouldn't go to AUB [the American University of Beirut] this morning, but I think he is overreacting. Hasn't he just told Micheline that throughout the whole civil war people continued their daily business as usual?

Saturday, July 15

All day long the girls watch TV, the terrible sickness of apartment life. We finally drag them out to take a walk on Faraya's natural bridge, joking that this is probably the only bridge in Lebanon not threatened by bombing. Afterward we go to dinner at Chez Shaker. The tabbouleh *is fine, the* kibbeh nayye *not so good, the television on—smoke plumes, rubble, sirens.*

Thursday, July 27

I walk with Naye to Bashir's for local gelato-style ice cream. There the man serving asks me, "Why haven't you left?" That is his way of greeting me! I reply that my home is here. Then he asks me an absurd question, "Shou akhathti [What did you take]?" I am thrown off-guard. If I hadn't already ordered the ice cream, I would have thought he meant flavors, but he meant what kind of husband, Christian or Muslim. I should have simply said, "Lebanese," but I want to have a conversation, so I say, "Well, he's not interested in such things and doesn't consider himself this or that, but socially he's considered a Muslim." The man "humphs," as if that solves an enigma for him. I ask him if he is going to leave. He says no, he can't because his only citizenship is Lebanese, but if he had another, he would go so fast.

Then he rather smugly mentions that here is safe anyway. I blurt, "You never know, America is so eager to have this bombing go on, and it's sending more bombs everyday, the Israelis may just have to use them everywhere." Then I ask how much our bill is, pay, and usher Naye out. I guess I had wanted to be a polite woman-who-married-a-Muslim, just to break his stereotype. In the end however, I am very unhappy because he successfully cornered me in his sectarian game.

One of the most notable things about the Israeli assault on Lebanon during the summer of 2006 was how it immediately highlighted the stark contrasts in Lebanese society. While people whom I was later to meet in villages like Zibqin were crushed by concrete as they sought secure sites, people whom I had planned on summering with were comfortably ensconced in their rental chalets and smug sectarian status as non-targets, innocents, viewing the war, via aerial transmitters, as little more than a continuation of the World Cup matches. Indeed, the Israelis seem deliberately to have used this social schism to wage their aggression, for they bombed first villages only kilometers over the southern border, then escape routes, including the coastal highway, major bridges, and Beirut's international airport. The effect was split-second panic: every person in Lebanon had to map the country into "safe" and "not safe" zones and grapple with the decision to make a move toward "safe" now or to accept being trapped. People became defined by their home address: targets in some zones, not targets in others only half a kilometer away. People with whom we had interacted on a daily basis became categorically different from us, and impossible to reach.

Wednesday, July 19
While sending e-mails from my house, I get a text message from Samah that Faraya heard a bomb; Teeta could even see the flames. I text back to ask if they know what the target was. It's ridiculous how we try to make logic out of what's happening to us. We act like there is an Israeli plan to immobilize certain sectors of Lebanon's life, but at least on one level, the target is simply Lebanon, and the Israelis don't care if they are "off-target." They are even deliberately "off-target" and hitting civilians at times to make us all surrender support for Hizballah. For me it has the opposite effect: I become more convinced that the only thing that will protect us is if Israel recognizes our parity, in might, in will to live, in ability to hurt our aggressors.

Sunday, July 23

We decide to all go as a family to Beirut. We spend the day and in the afternoon we leave the way we came. Once we are past the port I feel safer, but I keep looking back. Sariya asks me why. I say to see if Beirut is still there. Very few cars are on the road. 15 minutes later we hear the Israelis have started bombing the Dahiyeh again.

I have feared being bombed for so long now that I realize I feel left out. I am strangely curious about the experience of being attacked and surviving. So far my whole experience of this war has been basically vicarious, and that makes me feel cheap. Not that I am running toward the south, but still, I am not proud not to be targeted.

Friday, July 28

LBC is broadcasting direct from Dubai TV a musical video-clip composed of pictures of Lebanese civilian victims of the past two weeks of Israeli aggression: buildings crumpled, roads disintegrated, toys scattered, men crying, mothers screaming, children lifeless. The music is Anouar Brahem. On the lower portion of the screen a number flashes to which one can send an SMS for donating "money to Lebanon." Following this clip comes a list and voice-over of who has given how much money. Move over Haifa and Nancy, for here is truly a perverse form of entertainment, combining consumption, expense, and the promise of being part of a solution: watch the poor victims, experience some scenes that make you squirm, buy relief, reach a happy ending. And here we are supposed to be so thankful that our role as victim-stars has been appreciated, and bought.

In this essay I analyze the position I came to occupy quite by chance as an anthropologist living in Lebanon and a citizen of that nation by marriage. During the Israeli assault, I had to write about my situation as a means for conveying to concerned family and friends what I was experiencing and as a means for coping with the directed chaos around me. After the war, I write anew, more analytically, as a means of understanding the chaotic directions by which I have come to participate and experience the role of civilian and citizen activist. I seek to offer the testimony of an ordinary person, a person who was not an explicit target, but not safe; not politically aligned, but not politically removed; not an institutionalized relief worker, but not willing to sit back and take the role of passive, frightened spectator. My technique in this essay will be to tack between an experiential account, extracted from my diary entries (presented in italics) that record the discovery of my role in the war, and an analytical account (presented in non-italicized font) of the academic discussion of activism and civil society in the Arab world. The purpose of combining these two forms of knowing the role of civilian participants in the events of July–August 2006 will be to highlight various Lebanese investments in the war, the sense of helplessness that overwhelmed non-combatants, and the sense of urgency that spurred many to find a way to be agents of their future rather than passive spectators, or rather, I would suggest, active victims. This is not a tale of civil society overcoming imposed conditions but of the willful engagement by some with models of citizenship to confront those conditions in ways that allow people to realize new (or old) definitions of civilian, citizen, and activist. During the war I became involved in civilian efforts to bring aid and support to people targeted by Israeli warplanes. Following the war, I helped found an organization we eventually called the Civil Resistance Campaign (CRC).

Friday, July 14

Tonight we turn on the air conditioning—amazing that the electricity has not been hit yet. But we keep our bathroom window open to be able to know what is going on. After packing the washed clothes and replying to the e-mails of friends and parents, we go to sleep. At 3:30AM whooshing sounds wake me up. Soon there is a loud rumbling. A bomb drops, but not near. The whooshing is loud and going in multiple directions at once. What will they hit next? Samah is awake, too, and soon I get a text message on my cellular from Teeta: "Are u awake?"

"U bet."

"Girls scared?"

"No, sleeping like dogs."

We trade news until I go to watch TV. I bring in the rug that is drying on the balcony. What else can I do to get ready? What does it mean to get ready for bunker-buster bombs?

My testimony is not meant to divert attention from the efforts of other groups and individuals, whose numbers ballooned during the war and immediately after; rather, I seek to emphasize, as the starting point for any understanding of civil activism in the region, that ordinary Lebanese civilians were actively involved in resisting Israeli aggression and undermining Israeli designs. We did not embrace the position of the tearful, supplicating paradigmatic victim. In this sense we acted in contradistinction to government authorities. We didn't know what we could do as unarmed parties to the resistance effort, but we wanted to find out by trying.

Monday, July 17
*The Bou Khalil grocery store in Faitroun is packed. The first thing I ask is if they are accepting credit cards. Yes, thank god. There are no grocery carts; I substitute for one with a plastic trash bin. There is no milk, no flour, no sugar, no chicken, few vegetables, and no newspapers. What are available are ridiculous frozen delicacies, Chinese and Mexican ingredients, and alcohol of any flavor, suddenly quite cheap. In line someone asks about Candia milk. "*Allah yirhamha*" [Rest in peace], says the cashier. "Aren't you listening to the news?" He informs us that the Candia milk factory was one of the first buildings destroyed in the Beqaa Valley.*

At 9PM I tell Sariya and Naye to get their pajamas on, teeth brushed, and bodies in bed within five minutes and I will read to them. I look forward to reading to them, because we can imagine whole other worlds, and feel intellectual doing it. Fifteen minutes later, Naye is picking at a cherry that is too mushy to eat. I shout at her to get her teeth brushed and get in bed. She scurries to comply. Five minutes later she's playing with one of the pool noodles that is in the hall because I'm too lazy to put it in the closet with the outdoor toys. I am infuriated. I must sound just like my father. "I told you to get ready for bed in five minutes and you're still dicking around," I roar. She indignantly asserts that she was ready and was just waiting for Sariya. Now I don't want to read, but I don't want not to read. What if they die tomorrow, and I remember that I was such a shit to them. Or I die, and all they remember is this nasty mother who cared more about rules than enjoying being together. I approach Naye and hold her chin to turn her face to me, "Why can't you..." She cuts me off with her cries, protesting that I am holding her harshly. I am sure I wasn't, but I can't explain why I am so upset by her behavior. I'm such a shitty mom. What can I do for them anyway?

Wednesday, July 19
Down to Beirut, to go to the bank, use the internet, do the laundry, just be there. I keep my purse hanging across my chest the whole time I am at home, for fear I will have to fly out of the house at any minute. I keep the TV on to be able to know where the Israelis are targeting, how close, hoping there will be warning before a bomb suddenly drops on me. It is hard to concentrate on tasks and figure out the

best way to do my work. Every few minutes I stop and tour the house to see what I need to take with me to Faraya. Now that I am actually here it is so hard to do triage: look at all these things I have surrounded myself with, is any one very important? More important than the others? The vase Maher gave us for our wedding? The plates I received one of each year for Christmas since I was born? The paintings by Rim Jundi, Julie Bou Farah, my dear friend Hala? Sariya and Naye's paintings? The abaya I gave to my grandmother before she died of cancer? Our photo albums? All our books? Twenty minutes pass and two trucks are hit in Ashrafieh. I grab the rest of the laundry, still wet from the dryer, stuff it in a bag, turn off the computer and hot water (having not yet showered), run down to the car, come back up to make sure I have done all I just did, and then back down, and leave Beirut.

Monday, July 24

More burials in Gaza today. How ironic—there they dared to elect democratically a government antagonistic to the US. Here we democratically elected a government favorable, very favorable, as in may-we-kiss-your-feet-favorable to the US government. And the result is the same: siege, blockade, bombing, massacres of civilians—whatever happens to be useful to the Israeli government of the minute.

Tuesday, July 25

I have started buying food the way people embrace long-lost friends. I saw a bag of Lavax [laundry detergent] on the shelf in Faraya, and I grab it to myself like a dear playmate from childhood. I don't really need detergent, but I buy it anyway, for fear that I will not see it again. I realize I am absurd.

Wednesday, July 25

The cheery morning news on LBC shows medical aid coming from the US. It is literally draped in US flags. And why don't they drape the Apaches and F16s and "smart" bombs with such flags?

The year prior to this Israeli assault, I began teaching anthropology at the American University of Beirut (AUB). One of the courses I taught examined Arab culture and society and included a component on civil society in the Arab world. As Sheila Carapico observed in her 1998 book on Yemen, the main motive of studies of civil society in the Arab world has been to prove or explain its categorical difference from the Western model of "a public civic realm, a zone between the state and private sectors... a layer or buffer between government and households."[1]

Strict adherence to this model has encouraged analysts to assume that civic activism cannot flourish in a culture where family is often said to define the individual politically, economically, and socially, and government is structured as an overarching patriarchy. Arab cultural values and social structures are thus analyzed by many as the elements that both retard development of civil society and prohibit any possibility for radical change.[2] Carapico quotes the eminent anthropologist of Arab society Ernest Gellner, who, when comparing the Soviet Union and the Arab-Islamic world in 1992, called upon his decades of studying Islam, tribalism, and state structures among Arabs to assert that whereas European peoples of the former communist regime "craved civil society," their Muslim former compatriots simply lacked that desire (4).

Countering this essentialist assumption of an Arab character, political scientists have recorded numerous examples of Arabs attempting civil activism only to be repressed by their governments (often Western-backed). And yet, contrary to showing a healthy degree of civic-spiritedness among Arabs, this is taken to prove that repression is part of Arab character and that Arab peoples lack either the will or capacity to confront it.[3] Or again, when Arabs align to form non-governmental organizations that would seem to operate in that realm between the private family and the domineering state, they are analyzed for their adherence to the model of the Western NGO. If they do not conform precisely, this is seen as a weakness caused by Arab culture; if they do conform, this is seen as the importation wholesale of non-Arab culture. While Arabs thus have been condemned as passive, anti-social, ahistorical, and intolerant of public freedom, little research, Carapico shows, has been done to provide grounded analyses of civic action by Arabs.

Saturday, July 15
We watch Hassan Nasrallah's speech on TV. Most astonishingly, he closes by saying, "As you listen to me one of the Israeli war-ships is burning off the coast and is on its way to sinking." Sure enough, the ship appears on screen in flames. It is funny because Omar has just called Samah and said he is sick of seeing that warship off the Corniche and wishes someone would do something about it. I'm not sure who calls whom, me or Teeta, but we are quite pleased with the news, really very impressed.

Funny how views change quickly. We are able to call Beirut and learn that while Samah's family is happy about the ship being hit, they immediately fear that the response from Israel is going to be tremendously destructive to Beirut. They have cleaned out the shelter already and taken down there the armchair for Samah's invalid father, Suheil. I don't think that is a good idea and ask if they can't get him a room in the hospital. Raida says she has spent the day getting ready: gas, generator, new battery, food. "But what to do about Baba?"

In fact, the question is not simply one of analytical attitudes toward Arab culture but of how we understand the condition of self-control, self-determination, self-assertion. What does it mean to be in charge of one's life, determining one's future? Identifiable agency seems to assume a will that originates in an independent self and is able to overcome obstacles posed by others to realize individual goals. For landed intellectuals following Adam Smith, civil society arose when early capitalists denounced absolutist state claims on their assets and declared a public realm of self-interest that would promote communal interest. But is this historically specific model the only one? Does it mean that only individuals, and not families or governments, can enter the civil sphere? Anthropologists studying cultures not based in Enlightenment notions of individuality have shown that selves are not necessarily limited to singular physical bodies as houses for an independent will. Selves may be dispersed across bodies.[4] Being open-minded about agency allows for different conceptualizations of the self, of wills invested in and originating in others, even in forces or cultures. Following this trajectory, we may come to think of civil society less rigidly, in relation to cultural setting, thus encountering previously unrecognized forms of activism. Carapico argues that like agency, "civil society is not a binomial element, either there or not" (12), and following research based on extended anthropological fieldwork, political scientist Diane Singerman has argued that in urban Cairo, it is the family which provides the civic realm mediating between the individual and the broader public.[5]

Saturday, July 15
At the resort where I am "trapped," I take my children to the 3S Cottage to see friends who have an apartment by a swimming pool. Karim, the father of one of the friends, starts to talk about his wife's desire to leave. Five hundred years of state experience show what Arabs just don't get: sovereignty means controlling all internal

belligerence. Anyway, he adds, Hizballah is to be blamed for not knowing what they were getting into, for taking the country to a war it can't afford, for not concentrating on economic strength. Mostly, I listen, until Zayn shows up with his declared "soft spot" for Hizballah. When Zayn takes on Karim, I subtly remind the latter that he is Palestinian originally by asking him where his family is from. The Galilee (where Hizballah sent katyushas that are now falling). It kills me that such people came to Lebanon for help, insisting on cross-border support, and yet now that they are officially Lebanese, they are no longer interested in providing cross-border support.

Meanwhile, Nadia, Karim's wife, joins the discussion. She praises the Israelis for being "humane" in giving the people of Marwaheen an hour's warning to leave their homes. I wonder how much time she would think was humane to get ready to leave her house permanently. I am disgusted by how much people have accepted "their" role (not really theirs, because Nadia is accepting it for those in Marwaheen, not for herself) as victims of Zionism, as people whose life will be determined by the supremacist caprices of racist bigots.

Sitting this bright weekend morning at one of the fanciest compounds in Faqra, one of the most luxurious resorts in the country, I recall the sarcasm of the commentator on Al-Manar: What do we people of the Dahiyeh care about the airport, when we can't even afford to travel? What do we care about the tourists? They don't come to the Dahiyeh. What do we care about these new roads, bridges, hotels, etc., when we have been deliberately excluded from the national "prosperity" all along? I actually am not sure he said it so nastily, with such envy and anger, but he was icily uninterested in the infrastructure items about which other commentators were screaming. As some of my companions sit bemoaning their situation in Faqra, and the lack of security and investment now, I think only rich people are going to be upset by this war. The poor people have been systematically prevented from any security or prosperity anyway.

I think back to the play that Fairuz was scheduled to perform on July 15 in Baalbek. I heard the rehearsals were so good that "the performance would have been perfect," a friend had said. Where does perfection come from? A perfect play gone. Ninety-one Lebanese home-dwellers dead. I have gotten kind of philosophical, I guess because I have started think that the 91 who have died so far, like me, were not really alive. Just as we were not really in a state of peace for the past ten years. As long as we do not control the conditions of our life BUT we tell ourselves that we do, we are not really alive, we are borrowing our life from others: the people who control the conditions and the people who openly suffer due to our neglect and avoidance.

Situations of heightened threat, such as war, directly require defining what is at stake in selves, or more specifically, what or who must be protected versus left to peril. The Israeli aggression, then, provided the arena for putting into practice both my skepticism about the universalized concept of civil society and my awareness of the increasing importance of such a localized entity to confront a transnational belligerence that finds its justification, repeatedly, in the notion that forms of social organization in the Arab world are inherently inferior. Engaging repeatedly in discussions of the health of the nation, in formulating plans for the safety of my family, friends, and possessions forced me to consider the unexpected connections between myself and far-flung others; economic flows that generate prosperity, local knowledge that generates community, resource allocation that generates society. As a participant in contemporary Lebanese society, such connections mean that I am ever implicated in the actions of others. Likewise, this lack of boundedness means that we cannot be surprised by our vulnerability. I do not mean to dismiss as unimportant Israeli killings of Lebanese civilians but only to explore what it means to claim life in terms of being an active member of society. "They're killing innocent Lebanese," government spokespersons continually emphasized to the foreign press. Perhaps many of us are innocent of refusing to cooperate with Israeli strategy in the region, but are we innocent of being part of Lebanon where exclusion is a way of life?

Saturday, July 15
On the excuse of the children getting cold in the water (even with heated water, a pool gets cold at 1,850 meters), Zayn and I retreat from the debate and follow the kids to the "cottage." I ask Zayn about the possibility for local economic prosperity because he is in the curious position of locally producing electronics that are exported to the regional market. He has 29 employees to pay at the end of the month. All his orders are ready to go, but how can he get them out? Usually he sends them by DHL when he has an order in Kuwait, but DHL refused this time. Well, I ask, shouldn't there be a totally internally run economy, one that uses locally grown or gained material, one that sells to local customers. Zayn doesn't think that's realistic. He cites a friend of his who produces soap and wants to compete with Lifebuoy, an Indian product. He can't use olive oil, like they used to, because the production is too expensive, hand-harvested olive by olive. He imports the material to save money. My question is, save it from what? From whom? From the local economy? And for

what? For his own personal benefit? Then how can he complain about the weak economy? About not having local customers, if he's not willing to have the local people receive good salaries.

Thursday, July 20
Ramzi Hafez is on LBC. I can't believe this man is complaining about the "lost" Phoenician Village which never even existed, and we can't even protect southern villages from Israeli raids that occur daily. The Israelis used to test their new weaponry on shepherd boys in Wadi Ain el-Tineh! The only thing that stopped them from picking off Lebanese villagers for fun was the 1996 truce that Hizballah forced by proving it could keep sending katyushas to the Galilee. Ramzi is just like the proverbial milkmaid who goes off merrily skipping to the market, dreaming of all the things she will buy with her milk, so gay she cannot pay attention to the road, and trips on a stone. The dreams she cannot achieve are big in her head, but on the road they are only spilled milk. And as long as you cannot protect Lebanese civilians and structures from Israeli aggression, your celebrated losses in downtown Beirut are just spilled wealth. Carelessly, stupidly spilled—the difference is, you aren't losing anything but dreams, whereas taxpayers actually lose the money we have to pay for generations to come toward public debt resulting from projects that we cannot even use because security was not part of their construction.

Although the Israeli aggression treated the residential address of individual Lebanese citizens as an execution warrant, I, and many others, came to believe the ultimate target of such aggression was the entire Lebanese society. "Further, we feel strongly that if we repeat the mistakes of the post-liberation era (2000–2006) by leaving each residential community to mend its wounds in isolation, we will complete the aggression by paving the way to a civil war. To resist such a possible civilian culmination of military aggression, we have undertaken projects of joint reconstruction that bring people of areas hit by bombing together with solidarity-workers from across Lebanon." I typed the preceding and distributed it by e-mail as part of a statement to explain the new "civil activist" group that coalesced in the final weeks of the war, in my living room among others, over cups of coffee and tea.

Friday, August 4

Our meeting with activists and friends lasts six hours. The ISM-ers have a whole different experience of confrontation with Israeli occupation, so they have new ideas to offer; still, they want the lead to come from local people. But we have not thought about such possibilities, and as a people we have not thought about our responsibilities. It is almost inevitable that the ISM [International Solidarity Movement] is taking the lead but not finding willing local partners. I mean, we're excited but very skeptical.

They're late tonight, these Israelis. It's past twelve already and they haven't hit anything here yet. What's wrong with them? Don't they know we have a war to run? How is the world going to be rid of all terrorists and Arabs if the Israelis go and get lazy and soft after only 24 days of bombing the shit out of the place? I mean, I've been waiting awake all night, so the least they can do is deliver!

I like writing that. It makes me feel like I'm in control. Ha!

Primarily Lebanese but also from outside Lebanon, we chose, as teachers, doctors, writers, journalists, merchants, and engineers, to recognize our responsibility toward our fellow civilians and the reconstruction and repair of civil society. We launched a campaign that starts by covering the basic civilian needs created by Israeli aggression, but does so in a way and with an eye toward building permanent civilian networks to ensure the safety and prosperity of our civil society. Civil activism, we declared, would be using our civilian networks to make Israeli strategies in Lebanon impracticable. Structurally, our campaign capitalized on the liminal state created by the war, whereby people had been banished from their daily routines, like vacationers, but, unlike vacationers, utterly obsessed with the people and places that made up their daily lives. That condition brought together people who were well aware of their political differences: members of the Future Movement, the Communist Party, Hizballah, the Democratic Left, followers of Aoun, Jumblatt, Gemayel, and people nonaligned. We floated in a common boat of fear amidst a sea of anxiety and sadness. Jobless, we had time to spend with each other, planning, reconsidering, teasing, declaring. It was, as Victor Turner described in 1968, a time of "total confrontation" where we interacted as "concrete, historical, idiosyncratic individuals" exploring all possible imaginations of resistance to the aggression and pulling on all our personal resources as local residents.

Yet it is important to recognize that this liminal time was not purely extraordinary and anti-structural. It was, on the contrary, enabled and motivated by our family connections: we had in-laws or mothers to support us, spouses and children to encourage us. I would not have cared so very much, to be perfectly honest, about the war had I not been worried about my children, as disturbed by the idea of taking them away from their home as I was by that of leaving them exposed in it. By my experience as family guardian, I was sensitized to the pain of family members who lose their mundane minutiae or who see their relatives undignified. Clearly, I did not interact with the weeks of assault as an individual. It would have been absurd for me to interact with war as an individual because I did not experience the war as an individual, and my sense is that most of the people engaged in "relief" did not either. Our bodies were safe. Our addresses were not targeted. We could watch the war on TV; yet, we experienced it vicariously by living beyond the bounds of our bodies, by feeling the pain, agony, and frustration of people forced to leave their homes, livelihood, and family.

Saturday, August 5

A trip has been arranged to the Dahiyeh this evening. The ISM-ers want to set up a tent in a yet unbombed area, to prevent the Israelis from striking it, and they want to see the place first. Samah thinks they are insane. I want to go with them. I cannot explain why. I realize it is dangerous. I realize it must not be a form of tourism. I think I simply want to refuse the sense of a forced gap between me and other inhabitants of Beirut, between capital Beirut and its vibrant suburbs, between ways of life and discourses. Samah at first tells me fine, but then he becomes scornful. What will I accomplish by going there? Anyway (and this is how most decisions get made these days), they need my car. No public taxis are going to the Dahiyeh these days.

We pass the Kuwaiti embassy. The airport bridge is there above us, cut in half over the road. All the debris has been cleared away. It's a ghost town, but a clean one. Until we make a right turn. We reach the "security zone." Streets and apartments are indistinguishable. The rubble just a few feet in front of me reaches above my head. I am rooted at this corner. I cannot move beyond this spot. I have seen this on TV. It is not more real up close.

I try to study the wreckage, like an archaeologist: baking molds, strainers, stuffed animals, sandals, computer hard drives, a book about the Lebanese Phalangists, half of a child's scooter, mattresses, rug-beater, plastic water jug, rolled-

up carpet, wooden bed frames, so much stuff from ordinary houses. Even the Amnesty guy next to me, an older man with white hair and glasses who must have seen a lot of wars was flabbergasted by the vastness and brutality of the destruction. Whole city blocks gone.

As I pick my way through the wreckage, it occurs to me that this is the postmodern, global-era version of the volcanoes that produced the strange rock formations I climb over in Faraya. A tune rescues me from the sadness, "Wallah talla 'anahum barra" [By God, we kicked them out], a song Ahmad Qaabour arranged to commemorate 1982 and the expulsion of the Israeli forces from Beirut after a mere eleven days. What idiots these people are to think they can stay in Lebanon.

At home, I shower to wash away the connection that I so desperately sought.

Our campaign formed on the go, out of the spontaneous coalescence of individual attempts to be relevant, useful, and resistant. One idea that galvanized us was the plan to break the Israeli siege of the south. From the first bombings of roads and bridges and fleeing family cars, it was clear that Israel intended to split the country into isolated cantons. Bananas and lemons in one part of the country, bread and milk in another. Wounded and dying in one section, ambulances and medicines in another. We declared "Lebanon: An Open Country for Civil Resistance" and organized a convoy of 50 civilian cars carrying medicines, food rations, and diapers. Our destination was Tyre, but we got no further than Naameh, where we were stopped by the Lebanese internal security forces. They were concerned for our safety, but in an odd twist, they were apparently less concerned for the safety of a similar convoy headed for Saida [Sidon] and sponsored by Bahia Hariri: they were allowed to continue.

Though stopped momentarily, the thrust of our work remained to reroute the channeling of resources in Lebanon. Considering that Lebanese society is currently composed of socially isolated communities and that the vast majority of human resources are centered in Beirut, we seek to use our family, professional, and neighborly connections to redirect the investment of human resources to areas previously systematically neglected. We seek to activate all our social connections to overcome the isolation that many Lebanese feel from each other and that has enabled wars to be waged against the country under the slogan of removing undesired elements from the country (for example: 1860, World War I and the French Mandate, 1958, 1975, 1982, 1996, 2006).

Monday, August 14

With this cease-fire I don't really know what to do with myself. I got used to the war. It was a purpose and a system that came in and took over my life, and now that it's gone, I feel very empty. I actually miss the huge bombs—my appointment with stomach churning, racing pulse, and a rush of anger in my veins. I cannot believe that we can go outside without fear of being shelled. I do not believe it. I am not convinced that this victory is enough to keep the Israeli planes away. I want the war to continue until I can be sure. Maybe this is what Elizabeth was talking about, how victims become aggressors. I'm not satisfied with Israel's promise to attack "only in self-defense." Their army's name is the "Israeli Defense Force," so any time they hit is categorically "in self-defense." It's not that I want revenge for the civilians killed and the destruction wrought. I think anyway we have already gotten something akin to that by the damage imposed on Israeli property, economy, and pride. But we must have recognition that Israel set the scale of aggression and pursued it for unacceptable reasons. For that, we cannot be innocent victims but assertive people demanding our rights.

After a day of cleaning, I discover that I am restoring my house. I can bring out the vases and pictures and rugs and everything fragile or inflammable. We have survived a month of Israeli assault and discovered that it can do nothing to us militarily. And as long as we can stand unperturbed by broken bridges and crushed homes, Israel has no power to force us to do anything.

Tuesday, August 15

Bilal, who has finally left Tyre, tells us of the "mattress merkavas" clogging the road south. We debate back and forth what our group action should be. We are happy the cease-fire has held but a bit confused. Samah gets people excited about an idea to bring benefit jazz concerts to Baalbek, an area desperately in need of reconstruction but already basically forgotten by the nation. There is some question about the legality of having another festival series in Baalbek. We should call it "Off-Baalbek," I say. Or we may go south to Deir Kifa and work from there on villages where we can make contacts. Either way, we will be leaving Beirut again, but this time headed toward, not away from, the places Israel hit.

Civil activists without an action—where to go? How to get there? The basic idea of using civil connections provided an answer of sorts. At T-Marbouta, the café where our meetings moved, there was a waiter, Ali Yusif Khalaf, a handyman in his late fifties. As we wondered about what to do with all our communitas feelings and energy, we asked him where he is from. Abu Yusif explained that he is a native of Silaa village who sent his family to Syria ten days after the Israeli bombing commenced, and came to Beirut for temporary shelter and income. He brought us back to his village on August 19.

Saturday, August 19
Silaa is a relatively small community near Deir Kifa, in the Tyre district. While many of Silaa's families fled after the first week of bombing, a good number stayed, sharing shelter in homes in the village interior. They survived a month of siege only to be bombed anew in the last hours before the cease-fire of August 14. The town square today holds only four tall eucalyptus trees. Ten three-story apartment buildings that ringed these trees were completely reduced to rubble just minutes before the cease-fire went into effect. In total 35 homes were destroyed and 50 more gravely damaged. Eight people were killed, and four more are missing. The story of the missing is most disturbing: One 64-year-old man's body was never recovered. He was sleeping when the bomb fell. When his family removed the rubble, the mattress he slept on was found with all his clothing on it, but no body could be found beyond three bones.

We arrived as strangers in Silaa and similar villages. Only a few of us were from the south or had visited it regularly before this summer. Immediately we faced the awkward task of explaining why we had. No, we were not an international NGO or professional aid workers sent by a friendly government; no, we did not have family we were coming to assist. Nor had we been sent by a political party or some ambitious politician to prove some greater entity's inherent good. Without slogans emblazoned on our shirts or hats, our presence was anomalous and enigmatic. How could we expect to share in the recovery work, clearing the debris, cleaning what remained, finding potable water, caring for the children, and so on, if we did not have an identity explaining how people should relate to us? There was so much work to be done, but people will not let you offer them help unless it is clear what you will want in return. In that sense, our liminal character was highly problematic. Family can be allowed to give help because the help they may require in return is for your familial benefit. International NGO workers can be allowed because they come only for the present and leave soon. While many NGOs had been either ineffective or even dangerous during the war,[6] the NGO model of people doing good professionally was fundamental to the villagers' understanding of why we showed up in these off-road towns to walk through wreckage without knowing to whom it belonged. In those awkward moments when coffee was offered and we introduced ourselves for the first time, when we verged on insulting our hosts by saying we had come to help people who had given so much for the sake of sovereignty and dignity, the NGO model was quite readily embraced. We were assumed to be paid individuals seeking to feel good while earning a livelihood. Eventually, however, we came to present ourselves not as individuals with self-centered wills to implement but as people who felt angered by injustice, threatened by harm to homeland, impelled to respond to a vision of a larger group, the *watan* [nation]. In that sense, we explained, we were in need of something from our hosts beyond the coffee and tea they so generously offered.

Sunday, September 3

It is the 40th-day memorial of the killing of eight residents of Silaa by Israel. To concretize our vision of ourselves as members of the national "family," we arrange to provide a memorial lunch of lamb, rice, yogurt, and fruit following the religious services. We emphasized that though we had not met the departed, we felt them to be part of our national family and their mourning part of our national duty. This is what family members normally do to show respect for their dead, but the people in Silaa do not have the income to execute it. We have hired a restaurant in Bazouriya, ten minutes away from Silaa. About 500 villagers were expected to partake in the meal. We arrive at 11, only to find that the lunch has already been eaten! The services finished early, and people were hungry, the mukhtar explains. We feel shocked and foolish. The families of the departed tell us they were honored to be able to serve a proper meal on behalf of their beloved. They have saved some food for us and chat about the village as we eat.

In July, Ali Hussein had fled Blida, a border town, to Hamra Street. He used to come to our meeting place, T-Marbouta Café, for relief supplies, and we had known him as a refugee like any other: pale, tired, unshaven. When we met him again in Blida he was a transformed person, rosy, clean-shaven face, fresh clothes, dignified comportment. It was the difference between homelessness and belonging. He showed us his home, and though it had been blasted through by an Israeli–American rocket, he said, it was his. We joked about the Israelis engineering currents for the wind. Still, it will take more than humor to enable the residents of Blida to stay in the south as the winter rains roll in. This visit we delivered our supplies to the municipality—baby milk, diapers, and clothing for 116 children under the age of two. We were not able to satisfy their request for a 220-kva generator, but we are negotiating with UNIFIL to supply them. The mayor invited us for tea, at which we discussed the problems villagers face in returning, particularly cluster bombs, and the chances for creating a south economically free of products made by companies that support Israel.[7]

Saturday, September 17
For the fourth weekend in a row we offer children's entertainment activities in the Maqasid School in Silaa. Again about 80 children participate. There are more physical games on the playground led by Sami and Mohammad. Most of the older boys join them to play soccer and tag. Fida and Baha read from Samah's picture books to a group of children aged 3–5 and then play Qala al-qa'id [Simon Says] and toss water balloons. Maha and George lead group drawings of the children's favorite things about Silaa and changes wrought in Silaa by the Israeli bombing. Forty girls in their early teens competed in another boisterous round of Pictionary. When one girl picks the word "kite" [tayyara waraq], she asks Maha, "Is that the plane that drops papers?" referring to the pamphlets Israel had dispersed for propaganda and expulsion orders in the past weeks. Sariya leads the older girls in creating their own, personalized Monopoly game sets. The objective is multiple: to encourage the youth's self-reliance in the face of repeated threats to their homes and possessions, and to enable the boycott of the pro-Zionist toy company Hasbro.[8] *The girls enjoy most making up their own street names, chance cards, and currencies. The hit of the week, however, is musical chairs, and the claim that the kids are "dancing" provokes as many giggles as the contest to get a seat. As always, at the end of the hour-and-a-half play session, the children receive chocolate bars and either coloring books or picture books, and we organizers all receive invitations to stay in the children's homes.*

Navigating between the roles of guests, entertainers, tourists, aid workers, and aid seekers, we developed a set of steps that enabled us to provide effective initial aid and solidarity within two days of arrival and to form a basis for sustained interaction. After introducing ourselves to a resident, we would request introductions to members of the municipality and under their auspices hold an open meeting with villagers in order to solicit ideas for practical assistance guided by their own sense of their needs.

Our work generally fell into three categories: 1) gathering residential statistics on the homes destroyed during the assault; 2) assessing village-wide needs; 3) preparing a village-wide ceremony, as in a celebration of the war's end or a commemoration of those lost. In the first few weeks following the August 14 cease-fire, we concentrated on procuring drinking water as well as non-potable water for cleaning needs, renting electrical suction pumps and generators, notifying authorities of unexploded ordnances, and finding medical practitioners to deal with urgent or chronic health problems. We also engaged the village children in recreational activities to offer them something of the summer relaxation they sorely missed. With the residential statistics, we would secure (either through local purchases or donations) food, hygienic supplies, and properly sized clothing for each person whose home was destroyed, and distribute it in bags for each family, with toys for any children, in tagged bags dropped off at the municipality. In subsequent months we have moved on to longer-term projects that twin local institutions, such as elementary schools or ad-hoc clinics, and provide economic stimulus. What has continued to tie us to the villages we work in and welcome us back is not so much the goods we bring as the experiences we take away after sitting in newly repaired living rooms and listening to stories of survival and testimonies to tenacity. Yet our ties cannot only be southward and eastward, toward the direction of the bombing.

Wednesday, July 19
Samah and I feel like walking. We drive up the mountain and park the car near the Intercontinental Hotel. We see an eerie sight: a pool glimmering green in the night, a bar with a vine trellis overhead, a barbecue grilling meats, and gathered around holding drinks, people in their early twenties, conversing loudly: "Bedna nkhlas minhum ba'a!" *[Let's get rid of them already!]* "Eh, ana I think Hizballah…" *the speaker continues inaudibly in English. Samah shushes me to try to hear them. Their feelings are clear. What is this idea,* "nkhlas minhum?" *Its premise is that the Hezb is just a bunch of crazy fanatics, a deranged, marginal minority. Do these young people have no clue about why the Hezb came into existence? Do they not understand that for decades the government they think should be controlling the country did nothing for the south or other impoverished areas (not impoverished by fact or geography, but by the siphoning off of their resources and the unequal distribution of national investment that has led to the conglomerated wealth)? Who*

should be preparing to get rid of whom? The kids' conversation is practice for civil war. It motivates them to despise and disdain and even promote aggression against a group of people they think is small.

Monday, July 17

I admit I had not grasped how hard this is, to be on the side that takes the hitting, even here in Faraya. I had been thinking this would last a few days, a week or two. Most people around here, and about half who are interviewed at random by Al-Jazeera, are angry about "Hizballah dragging them into this mess." "We were happy, ya khay" [oh my brother], says Wadih, the engineer who built and runs the resort where we rent. I cut him off, turning to Samah, and say, "Let's take that walk now."

How can people who believe in a national economy, or national sovereignty, or a national presence to be ruled by a national government extricate themselves from the problems faced by others who live in their country, problems due to Lebanon's very composition? How can they be so alienated from the people who, they claim, compose their country? How can they feel that the vulnerability of the south to raids, the weakness of refugees, in the Dahiyeh or in the camps, has nothing to do with them? I feel all that, yet here I am, not knowing when I can go back to Beirut or why it isn't safe to do so now. I feel all that, yet what did I say to William about it? I just maneuvered my husband out of that confrontation. I don't like who I am in this situation.

The nationalist talk driving my encounters in Faraya during the war and in the south after it contradicts all my previous practice in skepticism toward "activist packages," to borrow Anna Tsing's phrase.[9] And yet, the experience of trying to disable war rendered my interaction with concepts like nation and civil society so very urgent. It is for this reason, ultimately, that our project of civil resistance is not just about the areas that were directly targeted by the Israeli army. The young barbecue guests, Wadih, Nadia, Karim, Zayn, and many other affirmed non-resistors must be equally part of this civil resistance project. In that sense, our project surpasses immediate relief. Our understanding of civil resistance, therefore, is that which calls upon existing civilian networks to resist attempts by belligerents to use military force to cripple society and cut short civilian lives, ambitions, and dreams. The biggest threat we see today is not Israeli bombing, ironically, but the loss of the connections between people that enable them to confront and survive belligerence, external or internal. To offer true civil activism, we have found, we must resist the current sectarian and classed structure of Lebanese civil society. What we have come up with departs from previous approaches to civil society and resistance. Instead of taking for granted that civil society exists or should exist, we ask how it might look if it actually worked for given, living civilians in their multifaceted lives.

Conceiving of civil resistance as including such a broad spectrum of Lebanese society raises the problem that for many, "resistance" [*muqawama*] is a dirty, dangerous word. The very concept that motivates southern villagers to invite Beirut-based strangers off the street and spend time with them formulating national strategy convinces other Lebanese that the speaker is a deranged radical. From our living room, to T-Marbouta meetings, to Silaa and other southern villages where we work with such different people, a common ground is created by our invocation of "duty," "urgency," and "nonconformity" to the Israeli–US articulated plans for a "New Middle East." We continually reconstitute this space as a place not for party belonging, religious adherence, or familial affiliation, but as a place for resistance. What we mean by this is the sense of asserting the relevance of one's life, of realizing one's inescapable non-redundancy. Here no one's life just is; everyone's life matters. Still, if we are serious about our project, then we must face the paradox of the term *resistance*, and do so without surrendering its goal.

In his study of the contradictory character of the Central American peasant activists, Charles Hale reminds us that in becoming anthropological commonsense, the awareness of paradox and fissure that cultural critique promotes may have naturalized contradiction to the extent that we blunt our will to engage it and surmount it.[10] What I take Hale to mean is that cultural critique could become a tool used by engaged activists to dissect and discredit the underpinnings of the packaged discourses they take up in their projects of assertion. This effort may, likewise, help activists interact with others who see activist discourses as packaged and artificial. I am reminded of Donna Haraway and Lila Abu-Lughod's respective responses to calls for academic objectivism: we are all always engaged and implicated, but if we highlight our awareness of that, we can produce accounts of action that foreground culture and make it a tool not just for intellectual critique but, as Haraway puts it, for "build[ing] meanings and bodies that have a chance for life."[11]

When last spring, while finishing up my course for AUB on Arab culture and society, I read Hale's call for a restructuring of the material relations of anthropological knowledge production that could combine the power of cultural critique and alignment with struggles against oppression, I was enchanted by the possibility, but very much caught up in planning a research program for the summer focusing on Lebanon's tourist festivals. According to that program, Fairuz's ungiven performance was perfect and the performance of Lebanese civil society seriously flawed. Quite unexpectedly, I found myself directly engaging Hale's recipe for academic research, and I was forced to consider the conflicting goals of Lebanese civil space, to see where participants could critique packaged discourses, and to strive to use those discourses effectively instead of being used by them.

In conclusion, I believe I can glean from my unintended participant observation a few lessons about civic activism in the Lebanese context: 1) Family is crucial both as an institution and metaphor to the pursuit of activism. Indeed, I have since noticed that the more we try to maintain the sense of liminality, of utter devotion to this extraordinary project, the less energy and commitment we have. Our numbers dwindle when we declare "full-time" activism. We are much more effective, both in terms of carrying out plans and in terms of enrolling a broad sector of the citizenry, when we enact our campaign as a small part of people's daily life as Lebanese. 2) Following on this, I would suggest there has been an over-emphasis in studies of Arab civil activism on individual will as motive and key to understanding social agency. 3) Finally, the model of host and guest, constantly needing each other and creating oneself in the other, may prove fruitful for rethinking social connections that construct workable civil society for dynamic citizens. Summarizing these three points is the conviction that we are all implicated and engaged in the articulation of active civil society; not one of us can or should claim the space of "innocent victim."

NOTES

1 Sheila Carapico, *Civil Society in Yemen* (Cambridge: Cambridge University Press, 1998) 2.

2 See Saad Eddin Ibrahim, "State, Women, and Civil Society: An Evaluation of Egypt's Population Policy," in *Arab Society: Class, Gender, Power, and Development*, Nicholas Hopkins and Saad Eddin Ibrahim, eds. (Cairo: American University of Cairo Press,

1997) 85–104; Elie Kedourie, *Democracy and Arab Political Culture* (Washington, DC: Washington Institute for Near East Policy, 1992); Bernard Lewis, *The Shaping of the Modern Middle East* (New York: Oxford University Press, 1995); Sara Roy, "Civil Society in the Gaza Strip," in *Civil Society in the Middle East*, vol. 2, Richard Augustus Norton, ed. (E.J. Brill, 1996) 221–258; Yahya Sadowski, "The New Orientalism and the Democracy Debate," *Middle East Report* 183 (July–August): 14-21, 40.

3 See Nawaf Salam, *Civil Society in the Arab World: The Historical and Political Dimensions* (Islamic Legal Studies Program, Occasional Publications, Cambridge, MA: Harvard Law School, 2002); Ernest Gellner, "Civil Society in Historical Context," *International Social Science Journal* 43.129 (1991): 495–510; Mustafa Kamil al-Sayyid, "A Civil Society in Egypt," in Richard Augustus Norton 269–294.

4 See Dorrine Kondo, *Crafting Selves* (Chicago: University of Chicago Press, 1990); Marilyn Strathern, "Self-Interest and the Social Good: Some Implications of the Hagen Gender Imagery," in *Sexual Meanings: The Cultural Construction of Gender and Sexuality*, S. Ortner and H. Whitehead, eds. (New York: Routledge, 1981) 64–89; Alfred Gell, *Art and Agency* (Oxford: Oxford University Press, 1998); Lila Abu-Lughod, *Writing Women's Worlds: Bedouin Stories* (Berkeley: University of California Press, 1993); Saba Mahmood, *Politics of Piety: The Islamic Revival and the Feminist Subject* (Princeton: Princeton University Press, 2005).

5 Diane Singerman, *Avenues of Participation: Family, Politics, and Networks in Urban Quarters of Cairo* (Princeton: Princeton University Press, 1995). See also Elizabeth Faier, *Organizations, Gender, and the Culture of Palestinian Activism in Haifa, Israel* (New York: Routledge, 2005).

6 As when Georges Khoury, the director of local charity organization Caritas, reported that the International Red Cross was requiring people in some villages to leave if they wanted aid and prohibiting other organizations from reaching those villages (Al-Jazeera, 1 August 2006). NGOs organize internationally and must maintain global credibility; they cannot be seen, they explain, to be siding with one group, or recklessly exposing their staff to danger. This summer that meant informing Israeli army officials of their plans and waiting for approval—thus, effectively taking permission from the aggressor to provide relief and avoiding the areas not approved for relief. When we organized our convoy we were called by the UN World Food Program and asked if we wanted this coordination. We categorically refused.

7 This passage derives from the unpublished diaries of fellow CRC activist Sami Hermez.

8 In response to an 84 percent drop in earnings in the year 2000, Hasbro re-introduced in 2001 its GI Joe line including its "Modern Day Israeli Defense Force Soldier" (see www.hasbro.com and http://enquirer.com/editions/2000/10/20/ fin_hasbro_inc_reports.html). Aimed at five-year-olds and armed with hand grenades and M-16s, this toy encourages children to play at brutally oppressing Palestinians while obscuring the truth of Israel's illegal occupation. CEO Alan Hassenfeld is a member of the Jerusalem Foundation (www.just-tzedakah.org/reports/JerusalemFoundation/ GS.html; www.jerusalem-foundation.org; and board of trustees, Trust for Jewish Philanthropy, www.thetrust.org/aboutus_home.html), which buys properties in Jerusalem and seeks to build up the Jewish presence there. He is also on the board of

directors of the Committee for Economic Growth Israel, which encourages American businesses to invest in Israel (see www.cegi.org/CEGIDirectors.html).

9 Anna Tsing, *Friction: An Ethnography of Global Connection* (Princeton: Princeton University Press, 2004) 234–235.

10 Charles Hale, "Activist Research v. Cultural Critique," *Cultural Anthropology* 21.1 (2006) 96–120.

11 Donna Haraway, "Situated Knowledge: The Science Question in Feminism as a Site of Discourse on the Privilege of Partial Perspective," *Feminist Studies* 14.3 (1989) 575–599; quoting from page 580; and Abu-Lughod (see note 4).

14. A FATEFUL VISIT TO LEBANON: A DIARY

Hiam Turfe-Brinjikji

Fifteen members of my immediate family were among the estimated 1.5 to 2 million tourists to visit Lebanon this summer. It had been 32 years since I visited my birthplace and I wanted to share the experience with my three children. We met my sister Mariam, her three young boys, my brother Ahmad, his wife, and their five children in Beirut. On Monday, July 10, we arrived in Bint Jbeil, which is just two-and-a-half miles from the Israeli border. The next day we visited my paternal grandmother and aunt and my maternal uncle and his family. We drove across southern Lebanon—along winding roads and across gentle rolling green hills dotted with beautiful villas. We visited the Kiam Israeli prison camp. We noticed the heavily fortified Israeli military outposts on the other side of the border fence and the United Nations posts inside the Lebanese border. Otherwise, life appeared normal, with no particular sign of hostility, although I did feel uneasy about the military presence at the border.

Day 1: Wednesday, July 12
On this day heavenly Lebanon began to turn into a burning hell. Breakfast in our hosts' beautiful garden was interrupted by news of the two Israeli soldiers captured by Hizballah. We were planning to return to Beirut that afternoon, but decided to leave earlier just in case. We were told not to worry too much—past incidents had been resolved through negotiations. We drove about fifteen minutes before receiving a call from my uncle imploring us to return immediately, because the Israeli military had bombed bridges and roads. Mariam and I remained in frequent contact with our husbands in Michigan, who told us that the US State Department advised all its citizens to stay off all roads in southern Lebanon and Beirut. For the next 36 hours we watched the Israeli bomber jets and helicopters drop bombs and missiles on the neighboring town of Maroun, just over the hill. Horrified by the plumes of black smoke and fires burning in the distance, we were assured by our hosts that the attacks would end soon and we would be able to leave.

Day 2: Thursday, July 13

At 7:30 in the evening, the first Israeli missile was launched on Bint Jbeil, about 100 yards from our location. We saw the explosion and inhaled its fumes; this was a turning point. We were horrified by the thundering noise of bombs and missiles impacting around us. We spread mattresses in the center of the house away from windows. Children cried and screamed while the adults reassured them they would be fine. A total of 25 people huddled on the floor, including 11 children under age 11. We soon learned that the first missile killed an 18-year-old coming home from evening prayers. Soon the electricity went out and the generators started. We dubbed this part of the war "Operation Bint Jbeil." We were certain that the missiles would hit the house and we would all die. We all prayed as children asked what would happen to them if they died. The thunder of outgoing and incoming fire was unbearable. We knew a missile hit nearby when the house rumbled and the earth shook. Sleep was not possible as the bombing continued throughout the night. We estimated that 70 Israeli missiles pounded Bint Jbeil in the first three hours.

Day 3: Friday, July 14

We lived through the night and began shifting into survival mode. The bombing stopped in the early morning and we stepped out into the smoke-filled air to help move supplies and mattresses into the second-level garage area beneath the house. Mattresses were spread on the floor of our "shelter"; food and cooking supplies, a TV, and a landline telephone were brought down. The street was visible through the large garage windows. We heard the wailing cries of the mother of the young man killed the previous night and watched the funeral procession tread up the hill to the cemetery. As we gathered necessary belongings from the house, two missiles struck a home 200 yards directly in front of us. I yelled at the kids to run down to the garage, as I tried to shake Mariam out of her frozen state of shock. In the garage, we sat in anticipation of more strikes. Through the garage windows we watched the rescue-and-recovery crew dig through the rubble, only to be attacked by another Israeli missile. Ambulances raced to take the dead and injured to the hospital. We couldn't understand why Israel was targeting civilian areas when the Hizballah rockets were clearly being launched from non-residential open fields in the distance. The bombing continued intermittently throughout the day.

Our relatives were working feverishly in Beirut and Dubai to facilitate our escape through the UN and Red Cross, but it was too dangerous for any organization to rescue us. We also remained in contact with my grandmother and aunt and pleaded with them to come with us if we were rescued. They told us they wanted to remain in their town because the war would end soon. Early Friday evening, the Israeli military dropped flyers in the town warning us to leave. But how could we leave?—the bombing continued, moving vehicles were being attacked, and the US State Department warned all Americans to remain off the roads. As night fell, we clutched our children and reassured them they would be okay, knowing full well that death could come for any of us with the next missile. Sleep was not possible for most of us, since along with the flurry of incoming missiles, outgoing rockets, and the ominous loud buzzing of spy planes looking for any movement on the ground, the Israeli bomber jets broke the sound barrier five times that night. We learned that this was a type of psychological warfare used by the Israeli military against the Lebanese in past wars.

Day 4: Saturday, July 15

The morning only brought more fear as we looked out onto the destruction of nearby buildings and roads. Our hope was linked to the telephone and television—our only connections to the outside world. My family in America, desperate for a cease-fire, went to the media to tell our story—to educate them about our predicament. Later that morning, several men burying the previous day's dead were targeted by missiles at the cemetery. They ran through our host's backyard seeking shelter and warning everyone to remain inside. We were in constant contact with family, who updated us on their efforts for a rescue. The US State Department continued to warn its civilians to stay off the roads as all moving vehicles were potential targets. This message was reinforced by the many news reports of civilians killed on the roads. Saturday night would prove to be another night of increasing horror. The Israeli bombing seemed to intensify with each passing night. We clutched closer to our children. We leaned on our children's bodies, hoping to protect them from the rubble if the house collapsed on us. We were living through a nightmare and feared that each breath might indeed be our last. We prayed that if we died, it would happen instantly and that we would not live to see our children or any of us suffer a long death trapped under the rubble. Mariam and I worried about our husbands, who were doing their best to save our lives, and we all worried about our family in America. How would they cope if fifteen members of our family were killed?

Day 5: Sunday, July 16

We learned that our uncle, who was very ill, was rescued and taken to Qana with his family by a local ambulance. The missile attacks and outgoing fire continued feverishly throughout the day. Our contacts in Beirut and Dubai seemed less confident about any rescue attempt. We now worried about an Israeli ground invasion. We discussed a plan of action and decided that if the Israeli soldiers found us, we would speak English, show them our American passports, and beg for our lives. Although we knew if they raided the town, we would be killed, but we had to hope.

Day 6: Monday, July 17

The morning dawn brought with it a thick black haze that filled the sky above and settled over the town. The garage was filled with smoke and chemical fumes. We were coughing and grasping our chests. Several people threw up. My son and several young children grabbed their asthma inhalers. Our throats were raw and our breath was forced. We were breathing and tasting the phosphorus from exploded missiles and the fumes of the burning gas station down the road. We experienced the war with all our senses.

Since Mariam and I are licensed counselors, we began to analyze the emotional and psychological effects of the war. We observed with each passing day that the younger children became more agitated and clung to their mothers, the teenage girls became quieter, while all the older boys and men slept a lot. Perhaps it was their way of coping with the despair and powerlessness to help their families. On the other hand, the women barely slept, our energy fueled by adrenaline and the need to nurture our loved ones through this horrific experience. My brother, a pharmacist, worried about the immediate and long-term health effects of breathing the poisonous air. The loss of our cell-phone connection only added to our panic and sense of helplessness. Would the landlines be next? We needed to leave—staying meant certain death. Leaving might also mean death, but it was our only chance. Either decision could mean life or death for our children.

During a brief respite in the attacks, we approached one of the men hiding with us and asked him if he knew a way out through the back roads. He fetched his wife, their thirteen-day-old baby, and seven other family members, and we left together. We were told that we might have to abandon the cars and run on foot, so we grabbed water bottles and snacks for the children. We had to plan to sleep in banana fields and olive groves and hope that we didn't trip an unexploded device. We piled in our cars and bid our farewells to our host family and my grandmother and aunt, who had decided it would be safer to remain. We drove through the black haze, shocked by the destruction and the singed black of the once-green earth. Our hearts beating feverishly with adrenaline, we were stopped in our track with a roadblock of metal and concrete debris. The other road out of town was also blocked by debris. We raced back to the house. Now, joined by 9 others, we were 34 people hiding in the garage. Would we all die together—7 men and 27 women and children? We were filled with hopelessness and despair. Pondering our fate, we resigned ourselves to the probability of death.

Hope came with a phone call from a relative in Beirut who found a taxi driver who was willing to come and rescue us. We contacted my grandmother and aunt, but they still wanted to stay. Everyone other than my immediate family decided to remain in the garage. They said the roads were too dangerous. We piled into the taxi and my brother's van. Every inch of road meant potential death since planes were flying above and devices on the road might explode if we drove over them. Some of the debris we had encountered earlier on the road had been moved. We felt like we were driving through hell. The destruction was merciless and unimaginable and the air was still hazy with smoke. A four-hour drive through the mountains would take us to Beirut. That night the bombing continued in the neighboring Beirut suburbs.

Day 7: Tuesday, July 18

The next morning we planned our escape from Beirut. Mariam wanted to leave with her children with the American evacuation to Cyprus. All foreign nationals were already being evacuated free of charge by their governments—except Americans. We learned that only minor children would be guaranteed departures with parents. This was not an option for me, because I had two older children who might travel alone or be left behind. Additionally, every US citizen would have to sign a $3,000 promissory note and secure their own flight out of Cyprus. This was later rescinded as heavy international condemnation of the US government's request grew. My sister and her three children were put on an evacuation waitlist while my brother tried to evacuate through his employer—the Saudi government. My children and I left by taxi for Damascus. Our trip involved a long detour through northern Lebanon since word came of missile attacks on fleeing cars on our original route. We arrived in Damascus eleven hours later. Two days later, Mariam and her children, who were still waitlisted by the US government, and my brother and his family, evacuated to Damascus with a 51-bus convoy. That evening we learned that the remaining 20 people in the garage had escaped to Beirut because the war had intensified and the phone lines were destroyed.

My husband flew to Damascus to help facilitate our return home. The Syrians opened their hearts, homes, mosques, churches, and schools to the war escapees.

Two weeks after our return home, we were notified of my grandmother and aunt's death. My grandmother's body was found under the rubble of her home, and my aunt's body was dismembered by a direct hit of an Israeli missile. This news was devastating for my family, especially my father. Our war experience was taken to the most horrific level—the death of loved ones. We also learned that the house and garage that had once sheltered us were hit by 35 Israeli missiles and bombs. Had we not escaped, we certainly would have been killed.

Part Four

INTERNATIONAL LAW AND WAR

15. INTERNATIONAL LAW AT THE VANISHING POINT

Richard Falk and Asli Bali

In the summer of 2006, two border incidents were invoked by Israel, with strong US diplomatic support and material assistance, to justify a prolonged military offensive in Gaza and a crushing "shock-and-awe" assault on Lebanon. The main international response, effectively orchestrated by Washington, was built around the bland assertion that Israel has the "right to defend itself."

Of course it does. But in the summer the unasked questions were "how," "with what limits," and "by what means"? It is the role of international law to provide answers to such questions, sometimes not very precise answers, but at least guidelines, which commanders and sovereign governments have considerable latitude to interpret with reference to considerations of "military necessity." What this means in practice is a rather broad margin of discretion in the international law of war that makes unlawful only clearly outrageous and unreasonable behavior, whether by states or by non-state actors engaged in armed struggle.

In the case of Israel's summertime conflicts on its southern and northern borders, the international community, again led by Washington, swiftly condemned the actions of Israel's "extremist" adversaries, and acquiesced in the tightening of existing sanctions upon them by legal and other means. Yet although Israel's actions in both Gaza and Lebanon were plainly unlawful by international legal standards, there was less condemnation and no material sanction imposed upon Israel, least of all by the chief arbiter of international peace and security, the UN Security Council. The imbalance in the international response has gravely undermined the credibility and, ultimately, the enforceability of international legal norms, which are only norms to the degree that they are enforced without fear or favor.

Lawful Limits of Self-Defense

On June 25, 2006, fighters belonging to three Palestinian factions, including Hamas, tunneled under the fence separating the Gaza Strip from Israel at the Kerem Shalom border crossing and attacked the army post on the Israeli side. The Palestinians killed two soldiers and snatched a third, whom they spirited back into Gaza, where he presumably remains captive. In an announced attempt to retrieve the soldier, Israel bombed bridges and a power plant in Gaza, stepped up artillery and aerial bombardment of sites believed to house the ineffective rocketeers of Hamas, launched multiple tank incursions into Gaza, arrested tens of Hamas parliamentarians without any charges and locked down the sole point of transit for people and goods between Gaza and the outside world. According to the UN, 280 Palestinians have been killed during the ongoing Israeli offensive, which lasted several months.

Global media attention shifted northward on July 12, when Hizballah militants crossed into undisputed Israeli territory, killing three Israeli soldiers and abducting two others, with five additional soldiers being killed on Lebanese territory in the course of an attempted rescue operation. In the ensuing month-long war, Israel bombed bridges, roads, power plants, and other civilian infrastructure in Lebanon, and also conducted multiple strikes upon Beirut neighborhoods and southern villages it dubbed "Hizballah strongholds." Israel also imposed a comprehensive land, sea, and air blockade upon Lebanon. Upward of 1,000 Lebanese were killed, and nearly one million displaced in the course of the bombardment, while 39 Israeli civilians were killed, and hundreds of thousands compelled to flee their homes, by Hizballah's retaliatory rocket fire. The UN Security Council brokered a "cessation of hostilities" between Israel and Hizballah in mid-August, but not between Israel and the fighters in Gaza, where a low-level war continues to rage.

Against the background of these events, a nasty mind game emerged: Israel's right to defend itself was improperly merged with Israel's supposed right to act in "self-defense" as generally understood in international law. The trouble here was that the UN Charter and international law have restricted valid claims of self-defense to situations where a major "armed attack" has occurred, precisely to avoid authorizing wars or excessive force as legal responses to border incidents. Indeed, the World Court found US claims of collective self-defense unlawful in the important 1986 case of Nicaragua vs. the United States on the grounds that Nicaraguan assistance to the armed insurgency in El Salvador fell short of an "armed attack." Understood in this context, Israel's claimed right to large-scale attacks on Gaza and Lebanon in response to border skirmishes involving the capture of three soldiers is certainly invalid under the international law of self-defense.

But there is a second layer of concern. It is assumed in diplomatic discourse and the media that once Israel invokes its right of self-defense, then anything goes. This negates the role of the law of war and international humanitarian law, the function of which is to set limits and provide guidelines for belligerents in wartime situations. That is, even if Israel had a valid basis to declare war on Lebanon, its conduct of that war would have to be constrained by the requirements of the laws of war.

More than international law is at stake here. To validate the Israeli responses to the Palestinian and Hizballah raids is to defy the rule of reason, which underpins world order and international law in crucial respects. It takes only a modest imagination to envision regions in flames if incidents of this, or even greater, magnitude were to be seized upon by the targeted country as occasions for general war.

If, then, Israel has a legal right to defend itself, but not a right of self-defense to justify acts of war, what was it entitled to do? A truly satisfactory answer to this question requires a consideration of the context, including the degree to which the raids were unprovoked rather than being part of a prolonged series of border incidents. But leaving aside context, Israel's right to defend itself clearly included steps, including border crossing, to catch and punish the perpetrators, and quite possibly to destroy their immediate base of operations. As Israel exceeded these measures within a day in both Gaza and Lebanon, the actual Israeli responses to the raids were grossly excessive, even if Israel is given the benefit of every doubt, by excluding context.

Mind games also emerged surrounding the proper body of applicable law. Israel has always maintained that Articles 47–78 of the Fourth Geneva Convention, laying out the duties of an occupying power, do not apply to its actions in the territories taken in the 1967 war. Though Israel is alone in this interpretation, it considers this legal argument greatly strengthened, with regard to Gaza, following its summer 2005 withdrawal of settlers and soldiers from the Strip. Further, it is Israel's claim that in both Gaza and Lebanon its enemy is not a state, but a non-state actor who is not a party to the four Geneva Conventions that constitute the body of international humanitarian law (IHL).

The First Geneva Protocol on the Protection of Victims of

International Armed Conflict (1977) supplements IHL by extending legal coverage to conflicts between a state and a non-state actor. Israel has not signed this widely ratified treaty, and so is not directly bound by it. But here also most of these obligations are now regarded as customary international law, which, like IHL itself, binds a state whether or not it has accepted a particular treaty. The 1977 protocol also binds non-state entities such as Hamas and Hizballah whenever they become participants in international conflicts. Thus, if the conflicts are understood as being between Israel and Hamas on one front, and Israel and Hizballah on the other, then both sides in both settings are bound at least by international humanitarian law recognized as customary.

Israel also insisted that the failure of Lebanon, as distinct from Hizballah, to deploy its army against the Israeli attack confirmed its claim that the Geneva Conventions were not applicable. This line of argument is contrary to international law as embodied in the Common Article 3 of these treaties, which declares that the conventions shall apply in "any armed conflict... even if the state of war is not recognized by one of them," and that parties to the conventions remain bound "even if the... occupation meets with no armed resistance."

The behavior of the various parties is all subject to customary international law of war (CILW), which has evolved over the centuries from its origins in the just war tradition, and has long been a recognized part of international law alongside treaties and conventions. There are four principles of CILW: the principle of proportionality, by which a legally valid military response must be proportional to the provoking occasion; the principle of necessity, by which a legally valid use of force must be necessary to achieve a lawful goal; the principle of discrimination, by which a legally valid use of force must discriminate between military and civilian targets; and the principle of humanity, by which a legally valid use of force must not rely on tactics that are cruel or widely perceived as inhumane. Obviously, these principles offer only very general guidelines that must be adjudged in specific circumstances, and whose proper application depends on a judicious application of the rule of reason.

The Gaza Offensive

Since its 2005 "disengagement" from Gaza, Israel has retained complete border control, including rigid regulation of entry and exit from the Strip, and control over Gazan airspace and offshore waters. It has also mounted frequent armed incursions into Gaza and launched air strikes at will. Given these realities, it would seem appropriate to consider Gaza as still subject to Israeli occupation until a withdrawal occurs that is fully respectful of Gaza's autonomy.

This conclusion bears upon the legal treatment of the border incident that Israel relied upon to launch its sustained Gaza offensive. The narrow legal issue is whether the Kerem Shalom raid was an act of terrorism or not. There is a strong basis in international law to affirm a Palestinian right of resistance, given the prolonged occupation by Israel, the refusal by Israel to respect UN resolutions calling for withdrawal to the 1967 borders, and Israel's persistent violation of IHL, inflicting great hardship on the Palestinians subject to the occupation.[1] Such a right of resistance does not accord impunity to Palestinian militants who use violence directly against Israeli civilian targets, of course. Such methods of resistance are criminal violations of the law of war. But since the targets on June 28 were military personnel, the incident does not qualify as an act of terrorism or a violation of the law of war.

At the same time, it is a violation of IHL and CILW to use the abducted Israeli soldier as a "bargaining chip," held illegally as a "hostage" for the sake of negotiating a prisoner release, especially if combined with a threat to his life. The severity of this violation by the Palestinian militant groups is somewhat diminished by their reiterated willingness to negotiate his release, the refusal of Israel to engage in diplomatic discussion with elected Palestinian leaders, and the fact that Israel has itself frequently abducted Palestinians whom it continues to detain without charge.

The big legal issue arises from the disproportion, excessiveness, and indiscriminate character of the Gaza offensive. Even if the Israeli interpretation of the abduction incident is fully accepted, there is scant legal justification for the Israeli response, either from the perspective of Common Article 3 of the Geneva Conventions, requiring respect for the sanctity of civilian life, or by the wider standards of CILW. There are two relevant norms set forth in the Hague Conventions that provide a basic standard against which to judge belligerents. First, Article 22 of the Fourth Hague Convention on Land Warfare states that "the right of belligerents to adopt means of injuring the enemy is not unlimited." This norm incorporates a measure of proportionality between the scale of provocation and response that was clearly absent from Israeli actions. Second, the so-called Martens clause in the preamble of the Hague Convention declares that

> [u]ntil a more complete code of the laws of war has been issued... the inhabitants and belligerents remain under the protection and the rule of the principles of the law of nations, as they result from the usages established among civilized peoples, from the laws of humanity, and the dictates of public conscience.

On this basis, responding to the following questions provides a legal assessment until, if ever, a duly constituted tribunal assesses the situation: Was the Gaza offensive a reasonable response, given the surrounding circumstances? Did its particular uses of force violate the limits imposed by IHL and CILW? The logical assessment is that it was unreasonable with respect to scale, scope, duration, and impact on the civilian population of Gaza, as well as with respect to targets and methods.

Such an assessment is reinforced by several other considerations. Treating the Kerem Shalom incident as the "cause" of Israel's offensive ignores prior and frequent Israeli provocations in the form of unlawful uses of force in Gaza. For instance, on June 9, 2006, Israel fired artillery shells that struck Palestinian civilians on the beach, killing 8 and wounding 32; on June 13, Israeli aircraft fired missiles at an ordinary van, supposedly a targeted assassination of a Hamas leader, that misfired and killed 9 Palestinian civilians; on June 20, in another assassination attempt that misfired, 3 Palestinian children were killed and 15 wounded. Even aside from the civilian casualties, these Israeli tactics are violations of Article 10 of the Universal Declaration of Human Rights that categorically prohibits extrajudicial executions and punishments. Moreover, with the Gazan population already beleaguered by denial of humanitarian foreign assistance for several months, the offensive is most convincingly regarded as an extreme form of collective punishment endangering civilian health and life. Article 33 of Geneva IV categorically prohibits collective punishments inflicted on civilians under occupation. The conclusion that Israel knowingly engaged in collective punishment is strongly reinforced by the deliberate bombardment of Gaza's only power plant, which provided an estimated 60 percent of Gaza's electricity and was crucial for the maintenance of the water purification system. Surely, this strike was a flagrantly unlawful act of war that could also be considered a crime against humanity.

The Attack on Lebanon

Unlike in the Palestinian case, Hizballah's raid was not immediately preceded by Israeli provocations, although Israel has repeatedly engaged in military operations inside Lebanon in alleged retaliation for Hizballah actions, and hundreds of Israeli violations of Lebanese sovereignty have been documented by the UN Forces in Lebanon (UNIFIL) since the Israeli withdrawal from southern Lebanon in 2000. Under the terms of Security Council Resolution 1559 (2004), the Lebanese government was under an international obligation to disarm militias operating within its territory—which it had failed to do. As the hostilities in Lebanon confirmed, Hizballah possessed an extensive stockpile of weaponry as well as the skill needed to inflict considerable harm on Israeli civilian society and military capabilities. So, the security threat posed to Israel was more substantial and more closely linked to the Hizballah initiating attack than in Gaza. With these conditions in mind, Israel could present a strong case under international law for a significant cross-border response designed to redress the July 12 raid and address the longer-term Hizballah threat.

And yet, the magnitude and scope of the Israeli response constituted clear violations of principles of proportionality and discrimination, and raised major concerns about the principle of humanity. Israel carried out heavy bombings and shelling to hobble the overall infrastructure of Lebanon, inflicted indiscriminate damage on villages and southern residential sections of Beirut where the Shiite population was concentrated, and imposed a massive air, land, and sea blockade on the entire country. To claim, as Israel did, that such targets were linked to the border incident because Hizballah had to be stopped from transporting the two abducted Israeli soldiers northward or outside Lebanon seems fatuous given the scale of destruction and the level of civilian suffering.

There were also credible reports of deliberate targeting of civilians, including people warned to leave villages who were later attacked from the air while fleeing in northbound convoys. The Israeli military's chief of staff, Lieutenant-General Dan Halutz, according to the *Jerusalem Post*, ordered ten multistory buildings in Beirut bombed for every rocket fired on Haifa (24 July 2006). This reported (and officially denied) order is a vengeful tactic that qualifies as terrorism, a collective punishment of intentionally disproportionate character that deliberately targets civilians in an urban setting. Finally, Israel used weapons—including cluster bombs and phosphorus bombs—that inflict cruel injuries, raising serious questions about legality under the principle of humanity. According to the head of an Israeli rocket unit, Israeli forces fired projectiles containing over 1.2 million cluster bomblets at southern Lebanon. "What we did was insane and monstrous," he said. "We covered entire towns in cluster bombs."[2] According to the *Washington Post*, UN officials believe that 90 percent of the bomblets fell in the last 72 hours before the war ended, meaning that many were fired in the two days between the passage of the UN cease-fire resolution and its implementation (26 September 2006). Possibly hundreds of thousands of the bomblets failed to detonate on impact, and lie unexploded in Lebanon.

Israel claimed that the government and people of Lebanon were legally responsible for the Hizballah attacks because, without their militia having been disarmed in accordance with Resolution 1559, Hizballah members hold seats in the Lebanese parliament and two cabinet positions. The Lebanese government clearly lacked the capacity to disarm Hizballah, and the departure of Syrian forces in 2005 removed what had been an effective control over its military operations. It is a notable fact that, after Israeli soldiers left Lebanon in 2000, not a single Israeli civilian was killed by Hizballah rockets, and only one by indirect Hizballah fire (an anti-aircraft round loosed at an Israeli jet in Lebanese airspace), until the summer 2006 hostilities commenced.[3] Beyond this, there is evidence that a major military attack on Lebanon was long in the works, and that the July 12 incident provided a pretext.[4] In any event, the World Court in the Nicaragua case set the bar very high in attributing to a state and its government responsibility for an armed movement, even when it has been financed, trained, and otherwise supported by the accused state, which is manifestly not the case with regard to Hizballah and Lebanon. From this perspective, the Israeli insistence on attributing accountability to Lebanon and its people seems completely without legal foundation, especially in view of the disproportionate response to the provoking July 12 incident. Some analysts have suggested that among Israel's objectives in attacking Lebanon was the completion of the "unfinished business" from their withdrawal in May 2000, namely the weakening of Hizballah in the domestic Lebanese political scene. The goal of altering the domestic political balance of a sovereign country as a corollary to a military engagement is, in effect, a policy of regime change by another name. To the extent that such contentions concerning Israeli objectives are correct, it would support the claim that the Israeli attacks on Lebanon were an aggressive war in violation of Article 2(4) of the UN Charter. In addition, Israel's wartime tactics violated fundamental rules of IHL, as well as infringing severely on CILW.

Resolution 1701

After a month of Israeli aerial bombardment and shelling of Lebanon and the introduction of Israeli ground forces on Lebanese soil, there appeared to be little prospect for Israel achieving its goals, namely the military defeat of Hizballah and the weakening of the party's political position within Lebanon. Contrary to repeated Israeli assertions, there was little evidence that Hizballah had either depleted its weapons stock or been significantly hampered in its operations. Further, the outrage provoked by the Israeli assault among the Lebanese civilian population had actually strengthened Hizballah's domestic stature and support. Having failed to secure its objectives through "shock and awe," Israel was left with two options: a protracted military campaign in Lebanon, for which the Israeli public appeared to have little appetite, particularly in light of Hizballah's retaliatory rocket attacks on northern Israel, or a negotiated cease-fire. Accordingly, Israel and the United States were forced to turn to the United Nations to generate a diplomatic exit strategy. The Israeli objectives were, however, unchanged. The idea was now to accomplish through diplomacy and US leverage at the UN what Israel had been unable to accomplish with the gun.

An initial draft cease-fire resolution was presented to the Security Council on August 5, following negotiations between the US, acting as Israel's proxy, and France, apparently acting on behalf of the Lebanese.[5] The key features of the draft were that it did not call for an immediate withdrawal of Israeli troops from Lebanese territory, that it demanded the cessation of all attacks by Hizballah but permitted Israel to continue military operations deemed to be "defensive," and deferred to a second resolution the authorization to deploy, under Chapter VII of the UN Charter, an international force on Lebanese territory to implement the cease-fire. By August 6, the Lebanese government had rejected the resolution as a capitulation document. By contrast, the Israelis indicated that they were very pleased with the terms of the resolution. In what was seen as a clear attempt to position the Lebanese government as the rejectionist party, Secretary of State Condoleezza Rice commented upon the release of the draft that reactions would demonstrate "who is for peace and who isn't." Following strong protest from the Arab League, the French withdrew their support for the maximalist Israeli position contained in the original draft and negotiations resumed. The modifications to the resolution over the next week were, however, more a reflection of Israel's ongoing failure to achieve military victory than any diplomatic dynamism.

The process that ultimately yielded UN Security Council Resolution 1701, passed on August 11, reflects the failure of international legal order. First, the 34-day delay in calling for an immediate cease-fire, despite pleas from the Lebanese government, represents the Security Council's complicity in permitting an aggressor to wage a military campaign unfettered by the obligations of the UN Charter and the prohibition on aggressive war. Indeed, even after the resolution was passed Israel was afforded another 48 hours to accomplish further military objectives in Lebanon, enabling the Israelis to greatly increase their ground forces in Lebanon prior to putting the cease-fire into effect. This 48-hour window was contrary to Security Council practice whereby resolutions come into effect immediately unless a specific time frame is contained in the text of the resolution. No such time frame is mentioned, suggesting that the 48-hour window was simply a final effort by the US to provide political cover for Israel to attempt to seize some vestige of military victory from the jaws of its defeat. Israel was not censured in any way for using the run-up to the cease-fire to further escalate its military presence in Lebanon. In this sense, the UN proved not only unable to restrain Security Council permanent members and their allies from violating the Charter, but actually seemed to collaborate with the violations. The circumstances of the passage of Resolution 1701 reflect the reality, especially acute in the post–September 11 era, that the UN is all too frequently a geopolitical tool for powerful states rather than an instrument for the enforcement of international law.

Beyond the process by which 1701 was negotiated, the terms of the resolution itself serve to undermine the UN's own authority. The very one-sidedness of the resolution is detrimental to the foundational principle of the UN Charter, which prohibits the waging of aggressive war. Resolution 1701 favors the country that blew up a border incident into an all-out war and attacked civilian targets in Lebanon in flagrant violation of the laws of war. The qualitatively discriminatory nature of the resolution, particularly when coupled with the failure to criticize Israel's tactics, appears to repudiate the central tenet of the international security system the UN was established to uphold.

Imbalances

Resolution 1701 adopts the Israeli narrative by singling out Hizballah as having initiated hostilities through a border attack on a single Israeli military patrol, while failing to criticize the disproportionate aerial bombardment and artillery campaign directed at all of Lebanon by the Israeli military. By identifying Hizballah as responsible for the initiation of the conflict, the resolution, which designates the conflict as a "threat to international peace and security," suggests that the Chapter VII authorization of UNIFIL to assist the Lebanese army in implementing the terms of the cease-fire might include a mandate to deal forcibly with Hizballah as the source of the threat to international security. This formulation not only fails to censure the party principally responsible for escalating the conflict, it actually rewards the Israeli use of force by suggesting that the Israeli response may have been within the bounds of legitimate military action. Whereas Security Council Resolution 1559 made reference to the disarming and disbanding of militias operating in Lebanon, the relevant provision was not governed by the Council's Chapter VII powers and could not be interpreted as permitting the use of force to accomplish such disarmament. By contrast, Resolution 1701 authorizes a peace-enforcement operation that, by its nature, is an exercise of the Council's Chapter VII powers. Despite subsequent indications by Secretary-General Annan that the resolution does not place the disarmament of Hizballah under a UN mandate,[6] the reference to disarmament in a resolution that itself is at least partially under Chapter VII authority provides fresh ammunition to the Israeli argument that intervention to disarm Hizballah might be authorized. Further, by failing to acknowledge the distinction between Israel's "right to defend itself" against border raids and the Israeli escalation of the July 12 skirmish into an all-out assault on Lebanon, the resolution comes dangerously close to turning an invocation of the right of self-defense into a license to use force aggressively and indiscriminately.

Another respect in which the resolution favors Israel is by prohibiting all attacks by Hizballah while requiring Israel only to stop "offensive military operations." A holdover from the previous draft, this imbalance permitted the Israelis not only to leave their troops on Lebanese soil despite the cease-fire but also to continue engaging in military activities in Lebanon, such as the "commando operation" conducted in the Baalbek valley a week after the cease-fire went into effect. Annan has identified this raid as a violation of the cessation of hostilities, along with numerous airspace violations by Israeli military aircraft that have been documented by UNIFIL. The Israeli response, however, has been that these actions are in compliance with Resolution 1701 because Israel deems them to be "defensive" operations. By failing to provide a definition of "offensive military operations," the resolution invites this kind of expedient definition by the Israelis.

Indeed, Resolution 1701 further favors the Israelis by imposing a disarmament obligation on Hizballah with no restriction of any kind on Israeli military policies. Arguably, with its Chapter VII authority and inclusion of an obligation to disarm Hizballah, this resolution is designed to be an implementation mechanism for Resolution 1559. The Lebanese domestic context that led to the passage of 1559 in 2004 has changed dramatically since then, not least as a result of Israel's war on Lebanon. Any attempt to forcibly disarm Hizballah today using the Lebanese army would risk a civil war by driving a wedge between the Lebanese government and the Shiite community, which represents over 40 percent of the Lebanese population. Attempts to disarm Hizballah are doomed unless the party itself, together with its supporters, consents. But in the wake of a war that demonstrated that an armed Hizballah may be the only force in Lebanon capable of deterring Israeli aggression, such consent is hardly likely. Further, to the extent that it could be secured, it would be through a process of national dialogue and not by deploying the Lebanese army or an international force to complete Israel's mission.

These considerations point toward another significant failure of 1701, namely the ill-defined mandate given to the more "robust" UNIFIL authorized by the resolution. The new authorization for UNIFIL appears to have been issued under the Security Council's Chapter VII authority, and as such may require the force to become involved in the disarming of Hizballah, designated by the resolution as the responsible party for the "threat to international peace and security" that arose from the war. The ambiguous mandate and the possibility that the force would be drawn into conflict with Hizballah or fired upon by Israel made it very difficult to persuade countries to participate in the mission. The French, who were initially expected to lead the force, were reluctant to commit a large contingent, and Israel vetoed the participation of contingents drawn from countries with which it does not have diplomatic relations, such as Indonesia, Malaysia, and Bangladesh, all traditionally strong contributors to UN peacekeeping operations. The Israeli conditions on peacekeepers coupled with the European desire for clear ground rules led to significant delays in the deployment of an international force.

The corollary to the failure to deploy a strengthened UNIFIL force rapidly was the Israeli refusal, until September, to lift the embargo it imposed on Lebanon, prolonging the war's burdens on Lebanon's civilian population. Indeed, arguably, the cease-fire was mainly designed to spare Israeli civilians the costs of war. Since the only threat Israeli civilians faced during the war was Hizballah rocket attacks, the danger to them was eliminated. While the implementation of the cease-fire brought aerial attacks by all sides to an end, the presence of Israeli troops on Lebanese soil left Lebanese civilians vulnerable to shelling from ground forces, particularly since Israel interprets the resolution as permitting "commando operations" in residential areas. The unexploded munitions scattered across the southern Lebanese landscape also imperil civilians there.

Indeed, Resolution 1701 did not address the use of prohibited weapons by Israel, or the use of certain permitted weapons in unlawful ways. Human Rights Watch (HRW) and other human rights organizations have been able to document the use by Israel of white phosphorus, not as an illumination device, but as an offensive chemical weapon. Israel has subsequently conceded that it deliberately used phosphorus shells offensively during its 2006 attack on Lebanon.[7] The Israeli use of cluster munitions in densely populated residential areas is another example of a prohibited usage of a weapon in violation of the laws of war. Indeed, the use of so many cluster bombs was equivalent to mining those civilian areas, because so many munitions normally do not explode on impact.

Following the conclusion of the war, UN mine clearance experts discovered over 100,000 unexploded cluster munitions in Lebanon and determined that "90 percent of the cluster bomb strikes occurred in the last 72 hours of the conflict"—that is, after the cease-fire resolution had been passed. As of September 28, 2006, HRW documented 18 deaths and 108 injuries from unexploded munitions in Lebanon after the cessation of hostilities. On the BBC, United Nations humanitarian chief Jan Egeland described the Israeli use of cluster munitions in Lebanon as "shocking and completely immoral" (30 August 2006). Despite these post-conflict denunciations of Israeli use of cluster munitions, the deafening silence of the UN Security Council about Israeli attacks on civilian infrastructure and residential areas in violation of the laws of war and use of prohibited weapons remains a deep indictment of the organization. Whether subsequent efforts, such as Amnesty International's call for a comprehensive and independent UN investigation of possible war crimes committed during the conflict, will correct this failure is yet to be seen.[8]

The remaining imbalances embedded in Resolution 1701 relate to the treatment of prisoners held on both sides, the treatment of occupied territory and the failure to address the root causes of the conflict. First, the resolution demands the unconditional release of two Israeli soldiers held by Hizballah but only "encourages efforts at settling the issue of Lebanese prisoners detained in Israel." These prisoners include four whose release Hizballah negotiated in 2004 only to have the Israelis renege at the last minute, another two dozen Lebanese who were disappeared during the Israeli occupation of southern Lebanon and are believed to either remain in Israeli custody or whose remains have been buried in secret by Israel, and the numerous Lebanese who were captured by the Israelis during the 2006 war. While no precise number is yet available for the Lebanese captured during Israel's 2006 attack, at least a half dozen were abducted during an Israeli commando raid on a hospital in Baalbek on August 1, 2006. Those seized included the unfortunately named Lebanese grocer, Hassan Dib Nasrallah, and his son, Bilal, who were quietly released by Israel after their interrogation revealed that the resemblance of the grocer's name to that of the Hizballah leader was purely coincidental. The others abducted in that raid have joined the ranks of Lebanese detainees held in Israel. The failure to impose symmetrical obligations with respect to prisoners and the failure to note that the Israelis being held are soldiers, while Israel abducted Lebanese civilians prior to and during the war, make a mockery of the Geneva Conventions' rules of detention. Taken together, the failures of Resolution 1701 reflect the UN's inability to protect a state that is the victim of aggressive war waged by the US or its close allies. In effect, Resolution 1701 demonstrates that where the permanent members and their allies are concerned, the Security Council will collaborate with the aggressor in the post-conflict situation to ratify the effects of the aggression.

But perhaps the most glaring failure is the absence of any consideration of the root causes of the conflict between Israel and its neighbors as part of any meaningful or tenable cease-fire. By failing to address the ongoing and related Israeli aggression in Gaza, the absence of a framework for a comprehensive peace settlement between Israel and Palestinians, and the continuing occupation of the Syrian Golan Heights (including the Shebaa Farms), the cease-fire resolution ensured that it could not be the basis of anything more than a temporary stalemate.

New Avenues

The implications of Resolution 1701, coupled with the course of hostilities among Israel, Hizballah, and armed Palestinian groups in the summer of 2006, suggest severe consequences not only for the civilian populations caught up in the conflicts but also for the enforceability of the international laws of war. In addition to the obvious need for a cessation of Israel's attacks in Gaza, further measures are required to address the violations of the laws of war that took place in these conflicts. The obvious inability of the Security Council to take effective steps to uphold the most basic norms of international law must be addressed with creative international proposals to supplement the Council when the arbiters of geopolitics undermine its authority to act.

Rather than retreating cynically from the limits imposed on the conduct of war by international law, concerned parties should look for new avenues for pursuing the implementation of international humanitarian law and the customary international laws of war. Three potential avenues are readily identifiable. First, the parties to the Fourth Geneva Convention should be convened to fulfill their obligation under Article 1 to protect the civilian populations of Lebanon and Gaza, and explore the grounds under Article 147 for the criminal prosecution of grave breaches of the convention. Second, a detailed request should be submitted to the prosecutor's office of the International Criminal Court to investigate all credible allegations of violations of the laws of war and commission of crimes against humanity during the Lebanon war. Indeed, this call was forcefully issued by the United Nations' Chief War Crimes Prosecutor for the former Yugoslavia, Carla del Ponte, when she complained in Agence France Press of international double standards in conflicts where "according to credible reports, serious violations of international humanitarian law were committed, for instance during the recent Israel–Lebanon conflict, but no independent criminal investigation is taking place" (6 October 2006). Finally, an emergency session of the UN General Assembly should be called to explore these allegations, and establish an international commission of eminent persons to assess the legality of Israel's response to border incidents, possibly including reference to the World Court for a relevant advisory opinion on the applicability of customary international laws of war to the Gaza offensive and the war in Lebanon.

The situation in Lebanon teeters on the edge of civil war, suggesting that there may be renewed and massive violence indirectly brought about by the Israeli war of aggression. It should be obvious in retrospect that Israel's war aims had little to do with border security, and mainly related to pushing forward their regional agenda, in partnership with the United States, of using military force to promote desired regime changes. Disturbingly, not even the utter failure of the approach in Iraq has lessened Israeli/American support for the pursuit of these strategic goals. What is painfully evident is that the norms of international law are put aside both by recourse to and conduct of war by the United States and Israel, and that the lawlessness exhibited in the Lebanon war is part of a wider pattern that increasingly threatens a disastrous war of regional scope.

NOTES

1 See Richard Falk and Burns H. Weston, "The Relevance of International Law to Palestinian Rights in the West Bank and Gaza: In Legal Defense of the Intifada," *Harvard International Law Journal* 32.1 (1991); and Richard Falk, "International Law and the al-Aqsa Intifada," *Middle East Report* 217 (Winter 2000).

2 *Ha'aretz* 12 September 2006. Human Rights Watch has documented two instances where Hizballah fired cluster munitions contained in Chinese-made rockets at the Israeli town of Maghar.

3 Augustus Richard Norton, "The Peacekeeping Challenge in Lebanon," *MIT Electronic Journal of Middle East Studies* 6 (Summer 2006) 76.

4 *San Francisco Chronicle* 21 July 2006.

5 The draft was printed in the *New York Times* 5 August 2006.

6 Kofi Annan stated explicitly that "disarming Hizballah is not the direct mandate of the UN" in an interview on Israel's Channel 2 television station. Gil Hoffman and *Jerusalem Post* staff, "Report: Lebanese Army to be Only Force to Bear Arms," *Jerusalem Post* 16 August 2006.

7 Meron Rappaport, "Israel Admits Using Phosphorus Bombs during War in Lebanon," *Ha'aretz* 22 October 2006.

8 Amnesty International, *Deliberate Destruction or "Collateral Damage"? Israeli Attacks on Civilian Infrastructure* (London, 23 August 2006).

16. THE LEBANON WAR IN THE UN, THE UN IN THE LEBANON WAR

Phyllis Bennis

In the middle of the 2006 Israeli war in Lebanon, a National Public Radio host asked me what I thought the war might mean for Condoleezza Rice's legacy as the first African-American woman to serve as US secretary of state. My immediate answer (perhaps too quick) was that Rice's legacy no longer had anything to do with her being a powerful African-American woman. From now on, I said, she would be remembered first as the highest-ranking US diplomat who told the United Nations, even as thousands of civilians continued to be made victims of a brutal war, that her government doesn't want a cease-fire, that a cease-fire would be "a false promise."[1]

At the United Nations, the US and Israel stood alone in defying the regional and global calls for an immediate cease-fire. According to the *New York Times*,

> American officials signaled that Ms. Rice was waiting at least a few more days before wading into the conflict, in part to give Israel more time to weaken Hizballah forces. The strategy carries risk, partly because it remains unclear just how long the rest of the world, particularly America's Arab allies, will continue to stay silent as the toll on Lebanese civilians rises.[2]

Instead, as the world demanded a new resolution to end the fighting, the US government declared instead that its goal was to implement the much earlier UN Resolution 1559, which had called only for the disarming of Hizballah and the deployment of the Lebanese army to southern Lebanon.[3]

The Israeli government itself recognized the importance of the world's response, and clearly counted on Washington's protection from any UN effort to hold Tel Aviv accountable. Speaking of the Gaza escalation that presaged the attack on Lebanon three days later, Israel's Ministry of Foreign Affairs reported that their assault

> does have an international dimension; the IDF has been fighting for almost two weeks and the international response to the results of the fighting has been low-key.... thus allowing Israel military freedom of action and maintaining its ability to receive international backing.[4]

Qana

It wasn't until the lethal Israeli assault on the Lebanese town of Qana on July 30, weeks into the war, that Rice declared on *ABC News*, "it is time for a cease-fire" (30 July 2006). The 2006 attack on Qana returned to stark reality the decade-long memory that was beginning to fade in much of the world, but which remained sharp and painful in Lebanon and inside the United Nations. Ten years earlier, in August 1996, during one of the frequent assaults that characterized Israel's then-18-year-long occupation of southern Lebanon, the Israeli air force attacked a UN peacekeeping center at Qana, a small Lebanese village in the south. The center was a long-established headquarters for UNIFIL, the UN's observer force in place since Israel's illegal occupation of southern Lebanon began in 1978; its mandate was to "confirm" the immediate Israeli withdrawal demanded by Security Council Resolution 425. But Israel had actually expanded its occupation throughout southern Lebanon, UNIFIL had been unable to do more than monitor Israel's continued occupation, and by 1996 Qana was a well-known UNIFIL headquarters.

When the August 1996 bombardments began, hundreds of Lebanese refugees from surrounding towns and villages, most of them women, children, and old people, had taken shelter at Qana, hoping the UNIFIL presence there would protect them from the bombardment. Instead, despite the presence (documented in UN photographs) of a high-tech surveillance drone directly overhead, relaying detailed information to Israeli air force commanders, the Israeli attack targeted the UN center and killed more than 100 Lebanese civilians, while wounding several Fijian peacekeepers serving with UNIFIL.

The Israeli attack on the UN center, and its aftermath, quickly came to symbolize the complicated relationship between the United States, Israel, and the United Nations, in which UN efforts to hold Israel accountable for violations of international law are repeatedly thwarted by US schemes designed to protect its key ally. Israeli officials had immediately claimed the Qana massacre was an "unfortunate mistake." UN Secretary-General Boutros Boutros-Ghali immediately commissioned an investigative report. When the report was completed, but before it was publicly issued, it included clear documentation of the presence of the Israeli drone surveillance plane in the immediate area during the airstrikes, thus rebutting the Israeli claim that the Qana attack was an accident. US diplomats moved quickly to try to prevent the information from being released, but eventually Boutros-Ghali, while carefully re-editing the report, allowed it to be made public. It was still unmistakably damning to Israeli claims. US officials were furious, and their anger at the secretary-general seemed to consolidate Washington's already intense effort to prevent Boutros-Ghali from serving a second term.[5]

For Lebanese, and so many others throughout the Arab world, the 1996 Qana attack came to signify the price civilians would continue to pay for Israeli occupation and domination. And for the United Nations staff, and for UN blue-helmet peacekeepers serving around the world, the 1996 Qana attack came to symbolize Israel's antagonism to the United Nations itself. So when Israel hit Qana again during the 2006 war against Hizballah and Lebanon, the anger and global outrage were even higher than the anger that inevitably would have answered the wanton killing anywhere of between 28 and 54 civilians, at least 16 of whom were children.

Within hours of the July 30, 2006 attack, the Security Council convened in emergency session. Secretary-General Kofi Annan called on the Council to condemn the attack "in the strongest possible terms." He called for immediate action to halt the spiraling violence "for the sake of the people of the region and of this Organization." Particularly concerned with the impact of Israel's war on "the people of the Middle East, the authority of the United Nations, and especially the Council," Annan went on to warn that, "the authority and standing of this Council are at stake. People have noticed its failure to act firmly and quickly during this crisis."

Recognizing the consequences of the US rejection of a cease-fire, Annan said that he was "deeply dismayed" that his own earlier calls for immediate cessation of hostilities had not been heeded, "with the result that innocent life continues to be taken and innocent civilians continue to suffer. ... This tragedy has, rightly, provoked moral outrage throughout the world," he said, regretting that some Lebanese, outraged over the world's refusal to call for a cease-fire, had turned their anger against the United Nations. Earlier that same day a large number of protesters had broken into the UN's Economic and Social Commission for Western Asia (ESCWA) headquarters in Beirut, and briefly set fire to it.[6]

Washington Holds the UN Back—Again

But while the UN secretary-general responded immediately, and a Security Council meeting was called on an emergency basis, it would be more than another week before the Bush administration would allow the Council to pass Resolution 1701 calling for a cease-fire. During that time, hundreds more civilians were killed, hundreds of thousands more displaced, and billions of dollars worth of Lebanese infrastructure were destroyed. And yet, Secretary Rice declared, the additional casualties caused by the delay were of little significance. The delay "has been time that's been well spent over the last couple of weeks," she said.[7]

For weeks, the Security Council discussion reflected very clearly Washington's insistence that Israel be given more time to finish its effort to destroy Hizballah in Lebanon, at whatever cost to the people, society, economy, environment of the country. US Ambassador John Bolton staunchly refused even to consider a cease-fire. Only after the Qana attack did the global horror and outrage at the civilian carnage force a still-reluctant Bush administration to give in and allow a cease-fire.

But the compromise call for a "cessation of hostilities" still missed the point. It called for "the immediate cessation by Hizballah of all attacks," but on Israel only of "all offensive military operations," thus giving only Israel the right of self-defense. The Associated Press recognized the text as a "major victory for the US and Israel" (5 August 2006). After pressure from veto-wielding France, and a visit to the Security Council of a high-level delegation of the Arab League led by key US allies, language was added that called for the withdrawal of Israeli troops from Lebanese territory only as Lebanese army and UNIFIL troops moved south.

Israel's justice minister, Haim Ramon, noting that the resolution did not call for the immediate withdrawal of Israeli troops, said that it was "good for Israel," but that Israel still had military goals to meet in Lebanon, and therefore "we have to continue fighting, continue hitting anyone we can hit in Hizballah." Even before the compromise resolution had passed in the Security Council, Ramon announced that after it was passed, Israel would not withdraw from a buffer zone several kilometers deep in southern Lebanon until the international force arrived.[8]

In fact, the UN's humanitarian chief, Jan Egeland, later reported that it was during the last hours of Council negotiations that Israel launched its most intensive and lethal attacks on Lebanese civilians. "What's shocking—and I would say to me completely immoral—is that 90 percent of the cluster bomb strikes occurred in the last 72 hours of the conflict, when we knew there would be a resolution," he said. "Every day people are maimed, wounded and are killed by these ordnance."[9]

When the resolution ultimately passed, it was with the barest support even from the pro-US government of Lebanon. Although the carnage at Qana and elsewhere across Lebanon, and the resulting international outrage, allowed enough changes in the draft text to reflect concern for the massive civilian casualties, the resolution's primary purpose was designed to suppress Hizballah's military positioning in southern Lebanon, as well as attempting to diminish its political power and growing influence in the country as a whole. It thus threatened to further destabilize the already shaky Lebanese state (Hizballah was a major force in Lebanon's parliament and politics), as well as to contain the militia's rising status throughout the Middle East. What it wasn't designed to do was force Israeli troops out of Lebanon and ensure a complete end to the war.

The Resolution

The first operative paragraph set the stage. It called for "a full cessation of hostilities based upon, in particular, the immediate cessation by Hizballah of all attacks and the immediate cessation by Israel of all offensive military operations." So right from the beginning there was no mutual cease-fire, only a discriminatory, uneven call for Hizballah to cease "all" attacks, while Israel was only required to stop "offensive" military activity. There was no definition of what Israel might consider "defensive" and therefore acceptable under the terms of the resolution, and crucially, no identification of any agency (the UN, UNIFIL, the Lebanese army, whoever) that would be authorized to determine what was offensive and what was defensive.

Overall the resolution was consistently one-sided, holding Hizballah responsible for the crisis, while failing to acknowledge any Israeli responsibility. This included the Security Council's view of the origins of the conflict: the resolution defined the hostilities beginning with "Hizballah's attack on Israel on 12 July 2006," ignoring Israel's role in transforming a small-scale border skirmish into a full-scale regional war. It reflected the tendency common in the US press of defining the responsible party by choosing when to start the clock. That is, by claiming the events of July 12 as the origin of the crisis, the Council ignored everything that had gone before, including Israel's constant overflights of Lebanese territory, its holding of hundreds of Lebanese prisoners, and the events in Gaza in the days and weeks earlier that had set the political stage for Hizballah's action.

Crucially, it also ignored Israel's role in creating a war out of a border incident. Hizballah's July 12 raid across the Israeli border may have violated the 1949 armistice agreement between the newly created state of Israel and Lebanon (there has never been an actual peace treaty signed), but it was limited to a military target. The only Israelis killed or captured were soldiers. Israel responded with a failed attempt to get the soldiers back, and then escalated immediately to massive airstrikes on Lebanese civilian targets—first the southern bridges, then the Beirut international airport. That escalation turned the border clash into a war—and it was that Israeli escalation that represented a clear violation of international legal prohibitions against targeting civilian infrastructure. Only after Israel had transformed a border skirmish into a war and escalated from military to illegal civilian targets, did Hizballah begin its own—also illegal—firing of rockets against Israeli cities.

Given the human devastation of the predictable Israeli response, one could certainly argue that the original Hizballah raid to capture the soldiers was what French Foreign Minister Philippe Douste-Blazy called an "irresponsible act." But it did not violate international law. According to Human Rights Watch, "the targeting and capture of enemy soldiers is allowed under international humanitarian law."[10] Israel's escalation, on the other hand, to a full-scale attack on civilians and civilian infrastructure, starting with the bombing of the Beirut international airport, was what Douste-Blazy, distinguishing it from Hizballah's raid, called "a disproportionate act of war."[11] The resolution even failed to condemn Israeli war crimes with the legalistic term "disproportionate."

The resolution was seriously flawed in other ways as well. There was no reference to a prisoner exchange, despite widespread understanding that Israel's long-term holding of Lebanese prisoners seized by Israeli commandos inside Lebanese territory was one of the key factors underpinning the conflict. There was a specific demand on Hizballah for the "unconditional release of the abducted Israeli soldiers," but only a vague reference to "encouraging the efforts aimed at settling the issue of the Lebanese prisoners detained in Israel." That meant no actual pressure on Israel at all. There was no mention of the 9,400 Palestinian prisoners then held by Israel, whose release (starting with the release of the 300 or so children and over 125 women among them) was part of the first demand by Hizballah in exchange for the captured soldiers, even before Israel escalated the border skirmish to full-scale war.

In fact, the resolution completely ignored the link between the Lebanon war and the parallel crisis then raging in Gaza; the text does not mention the Palestinians at all. In its assertion that the only cause for the Lebanon war was the Hizballah attack of July 12 (when the two Israeli soldiers were captured), the resolution delinked the Lebanon war from its Palestinian origins, and implicitly continued Israel's US-granted green light to continue its ongoing assault in Gaza.

There was also no reference to Israel's use of weapons internationally designated as illegal. The resolution did call on Israel to turn over to the UN maps of its minefields in southern Lebanon (remaining from its eighteen years of occupation) but there was no requirement that it cease its current use of prohibited cluster bombs (which become land mines when they do not detonate immediately) and white phosphorous ammunition against civilian targets. UN Undersecretary-General for Humanitarian Affairs Jan Egeland, who called Israel's use of cluster bombs "completely immoral," reported to the Security Council that Israel had dropped so many cluster bombs during the last 72 hours before the UN cease-fire that more than 100,000 remained unexploded—which meant more than one million were originally dropped. The cluster bombs each contain small "bomblets" powerful enough to blow off a foot, a leg, a child's head—and the 10 percent or so that fail to detonate when they hit the ground turn into landmine-like anti-personnel weapons.

While the resolution called on all states to prevent "the sale or supply to any entity or individual in Lebanon of arms and related materiel of all types, including weapons and ammunition, military vehicles and equipment, paramilitary equipment, and spare parts for the aforementioned, whether or not originating in their territories," it was understood that this prohibition was aimed at Hizballah and its Iranian suppliers. No one took the reference to apply to Israel's arms suppliers even while Israeli troops remained in Lebanon. This was particularly relevant since UN High Commissioner for Human Rights Louise Arbour told the world that war crimes had been committed on both sides, and warned that political leaders of supporting countries could be held personally liable. Human Rights Watch called Israeli violations against civilians in Lebanon "war crimes."[12]

But the US government faced no UN or other international sanction for its complicity in Israeli war crimes, achieved by providing military hardware, fuel, and weapons to Israel, knowing that they were being used in violation of international and US domestic law such as the Arms Export Control Act. Instead, Washington's escalation of the militarization of the region remained unchallenged by the United Nations. During the Israeli assault Washington ratcheted up its provision of both emergency (jet fuel), and "ordinary" military equipment (including a replacement batch of 600-pound "bunker-buster" bombs) to Israel.[13] And in the midst of the war in Lebanon, the Bush administration approved $6 billion worth of new US arms sales to the Saudi government, including Black Hawk helicopters, armored vehicles, and other military equipment. That was separate from the $2.9 billion sale, announced at the same time, of M1A1 tanks for the Saudi military.[14] The administration justified the sale to Congress claiming that the sale would help strengthen Saudi Arabia's military and its ability to help the US fight terrorism around the world.

It was particularly telling that the only cause mentioned in the resolution's reference to "the need to address urgently the causes that have given rise to the current crisis" was "the abducted Israeli soldiers." There was no acknowledgment of the widespread evidence that Israel, with certain US approval, had planned its assault against Lebanon more than a year earlier, and was simply waiting for the right provocation. "Of all of Israel's wars since 1948, this was the one for which Israel was most prepared," said Gerald Steinberg, professor of political science at Bar-Ilan University. "In a sense," he told the *San Francisco Chronicle*, "the preparation began in May 2000, immediately after the Israeli withdrawal [from Lebanon] ... and, in the last year or two, it's been simulated and rehearsed across the board." In fact, the *Chronicle* article went on,

> more than a year ago, a senior Israeli army officer began giving PowerPoint presentations, on an off-the-record basis, to US and other diplomats, journalists and think tanks, setting out the plan for the current operation in revealing detail. ... In his talks, the officer described a three-week campaign: The first week concentrated on

destroying Hizballah's heavier long-range missiles, bombing its command-and-control centers, and disrupting transportation and communication arteries.[15]

Israeli strategists appeared confident enough of US protection in the United Nations that they remained unconcerned that attacking Beirut's international airport and destroying key civilian-use bridges across Lebanon's rivers constituted clear violations of international humanitarian law, particularly the Geneva Conventions' prohibitions on attacking civilian targets. And the Israelis were right—the UN resolution said nothing about the possibility of war crimes. It called for deployment of an international peacekeeping force only on the Lebanese side of the border—clearly aimed at suppressing Hizballah—but never even considering a similar deployment on the Israeli side.

The Precursor: Israel's War in Gaza

It is impossible to examine the UN's response to Israel's 2006 Lebanon war without taking into account its response to the earlier Israeli assault on the Gaza Strip, which began just weeks before the latest Lebanon crisis broke out. While it is clear that Israel had already planned its anti-Hizballah attack in Lebanon, the Hizballah capture of the two Israeli soldiers that provided Israel with its claimed justification was directly linked to the crisis unfolding in Gaza. In the first hours after the soldiers were seized on the Lebanese border, Hizballah's leader, Shaykh Hassan Nasrallah, publicly announced that the organization wanted to negotiate a prisoner swap with Israel, in which the soldiers, including the one captured by Hamas just outside the Gaza Strip two weeks earlier, would be exchanged for Palestinian and Lebanese prisoners being held in Israeli jails. Hizballah made clear that it had carried out its raid to provide the Palestinians with stronger bargaining chips for their negotiations with Israel—aiming at the kind of negotiated prisoner swap that had been carried out numerous times before between Israel and various Lebanese and Palestinian forces. (The hyperbolic Israeli claim that "we never negotiate with 'terrorists'" never had any basis in historical fact.)

The crisis sharpened six months after the Palestinian elections that had brought Hamas to power were answered by an Israeli- and US-led international boycott and economic sanctions against the Palestinian Authority. The 2005 Israeli "disengagement" from Gaza had resulted in settlers being moved out and Israeli soldiers redeployed from the Gazan territory to positions surrounding the strip. But under international law, which defines occupation as control of territory by an outside power, Gaza remained occupied, with Israel continuing to control all borders and entry and exit of people and goods, controlling Gaza's airspace and coastal waters, and preventing the construction of a seaport or the rebuilding of the Israeli-bombed airport. The humanitarian crisis throughout the occupied Palestinian territories, but especially in Gaza, was already at crisis proportions, as the US-orchestrated sanctions ostensibly aimed at the Hamas-dominated Palestinian Authority (PA) in fact imposed a brutal collective punishment on the entire Palestinian population of the occupied territories.

Hamas had maintained a unilateral cease-fire for sixteen months. But as Israeli attacks continued to escalate, the organization announced its intention to end the cease-fire. When Israeli fire killed nine people on a Gaza beach, seven of them from one family and five of them children, Hamas responded with a June 25 raid to capture a soldier at a military checkpoint just outside the Gaza Strip.

Following the soldier's capture, Israel intensified its military assault on Gaza, beginning with the destruction of the only power-generating plant in Gaza, the only source of power for half of the 1.4 million residents. During the massive escalation, Israeli Prime Minister Ehud Olmert admitted on the BBC that Israel remained in control and would continue to act militarily in Gaza as it sees fit. "We will operate, enter and pull out as needed," he said (9 July 2006). Israel continued its air strikes and ground attacks on people and infrastructure throughout Gaza, and continued its nightly barrage of sonic sound-bombs across Gaza's population centers.

During the Gaza crisis, United Nations humanitarian agencies working on the ground played a key role in informing the world about the catastrophe facing the Palestinians. Israel's attacks represented a massive collective punishment against the 1.4 million people of Gaza, and thus under international law constitute a war crime, violating Israel's obligations as occupying power under the Geneva Conventions. The deliberate targeting and destruction of the electricity generating plant, especially at the height of summer and at a moment in which the already in-place siege of Gaza meant there were virtually no fuel stocks available for local generators, guaranteed widespread humanitarian disaster for a civilian population, something specifically prohibited under the Geneva Conventions. The same was true for the deliberate destruction of the already-eroded water system meant that already borderline-saline water became scarcer than ever. The humanitarian situation quickly moved from terrible to catastrophic.

The UN's humanitarian organizations working on the ground in Gaza issued statements expressing deep alarm. In a rare joint statement, the agencies said they were

> alarmed by developments on the ground, which have seen innocent civilians, including children, killed, brought increased misery to hundreds of thousands of people, and which will wreak far-reaching harm on Palestinian society. An already alarming situation in Gaza, with poverty rates at nearly eighty per cent and unemployment at nearly forty per cent, is likely to deteriorate rapidly, unless immediate and urgent action is taken.

According to the high commissioner for human rights, "the use of force by Israel during its military operations into the Gaza Strip has resulted in an increasing number of deaths and other casualties amongst the Palestinian civilian population, and significant damage to civilian property and infrastructure." UNRWA, which cares for 980,000 Palestinian refugees, "believes that Gaza is on the brink of a public health disaster." The World Health Organization (WHO) stated that

> the public health system is facing an unprecedented crisis. WHO estimates that though hospitals and 50 per cent of Primary Health Care Centers have generators, the current stock of fuel will last for a maximum of two weeks. ... According to WHO in the last week, there has been a 160 per cent increase in cases of diarrhea compared with the same period last year. Compounding these problems, WHO estimates that 23 per cent of the essential drug list will be out of stock within one month.

The World Food Program (WFP) estimated that "in June 70 percent of the Gaza population were already unable to cover their daily food needs without assistance. The escalation of hostilities has made food an increasingly critical issue. Wheat flour mills, food factories and bakeries, reliant on electricity, are being forced to reduce their production due to power shortages; furthermore the loss of capacity to preserve perishable food in the Gaza heat is resulting in high food losses in the home." And UNICEF stated that children in Gaza are living in an environment of extraordinary violence, insecurity, and fear.

> ... The ongoing fighting is hurting children psychologically. Caregivers say children are showing signs of distress and exhaustion, including a 15–20 percent increase in bedwetting, due to shelling and sonic booms. ... UNICEF stressed that children are always most vulnerable to outbreaks of communicable disease brought on by lack of water and sanitation.

OCHA, the overall humanitarian coordinating agency, called on Israel to allow UN deliveries of emergency supplies, but recognized that

> humanitarian assistance is not enough to prevent suffering. With the bombing of the electric plant, the lives of 1.4 million people, almost half of them children, worsened overnight. The Government of Israel should repair the damage done to the power station. Obligations under international humanitarian law, applying to both parties, include preventing harm to civilians and destroying civilian infrastructure and also refraining from collective measures, intimidation and reprisals. Civilians are disproportionately paying the price of this conflict.[16]

OCHA's mention of international humanitarian law referred to the Fourth Geneva Convention. Article 3(1)(a) prohibits "violence to life and person" and "murder of all kinds." Calling murder "targeted assassination" does not make it legal. Article 33 states that "No protected person may be punished for an offense he or she has not personally committed. Collective penalties and likewise all measures of intimidation or of terrorism are prohibited." In Article 36 the "taking of hostages is prohibited." That would include the Israeli arrests of about one-third of the elected Palestinian Legislative Assembly and about one-half of the Palestinian Authority's cabinet ministers, who were being held at least partly to serve as bargaining chips.

But no specific response to these specific violations of international law, despite their having been documented by key United Nations humanitarian agencies, was forthcoming from the UN's most powerful political body, the Security Council. It was not for lack of trying. During the week before Hizballah's capture of the two soldiers, the Council debated a Gaza resolution proposed by the Arab Group at the UN, which called for an end to Israel's "disproportionate" military attacks that were already responsible for numerous deaths and injuries among Palestinian civilians. The resolution also called on Palestinians to stop the firing of rockets from Gaza into Israel, and demanded the "unconditional" release of the captured Israeli soldier. But despite that careful language and the deliberate inclusion of demands on the Palestinians, the US used its veto to prevent passage of the Council resolution. US Ambassador John Bolton claimed it was "unbalanced" and that it would put "demands on one side of the Middle East conflict but not the other."[17]

And Before: The UN in Lebanon

Almost two decades before Israel's 2006 war against Hizballah in Lebanon, it had engaged in a similar effort to wipe out a perceived challenge to Israeli hegemony and control of the region. In 1978 the challengers were not Lebanese but Palestinians, specifically the Palestine Liberation Organization and hundreds of thousands of Palestinian civilians, who had regrouped in Lebanon after the PLO's expulsion from Jordan in 1970. In March 1978, Israel launched what it called Operation Litani, an invasion of southern Lebanon that was officially described as an effort to expel PLO fighters, between the Israeli border and the Litani River, about 20 miles north.

Five days later, the UN Security Council passed Resolution 425, calling for an immediate withdrawal of Israeli troops, and the creation of a peacekeeping force, known as UNIFIL, to "confirm" Israel's withdrawal and assist the Lebanese government in restoring its authority in the area. Israel did not withdraw, although it redeployed most of its troops to areas much closer to the Israeli border, and UNIFIL remained limited to monitoring the continuing Israeli occupation.

Then, four years later, Israel invaded again. Israel claimed its June 6, 1982 invasion was in response to an unsuccessful assassination attempt against the Israeli ambassador to London. But it was widely known that the would-be assassins were partisans of the renegade anti-PLO organization run by Abu Nidal, whose usual targets included the PLO leader Yasir Arafat himself. It was a false pretext; the PLO had no connection to the failed plot. The 1982 invasion was far bigger than that in 1978; 60,000 Israeli troops seized and occupied all of Lebanon's territory from its southern border to the suburbs of Beirut, laying siege to the capital for weeks throughout the summer. The US sponsored a cease-fire in August, under which the PLO agreed to leave Lebanon for Tunis, Israel agreed not to move further into Beirut, and the US agreed to provide security for largely Muslim West Beirut, including Palestinians left behind when the PLO fighters left.

Two days after the PLO had boarded ships out of Lebanon's harbors, Israeli troops surrounded the Palestinian refugee camps south of Beirut. After the assassination of the just-elected Lebanese President Bashir Gemayel, on September 14, the Israeli army broke its agreement with the US and reoccupied West Beirut. Israel sealed off the refugee camps, and Israeli leaders including then Defense Minister Ariel Sharon invited right-wing Lebanese Phalangist and South Lebanon Army militias, long allied with Israel, to "clean out" alleged PLO fighters from the Sabra and Shatila camps. The militias entered the camps on September 16, as Israeli soldiers lit the skies with flares to light their way. The massacres went on for two days, with up to 2,000 civilians slaughtered.

While the massacre was beginning, on September 16, the Security Council met and passed Resolution 520, which condemned the assassination of Gemayel, and called for "the strict respect for Lebanon's sovereignty, territorial integrity, unity and political independence under the sole and exclusive authority of the Lebanese Government through the Lebanese Army throughout Lebanon." It condemned "the recent Israeli incursions into Beirut in violation of the cease-fire agreements and of Security Council resolutions" but demanded only "an immediate return to the positions occupied by Israel before 15 September 1982, as a first step toward the full implementation of Security Council resolutions." It made no reference to the massacre then underway.

On December 16, 1982, the UN General Assembly, "appalled at the large-scale massacre of Palestinian civilians in the Sabra and Shatila refugee camps situated at Beirut, recognizing the universal outrage and condemnation of that massacre... Condemns in the strongest terms the large-scale massacre of Palestinian civilians in the Sabra and Shatila refugee camps; [and] resolves that the massacre was an act of genocide."[18]

Israel consolidated its occupation forces in the strip of southern Lebanon between the Israeli border and the Litani River. Throughout eighteen years of occupation, there was little serious effort by the UN to end the occupation, although UNIFIL troops became a permanent United Nations fixture in the area. The continuing resistance, led by

Hizballah, which had only come into existence months after the 1982 invasion, took an ongoing toll on Israeli troops, leading to a major pull-out of troops in 2000.

Israel claimed its 2000 withdrawal completed its compliance with the long-violated 1978 Resolution 425, but it maintained control of the disputed Shebaa Farms. This was an area of land long claimed by Lebanon but which Israel claimed was actually Syrian territory and therefore subject to Israel's ongoing occupation of the Syrian Golan Heights. The status of Shebaa Farms remained contested, and the presence of Israeli troops there provided a key justification for Hizballah maintaining the independence of their militia in the area. Later, Resolution 1701 would call for resolution of the status of Shebaa Farms within 30 days, but it remained unresolved.

In 2004 the US, with French support, sponsored Security Council Resolution 1559, which called for the disarmament of Hizballah and for Syria to withdraw its troops from Lebanon (Syria had first entered Lebanon with Arab League permission during the Lebanese civil war in 1976, at the time on the side of anti-Palestinian forces within the fractious Lebanese polity). The resolution was widely viewed as part of rising US pressure on Syria in the context of the Bush administration's "global war on terror," in which Syria had emerged as a second-tier member of Washington's so-called axis of evil.

In February 2005, Lebanon's Prime Minister Rafiq Hariri was assassinated in Beirut. For many, Syria was the most likely culprit, as Hariri had moved away from an earlier pro-Syria stance. Competing protests filled the streets of Beirut, some calling for an end to the Syrian troop presence in Lebanon, others demanding an end to outside (read: US) pressure on Lebanon's decision-making. The US, looking for ways to ratchet up the pressure on Syria, which it blamed for allowing arms and fighters to cross from Syria into US-occupied Iraq, quickly made the anti-Syria protesters its own. Soon dubbed the "cedar revolution," the protests became central to Washington's move in the UN to force the Security Council to establish an international commission of inquiry into the Hariri assassination.

Resolution 1636 was the result. It called for Syrian cooperation with the commission, and imposed sanctions against individuals designated by the commission as suspected of involvement in the killing of Hariri. From its beginnings, the resolution was widely seen as reflecting US pressure on the Council; whatever Damascus's actual involvement in the assassination, it was understood that Washington's goal was grounded far more in isolating Syria and weakening it in the region, than it was concerned with justice in Lebanon.

Early in Israel's Lebanon war, the US focused on Resolution 1559 as an alternative to supporting the rising global calls for a new resolution that would impose a cease-fire and end the havoc being wrought on Lebanese lives and country. According to Bush's logic, 1559's call for "the disbanding and disarmament of all Lebanese and non-Lebanese militias" made a lot of sense for an administration committed to keeping the focus on destroying Hizballah, while protecting Israel's violations of international law.

But the narrow focus also revealed a key weakness of US strategy. The US had long used the pretext of violations of Security Council resolutions to provide political cover for unilateral interventions—in Iraq, most egregiously. And Bush's favored resolution on Lebanon, 1559, did indeed call for the disarming of Hizballah. But in that 2004 resolution the Security Council also included crucial language "reiterating its strong support for the territorial integrity, sovereignty and political independence of Lebanon within its... recognized borders, [and] noting the determination of Lebanon to ensure the withdrawal of all non-Lebanese forces from Lebanon." It called on "all parties concerned to cooperate fully and urgently with the Security Council for... the restoration of the territorial integrity, full sovereignty, and political independence of Lebanon." Clearly, no one felt it necessary to point out the hypocrisy of the US claims of concern regarding the "territorial integrity" of Lebanon, while Washington's own key Middle East ally was bombing Lebanon's infrastructure to rubble and was sending its troops into southern Lebanon as if the border of Lebanese territory did not exist.

But it was here that the ideologically driven anti-UN approach of the Bush administration—unilateralism and militarism to trump multilateralism and diplomacy—crashed against the political shoals of their strategy. Double standards remained consistent in Washington's approach to the enforcement of UN resolutions. But global familiarity with those double standards simultaneously undercut the international legitimacy that the US hoped, however grudgingly, that the United

Nations could provide for Washington's chosen "solutions" to Middle East crises.

Ultimately, the UN in Lebanon remained in the ambivalent position of political weakness—unable to challenge the US framework of Lebanon as part of the "war on terror" in the "new Middle East"—but operative importance. On October 31, 2006, UN humanitarian agencies were wrapping up their emergency relief operations in Lebanon, as recovery and reconstruction moved to center stage. Much of the post–civil war reconstruction of Lebanon, with its glittering new tourism, banking, and high-tech development, had been shattered under Israel's summer bombardment. Lebanon's recreated wealthy elite lost almost everything they had. It was the UN's World Food Program, throughout the summer's cataclysm and the autumn's gingerly rebuilding, that had fed 810,000 people, almost a quarter of Lebanon's entire population.[19]

NOTES

1 Ashish Kumar, Sen, "Rice Rejects Lebanon Cease-fire," *Tribune* (Chandigarh, India) 23 July 2006.

2 Helene Cooper and David E. Sanger, "US Seen Waiting to Act on Israeli Strikes in Lebanon," *New York Times* 19 July 2006.

3 Helene Cooper and David E. Sanger, "US Plan Seeks to Wedge Syria Away From Iran," *New York Times* 23 July 2006.

4 Cabinet Communique, Israeli Ministry of Foreign Affairs, 9 July 2006 (www.mfa.gov.il/MFA/Government/Communiques/2006/Cabinet+Communique+9-Jul-2006.htm).

5 It should be noted that the campaign against Boutros-Ghali had earlier origins. Even before the Qana debacle, then US Ambassador to the UN Madeleine Albright was engaged in an unacknowledged but high-stakes campaign of her own. She had correctly recognized that no one ever lost points in official Washington by being too protective of Israeli interests, or being too antagonistic toward the UN. She launched a series of attacks designed to demonize Boutros-Ghali as responsible for everything in the UN that Washington loved to hate, to orchestrate his downfall, to claim credit for it, and to reap her just reward—in this case appointment by a victorious President Bill Clinton as secretary of state in his second term. Boutros-Ghali's refusal to disguise Israel's responsibility for the Qana attack only escalated his value to Albright as a symbolic target.

6 "Security Council Holds Emergency Meeting Following Israeli Attack on Qana: Secretary-General Says Act Must Be Condemned in Strongest Possible Terms," UN Department of Public Information, 30 July 2006.

7 "President Bush and Secretary of State Rice Discuss the Middle East Crisis," 7 August 2006 (www.whitehouse.gov/news/releases/2006/08/20060807.html).

8 Herb Keinon, "Jerusalem Pleased with Cease-Fire Draft," *Jerusalem Post* 5 August 2006.

9 Rory McCarthy, "Cluster Bombing of Lebanon 'Immoral' UN Official Tells Israel," *Guardian* 31 August 2006.

10 "Questions and Answers on Hostilities Between Israel and Hizballah," *Human Rights News*, Human Rights Watch, 2 August 2006.

11 Kertsin Gehmlich, "Bush Defends Israel; EU, Russia Condemn Attacks," Reuters, 14 July 2006.

12 "Attacks on Fleeing Civilians," Human Rights Watch, 6 August 2006 (www.hrw.org/reports/2006/lebanon0806/6.htm).

13 "Frieda Berrigan on the Weapons Trade as Entertainment," TomDispatch.com, 31 July 2006 (www.tomdispatch.com/index.mhtml?pid=106939).

14 "Pentagon Approves $6 Billion in Saudi Arms Sales," US–Saudi Arabian Business Council, 8 August 2006 (www.us-saudi-business.org/NewsBulletinsDetail.asp).

15 Matthew Kalman, "Israel Set War Plan More Than a Year Ago," *San Francisco Chronicle* 21 July 2006.

16 Statement by the United Nations Agencies working in the occupied Palestinian territory, 8 July 2006 (www.un.org/unrwa/news/UN_agencies_8Jul06.htm).

17 Simon Tisdall, "Tying the Hands of the United Nations," *Guardian* 28 July 2006.

18 "The Situation in the Middle East," General Assembly Resolution A/RES/37/123, 16 December 1982 (www.un.org/documents/ga/res/37/a37r123.htm).

19 "Lebanon: Disarming Hizballah is Key to Permanent End to Conflict," UN News, 31 October 2006.

17. US MILITARY ASSISTANCE AND ARMS TRANSFERS TO ISRAEL

Frida Berrigan and William D. Hartung

Israel's summer 2006 intervention in Lebanon was tacitly supported by the United States, as evidenced by the Bush administration's opposition to a cease-fire until the Israeli military had "achieved" what it wanted to achieve. The Israeli intervention was a political and strategic failure—Hizballah was left with significant military capabilities while garnering unparalleled status in the Arab world for holding the Israeli Defense Force at bay. The Israeli strategy of destroying large parts of Lebanon's infrastructure in hopes of turning the Lebanese government and public against Hizballah backfired dramatically, as might have been expected.

The real victims of the war were Lebanese civilians, who were killed and displaced in large numbers, including at least 1,000 civilian deaths. This is about five times the number of Hizballah and Lebanese army civilian personnel who died in the 34-day war. As Helena Cobban has noted in her analysis of the conflict, the UN estimates that Israel "destroyed 15,000 homes, 900 businesses, 77 bridges, and 31 utility plants" throughout Lebanon.[1] This roster of devastation does not include the postwar problem of unexploded cluster bomb munitions that have prevented many Lebanese farmers from planting their fields until they have been cleared of these deadly explosives.

The United States is the primary source of Israel's military arsenal. For more than 30 years, Israel had been the largest recipient of US foreign assistance and since 1985 has received about $3 billion in military and economic aid each year from Washington, meaning that US aid accounts for more than 20 percent of Israel's total defense budget. The billions of US arms and aid it provides every year gives the Bush administration substantial leverage over its ally. A discussion of US military support for Israel is a crucial component of understanding the Middle East crisis.

Press coverage of the war barely mentioned the role of the United States as Israel's primary weapons supplier, and the leverage Washington could have used to curb the Israeli attack on Lebanese society—leverage that the Bush administration chose not to use.

A Special Relationship: US Military Aid to Israel

Despite its relatively small size, Israel is the largest recipient of US foreign military assistance. Over the past decade, the United States has transferred more than $17 billion in military aid to this country of just over 6 million people. In 2005, Israel received $2.25 billion in Foreign Military Financing (FMF), and President George W. Bush's budget request for 2007 includes an additional $2.24 billion in FMF aid for Israel.

The United States sees its military aid as going to "help foster stability in a historically volatile region," and to support Israel's "multiyear defense modernization plan." In its 2007 request for military aid submitted to Congress, the Department of Defense also mentioned helping its ally "meet cash flow requirements" to procure F-16 fighter planes, Apache Longbow Attack helicopters, field vehicles, and advanced armaments.

FMF represents a significant chunk of the Israeli defense budget, most of which is spent in the United States on US weapons. In addition to this "special relationship," the Congressional Research Service report on US foreign assistance to Israel enumerates a number of other special aid concessions from the United States. Unlike other countries, Israel receives its Economic Support Funds (ESF) in one lump sum early in the fiscal year rather than in four quarterly installments. This forces the US to pay more in interest for the money it borrows to make lump-sum payments—between $50 million and $60 million per year, according to Agency for International Development officials.

While other countries primarily deal with the Department of Defense when arranging to purchase military hardware from US companies, Israel deals directly with US companies for the vast majority of its US military purchases. Other nations have a $100,000 minimum purchase amount per contract, but Israel is allowed to purchase military items for less than $100,000.

The United States underwrites Israel's research and development of weapons—and has contributed a few billion dollars to Israeli systems like the Merkava tank and the Lavi ground-attack aircraft. Finally, Israel and the United States have collaborated on an indigenous version of Lockheed Martin's F-16 fighter plane, the Sufa ("storm" in Hebrew). The $45 million per copy F-16I Sufa is part of a $4.5 billion deal between the US manufacturer and Jerusalem.[2]

Fuel for the Fire: Weapons Sales and Grants

The bulk of Israel's current arsenal is composed of equipment supplied under US military aid programs. For example, Israel has 226 US-supplied F-16 fighter and attack jets, 89 F-15 combat aircraft, over 700 M-60 tanks, over 6,000 armored personnel carriers, and scores of transport planes, attack helicopters, utility and training aircraft, bombs, and missiles of all kinds—air-to-air, air-to-ground, surface-to-air, and air-to-surface.

Israel is one of the United States' largest arms importers. Between 1996 and 2005 (the last year for which full data is available), Israel took delivery of $10.19 billion in US weaponry and military equipment, including more than $8.58 billion through the Foreign Military Sales program, and another $1.61 billion in Direct Commercial Sales.

In 2005 alone, documents from the Departments of Defense and State show that Israel received $2.76 billion in weaponry and military hardware from the United States, and another $629 million in defense services like maintenance and training. This figure includes transfers of $188 million in miscellaneous missile spare parts, $7.1 million in tank components, $155 million in ship components, $1.3 million in explosives, and $720,000 anti-personnel riot-control chemicals.

Recent military sales to Israel include propulsion systems for "fast patrol boats" worth more than $15 million from MTU Detroit Diesel; an $8 million contract with Lockheed Martin for high-tech infrared "navigation and targeting" capabilities for Israeli jets; and a $145 million deal with Oshkosh Truck Corp. to build more than 900 armor kits for Israel's Medium Tactical Vehicles.

Israel's dependence on Washington for aid and arms means that the Israeli military relies on spare parts and technical assistance from the US to maintain optimum performance in battle. This point was underscored on July 14, 2006, when the Pentagon's Defense Security Cooperation Agency supported an Israeli request for JP-8 jet fuel worth up to $210 million. Although this fuel was not to be delivered immediately, it allowed Israel to replace fuel used in bombing runs in Lebanon. The Pentagon describes the deal as follows:

> The proposed sale of the JP-8 aviation fuel will allow Israel to maintain the operational capability of its aircraft inventory. The jet fuel will be consumed while the aircraft is in use to keep peace and security in the region. Israel will have no difficulty absorbing this additional fuel into its armed forces.

Israel's War against Lebanon: Cluster Bombs on Display

On August 14, 2006, Israel and Lebanon signed a peace agreement ending their 34-day war, yet the body count continues to rise. According to a November Handicap International report, since the cease-fire in mid-August, unexploded ordnance has killed 21 and wounded another 121 Lebanese civilians.

An Israeli Defense Force (IDF) spokesman insists that "all of the weapons and munitions used by the IDF are legal according to international law and their use conforms to international standards." That is cold comfort for the family of eleven-year-old Ramy Shibleh, one of the postwar victims. He was gathering pinecones outside Halta, a small southern town where the Lebanese army had already cleared mines twice. But more bombs remained, including the one that Ramy and his brother hit with their cart of pinecones. Reuters reports that Ramy tried to toss the rock-like object out of the way, but it exploded, tearing off his right arm and the back of his head and killing him instantly. His mother keeps the shreds of the yellow shirt Ramy was wearing when he died. "He was only picking the pine nuts to buy the toys he loved," she told reporters.

At least two of Israel's cluster bomb and launch systems are US-manufactured. Human Rights Watch discovered remnants of the M483A1 155mm-artillery projectiles, which each contain 88 M42 and M46 submunitions. The projectiles are known as "Dual-Purpose Improved Conventional Munitions" (dual in the sense that they are anti-personnel and anti-vehicle) and were developed at "the Army's Center of Lethality"—the Armament Research, Development and Engineering Center in Picatinny, New Jersey. The researchers also found M26 rockets fired from Lockheed Martin's Multiple Launch Rocket System (MLRS). Each MLRS can fire up to 12 rockets at once, and each rocket contains 644 M77 submunitions.

While the IDF is responsible for the vast majority of the millions of cluster bombs used throughout the war, reports from Human Rights Watch assert that Hizballah shot 100 or more Chinese-made rockets packed with cluster submunitions. During the war, three civilians in northern Israel were wounded, but as of this writing, there have been no reports of post-conflict casualties from these Hizballah weapons.

Secret Agreements, Open-Ended Investigations

The State Department is investigating Israel's use of American-made cluster bombs during the war in Lebanon—in particular, whether Israel broke a secret agreement made with the United States in 1967 not to use cluster bombs against civilians. In their October 2006 report "Foreseeable Harm," Landmine Action disclosed the conditions of the agreement, including the stipulation that Israel was to use cluster munitions "only for defensive purposes, against fortified military targets, and only if attacked by two or more 'Arab states.'" Additionally, the secret provisions prohibit use of the bombs except against "regular forces of a sovereign nation" and in "special wartime conditions," according to the administration and congressional officials. The arrangement gave the IDF greater latitude than the typical regulations that require foreign governments to use US-origin military items solely for internal security and legitimate self-defense.

There have not been any follow-up reports in the media on the status of the State Department's investigation, or its conclusions. Calls to the Office of Defense Compliance by *In These Times* requesting more information were not returned. But it does not take months of careful study to conclude that the IDF flagrantly violated US law as well as the secret agreement made to skirt that law, to say nothing of the Geneva Conventions.

72 Hours of Cluster Bombs

And then there is the timing. During the last three days of the war—as the final touches on the peace agreement were being made—Israel dumped an estimated 1.2 million bomblets throughout Lebanon, a country smaller than Connecticut. With their failure rate of up to 40 percent, more than one of every three bombs may not detonate immediately—and so it lies in wait for children, trucks, and livestock.

While the IDF has not explained their decision to saturate southern Lebanon with bombs, an October 6 *New York Times* article posits that Israel wanted to inflict as much last-minute harm on Hizballah as possible and slow the repopulation of border communities. An unnamed Israeli commander of a rocket unit in Lebanon told *Ha'aretz* on September 12 that the saturation bombing with cluster weapons was "insane and monstrous; we covered entire towns in cluster bombs."

The saturation bombing has effectively crippled agriculture. Farmers' fields and orchards are now minefields and their crops are rotting on the stalk. The summer tobacco, wheat, and fruit, as well as late-yielding crops like olives, cannot be harvested and winter crops, like lentils and chickpeas, have not been planted because farmers cannot plow their fields. Many of the two to three daily casualties are poor farmers desperate to feed their families.

Rida Noureddine, an olive and wheat farmer whose land is littered with cluster bombs, feels the frustration of many southern Lebanese who are dependent on the land. He told the *New York Times*, "I feel as though someone has tied my arms, or is holding me by my neck, suffocating me because this land is my soul."

Cluster Bombs in the Eyes of the World

With the spotlight on Israel's use of cluster bombs in Lebanon, the call for a ban on cluster bombs similar to the prohibition on landmines is growing louder. Belgium instituted a ban and Germany announced their troops will no longer use cluster weaponry. Australia and Norway have declared a moratorium. Sweden, Mexico, the Vatican, and the International Committee of the Red Cross are all calling for a ban.

The model for their efforts is the Landmine Ban or "Ottawa Treaty," which entered into force in March 1999. The treaty prohibits the manufacture, trade, and use of anti-personnel mines, obliges signing countries to destroy stockpiles within four years and clear their own territory within ten years, and urges governments to help poorer countries clear land and assist landmine victims. Non-governmental organizations like Landmine Action and the Mennonite Central Committee argue that once a cluster submunition hits the ground, it is essentially a landmine and should be barred under the treaty.

The United States is not among the 151 states that have ratified the Landmine Ban, and the Bush administration's February 2004 landmine policy reserves the right to use so-called self-destructing mines through 2010. Israel, Burma, North Korea, and 36 other countries also remain outside the international consensus banning landmines.

Another possible tool for anti-cluster bomb campaigners is the 1980 Convention on Certain Conventional Weapons (CCW). As ratified, the Convention prohibits or restricts the use of weapons that cause excessive injuries or have indiscriminate effects on people—including weapons that leave undetectable fragments in the human body, mines and booby traps, incendiary weapons (such as white phosphorus, used by the United States in Iraq and Israel in Lebanon) and blinding laser weapons.

In November 2003, a fifth protocol, addressing "Explosive Remnants of War" like cluster-weapon duds, was added. So far, only 26 nations have signed on to Protocol V and agreed to negotiate responsibility for clearance, provide risk education to the local population, improve the reliability of munitions through "voluntary best practices," and continue to implement existing international humanitarian law. These are useful measures, but they do not address the use of cluster bombs, just what to do after they have landed. In addition, ratification by many more countries—especially by countries like Israel and the United States that are using these weapons—is needed for the effort to be more than symbolic.

The CCW's Third Review Conference ran from November 7–17, 2006 in Geneva. The International Committee of the Red Cross (ICRC) and other key NGOs and nations see an immediate freeze on the use of inaccurate and unreliable cluster munitions as a worthy outcome of the meeting, along with the elimination of stockpiles of legacy systems, and a complete ban on the use of cluster munitions against military targets in populated areas. ICRC will hold an "international expert meeting" in 2007 as a first step toward a new global pact on cluster weapons. Against the backdrop of Lebanon's suffering, there is broad support for these steps.

Unfortunately, maintaining the sense of urgency will not be easy, especially in the face of diplomatic foot-dragging by key states like the United States, which says Protocol V is an adequate response to cluster weapons (even though the United States has not yet ratified the measure). In advance of the meeting, the State Department asserted support for Protocol V, but cautioned that it is not interested in "negotiating new rules on cluster munitions or other explosive remnants of war."

Law and Israel

The laws governing weapons sales are clear. The US Arms Export Control Act of 1976 stipulates that arms transfers can only be used by the recipient nation for self-defense, internal security, and in United Nations–sanctioned operations. The Foreign Assistance Act of 1961 bars military aid and arms sales to countries that demonstrate "gross and consistent" patterns of human rights abuses. And the Export Administration Act, passed in 1979, regulates the sale of "dual-use" items that could have civilian or military application.

These two laws are clearly worded, and yet are not uniformly enforced with regard to Israel. The United States' need for a strong ally in the Middle East appears to repeatedly trump concerns about human rights. But, there are precedents for US criticism of Israel's use of US-origin weaponry in human rights abuses, including "extrajudicial killings" and "excessive use of force."

In the State Department's human rights reports for 2003, 2004, and 2005, incidents mentioned include missile strikes on a refugee camp that killed six people and wounded nineteen; the shooting and killing of four Palestinian children; the demolition of Palestinian homes using tank shells, heavy machine guns, and rockets (deemed an excessive use of force); the use of rocket fire in targeted killing of leaders of Hamas; the killing of 47 civilian bystanders in an operation aimed at suspected terrorists in the occupied territories; and the use of tank shells, machine-gun rounds and rockets fired from aircraft against Palestinian towns and cities that were sources of Palestinian shooting attacks. The human rights reports do not indicate the origins of the weapons used in these cases of excessive force, targeted assassinations, and failure to protect civilians in retaliations against Palestinian attacks. But given that many of Israel's tanks, ground-attack planes, attack helicopters, and air-to-ground missiles are of US origin, it is likely that US weapons were used in at least some of these attacks.

During the last major Israeli incursion into Lebanon, in 1981, the Reagan administration cut off US military aid and arms deliveries for ten weeks while it investigated whether Israel was using weapons for "defensive purposes," as required under US law. At the end of that period, then Secretary of State Alexander Haig suggested that one could "argue until eternity" about whether a given use of force was offensive or defensive, and the ban was lifted.[3] But at least the Reagan administration took some action, which is more than can be said thus far about the administration of George W. Bush.

Conclusion

The United States is the one country in the world that has both the carrots and the sticks to bring lasting peace to the Middle East.

Washington has high-tech weaponry and advanced systems that Jerusalem covets, and it has the legal precedent to withhold them from a country that has again and again used them in contravention of US and international law.

But, even as it brandishes sticks and dangles carrots all over the world, the United States seems completely unwilling to bring its diplomatic power to bear on the most vexing problem in the post-9/11 world: the source of so much grievance and violence. And as tensions grow, exacerbated by the rising threat of nuclear proliferation in the region, the United States can no longer afford the status quo of arming Israel while pretending to play neutral outsider and "honest broker."

NOTES

1 Helena Cobban, "The 34-Day War: Hizballah's Victory, Israel's Choice," *Boston Review* 31.6 (November/December 2006) 31.

2 Data on the Israeli arsenal and US support for it used throughout this article are drawn from the following sources: International Institute for Strategic Studies, *The Military Balance 2006* (London: IISS, 2006) 191–193; US Department of Defense, Defense Security Cooperation Agency, *Foreign Military Sales and Military Assistance Facts*, 2001 through 2005 editions; US Department of State, *Congressional Presentation on Foreign Operations*, FY 2001 through FY 2007 editions; US Department of Defense, Defense Security Cooperation Agency (DSCA), and data on Foreign Military Sales offers and Commercial Sales deliveries posted on the DSCA web site at www.dsca.org.

3 On Haig's statement, see Steven R. Weisman, "Reagan Ends Ban on Sending Israel F-16 Warplanes," *New York Times* 18 August 2001; and Lee Lescaze, "Reagan Lifts Ban on Delivery of F-16 Jets to Israel," *Washington Post* 18 August 1981. For a capsule history of the US–Israeli arms sales relationship, see William D. Hartung, *And Weapons for All* (New York: HarperCollins, 1994) 217–221.

Part Five

THE DECONSTRUCTION OF ISRAELI POWER

18. YOU ARE TERRORISTS, WE ARE VIRTUOUS
Yitzhak Laor

This essay was originally published in the London Review of Books *28.16 (17 August 2006).*

As soon as the facts of the Bint Jbeil ambush, which ended with relatively high Israeli casualties (eight soldiers died there), became public, the press and television in Israel began marginalizing any opinion critical of the war. The media also fell back on the kitsch to which Israelis grow accustomed from childhood: the most menacing army in the region is described here as if it is David against an Arab Goliath. Yet the Jewish Goliath has sent Lebanon back twenty years, and Israelis themselves even further: we now appear to be a lynch-mob culture, glued to our televisions, incited by a premier whose "leadership" is being launched and legitimized with rivers of fire and destruction on both sides of the border. Mass psychology works best when you can pinpoint an institution or a phenomenon with which large numbers of people identify. Israelis identify with the IDF, and even after the deaths of many Lebanese children in Qana, they think that stopping the war without scoring a definitive victory would amount to defeat. This logic reveals our national psychosis, and it derives from our over-identification with Israeli military thinking.

In the melodramatic barrage fired off by the press, the army is assigned the dual role of hero and victim. And the enemy? In Hebrew broadcasts the formulations are always the same: on the one hand "we," "ours," "us"; on the other, Nasrallah and Hizballah. There aren't, it seems, any Lebanese in this war. So who is dying under Israeli fire? Hizballah. And if we ask about the Lebanese? The answer is always that Israel has no quarrel with Lebanon. It's yet another illustration of our unilateralism, the thundering Israeli battle cry for years: no matter what happens around us, we have the power and therefore we can enforce the logic. If only Israelis could see the damage that's been done by all these years of unilateral thinking. But we cannot, because the army—which has always been the core of the state—determines the shape of our lives and the nature of our memories, and wars like this one erase everything we thought we knew, creating a new version of history with which we can only concur. If the army wins, its success becomes part of "our heritage." Israelis have assimilated the logic and the language of the IDF—and in the process, they have lost their memories. Is there a better way to understand why we have never learned from history? We have never been a match for the army, whose memory—the official Israeli memory—is hammered into place at the center of our culture by an intelligentsia in the service of the IDF and the state.

The IDF is the most powerful institution in Israeli society, and one which we are discouraged from criticizing. Few have studied the dominant role it plays in the Israeli economy. Even while they are still serving, our generals become friendly with the US companies that sell arms to Israel; they then retire, loaded with money, and become corporate executives. The IDF is the biggest customer for everything and anything in Israel. In addition, our high-tech industries are staffed by a mixture of military and ex-military who work closely with the Western military complex. The current war is the first to become a branding opportunity for one of our largest mobile-phone companies, which is using it to run a huge promotional campaign. Israel's second biggest bank, Bank Leumi, used inserts in the three largest newspapers to distribute bumper stickers saying: "Israel is powerful." The military and the universities are intimately linked too, with joint research projects and an array of army scholarships.

There is no institution in Israel that can approach the army's ability to disseminate images and news or to shape a national political class and an academic elite or to produce memory, history, value, wealth, desire. This is the way identification becomes entrenched: not through dictatorship or draconian legislation, but by virtue of the fact that the country's most powerful institution gets its hands on every citizen at the age of eighteen. The majority of Israelis identify with the army and the army reciprocates by consolidating our identity, especially when it is—or we are—waging war.

The IDF didn't play any role in either of the Gulf wars and may not play a part in Bush's pending war in Iran, but it is on permanent alert for the real war that is always just around the corner. Meanwhile, it harasses Palestinians in the West Bank and Gaza, to very destructive effect. (In July it killed 176 Palestinians, most of them from the same area in Gaza, in a "policing" operation that included the destruction of houses and infrastructure.) They shoot. They abduct. They use F-16s against refugee camps, tanks against shacks and huts. For years they have operated in this way against gangs and groups of armed youths and children, and they call it a war, a "just war," vital for our existence. The power of the army to produce meanings, values, desire is perfectly illustrated by its handling of the Palestinians, but it would not be possible without the support of the left in Israel.

The mainstream left has never seriously tried to oppose the military. The notion that we had no alternative but to attack Lebanon and that we cannot stop until we have finished the job: these are army-sponsored truths, decided by the military and articulated by state intellectuals and commentators. So are most other descriptions of the war, such as the Tel Aviv academic Yossef Gorni's statement in *Ha'aretz*, that "this is our second war of independence." The same sort of nonsense was written by the same kind of people when the 2000 intifada began. That was also a war about our right to exist, our "second 1948." These descriptions would not have stood a chance if Zionist left intellectuals—solemn purveyors of the "morality of war"—hadn't endorsed them.

Military thinking has become our only thinking. The wish for superiority has become the need to have the upper hand in every aspect of relations with our neighbors. The Arabs must be crippled, socially and economically, and smashed militarily, and of course they must then appear to us in the degraded state to which we've reduced them. Our usual way of looking at them is borrowed from our intelligence corps, who "translate" them and interpret them, but cannot recognize them as human beings. Israelis long ago ceased to be distressed by images of sobbing women in white scarves, searching for the remains of their homes in the rubble left by our soldiers. We think of them much as we think of chickens or cats. We turn away without much trouble and consider the real issue: the enemy. The Katyusha missiles that have been hitting the north of the country are launched without "discrimination," and in this sense Hizballah is guilty of a war crime, but the recent volleys of Katyushas were a response to the frenzied assault on Lebanon. To the large majority of Israelis, however, all the Katyushas prove is what a good and necessary thing we have done by destroying our neighbors again: the enemy is indeed dangerous, it's just as well we went to war. The thinking becomes circular and the prophecies self-fulfilling. Israelis are fond of saying: "The Middle East is a jungle, where only might speaks." See Qana, and Gaza, or Beirut.

Defenders of Israel and its leaders can always argue that the US and Britain behave similarly in Iraq. (It is true that Olmert and his colleagues would not have acted so shamelessly if the US had not been behind them. Had Bush told them to hold their fire, they wouldn't have dared to move a single tank.) But there is a major difference. The US and Britain went to war in Iraq without public opinion behind them. Israel went to war in Lebanon, after a border incident that it exploited in order to destroy a country, with the overwhelming support of Israelis, including the members of what the European press calls the "peace camp."

Amos Oz, on July 20, when the destruction of Lebanon was already well underway, wrote in the *Evening Standard*: "This time, Israel is not invading Lebanon. It is defending itself from a daily harassment and bombardment of dozens of our towns and villages by attempting to smash Hizballah wherever it lurks." Nothing here is distinguishable from Israeli state pronouncements. David Grossman wrote in the *Guardian* the same day, as if he were unaware of any bombardment in Lebanon: "There is no justification for the large-scale violence that Hizballah unleashed this week, from Lebanese territory, on dozens of peaceful Israeli villages, towns and cities. No country in the world could remain silent and abandon its citizens when its neighbor strikes without any provocation." We can bomb, but if they respond they are responsible for both their suffering and ours. And it's important to remember that "our suffering" is that of poor people in the north who cannot leave their homes easily or quickly. "Our suffering" is not that of the decision makers or their friends in the media. Oz also wrote that "there can be no moral equation between Hizballah and Israel. Hizballah is targeting Israeli civilians wherever they are, while Israel is targeting mostly Hizballah." At that time more than 300 Lebanese had been killed and 600 had been injured. Oz went on:

> The Israeli peace movement should support Israel's attempt at self-defense, pure and simple, as long as this operation targets mostly Hizballah and spares, as much as possible, the lives of Lebanese civilians (this is not always an easy task, as Hizballah missile-launchers often use Lebanese civilians as human sandbags).

The truth behind this is that Israel must always be allowed to do as it likes even if this involves scorching its supremacy into Arab bodies. This supremacy is beyond discussion and it is simple to the point of madness.

We have the right to abduct. You don't. We have the right to arrest. You
don't. You are terrorists. We are virtuous. We have sovereignty. You don't.
We can ruin you. You cannot ruin us, even when you retaliate, because we
are tied to the most powerful nation on earth. We are angels of death.

The Lebanese will not remember everything about this war. How
many atrocities can a person keep in mind, how much helplessness can
he or she admit, how many massacres can people tell their children about,
how many terrorized escapes from burning houses, without becoming a
slave to memory? Should a child keep a leaflet written by the IDF in
Arabic, in which he is told to leave his home before it's bombed? I cannot
urge my Lebanese friends to remember the crimes my state and its army
have committed in Lebanon.

Israelis, however, have no right to forget. Too many people here
supported the war. It wasn't just the nationalist religious settlers. It's
always easy to blame the usual suspects for our misdemeanors: the
scapegoating of religious fanatics has allowed us to ignore the role of the
army and its advocates within the Zionist left. This time we have seen
just how strongly the "moderates" are wedded to immoderation, even
though they knew, before it even started, that this would be a war against
suburbs and crowded areas of cities, small towns and defenseless villages.
The model was our army's recent actions in Gaza: Israeli moderates found
these perfectly acceptable.

It was a mistake for those of us who are unhappy with our country's
policies to breathe a sigh of relief after the army withdrew from Lebanon
in 2000. We thought that the names of Sabra and Shatila would do all
the memorial work that needed to be done and that they would stand,
metonymically, for the crimes committed in Lebanon by Israel. But, with
the withdrawal from Gaza, many Israelis who should be opposing this
war started to think of Ariel Sharon, the genius of Sabra and Shatila, as a
champion of peace. The logic of unilateralism—of which Sharon was the
embodiment—had at last prevailed: Israelis are the only people who
count in the Middle East; we are the only ones who deserve to live here.
This time we must try harder to remember. We must remember the
crimes of Olmert, and of our minister of justice, Haim Ramon, who
championed the destruction of Lebanese villages after the ambush at Bint
Jbeil, and of the army chief of staff, Dan Halutz. Their names should be
submitted to the Hague so they can be held accountable.

Elections are a wholly inadequate form of accountability in Israel: the people we kill and maim and ruin cannot vote here. If we let our memories slacken now, the machine-memory will reassert control and write history for us. It will glide into the vacuum created by our negligence, with the civilized voice of Amos Oz easing its path, and insert its own version. And suddenly we will not be able to explain what we know, even to our own children.

In Israel there is still no proper history of our acts in Lebanon. Israelis in the peace camp used to carry posters with the figure "680" on them— the number of Israelis who died during the 1982 invasion. Six hundred and eighty Israeli soldiers. How many members of that once sizeable peace camp protested about the tens of thousands of Lebanese, Palestinian, and Syrian casualties? Isn't the failure of the peace camp a result of its inability to speak about the cheapness of Arab blood? General Udi Adam, one of the architects of the current war, has told Israelis that we shouldn't count the dead. He meant this very seriously and Israelis should take him seriously. We should make it our business to count the dead in Lebanon and in Israel and, to the best of our abilities, to find out their names, all of them.

19. TRAVELS IN ISRAEL
Gabriel Piterberg

This essay was originally published in the London Review of Books *28.18 (21 September 2006).*

On the road to Kiryat Shmona in northern Israel, on Sunday, August 13, just before the cease-fire is declared, my mobile phone buzzes incessantly: my mother would just like to know if I think that either Jews or Arabs are worth dying for. Woody Allen's line about being brought up by a castrating Zionist mother comes to mind. My own was an active Communist as a medical student in Buenos Aires in the late 1940s and early 1950s, and recalls that era somewhat righteously to justify her failure to take part in any similar activity in Israel ("I have already done my share of trying to make this a better world"). Her politics are normally more than reasonable, but this recent war has played havoc with her judgment. She is not alone.

As I get close to the town, military radio lists a host of northern locations and instructs their inhabitants to make for shelters and safe places, an announcement whose wisdom is confirmed by the heavy sound of explosions. I am just a couple of kilometers south of Kiryat Shmona and keep on going. The blasts get louder the closer I get, but from the car I can't spot any points of impact or even a column of smoke. At the southern edge of the town, however, the Katyusha shelling seems truly threatening, so I pull over at a petrol station which has a sort of open-air shelter where drivers and employees are huddling. This is an ideal site, for it indemnifies me from my mother's accusation of recklessness, enables me to see what's going on, and doesn't have the heat or stench of the proper public shelters I will soon get to know. Within minutes the station employees have taught me how to distinguish between "the motherfuckers' rockets" and "our artillery," whose rough location one can judge after a few minutes. Listening to the fury of our ordnance blasting into Lebanon I think of the chutzpah of Israeli allegations that Hizballah places fighters and weapons among the civilian population. The clouds of smoke rising from Katyusha impacts seem to be mainly on the mountain above the town. In the shelter, we decide that the targets were probably Manara (a kibbutz) and Margaliot (a moshav).

In the mid-1970s I used to pass through here quite often: part of my military service was spent on Mount Hermon. Kiryat Shmona was a place where one waited apathetically to hitch a ride back to base, or more impatiently, to get a ride home at the start of a longish leave in the hope that one would get there early enough to pick up a date. There was a bus station—it's still there, where it was—but only losers traveled on public transportion. Although I notice a few changes—a new shopping mall, for example—the city remains familiar and just as unattractive as it was then.

Kiryat Shmona was founded in 1950, named after the eight men who died defending Tel Hai against an Arab attack in 1920. (The most famous was Joseph Trumpeldor, whose last words are supposed to have been: "Never mind, it is good to die for our country.") One of the ways the state dealt with the massive immigration from North Africa and the Middle East after the founding of Israel was to move people into places that became known as "development towns." Some have been more successful than others, but there are no boomtowns. A sociological rule of thumb: if a given development town was located in an area of thriving cooperative agricultural settlements (kibbutzim and moshavim), its own "development" would be arrested. Kiryat Shmona could never be described as a success story. To its population of predominantly North African and Middle Eastern Jews have been added, in the last two decades or so, immigrants from the former Soviet Union. In socioeconomic terms, it is a weak community, and the fact that it's the site most heavily targeted by Hizballah's Katyushas and other rockets may not be coincidental. Raining missiles on Israel's deprived communities is intended as a frightening piece of consciousness raising.

My first appointment with the municipality is at the emergency headquarters or "war room" (the male occupants of these offices tend to prefer the latter designation). Policemen guard the doors to the switchboard and the main meeting room. The "threat" soon becomes clear: raging inhabitants, who have lost their wits and patience, congregate here after each volley of Katyushas. A woman in a nightdress (it is nearly noon) is screaming and gesticulating wildly. She's had it, she says, with Katyushas, sirens, and public shelters stinking of urine; the other day a cat gave birth in the shelter and the aggressive mother was making it impossible for anyone to get inside; in conclusion, she'd like to stick a few Katyushas up the mayor's arse (my impression is that the poor man is doing the best he can). I am squeezed through the crowd to talk to the municipality spokesman, Doron Shanfer. He treats me to a hardline racist speech, denouncing Arabs, Muslims, Hizballah, insisting on the pointlessness of any agreement or cease-fire that might preempt the destruction of Hizballah.

Some information is nonetheless forthcoming. Of 24,000 inhabitants, between 7,000 and 9,000 had stayed put; the rest had gone to central or southern Israel. Three or four thousand more have recently been evacuated by the authorities. My spokesman then cites the fantastic figure of more than 1,600 homes destroyed, a brazen exaggeration, it seems to me, unless "destroyed" is run through some strenuous hermeneutics. Of eleven schools, four were hit; sports facilities, playgrounds, a handful of industrial sites and the main shopping mall have also sustained damage. By chance, I learn that unemployment in Kiryat Shmona is much higher than the official 8.5 percent. My interest catches the spokesman offguard, or so it seems to me. The figure seems likely to rise, he says, regardless of the war.

I decide modestly to emulate the Almighty, and to drive through the city "and see whether they have done altogether according to the cry of it, which is come unto me; and if not, I will know" (Genesis 18.21). After almost two hours of touring the city, which is not that large, it's clear to me that talk about physical destruction caused by Hizballah shelling is a grotesque puff for the rhetoric of reciprocity. It is true that buildings and roads have been hit, and there have been casualties, but even to begin to compare this to the devastation in the south of Lebanon and Beirut under Israeli air force "surgical" bombardment is disgraceful.

What I do see as I go up and down the streets of Kiryat Shmona, between intermittent bursts of Hizballah fire, is an order of social despair to which the war may have given added poignancy, but which is not, in itself, a result of the war. The people I run into and converse with are clearly unable to leave. They are disoriented and depressed by weeks of scrambling into and out of shelters without much else to do. The two public shelters I go into confirm the comic-strip description of the angry woman at the municipal offices. I see a few people reluctantly leaving their apartments to collect the food that the municipality distributes. Their clothing betrays their bewilderment. They have lost track of whether it's day or night, whether they're in the private or the public sphere. Those who have remained are the poorer inhabitants, veteran Mizrahis or relatively recent immigrants. A man from St. Petersburg tells me that his wife and granddaughters are in Bat Yam, just south of Jaffa, lodging with acquaintances. (In popular Israeli culture, Bat Yam is the equivalent of Milton Keynes.) He had gone with them, but then decided to return. "Why?" I ask.

"Are you not from this country?" he replies.

"Of course I am," I say. "But I no longer live here."

He smiles. "So how come you're asking why I prefer Kiryat Shmona with Katyushas to Bat Yam without?"

It had occurred to me as I drove to Kiryat Shmona to think of what is happening here in terms of a "Katrina syndrome": this was the first war the state had conducted after a vigorous campaign of neoliberal privatization and the final dismantling of what had once been a highly interventionist state; Sharon had shrewdly duped Netanyahu into finishing the makeover when Netanyahu was his finance minister; the poor and the Galilee Palestinians would surely be paying the price for the collapse of adequate state institutions and infrastructure, in wartime especially. But each encounter with the social and physical landscape weakened my flirtation with the Katrina analogy. The sheer magnitude of death and destruction on the Gulf Coast compared to northern Galilee made it improper. Then again, Israeli state institutions were not as careless and derelict as their American counterparts. Finally, Israel was making use of the suffering and destruction it was experiencing as a result of a war it had unleashed for propaganda purposes. America derived no PR value from the devastation of New Orleans.

In 1982 I was a reserve officer in the IDF. I took part in the terrible war in Lebanon, to my shame. I was demobilized at the end of the blitzkrieg, just before the siege of Beirut. My own involvement is reason enough for me to ask why, in the torrent of punditry and analysis occasioned by the present war, no one can be bothered to explain when and how Hizballah came into existence.

Driving back from the Galilee to Jerusalem one evening, I tune the radio to the news and hear Eyal Zisser of Tel Aviv University's Moshe Dayan Center announcing that one would have to go back "a thousand years" in order to understand Lebanon's confessional structure. The literature on the shifting historicity of national, ethnic, religious, and other forms of collective belonging is vast, and a scholar nowadays has no justification for assuming that the existence of Shias, Druze, and Maronites many centuries ago somehow explains the confessional underpinning of modern Lebanon. It's clear, for example, from Ussama Makdisi's *The Culture of Sectarianism* (2000) that Lebanon's confessional arrangement is modern, coalescing in the 19th century and completed by French colonial rule in the 20th. A strain of Orientalism compounds our refusal—for political and propaganda reasons—to describe Hizballah with any accuracy. The behavior of Muslims, Arabs, and Orientals in general is the expression of an impermeable essence, dating back many centuries, with the result that only the remote past or the present and very recent past can ever be "understood." A passing acquaintance with Hizballah's history, and Israel's involvement in Lebanon, is a useful antidote to Israeli nostrums about the nature of the Middle East/Islam/ Lebanon/the Palestinians, and the facile characterizations that govern our actions while blinding us to their meaning—as if what Israel does and what the Middle East is were completely unrelated.

Hizballah is not only a guerrilla force, but a political movement with social and economic capacities, and a parliamentary party.[1] It is not only a Shia phenomenon but very much a Lebanese one. When the confessional logic of modern Lebanon was enshrined in the National Pact of 1943, the Shia community got a raw deal. Whereas the Maronites were given the office of president and the Sunnis that of prime minister, the Shias had to make do with speaker of the house. More significant in the long run, this dispensation didn't take account of the possibility of demographic change: however much the Shia proportion of the population grew, they would remain underrepresented and get a smaller share of state funds. A wave of urbanization in the 1960s led many Shias to leave their rural communities in the Beqaa Valley and southern Lebanon, and migrate to Beirut's poor neighborhoods. This was a turning point in the sociology of the country.

Politicization, among the Shias, took the form of support for the Lebanese Communist Party and the Syrian Socialist Nationalist Party, at least until the 1970s when an able cleric by the name of Sayyid Musa al-Sadr, who would later disappear in Libya, set up the Movement of the Deprived and began to lure the Shia masses away from the left-wing parties. The replacement of the secular left by political Islam has had two depressing consequences: intellectually, it seems to vindicate the Orientalist "truth" that the authentic, timeless affiliation of Muslims is to religion, ethnicity, and the tribe, and that anything else is merely a veneer; politically, it makes it easier to consign people to dangerously rigid identities.

One of the tangible results of Musa al-Sadr's success was the formation of a militia—a sine qua non in Lebanese politics of the period—to go with his movement. It was known as Amal (both an acronym that stands for Detachments of Lebanese Resistance and a noun that means "hope"). Another was the rapid ascendancy of two Shia religious leaders, who, like al-Sadr, studied in the holy Shia city of Najaf in Iraq: Sayyid Mohammad Hussein Fadlallah and Sayyid Hassan Nasrallah. The decisive factor in the shift from Hope (Amal) to the Party of God (Hizballah) was Sharon's invasion in the summer of 1982, the attendant battle of Beirut, and the massacres at Sabra and Shatila, where roughly a quarter of the refugees were Shiites from southern Lebanon.

Growing numbers of Shias became disenchanted with Amal in the aftermath of the invasion because it failed to redress their socioeconomic hardship or to resist the Israeli occupation. All the emerging Shia groups, whether in Beirut's poor neighborhoods, the Beqaa Valley or the south, were religious; all resisted the Israeli occupation, and joined the militia-infested fray. Within less than three years and with Iran's material support, these groups came together—in February 1985—to form Hizballah and its military wing, the Islamic Resistance. The Israeli–Hizballah relationship has been a dialectical affair. Hizballah's existence is unthinkable without Israel's invasion of 1982; now it is a major obstacle to Israel's military and policy adventures in Lebanon.

Israel's attempts to shape Lebanon's fortunes began many years before Sharon's war, however. Ben Gurion's notion of an alliance of minorities in the Middle East is a useful starting point. This logic assumes a priori shared interests among groups that are not Arab–Sunni Muslim, such as the Kurds—Sunni but not Arab—and the Maronites, who are Arab but not Muslim. The concept of Middle Eastern "mosaic states" is a variation on this theme. In *The Tragedy of Lebanon* (1983) an unnamed Israeli Arabist explained to *Washington Post* journalist Jonathan Randal that

> only when Israel raises money from American Jews do we Israelis claim
> that the entire Arab world is a united juggernaut determined to drive
> poor little Israel into the sea. In fact, the Middle East is a jigsaw puzzle

of peoples and cultures. Minority regimes run Syria and Iraq. King Hussein and his Bedouin are a minority in Jordan, outnumbered by Palestinians. Sudan has a large animist and Christian minority. Algeria and Morocco have large Berber minorities. If Israel could succeed in contacting all these groups which oppose Arabism and Islam, then it could break the Islamic world into pieces.

Aggressive and grandiose Israeli aspirations unilaterally to mold their environment are not new. The instability of the Middle East in the mid-1950s brought the clash between Ben Gurion and Moshe Sharett, Israel's second prime minister, to a head. In the winter of 1954 Ben Gurion had retired—temporarily, it turned out—from the premiership, but continued to press for the destabilization of Lebanon. Tensions between Syria and Iraq were running very high, and sticking to his conviction that times of crisis are opportunities for the bold (as they had been in 1948), Ben Gurion argued that this was "the time to arouse Lebanon—that is to say, the Maronites—to proclaim a Christian state." He later said:

> Maybe (of course nothing is certain in politics) now is the propitious moment to bring about the establishment of a Christian state as our neighbour. Without our initiative and our energetic help it will not come about. And it seems to me that this is now the central task or at least one of the central tasks of our foreign policy, and we should invest means, time and energy and act in all ways likely to bring about a fundamental change in Lebanon. [Eliahu] Sassoon and the rest of our Arabists must be mobilised. If money is needed, dollars should not be spared, even though the money may go down the drain. All our energies must be concentrated here.

More than a year later Ben Gurion was back as defense minister, as keen as ever to realize what Sharett called "his old dream" of reshaping Lebanon. Now he had the assistance of his young chief of staff Moshe Dayan. According to Sharett's report of a meeting in May 1955, Dayan felt that the trick was to find a suitable Lebanese officer—a captain would suffice.

> We should win his heart or buy him, to get him to agree to declare himself the saviour of the Maronite population. Then the Israeli army would enter Lebanon, occupy the necessary territory and set up a Christian regime allied to Israel and everything would turn up just fine . . . Ben Gurion was quick to stress that his own plan is intended to be put into effect only in the wake of Syria's conquest by Iraq.

The actual Christian army officers who were found and who served as Israel's buffer policemen in southern Lebanon were, first, Major Saad Haddad and his South Lebanon Army, and then General Antoine Lahad. Israel's arrangements for the North Bank (that is, south Lebanon from the international border to the Litani River) and later for the West Bank share the same logic: in each case, a proxy polices the locals to satisfy the regional empire's "security needs." The services rendered by Haddad and Lahad are scarcely different from those that have been expected of Arafat and Abu Mazen since the Oslo process got underway.

Syria became another of Israel's policy partners when the latter's involvement in Lebanon began in earnest in 1976. In that year, as the civil war began to get out of hand, Israel and Syria with Washington's blessing put down their markers. An unwritten agreement known as the Red Lines stipulated Israeli control up to the Litani River and a Syrian force policing much of the rest of the country, but without deploying surface-to-air missiles that might have stood in the way of the Israeli air force. For the rest, in a proper Talmudic spirit, the agreement was largely a matter of interpretation and, as Rabin reportedly told Randal, "any interpretation of the tacit understanding is correct." The Red Lines held until the summer of 1982. In that time, Israel sought to bring three groups under its wing, and to use them against its enemies in Lebanon— that is, the Syrians and the Palestinians. These groups were the Shias, the southern Christians, and the northern Christians. Among the latter group, the Israelis initially favored the seasoned politician Camille Chamoun, with whom they had already had contact, and his son Dany, commander of the Tiger militia. Gradually the Mossad preference for Pierre Gemayel and his extreme right-wing Phalangist militia (later to become the Lebanese Forces) prevailed. Pierre Gemayel had been to the 1936 Olympics in Berlin and had found the Nazis inspiring; his militia was now being seen as the protector of the Jewish community in Lebanon. Sharon installed Gemayel's son Bashir as Israel's puppet president in 1982. After his assassination, he was replaced by his brother Amin. It was the Phalangists who committed the Sabra and Shatila atrocities of September 1982, while the IDF sealed off the camps.

Jerusalem's German Colony on a blazing August morning. I used to come here in the old days: a cousin of my mother's lives on Emek Refaim Street, the colony's main avenue. The neighborhood was built in the second half of the 19th century, one of several German colonies in Palestine whose European population was increasing as the twin expansion of empire and capital approached its climax. It was designed as a German village, but the architecture and local stone give it an Arab quality. German gentiles and wealthy Arab Jerusalemites used to live here; they were joined by Jews in the 1930s. As in so many neighborhoods, 1948 put an end to the Arab presence. I used to think of this as one of West Jerusalem's most attractive districts and I'm struck now by the transformation of its human landscape: it is overwhelmingly dominated by American settlers. They are conspicuous by their appearance and accent (in English and Hebrew). Quite a few of the men, I notice, carry discreet personal firearms. They walk about confidently, with an air of ownership, or perhaps resentment is clouding my ethnography. The relative newcomers are easily distinguished from the older social strata: middle-class European Jews in the more northern section of the colony, and North African and Kurdish as one walks further south into Rachel Imenu Street. The change makes the colony much less desirable as far as I'm concerned, and leads inevitably to dark thoughts about the multifaceted process of Palestinian dispossession.

Café Masaryk stands at the intersection of Emek Refaim and Masaryk. It is a testimony to the quality of Israeli coffee culture, which Starbucks has never been able to penetrate. I am joined by Amira Hass, the distinguished *Ha'aretz* correspondent, whose coverage of the occupation, sparing neither side, is a model of what free and critical media ought to be. The underlying purpose of Israeli policy, from Peres to Sharon, she argues, is to wreck the Palestinian national project, since its success, however peaceful, would undermine the viability of the Jewish state. She was not surprised by Israel's insincerity in the Oslo process, which it had never envisaged as bilateral—the stratagem was to get the PLO to acquiesce in a unilaterally imposed settlement—though she was surprised by Fatah's susceptibility, by which I think she means corruption. To play devil's advocate, I say that, if we put Oslo itself aside, a viably independent Palestinian state ought to make Israel's existence as a Jewish state more secure. Hass is not impressed: whatever the initial logic inscribed in an agreement of two ethnic states coexisting more or less peacefully, history does not recognize finality. An agreement of that sort would quickly erode Israel's ability to act unilaterally by producing the conditions for a proper bilateralism, perhaps even equality; there would be talk of federal arrangements and, inside Israel itself, of territorial rather than ethno-religious citizenship as well as universal suffrage, all of which are inimical to the concept, but more important the operation, of the Jewish state. The innate Zionist anxiety about the state continuing to be a Jewish one, and the resolve to establish that in perpetuity, were confirmed by the point on which Barak was most adamant at Camp David in 2000: the absolute and irrevocable finality of whatever was agreed.

There are frightening continuities between Israel's unilateralism in Lebanon and in the occupied territories. Some of them are pointed up in Jean Said Makdisi's extraordinary war memoir, *Beirut Fragments* (1990), which I have with me and find I cannot put aside. The book also brings home the continuity between present and past. "Always the Israelis announced that they bombed 'Palestinian targets,'" she writes of the 1982 war. In 2006, read "Hizballah infrastructure." Or that they were eliminating "terrorist bases."

Always there would be terrible anger and bitterness, not only at the raids themselves but at the hypocrisy of the announcements. If the targets were often Palestinian refugee camps, they were as often Lebanese villages; if some fighters were killed, the majority of the victims in either case were civilians. The pictures in the papers were always the same: babies and old men, Palestinian and Lebanese, lying dead or dying; bits of bodies, shops and cars, houses reduced to unrecognizable rubble.

Then there are the symbolic and anecdotal connections. One is the thick-skinned Israeli resort to music. The keen-eyed Jonathan Randal was in Lebanon at the time of the March 1978 invasion, code-named by Israel "Stone of Wisdom." Returning to the south a few days after an onslaught on Tyre, he

> ran into an Israeli string quartet playing Mozart in a field for the benefit of the troops. It was as if some Israeli Buñuel were trying to find the equivalent of those USO shows that so delighted American troops in the field in Vietnam. Yet the Israeli troops seemed ill at ease, almost ashamed of the destruction they had wrought.

Twenty-four years later, in April 2002, the Battle of Jenin was waged as part of a ferocious Israeli re-invasion of the occupied territories, chillingly named Defensive Shield. Dozens of Palestinians were killed. As those in the Jenin refugee camp were digging with their fingers in search of survivors and corpses, Israel's Channel One broadcast its Friday-night variety show *Taverna*, which mostly consists of Mediterranean music, from a hill overlooking the camp.

That's bad: this is worse. After the withdrawal from Beirut in 1982, Said Makdisi writes, it emerged that "the Israeli soldiers, wherever they had been, had defecated in choice places. On books, furniture, clothes and carpets; on bedroom floors; near toilet seats and in bathtubs; on school desks; and in shop windows, people found the rotting faeces." The same phenomenon was amply reported after Defensive Shield, with two additions: this time soldiers defecated in the presence of the people whose homes they had invaded, and, presumably to keep abreast of technology, they defecated on computers too.

I went back to northern Galilee to meet the local kibbutzim administration, known as the Upper Galilee Regional Council, on the southern side of Kiryat Shmona. It is the authority for the Upper Galilee's 29 kibbutzim (16,500 inhabitants all told). The council's neat, well-swept yard, dining hall, and emergency headquarters instantly make me think of Gershon Shafir's masterly study of the kibbutzim's foundation in *Land, Labour and the Origins of the Israeli–Palestinian Conflict 1882–1914* (1989). Shafir understands the kibbutz in the context of the settler colony, defined initially by the exclusion of the indigenous people from everything to do with the land and, then, by the exclusion of late-coming settler-immigrants. Even now the most significant thing about the kibbutz, its disintegration notwithstanding, is that there are no Arab members and few Mizrahis.

The contrast between the regional council and Kiryat Shmona's municipal offices—the two are very close—is so stark that we might as well be talking about different planets. Where the former is clean, relaxed, spacious, well-equipped, and properly air-conditioned, I remember the latter as hot, noisy, and confused, with the mayor almost besieged in his chamber. What I hear now confirms the artificial barrier between "development towns" and kibbutzim: according to the council's head, Aharon Valency, and his colleague Yaara Kadosh, around 550 rockets landed within the kibbutzim's orbit. Thanks to a very efficient infrastructure only 20 percent of the kibbutzim members have left and most of those were only renting accommodations. One may wonder why it is necessary to have two Katyusha counts, one for the kibbutzim and another for Kiryat Shmona, if this is all one area, and Kadosh and Valency begin to move uneasily in their seats when I ask them to explain. Both officials are aware of political correctness, of course, and almost say that they can't say what they'd really like to say. Instead I get vague allusions, which I immediately understand since I share the same cultural references, to social texture, historical ethos, behavioral codes, Zionist values, and so forth. This is emphatically about class superiority and a higher national consciousness, neither of which, since the Begin era, dares speak its name. What accounts for their wriggling is Labor's demise. Labor had dominated the Zionist movement and the state of Israel since the 1930s. But the mass immigration of the 1950s and the delayed response to the trauma of the 1973 war were bound to favor the right. Begin was a populist demagogue. He appealed to his supporters, a crucial portion of whom were Mizrahim—quite a few from development towns like Kiryat Shmona—by telling them how wronged they had been by the haughty millionaires from the kibbutzim with their sumptuous lifestyles and big swimming pools, and how proud they should be of who they were. Ever since Begin tapped into it, the Ashkenazi–Mizrahi schism has become explosive, and politicians and public officials who flirt with it may not survive the consequences.

Valency concludes with a programmatic speech on the need for national regeneration and a renewal of Zionist values. Kadosh thinks that the war may have a positive consequence: "The way we have looked after our community and kept it together will engender a revivial of the kibbutzim and their way of life, and will propel us forward." She goes on to describe the "gut-wrenching" experience of seeing dead animals after Kibbutz Amir's cowshed had been hit by a Katyusha. "I couldn't bear to look at it again," she says.

As I leave the regional council's war room I take another look at a quote from Golda Meir pinned up on the noticeboard: "We can forgive the Arabs for killing our children. We cannot forgive them for forcing us to kill their children. We will only have peace with the Arabs when they love their children more than they hate us."

I spent two exhilarating days traveling in the Palestinian communities of the Galilee with my friend Ilan Pappe. One of the reasons I enjoyed it, despite the grim realities of the place, was made clear to me by something Amira Hass had said in Jerusalem. All Israeli Jews are "collaborators," she'd told me; the question is how "we delimit the scope of collaboration" (she has recently published an editorial along these lines in *Ha'aretz*). Of herself, and her own place on the spectrum, she said—or intimated— that she had struggled for the Palestinians under occupation and sympathized with their suffering, but the fellow citizens with whom she truly belonged were the Palestinian Israelis.

I am having an evening coffee on Salman Natur's balcony in Daliyat al-Karmel, a Druze town southeast of Haifa. His house is two-thirds of the way up a mountain—just the height we were taught to walk at in the army—with the town spread beneath. Natur is an unusual figure: an anti-Zionist Druze. He developed a fondness for *Al-Ittihad*, the Communist Party's newspaper, when he was twelve, as a protest against people who had told him to throw stones at its readers, and eventually became its culture editor. He is now the editor of a quarterly in Ramallah. Natur remarks that out of 41 Israeli civilians killed, 18 were Arabs. Like all my interlocutors, he expresses the complexity and delicacy of the Palestinian Israeli position: "Whatever we do or say and however we express it, Israeli Jews will find fault with us." Israeli Palestinians support Nasrallah and Hizballah for standing up to Israel, even if their lives are more directly threatened by Hizballah's Katyusha rockets than they are by the Israeli state. Natur believes that the war has strengthened Israeli Palestinians' sense of themselves as part of the Arab world. It has also further undermined the already low standing in that world of its corrupt and dictatorial regimes. But, belonging as he does to the old left, Natur is deeply frustrated that the ideological basis of the opposition to Israel and the US is "Islamic and not secular-progressive."

On the way to Shaab, a large village deep in the Upper Galilee, I find myself thinking of the Galilee as one of Zionism's major failures, since the 1948 operations left it substantially uncleansed. Ben Gurion realized this and in December 1954 said: "We must settle not only the south, but also the north. The Negev is empty and desolate; the north is not as desolate, but empty, empty of Jews." The state project of Judaizing the Galilee began in the 1970s. One of its main results has been the spread of settlements for Jews only called *mitzpim* [singular *mitzpeh*, literally "lookout"], built on mountain tops overlooking Arab towns and villages, and designed to prevent them growing normally. Like the settlements in the occupied territories, the mitzpim are architecturally obtrusive and their superior infrastructure (e.g., electricity and roads) is immediately evident. Two mitzpim tower over Shaab to the north, and another can be seen further to the east, not far from the city of Karmiel, founded in 1964 after a massive appropriation of land from the Galilee Palestinians.

Asad Ghanim, in whose magnificent house on the hillside we have lunch, teaches political science at Haifa University. The house seemed to have been lost to Ghanim's grandfather and father, but Ghanim's tenacity won it back and some of the original stones have been built into the newer edifice. As always with Palestinian Israelis, the sword of demolition for putatively illegal building hovers over it. Ghanim surprises me by confessing that the way south Lebanon was scorched and the attempt at "ethnic cleansing" (his expression) has awakened 1948 anxieties in him. The chauvinist, anti-Arab militancy with which Israel's society is awash, and the increasing support for Avigdor Liberman (whose party has eleven Knesset seats and advocates the transfer of Israel's Palestinian citizens), have made him wonder about his status. I am surprised because Ghanim is a generation younger than Salman Natur and was presumably born into the state. I'd heard a similar sentiment the day before from Mary Totry, who also teaches at Haifa University, and I'd thought it was unusual. On reflection I shouldn't have been surprised. Nothing that the state of Israel has done since 1948 has given its Palestinian citizens reason to take their citizenship for granted.

Ghanim's house borders the edge of yet another mitzpeh, Yaad, built on the ruins of Miaar in the 1980s. Miaar's inhabitants were expelled in 1948, but the village itself was not destroyed until the 1950s, and a number of ruins were preserved, along with the cemetery. In May 2004 the American-based International Institute for Mediation and Historical Conciliation brought together the current inhabitants of Yaad and the former inhabitants of Miaar for a series of meetings and conversations, which were recorded in a documentary entitled *Miaar–Yaad: One Hill, Two Villages*. Does Miaar–Yaad offer some solace, is it a source of measured optimism? I really don't think so, but beggars can't be choosers.

NOTE

1 In the original text the author refers to the work of Lara Deeb, published in *Middle East Report* (31 July 2006). Lara Deeb's essay was revised and expanded, and can be found in Part I of this volume—Ed.

20. THE CULTURE OF ANNIHILATION

Azmi Bishara

This essay was originally published in Al-Ahram Weekly *806 (3–9 August 2006).*

The fighter plane is the quintessence of modern civilization, the modern goddess. It is the product of the collective input of all the sciences and the neutralization of all morals and values. In it converge the laser, micro-optics, microelectronics, and high-tech aerodynamics, allowing for precision flying, hairline fine guidance, dead-on targeting, and surgical destruction. It is hygienic and ultra-precise and its factories, hangars, and assembly plants are as tall and spacious as cathedrals. These planes are only manufactured in the most industrially developed states, assembled by huge corporations whose employees inhabit equality-oriented societies and receive high salaries. They can only be piloted by highly qualified individuals. They are simultaneously the product of absolute individualism and institutionalized collective labor. The employees who contribute to their manufacture embody societies that have achieved much; they are the elite, a cut above the rest, the chosen ones, the new Aryan race.

As with any goddess of consumerist society it has a built-in obsolescence; a new plane has to be produced every two or three years in order to keep up with demand, incorporating the latest technological developments and scientific discoveries in order to preserve her superiority over the gods of other people.

The fighter plane makes the immoral moral. It soars above good and evil, a celestial goddess with an insatiable thirst for sacrificial tribute. The pilot does not see the blood; he doesn't see the bayonet or the bullet piercing through the body of the victim. He does not get dirty because he does not have to crawl. Or see the eyes of his victims. Nor does he break the commandment *thou shalt not kill*. All he does is press a button from a long way away.

All the victims hear is the screech of the oncoming missile. Then the world shakes around them and they topple over, without so much as swaying. Perhaps they feel excruciating pain before passing into nothingness. All people are helpless before the fighter planes; no father or mother can protect their child. Children are torn to pieces, or buried beneath the rubble of buildings that collapse with an echoing groan that blends with the sound of limbs being torn. Stones, planks of wood, shreds of steel crash into human bone and pulverize skulls—all in the twinkling of an eye.

Meanwhile, from up there in the pilot's seat, all that can be seen are a plume of smoke and a cloud of dust. "Mission accomplished," radios the pilot to the base, as he executes a neat turn overhead in skies beyond the sea of morals. Then he lands, jumps out of the plane and heads to the barracks, helmet tucked under his arm like a motorcyclist. He goes for coffee in the cafeteria, exchanges jokes with his fellow pilots, with the female staff on the base, and with the mechanics who will be getting his plane ready for another sortie of death. Then he heads home. On his way he listens to some music, clowns around with some children and, maybe, engages in a conversation about politics. He might be earnest, or indifferent or incensed. He could be a leftist or a rightist, in support of gay rights or against them, a self-acclaimed dove or a rabid hawk. But these are not the criteria that qualified him to push the button. All such thoughts and criteria fade into meaninglessness in the religion of the fighter bomber.

The peoples of the world are divided into the haves and have-nots of F-15s and F-16s.

The haves are divided into countries that own these planes and countries that are possessed by them. The Arabs are divided not only into the have-nots, but those who don't have and yet have made the planes into golden cows.

These fighter planes are omnipresent. They can be visible or invisible. But there is no escaping their venom, nowhere to hide from their missiles. The planes remain in the air but their missiles will swoop down on the passengers of a fleeing car, a bus, an ambulance, and they will bore through the ceilings of bunkers and shelters until they reach the tender bodies within. Human flesh stands no chance against a missile flying toward it from a fighter plane. The body stands naked before the goddess who roams the heavens as edifices of stone and reinforced cement crumble before her.

The planes wreak massive destruction, but they cannot resolve the battle against those who have right on their side. To do that the goddess's followers have to fight a ground war. But once the inhabitants of that civilization start fighting on the ground, they start to die and begin to cry. This phenomenon has given rise to a curious belief, which is that while their soldiers have the right to kill, others do not have the right to kill their soldiers, even in war. This is why when one of their soldiers is struck, they are overcome by shock, and why when their armies suffer a defeat at the hands of the forces of the weak and oppressed, they take it as an affront to the prestige of their army and their military superiority. At such a point Israel stealthily withdraws the ground forces and unleashes the F-16s to bomb "terrorist" locations, be they homes or villages. It is a cowardly and vindictive way to behave, open to those who possess an air force that enables them to become arrogant airborne tyrants. On the ground they are human beings like everyone else: fragile and brittle. But in the air, with the protection of their goddess, they can stomp around, invisible to the naked eye but certain to make their thunder heard as they pass overhead, taking full advantage of the fragility of those who are left on the ground without planes, and even those who have taken refuge in the holes in the ground. They avenge themselves not just because they have the will to do so—they hold no monopoly on will—but because their goddess makes it possible for them to do so.

> And the Lord said unto Joshua:
> "See, I have given into thine hand Jericho, and the king thereof, and the mighty men of valor.
> "And ye shall compass the city, all ye men of war, and go round about the city once. Thus shalt thou do six days.
> "And seven priests shall bear before the ark seven trumpets of rams' horns. And the seventh day ye shall compass the city seven times, and the priests shall blow with the trumpets..."
> ...[A]nd it came to pass, when the people heard the sound of the trumpet, and the people shouted with a great shout, that the wall fell down flat, so that the people went up into the city, every man straight before him, and they took the city.
> And they utterly destroyed all that was in the city, both man and woman, young and old, and ox, and sheep, and ass, with the edge of the sword...
> And they burnt the city with fire, and all that was therein. Only the silver, and the gold, and the vessels of brass and of iron, they put into the treasury of the house of the Lord.

And Joshua saved Rahab the harlot alive, and her father's household, and she dwelleth in Israel even unto this day; because she hid the messengers, which Joshua sent to spy out Jericho. (Joshua 6)

It is destructive power that fills them with pride... the sort that comes before the fall. The death of a child, two children, three; the death of a woman or two; the destruction of an ambulance—when does brute force against innocent people become unacceptable? Thirty children? Fifty? In front of the cameras? How many when there are no cameras at hand? At what point do the scales tip? Cameras, incidentally, do not transmit the putrid odor of bodies crushed beneath the rubble.

It is difficult to pinpoint exactly when the cup slips out of the hand of an Arab or Western official as he stares at the television screen. Which image of dying children got through to him? Did his mouth drop agape as his cup crashed to the floor? Did he choke on the food he was eating? Does he think that he should have listened to his aides sooner and called for an immediate cease-fire? Does he groan at the horror of the crimes committed by Israel or slump in despair at Israel's folly in forfeiting yet another opportunity?

Israel was built on targeting civilians. In 1948 it targeted them in order to displace them and usurp their land. It targeted entire villages that it alleged were *fedayeen*—resistance fighter—bases. The "strategy" was founded upon two tenets: the need to deter civilians from supporting the resistance, which is to say to repress the expression of any political or social position, and the need to feed and quench the Israeli thirst for revenge. This two-pronged military creed was epitomized by Unit 101, led by Ariel Sharon in the early 1950s. It raided villages, blew up houses, and slaughtered the residents. Among the most notorious fruits of this philosophy were the massacres of Qubya, Nahalin, and al-Bureij in the 1950s, and the massacres of Jabalya, Beit Hanoun, al-Shajalya, Qasba in Nablus, and Jenin in more recent times. To perform these deeds Israel needed butchers, though it called them "legendary warriors." It was a hands-on approach. It did not involve F-16s. With these all that are needed are spoiled youths of the appropriate religious affiliation and with their hearts set on an American consumerist lifestyle.

Israel is deliberately targeting civilians in Lebanon, capitalizing on an expedient moment. Its aims are to punish anyone who might have supported the resistance, to displace civilians northward in order to aggravate sectarian tensions in the country and to quench its barbaric thirst for revenge. The current attack, in all its ferocity and with its toll of innocent victims, was planned well in advance, with malice aforethought. Israel is a terrorist state. The diabolical logic of this state is actively supported by another terrorist state led by George Bush, a very dangerous, pathologically violent and sadistic man surrounded by a gang of cool and calculating Machiavellians and apologists for state terrorism. They ardently believe that civilians who don't own fighter planes are so far down the rungs of the ladder in the survival of the fittest that if they die, well—that's their own fault, a result of their own lack of realism.

This logic has one flaw that makes it unpardonable, a curse that will haunt that civilization, a permanent indictment of its control of the skies: how can children be expected to be "realistic"? How can anyone blame them for their own death?

It is wrong to sing the praises of dead children as if they were heroes, a disgrace to put their bodies on display. These children were not warriors. They were not in the resistance. They did not die in order to achieve a victory for others who didn't die and who hadn't put their lives on the line. These children died because they couldn't escape in time or manage to hide from the planes. They are the victims of the criminally barbaric civilization of fighter planes. Their murderers must be brought to account and the resistance against the aggression must be sustained.

21. ILLUSIONS OF UNILATERALISM
DISPELLED IN ISRAEL

Yoav Peled

This essay was originally published in the Middle East Report *online,*
11 October 2006.

In 1967 Israel's government was headed by Levi Eshkol, a politician said to be easygoing, weak, and indecisive, who four years earlier had replaced the country's founder, David Ben Gurion, as prime minister. The Israeli public, tired of Ben Gurion's authoritarianism and constant exhortations to greater and greater sacrifice, had greeted Eshkol's appointment with a sigh of relief. Israel's chief Arab adversary at the time, Egyptian President Gamal Abdel Nasser, sought to take advantage of the Eshkol government's reputed lassitude in order to annul Israel's achievements in the 1956 Suez campaign: the demilitarization of the Sinai Peninsula and the opening of the Strait of Tiran to Israeli shipping. On Nasser's orders, Egyptian soldiers moved into the Sinai, and Egyptian gunboats blocked the narrow waterway.

Nasser's actions were largely symbolic—only some 3 percent of Israel's international trade moved through the Strait of Tiran, and the Egyptian forces in the Sinai did not pose any immediate threat to Israel—but the Israeli military argued that the credibility of its deterrence doctrine must be restored, and that effective deterrence could only be restored by military means. After resisting the generals' urgings for three weeks, Eshkol's government caved in and, in the ensuing six-day war, the Middle East was transformed.[1] Nasser's mistake was that he did not realize that, with a weak civilian government in Israel, nobody would stand up to the military's belligerent designs. (Ben Gurion, it should be noted, advised very strongly against launching the 1967 war, but his advice was ignored.)

In July 2006, by his own admission, Hassan Nasrallah, secretary general of Hizballah, made the same mistake. Under the two most recent prime ministers, Ehud Barak and Ariel Sharon, both of whom were retired generals, Israel had met minor Hizballah operations with carefully measured responses, designed not to escalate conflict on the Lebanese border while Israel was busy fighting the Palestinians in the West Bank and

Gaza. Based on that experience, Nasrallah estimated that the government of Prime Minister Ehud Olmert, headed by "rookies" (his term) and committed to a "civilian agenda" (their term), would not react very strongly to a brief incursion across the border and the capture of a few Israeli soldiers. Nasrallah was probably assured in his assumption by the facts that, on June 25, militants of Hamas and associated forces had launched a similar attack on Israel from inside Gaza, and that, as a result, the Israeli military was engaged in a massive attack on the Palestinians. From this, Nasrallah must have concluded that Hizballah's action would alleviate the pressure upon the Palestinians, without too much risk to the Shiite militia or to Lebanon as a whole.

Nasrallah's decision turned out to be a huge miscalculation. The two figures at the head of the Israeli government—Olmert and Defense Minister Amir Peretz (formerly of Peace Now)—proved to be totally incapable of standing up to the military, which was itching to avenge its humiliation at the hands of Hizballah, as well as Hamas. In fact, Olmert and Peretz abdicated their leadership role in favor of Lieutenant-General Dan Halutz, chief of staff and a former air force commander, made famous by his remarks after an Israeli jet dropped a one-ton bomb on an apartment building in Gaza, killing Hamas leader Salah Shehadeh and fifteen civilians. Asked by a journalist what he felt after such "targeted killings," he said he felt "a slight bump to the plane as a result of the bomb's release.... That's what I feel."

The Israeli military took advantage of Nasrallah's miscalculation in order to visit death and destruction upon Lebanon, on a scale unknown since Sharon's invasion of that country in 1982. Halutz vowed to set Lebanon back 20 years, and he probably did, but not before liquidating his personal stock portfolio, just in case things did not go as smoothly as expected. Indeed, things did not go smoothly at all from Israel's point of view.

Dual Failure

Israel's failure in the 2006 Lebanon war was twofold—military and civilian. The dual failure brought to the fore in a dramatic way the time bombs bequeathed by Ariel Sharon to his successor: the ongoing war against the Palestinians and the social crisis created by the neoliberal economic policy of the last two decades. Militarily, Israel failed to achieve any of its three (totally unrealistic) declared war aims: release of the two soldiers captured by Hizballah, dismantling of the military arm of that organization, or, failing that, its complete removal from southern Lebanon. Most devastating, however, was the military's failure to halt the barrage of Katyushas and other rockets that kept falling on northern Israel at a rate of 100 to 200 per day until the very last day of the war, and that effectively brought life in that region to a standstill for an entire month. The civilian aspect of the failure was just as severe. The state failed to evacuate the civilian population of northern Israel in an orderly fashion, and did not even attempt to provide essential services to those—the poor, the old, and the infirm—who could not evacuate themselves. In both cases, the responsibility fell to private charities that, naturally, could provide only partial solutions.

The specific causes of Israel's military failures are now being investigated, debated and fought over, but the underlying reason is clear to anyone who wants to look. For the last 40 years, but especially since September 2000, the main task of the Israeli Defense Force (IDF) has been what Ze'ev Schiff, the eminent military analyst for the daily *Ha'aretz*, has euphemistically called the "violent policing" of the occupied territories. Given the limited resources put at its disposal by a society that is fast becoming economically liberal, affluent, and individualistic, the IDF (with the exception of the air force) could not engage in "violent policing" while at the same time maintaining fighting capabilities at the pre-1967 level. Revealingly, after one repulsed advance on a southern Lebanese village, some soldiers expressed genuine amazement that Hizballah fighters in the village actually shot back at them.

The civilian failure had its roots in the neoliberal economic policy pursued by the Israeli state since 1985, designed to shift resources from the public sector to the market. This policy has led to extensive privatization of public services and the gradual degeneration of those that cannot be made profitable enough to be privatized. Maintenance of public bomb shelters and provision of food, water, and medical assistance to the people who find refuge therein at times of war are not activities that can be privatized, however. So these services were not provided at all, or were provided very inadequately by private charities or NGOs. The low point of this benign neglect by the state was the failure to declare a state of emergency in the northern part of the country, a measure that would have committed the state to provide essential services and pay adequate compensation to businesses and individuals who suffered economic losses because of the war. (A less far-ranging "special state" was declared, but the needs of most residents of the affected region were not met.)

In a deeper sense, though, Israel's failures in the Lebanon war signified the divorce of two political objectives—economic liberalization and war—that Sharon had managed to wed though they had been believed, historically, to be at odds. Sharon's ability to defeat the second intifada while pursuing a policy of aggressive economic liberalization made him Israel's most popular prime minister since the introduction of public opinion polls in the late 1960s (well after Ben Gurion's time). But the mechanism for this seemingly historic achievement, the promised unilateral solution to the Israeli–Palestinian conflict, was actually sleight of hand. And the Lebanon war, coupled with the summer's events in Gaza, exposed the trick.

An Illusion Banished

Sharon borrowed the idea of a unilateral solution, like many of his other bits of political prestidigitation, from his Labor party rivals. In 2000, Prime Minister Barak declined to sign a peace agreement with Syria that would have provided for Israel's withdrawal from the Golan Heights and southern Lebanon in return for peace and security arrangements, because he feared he would lose popularity with the Israeli public.[2] Instead, he decided to withdraw from southern Lebanon unilaterally, promising fire and brimstone to anyone who dared attack Israel across the UN-demarcated Blue Line. In the 2003 election campaign, Amram Mitzna, then Labor party leader, proposed to apply the same logic to Gaza. Sharon adopted Mitzna's proposal after his election victory and carried it out successfully, thus changing his image from warmonger to peacemaker at the twilight of his active life.

The attraction of unilateral withdrawals was that they promised to stabilize areas of confrontation, thus cutting back on military expenses, without the need for Israel to give up territory that it really valued: the Golan Heights, in one case, and much of the West Bank, in the other. For six years following the unilateral pullout from Lebanon, the northern border was indeed quiet, with a few interruptions from skirmishes with Hizballah that the Barak and Sharon governments knew how to contain. That experience was the basis of Sharon's decision to implement similar unilateral arrangements, first in Gaza and then in the West Bank, where a complex of concrete walls and barbed-wire fences is being built to mark the line of withdrawal.

"Disengagement" from Gaza, however, did not end Israel's control over that strip of land; it only changed the form of control. Instead of ruling Gaza from the inside, Israeli forces have kept the territory under siege, gradually suffocating economic and social activity there, until the present moment, when the population busies itself with bare survival. Based on this "success," Sharon planned to implement a similar arrangement in parts of the West Bank. For that purpose he split his political party, Likud, and set up Kadima, a new party that ran in the March 2006 elections solely on the "disengagement" platform and gained a plurality of the seats in the Knesset. (Unlike the less astute Olmert, however, Sharon never committed himself publicly to further disengagement in the West Bank.)

Sharon was incapacitated before the 2006 elections, and his successor declared that through disengagement in the West Bank (later renamed "convergence," and still later "realignment"), he would turn Israel into "a fun place to live in" by 2010. That fantasy never had a real political chance, but before it could even be tested, Hamas and their fellow militants banished Olmert's illusion. The disengagement has not caused the Gazan resistance forces to stop shooting Qassam rockets into Israel, terrorizing in particular one small town, Sderot, which happens to be Defense Minister Peretz's hometown. Evidently, and like much of the rest of the world, these fighters have not been persuaded that Israel has really relinquished its control over Gaza. Finally, a daring attack on an Israeli military outpost and the capture of one soldier lured Israel back into the Gaza Strip.

By the Sword Or...

From the beginning, Israel's security establishment, which lives off the occupation of lands taken in the 1967 war, objected to the idea of unilateral (or any other) withdrawal, but eventually abided by Barak's and Sharon's authority. The most dramatically public expression of this attitude to date came from Maj. Gen. Yiftach Ron-Tal, until recently commander of the Land Branch of the IDF (a position roughly equivalent to the US Army chief of staff), and who was on leave before retiring, but still officially on active duty. In unauthorized interviews with several Israeli media outlets on October 4, Ron-Tal, whose son, it turns out, was a Gaza settler, blamed Israel's failure in Lebanon on the disengagement from Gaza and claimed that a people that gives up parts of "its" land commits suicide. Now, with the developing civil war in Gaza, caused by the policy of economic strangulation of the Palestinians pursued by Israel with the aid of the US and the European Union, there is talk in IDF circles of reoccupying Gaza in order to bleach the stain of defeat in Lebanon.

With the illusion of unilateral withdrawal dispelled, the old dilemma of war vs. economic prosperity has reared its ugly head again. Israel clearly has only two options left: it can try to achieve peace, stability, and prosperity through negotiated agreements with its Arab neighbors, or it can continue to live and die by the sword. But in order to live, rather than die, by the sword, the country's course of development over the last 20 years must be reversed, and a Ben Gurionesque, mobilized society must be restored. Such a turnabout is being advocated now not only by the West Bank settlers, who have always yearned for it, but also by erstwhile liberal commentators such as *Ha'aretz*'s Ari Shavit. "What the hell happened to us?" Shavit implored in a widely reproduced column that appeared in English on August 16. He proceeded to blame "political correctness" for Israel's military failings. Not only was the defense budget cut, but also "the Israel Defense Forces was identified as an army of occupation—rather than as an army defending feminists and homo-lesbians from the fanaticism of the Middle East.... In the spiritual world of political correctness, power and army have become dirty words."

A softening of manliness, a yearning for normalcy, a pursuit of bourgeois individual pleasures at the expense of the rugged Zionist collective—all these decadent indulgences, in Shavit's estimation, lulled Israel to sleep and presaged its rude reawakening in the "Lebanese mud" (the Israeli equivalent of the American expression, the "rice paddies of Vietnam"). "Israel tried with all its soul and all its might to be Athens. However in this place, in this era, there is no future for an Athens without a speck of Sparta." But how is Ben Gurion's Israel to be conjured anew, in the globalized, liberalized country that actually exists? Ben Gurion did not even allow television broadcasting in his time; in 2006, Israeli soldiers blogged, completely uncensored, from the front. The fact that turning Israel from whatever it is (certainly not Athens) back into Sparta, if at all possible, would require the institution of a quasi-fascist state, does not seem to bother Shavit.

The other option, a move toward negotiated, comprehensive peace, would require a major realignment of the public mood, which blames the government not for launching a totally unnecessary and ill-conceived war, but for conducting that war so ineptly. Hence this option presently seems unavailable. Yet the past popularity of unilateral withdrawals, manifested in the electoral success of Kadima, indicates that a significant segment of the Israeli Jewish public—the beneficiaries of economic liberalization—have tired of paying the price for the ongoing conflict. Given that unilateral arrangements are off the table, these elements—symbolically designated "Tel Aviv" in the current public discourse—may migrate back to the political camp to which they belonged before the breakdown of the Oslo process: the one that advocates peace through negotiated settlements. The idea of negotiated peace with the Palestinians is not, in fact, dead among the broader public. In the monthly poll conducted by the Tami Steinmetz Center at Tel Aviv University, the "negotiations index" that measures willingness among Israeli Jews to negotiate with the Palestinians, combined with confidence in the utility of such negotiations, stood at 43.2 in June 2006, right before the war, declined to 41 in July, and climbed back to 41.8 in August and 42.2 in September.[3] This is not a majority, but it is a constituency upon which to build.

The peace course is already urged by what is left of Israel's liberal punditry, and the Olmert government, desperate to hold on to power, has released a few trial balloons in that direction, as well as in all others.[4] It is still quite difficult to imagine the peace camp being revived, or what its concrete political program would look like. But the elimination of the unilateral option by the actions of Hamas and Hizballah raises the hope, for the first time in six years, that this line of development is at least possible.

NOTES

1 For details, see Tom Segev, *Israel in 1967* (Jerusalem: Keter, 2005), especially 243–358 [Hebrew].

2 Gilead Sher, *Just Beyond Reach: The Israeli–Palestinian Peace Negotiations, 1999–2001* (Tel Aviv: Yediot Aharonot, 2001) 65–66 [Hebrew]. See also Akiva Eldar's interview with Uri Sagi, the retired major general who headed the Israeli delegation in the negotiations with Syria, in *Ha'aretz* 18 July 2006 [Hebrew].

3 On the other hand, in August 2006 only 14 percent of Jewish Israelis favored full

withdrawal from the Golan Heights in return for peace with Syria, compared to 21 percent in January 2005, the last time this question was asked in this poll.

4 On just one day, October 1, 2006, the following op-eds appeared in *Ha'aretz* [all in English]: Uzi Benziman, "Is Israel a Partner?" Gideon Levy, "Operation Peace for the Winery," Daniel Gavron, "Let's Prevent the Next Round." See also the column by another retired major general, Avraham Tamir, "Yes to the Saudi Plan," *Ha'aretz* 3 October 2006 [Hebrew].

22. ISRAEL IN LEBANON:
THE FOREIGN POLICY LOGIC OF
JEWISH STATEHOOD

Virginia Tilley

This chapter first appeared in the MIT Electronic Journal of Middle East Studies *(Summer 2006). Research was supported by grants from the Friedrich Ebert Stiftung Foundation and the Foundation for Human Rights (South Africa), under the auspices of the Centre for Policy Studies (Johannesburg).*

To date, Israel's motives in the 2006 war with Hizballah have not been clarified by the rush of academic analyses. The dominant explanation, that Israel sought simply to end the threat of Hizballah's rocket attacks, is narrow to the point of inaccuracy, particularly since those attacks had taken no Israeli casualties over the past decade. Some scholars have described background motives: Ilan Pappe, for example, described on the Electronic Intifada an underutilized Israeli military seeking to justify its budget and demonstrate its prowess (14 July 2006). Some offer close analyses of proximate security logics, such as Robert Blecher's piece in the *Middle East Report* about how Israel's strategy toward the Palestinians has influenced its response to Hamas and Hizballah (18 July 2006). Other explanations decline toward motives and identities that derive more from polemics than scholarship, such as generic accusations of Israeli expansionism, US imperialism, and radical Islam (or "Islamo-fascism"). Attempts to deepen these models too often psychologize the conflict by blaming primordial ethnic hatreds or cultural clash: Arab prejudice against Jews, Jewish-Zionist racism against Arabs, Muslim "rage," or an East–West "clash of civilizations."

Many of these factors, even when imaginary, are not precisely incorrect or irrelevant, as they shape the behavior and influence of key actors. But most lack theoretical and empirical rigor as explanations, for they focus not on the causes but the effects of a more fundamental problem. At root, Israel's motives in Lebanon trace to one primary source: the ethnic imperative of Jewish statehood—the belief that a Jewish state requires an overwhelming Jewish-ethnic majority within Israel's territory—which has been incorporated into the Israeli government's understanding of state security.

Focusing on Israel's domestic ethnic doctrines might seem counterproductive at this juncture, diverting energies away from urgent conflict resolution in southern Lebanon and toward an ideological dispute that has long proved irreconcilable. The purpose here is not to engage in moral or ideological contest, however, but to redirect analysis toward the strategic logics that steer Israel's foreign policy, which are inseparable from its domestic geostrategy. So far, the international community has proved unwilling to tackle this "third rail" of Middle East politics. But until Israel's doctrine of ethnic statehood is addressed, none of its spin-off effects, including Israel's continuing military ambitions in Lebanon, can be addressed effectively either. This discussion will briefly explain why international pressure on Israel to democratize and enfranchise Palestine's native people is not only essential to resolving the Palestinian–Israeli conflict but is also fundamental to collective security.

National Identity and Foreign Policy

Classical realist theory (and its rational-choice and game-theory derivatives) assumes that state behavior in international affairs is driven by self-help and concerns with power (whether political or economic). In Lebanon, this lens brings focus on such questions as Israel's need to eliminate Hizballah's capacity to attack its northern towns or its need for security guarantees before it agrees to peace talks with the Palestinian Authority. The present United Nations intervention to orchestrate a cease-fire in Lebanon, Security Council Resolution 1701, reflects this view by concentrating narrowly on separating the warring parties, disarming Hizballah, and securing Israel's withdrawal from Lebanese land. Lebanon's internal politics are implicated only in so far as they are relevant to extending "the authority of the government of Lebanon" over all of Lebanese territory. Israel's internal politics are not addressed or implicated at all.

A constructivist approach reveals the inadequacy of this approach to generating a stable peace. Other factors can drive state behavior, such as knowledge systems that shape perceptions and related logics. Especially, the domestic discourse of the national identity can inform government and popular conceptions of the national interest, which in turn informs the state's foreign policy. Within Israel, the shared understanding among Israeli Jews that Israel must remain a "Jewish state" is such a discursive formula. This perceived imperative has shaped Israel's regional strategy regarding borders, water, immigration, military occupation, and external security in ways that authorized or even mandated the policy to attack Hizballah and therefore must now dominate international concerns. Understanding Israel's demographic imperative is therefore the sine qua non for addressing the policies that logically derive from it.

The "Demographic Threat"

Israel's ethnic imperative (Jewish statehood) is often promoted as sui generis, deriving from the unique experience of Jews in Europe and especially the Holocaust. In fact, its intellectual history is firmly rooted in the early decades of the 20th century, when the new "nation-state" concept and the racial pseudo-sciences intersected to propose an organic (racial-spiritual) quality to nations.[1] From about 1880 through the 1930s, nation-builders in all world regions globally absorbed the tenet, promoted by some European racial and political theorists, that racial homogeneity was essential to healthy and viable nation- and state-building. This premise led state-builders globally to seek various coercive methods—whether assimilationist, ethnocidal, or genocidal—to achieve such homogeneity on whatever terms made local social and political sense. Hence Zionist founder Theodor Herzl understood that a Jewish state in Palestine would have to consolidate a Jewish majority, and by the 1930s this demographic imperative was embedded in Zionist doctrine as a central strategic goal (although not without contemporary controversy) For Jewish-nationalist architects like Ben Gurion, the imperative of ethnic homogeneity was understood both to necessitate and legitimate ethnic cleansing: that is, the expulsion of the non-Jewish Arab population from their cities and villages in what became Israel and subsequent refusal to allow the refugees to return.

By mid-century, however, the old racial concept of nationhood was discredited by experience of its inherent predilection to generate precisely such discrimination and human rights abuses. Especially, the horrors of Nazi and Japanese racial nationalisms forced the international community to abandon ethno-racial premises for nationhood in favor of territorial definitions (even as they greatly stoked Zionist commitment to the ethnic formula).[2] Changing norms did not transform social views entirely, of course: today, racial and ethnic biases certainly persist everywhere in popular nationalist thought just as they persist in nationalist canons (imagery, founding narratives, heroes, and so forth). Immigration quotas in many countries also reflect continuing nervousness about preserving the nation's established (or imagined) ethnic character. But constitutional provisions to enforce a titular ethnic majority are abjured on grounds that conflating territorial statehood with ethnic nationalism will inevitably discriminate against minorities and foster conflict that could spill into regional unrest. Even in ethnic hotbeds like Serbia, constitutional or basic law provides ethnic-neutral rights, which domestic minorities (or majorities) can use in the *longue durée* fight against discrimination.

Israeli law and Zionist discourse that insist on Jewish-ethnic dominion within Israel are therefore both anachronistic and unique in continuing to laud the state's founding ethnic premise with full early-20th-century ardor.[3] One manifestation of this ardor is its invention of the so-called demographic threat: the possibility that Arabs may someday constitute a majority in Israel and vote Jewish statehood—that is, the body of laws that secures Jewish-ethnic privilege in Israel—out of existence. Since Jewish-ethnic statehood and "Israel" are considered the same thing in Zionist discourse, this "threat" is perceived as a threat to Israel's "survival"—a rhetorical twist that converts easily, for propaganda purposes and within the psychology of many Zionists, into equating full non-racial democracy in Israel with physical Jewish-Israeli extermination. Again, this formula is not new: it is precisely the understanding that once dominated nationalist thought everywhere (generating, for example, the extermination campaigns against Native Americans in the United States, which some Zionist polemicists cite today as a legitimizing precedent).

Hence Israel's latitude to pursue the domestic demographic policies that ensure the state's Jewish "character" is translated into an imperative for its foreign policy. In other words, Israel's security, in a military-strategic sense, is understood to require a regional security environment that secures its capacity to preserve a domestic Jewish majority. For theorists of nationalism and international relations, the case is absorbing: no other state today defends its ethnic character to the point of regional war-making. For those concerned with its implications for international stability, however, Israel's demographic imperative must be seen as untenable due to its implications for international instability. Some precise links between Israel's domestic and foreign policy are traced below.

Identity, Borders, and Hizballah: The "Convergence Plan"

The demographic threat requires that Israel control and/or partition historic Palestine in ways that exclude the Palestinian population making any claims on citizenship. Exactly how to do this remains debated, however, and the latest solution has been sabotaged by the war with Hizballah.

The problem derives from a basic quandary: how to obtain land without people. Some leftist-liberal thought has held that the best way to obviate the threat of an Arab majority is to give up land: that is, withdraw from the West Bank and Gaza Strip and consolidate Israel's permanent borders within the 1948 Green Line. This maneuver would secure a roughly 75-percent Jewish majority.[4] It also has the advantage of according with the directives of SC Resolution 242 and most international consensus about a just resolution to the conflict. (From the Zionist perspective, natural increase of Arab Israelis throws an obvious wrench into this solution, but no clear answer to that problem has yet gained Israeli consensus.)

Full withdrawal has run afoul of several currents of Zionist thought that view withdrawal from the West Bank as an anathema: for example, some Orthodox religious beliefs that the biblical West Bank highlands are the spiritual heartland of Jewish life; secular nationalist beliefs that the highlands are an inextricable part of Israel's geographic imaginary (Eretz Israel); and security arguments that the highlands comprise a vital buffer zone against Arab attack. Control of the West Bank aquifer adds a more purely material dimension to this attachment, as does the immense economic cost of withdrawing a half-million people from sizable cities. Assembling these disparate views into a "neo-Zionist" alliance, right-wing Israeli thought has therefore sought to retain the West Bank, including Greater Jerusalem. Yet annexing all of the West Bank and Gaza Strip would convert 3.5 million Palestinians into a disenfranchised domestic population, on an openly apartheid model. The South African example is cautionary here: inevitably linking politically to Israel's Arab citizenry, the Palestinians would quickly comprise a civil rights movement that Israel's democracy (like all other racial democracies) would find impossible to defeat. (Forced transfer remains one option urged by some, but is vetoed by those who believe transfer inhumane or simply that it would too seriously damage Israel's international standing or security.)

Israel's "convergence" plan, launched by Prime Minister Ariel Sharon and continued by Prime Minister Ehud Olmert through the Kadima Party, proposed to resolve this dilemma through a new partition: aggregating the smaller outlying West Bank settlements into a few large settlement blocs that cut across the West Bank highlands, retaining the entire Jordan Valley (except for an enclave around Jericho), and allowing autonomous Palestinian governance in the remaining enclaves. The plan is premised on the assumption that sealing 3.5 million Palestinians behind the "security barrier" (Wall) in disarticulated chunks of territory called a "state" will satisfy Palestinian political aspirations and allow Israelis to live peacefully within settlement cities annexed to Israel, such as Ariel and Ma'ale Adumim. The Wall itself is essential to this plan, preventing the two juxtaposed populations from mixing and thereby permitting Israel to remain "Jewish and democratic"—a democracy that preserves its pro-Jewish legal system through majority-Jewish rule. On the other side of the Wall, Palestinians are expected eventually to normalize their society, economy, and politics, probably by reorienting both toward Jordan. Demographic separation would then be ensured by watch towers and electronic surveillance for which Palestinian authorities would also be held responsible. Ironically, this plan requires that Israel postpone peace talks long enough to complete the Wall and consolidate the Palestinian population within their autonomous enclaves, where their separation will be ensured, but with US assistance these delays have proved easy to orchestrate. The convergence plan is already well underway, pursued through accelerated expansion of the major settlement cities and especially construction of the Wall.

Removing or neutralizing Hizballah became integral to the convergence plan as it became plain to Israel's leadership that the plan could not be implemented without violent repression of the Palestinians, who are losing land, livelihoods, and social cohesion to it and therefore continue to resist it. A general collaboration is the first problem: Hizballah and Hamas routinely share intelligence and resources. Although direct aid from Hizballah inside the Palestinian territories is limited, it still provides crucial support, frustrating Israel's attempts to strangle Hamas financially. Hizballah is also positioned to lob Katyushas and larger missiles at Israel as conditions in the Palestinian territories deteriorate. Although for the past decade this threat has been latent (Hizballah has restrained its attacks to retaliating against Israeli incursions into Lebanon), Hizballah's capture of two Israeli soldiers on July 12 was suggestive of this solidarity. The Gaza Strip had then been under several weeks of a concerted Israeli attack, including destruction of Gaza's only power plant, intended to terminate the ineffectual but (for Israelis) demoralizing stream of homemade Hamas missiles regularly lobbed from northern Gaza into Israel's southern communities. Some reports have confirmed an agreement between Hamas and Hizballah to "warm up" the northern border and take pressure off Hamas, although the scale of Israel's response was clearly not anticipated.[5] A truly free hand for Israel regarding its occupation policy requires that this threat be eliminated.

The second problem, however, is far more important for the Israeli government. Within Israel, political support for the government's convergence plan relies on Israeli–Jewish public belief that a unilateral "sacrifice" of West Bank territory will ultimately result in a stable peace. Hizballah's capacity to launch rockets into Israel has raised the specter that Hamas will also grow to constitute a serious guerrilla threat in the Palestinian areas of a partly evacuated West Bank.

The Israeli government was already plagued by this political problem after orchestrating the withdrawal from Gaza. Israel's withdrawal of its Gaza settlements was argued to be a "sacrifice" justified by the promise of peace. But Israel retained control of Gaza's borders and cut off trade and monetary transfers, generating prison-like conditions in which Palestinian social conditions deteriorated rapidly and Palestinian resistance continued. Among other measures, Hamas militants regularly fired primitive rockets from the Gaza Strip into proximate Israeli towns. Ineffectual in damaging Israel directly, these symbolic attacks nevertheless belied Israeli government promises that unilateral withdrawal would pacify Palestinian militancy. Hizballah's blooming military capacity on Israel's northern border further suggested that, under conditions of genuine Palestinian sovereignty, Palestinian rocket attacks could make the Wall ineffectual as a security barrier and develop into a similarly serious threat.[6]

It was largely out of anxiety to discredit these dire omens for the convergence plan that, in late June, the Israel government launched its military campaign to crush Hamas in the Gaza Strip—a campaign that, by early July, was wreaking unprecedented levels of destruction and, at this writing, has cost 191 Palestinian lives. The same concern prompted Israel to prepare for an attack on Hizballah as much as a year before the border incident provided the pretext for it.[7]

In sum, eradicating Hizballah has become fundamental to Israel's strategy for averting the demographic threat. First, the Israeli government needs to eliminate a Palestinian ally that was impeding its capacity to repress Palestinian resistance. Second, the government urgently needs to retain Jewish-Israeli political support for the all-important convergence plan, by dispelling rising Jewish-Israeli fears that Hamas will emulate Hizballah by building a serious guerrilla force within vacated West Bank enclaves. Hence Israeli's failure to eliminate Hizballah in the recent war has probably spelled the ruin of the convergence plan. On the same grounds, however, it has also spelled the ruin of leftist arguments for withdrawing from the West Bank completely, as the same risk of a hostile guerrilla force could arguably develop across a Wall positioned along the Green Line. Israel's need to eradicate or at least disarm Hizballah and Hamas therefore remains salient as long as its Jewish-ethnic imperative remains operative.

The Ethnic Imperative and Iran

The US and Israel have been planning to attack Iran, and seeking political cover for doing so, for the past year.[8] From Israel's perspective, Iran is the primary supporter (in arms, training, and some finances) of Hizballah and Hamas. Iran also runs its supply lines through Syria, the only frontline state not to have made peace with Israel and whose insistence on return of the Golan Heights presents difficult dilemmas for Israel (especially concerning the Golan's important watershed). Syria is militarily weak, but Iranian connections to Hizballah create a geopolitical "arc" of anti-Israeli networks that facilitate anti-Israeli militancy and limit Israeli ambitions in the entire Middle East.[9] Installing a pro-Western regime in Iran would both cut off support to local guerrilla groups and isolate Syria, allowing Israel to pursue regime change in Syria as well. Iran is therefore the last serious obstacle to consolidating the pacified and compliant Middle East that the Zionist movement has sought to create since the 1930s and that would now allow Israel full latitude to set its borders as it wishes.[10] This agenda has become more urgent, however, as Iran has developed a nuclear energy program. If Iran uses enriched uranium to develop a nuclear weapon, it could deter an Israeli attack on Iran or any other regional target. One of the world's largest nuclear powers, Israel has been determined to preserve its regional monopoly on nuclear deterrence.

From the perspective of the Bush administration, Israel's agenda regarding Iran is fully compatible with US interests. Since the fall of Saddam Hussein and dissolution of Iraq's army, Iran has emerged as the sole regional power capable of contesting unfettered US hegemony in the world's richest oil region. The US therefore seeks regime change in Iran for classic realist reasons. Installing a pro-Western Iranian government is also a longstanding goal in the neocon vision of a "new Middle East," which is informed by a conflation of corporate interests, militarism, Zionism, and recidivist notions that the US must play a vanguard role in the West's anti-Islamic civilizing mission.[11] For the past two years the White House has been consulting with Pentagon and air force advisors about how to destroy Iran's nuclear facilities, partly on the belief that such a strike would trigger domestic outrage, revolution, and ascension of a pro-Western regime. (This fantasy remains impressively immune to past experience in Iraq and Lebanon, as well as all independent expert advice, including the Pentagon and the State Department.)[12]

A major air strike on Iran requires a sufficient casus belli, however, or at least sufficient political cover to secure international passivity. Public statements by Israel and the US over the past year have therefore attempted to cultivate an international consensus conducive to military intervention against Iran: especially, through a disinformation campaign exaggerating intelligence about Iran's intentions and capacity to develop nuclear weapons, coupled with a push in the Security Council (SC) to pass a resolution that will legitimize force against Iran if it does not abandon its uranium enrichment program (on the apparent expectation that Iran will refuse to do so).

Throughout 2006, Israel has also been stoking domestic and international belief that Iran is threatening to "annihilate" Israel, especially by promoting mistranslations of President Ahmadinejad's statements that falsely cast him as openly threatening to "destroy Israel" or "wipe Israel off the map." (Ahmadinejad's statements have actually indicated a desire for, or fatalistic expectation of, regime change in Israel, not plans for a military attack. Mistranslations have distorted these statements, but the discursive conflation noted above—of Jewish statehood and Israel's material survival—also serves Israeli propagandists here.) Together, these measures portend a reprise of the Iraq strategy: whipping up international tensions about an imminent nuclear threat, followed by a unilateral US strike that adopts the mantle of UN legitimacy while dismissing SC reluctance to authorize military intervention.

Relevant here is that neutralizing Hizballah is prerequisite to a US attack on Iran, because Hizballah is too well positioned to bombard Israel's northern cities in the event of an attack on its Iranian ally and patron. Supporting Hizballah's capacity in this regard indeed provides Iran with an important deterrent to attack by Israel or the US. (Cast as "evil" by the Bush administration, this satellite maneuver reflects a classically realist strategy on Iran's part.)

Hizballah's deterrent would matter even if the US attacks Iran, as Israel is understood to be a key ally of the US. But it is especially important if Israel attacks Iran. Striking Iran is difficult for the US to do directly, as its occupation forces in Iraq and naval bases in the Gulf would be vulnerable to the impassioned anti-US (and anti-British) guerrilla campaign that would immediately erupt. Hence, the Israeli air force might strike Iran instead. In recent years, Israel has purchased new "bunker-busting" missiles, a fleet of new F-16 fighter jets, and five leading-edge German Dolphin submarines—i.e., the appropriate weaponry for striking Iran's nuclear installations and deterring its retaliation. In 2005, the *Times* of London reported that Israel had constructed a mock-up of Iran's Natanz facility in the desert and was conducting practice bombing raids.[13] In recent months, Israeli officials have openly stated Israel will unilaterally bomb Iran if the UN fails to take decisive action to terminate Iran's nuclear energy program.

But Israel's failure to disarm Hizballah by aerial bombing has seriously impacted all options for military action against Iran, in several ways. First, Israel's massive bombardment of Lebanon could not remove Hizballah's underground facilities even using the latest bunker-busting technology, and so has discredited rather than supported White House arguments that the US Air Force will be successful regarding Iran's vastly larger and deeper nuclear complexes. Second, by leaving a proximate armed threat on Israel's northern border (and demonstrating the actual size of that threat), it has left Israel's flank vulnerable to retaliation by Iran's regional ally, making it dangerous for Israel itself to attack Iran. Third, by galvanizing new Lebanese political unity in collective loathing for Israel, it has further belied the already strained neocon assumption that military intervention, whether by Israel or the US, will trigger an internal coup or revolution in Iran that will install a pro-Western government. Finally, it has caused delay. With only two years before the elections, time may now be too short to orchestrate the strike on Iran before Bush leaves office.

In sum, Hizballah's successful resistance has damaged Israeli and neocon hopes to create a "new Middle East" uniformly supine to US and Israeli interests. While Iran's Islamic government survives, Hizballah will survive. While Hizballah survives, the attack on Iran is stalled. While the Iran–Hizballah axis endures, the Israeli government cannot pursue the program of land annexation and ethnic engineering that will secure Jewish statehood. That prospect may only inspire more extreme measures, however, for the present impasse raises the stakes. With the costs of the occupation rising, repression of Palestinian resistance increasingly costly, and Israel's international image deteriorating rapidly, Israel's need to defeat Palestinian resistance and secure its final borders in ways that secure its Jewish majority is becoming more urgent.

Using the United Nations: Resolution 1701

Possibly the most far-reaching effect of Israel's demographic imperative is how it has shaped its relationship to the United Nations and ultimately affected the UN itself. Israel has a long history of ignoring Security Council (SC) resolutions related to territorial withdrawal and the return of Palestinian refugees, and has even formally announced its autonomy from UN authority.[14] Israel has also consistently rejected any suggestion that an international force might assume responsibility for monitoring peace in southern Lebanon or the Palestinian occupied territories. These stands have contributed to UN weakness, as the US has consistently supported Israel prerogatives through use of the SC veto.

With its unexpected defeat in its attempt to disarm Hizballah, however, Israel now needs precisely the intervention it has long rejected: an effective international peacekeeping force on its border. Israel's real strategic goal in the war with Hizballah was not precisely to destroy or even necessarily disarm Hizballah but to remove its capacity to attack Israel at will. The last hope for this plan is UN Resolution 1701, written primarily by the US with Israeli input, which makes the entire international community responsible for this outcome. But by enlisting the SC to serve Israel's foreign policy agenda, first by delaying the resolution and then through its wording, Israel has made the UN not merely passive or ineffectual but complicit in its project of preserving ethnic statehood. The effect on the UN has been a serious loss of credibility.[15]

The wording of 1701 is complicated and even slippery, but its essential formulas are clearly in service to Israeli agendas. The resolution establishes that Israel's withdrawal should happen "in parallel" with the arrival of the Lebanese army, but does not specify whether the army's arrival is sufficient for Israel's withdrawal or must be associated with Hizballah's effective disarmament. The resolution establishes no arbiter to monitor this question, leaving Israel to determine when "the authority of the government of Lebanon" has been truly imposed. The resolution also confirms that rebuilding Lebanon must not translate into Hizballah's resupplying and rebuilding its military capacity in the south. If Israel deems that reconstruction is serving Hizballah's military capacity (which it doubtless will, as Hizballah and the army will necessarily collaborate in the reconstruction of heavily Shiite areas), then under the terms of 1701, Israel can declare Hizballah in breach and itself authorized to stop or even bomb reconstruction efforts that contribute to Hizballah's capacity. Since Israel has already clarified that all civilian infrastructure falls into this category, reconstruction could be effectively stopped or reversed.

The resolution also provides Israel with an external guarantor of Hizballah's disarmament: an expanded UNIFIL. UNIFIL also provides the Lebanese government with a friendly international force that can monitor and even oppose any Israeli intervention. Yet UNIFIL lacks any real capacity to implement authority over Hizballah or to repel Israeli aggression. Its primary responsibility—to "ensure that its area of operations is not utilized for hostile activities of any kind"—pertains solely to containing Hizballah. Since the rest of the resolution provides multiple loopholes for Israeli aggression (e.g., redefining it as "defense"), this clause sets up UNIFIL for failure to protect civilians from any action Israel may want to take. It also sets up international troops for targeting by Hizballah, whose leadership will accurately perceive their true role as Israeli surrogates.

In sum, Resolution 1701 is designed to accomplish Israel's strategic goal through a method far better (and cheaper) than direct Israeli military occupation: by installing Lebanese government and international forces in southern Lebanon that are obligated by the UN to render Hizballah incapable of launching any attack on Israel on its own authority. Hence Israel has not precisely "lost" a war that resulted in UN endorsement for Israel's original objective. Israeli military chief Lieutenant-General Dan Halutz's comment indicates this view: "Tallying up the points, it is definitely a victory, perhaps not a knockout, but in terms of achievements, it is [a victory]."[16] If the provisions of 1701 do achieve Israel's goals, the Israeli government's plans to seal the Palestinians within ethnic enclaves and the US–Israeli plan to attack Iran will again be viable.

Conclusion

Israel's recent aggression in Lebanon, still simmering in its first fragile cease-fire at this writing, is now routinely called a "war." The term is apt, given the scale of events, but its use is nevertheless significant. This conflict was not between two states, the usual meaning of "war." Nor is it a "guerrilla war" in the usual sense—guerrilla resistance to a state's government or military within the state's territory, as presently is happening in Iraq. Indeed, from Israel's perspective, its attack was never meant to be a "war." Israel and the United States clearly anticipated a swift unilateral aggression that would eradicate Hizballah's military capacity within days, approximating the speed and success of Israel's invasion of Lebanon in 1982. The venture was designed and expected to be a one-sided bombing campaign with little risk to Israel, taking NATO's bombing of Kosovo as its model. In the event, the venture "failed." But failure has altered only the means, not the goals, of Israel's larger strategy, which is driven by its ethnic imperative and will remain largely unchanged as long as that imperative endures.

Consequently, Israel's demographic doctrine is the proverbial elephant on the table. Far from an ideological or even moral question, that doctrine must be addressed as a matter of international security, as it is central to Israel's realist geopolitics. The logic boils down to linked contingencies:

—Israel cannot sustain a Jewish majority without excluding the Palestinians from citizenship.

—It cannot exclude the Palestinian population from citizenship within the state in apartheid-like conditions without confronting their eventual insistence on citizenship.

—It cannot fix its permanent borders in ways that consign the Palestinians to autonomous (yet unviable) cantons without committing serious human rights abuses and generating violent Palestinian resistance.

—It cannot muster sufficient domestic Jewish-Israeli support for creating the cantons as long as the Palestinians are resisting it.

—It can neither repress Palestinian resistance nor reassure the Jewish-Israeli public while Hizballah is positioned on its border with a significant arsenal and links to Hamas.

—It cannot eradicate Hizballah and Hamas (or any similar groups that may arise) until their sources of support (Syria and Iran) are also eliminated.

Hence Israel's ethnic imperative to maintain a Jewish state necessitates its program of regional aggression. The imperative has already inspired Israel to demolish much of Lebanon and now pose an imminent threat to Iran. It is even arguably dangerous to Israeli security, as it is galvanizing unprecedented degrees of threat to Israel. The only interest it serves is ethnic statehood—which is not only anachronistic in today's world but is demonstrating, as it does everywhere, its inherent propensity to violence.

The ethnic demographic is certainly not the only factor driving Israeli foreign policy: the variables noted at the beginning of this paper are all relevant, if some exist only as imagined identities or emerge from racial stereotyping. But their study distracts from the underlying problem. Only by addressing the originating logic of Israel's geostrategy—Zionist dedication to preserving a Jewish-ethnic majority in a land holding an equal number of non-Jews—can the determinants of violence be unmasked and, with care, dismantled.

The task for international intervention is therefore dual: (1) to impose international human rights standards on Israel in the urgent interests of international stability; and (2) to create (or compel) a process of consultation and negotiation that can adequately allay Jewish-Zionist fears about what will befall Jews if the Jewish state morphs into a secular democracy. The South African experience has much to say about appeasing an aggressive ethnic nationalism through negotiation and compromise. The international community will, however, have to muster the necessary political will to orchestrate a workable process—not out of humanitarian concern for the Palestinians (a motive that has proved demonstrably inadequate), but in the interest of collective security.

NOTES

1 Zionism is a complicated doctrine with many internal currents, some of which have contradictory implications for land policy and governance, but this discussion is beyond the scope of this article; see bibliography and discussion in Virginia Tilley, *The One-State Solution: A Breakthrough for Peace in the Israeli–Palestinian Deadlock* (University of Michigan Press and Manchester University Press, 2005) 131–182.

2 On this normative switch, see J. S. Barkin and Bruce Cronin, "The State and the Nation: Changing Norms and the Rules of Sovereignty in International Relations," *International Organization* 48 (1994) 107–130.

3 Tony Judt has highlighted this "anachronistic" quality in his "Israel: The Alternative," *New York Review of Books* 50.16 (23 October 2003).

4 The last Israeli census found that 19.5 percent of Israel was Arab. Another 4 percent were non-Jewish and non-Arab. This population includes non-Jews who entered with the Russian "Jewish" immigration in the early 1990s. Studies of the Russian population suggest that as much as 70 percent may be non-Jewish. If just half (about 500,000) are non-Jewish, then the non-Jewish population of Israel is closer to 30 percent.

5 Seymour Hersh, "Last Stand: The Military's Problem with the President's Iran Policy," *New Yorker* 10 July 2006.

6 Numerous commentators have observed this connection: see, for example, Robert Blecher, "Converging Upon War."

7 Matthew Kelman, "Israel Set War Plan More Than a Year Ago," *San Francisco Chronicle* 21 July 2006; Seymour Hersh, "Watching Lebanon: Washington's Interests in Israel's War," *New Yorker* 21 August 2006.

8 Some administration officials have urged this attack since the 1990s; Israeli planners since the 1980s. See discussion in Tilley, *The One-State Solution* 111–113.

9 BBC News, "Blair Warns of 'Arc of Extremism'," 2 August 2006: available at http://news.bbc.co.uk/2/hi/uk_news/5236862.stm.

10 This argument traces from Vladomir Jabotinsky, whose writings were very influential for Arial Sharon and the line of political leaders that created the Likud Party. See Avi Shlaim, *The Iron Wall: Israel and the Arab World* (New York: W.W. Norton & Co., 2001).

11 The nature of this worldview is suggested by President Bush's fondness for biographies about Theodore Roosevelt, who presided over the US imperialist expansion into Latin America and the Philippines. It is also articulated by Daniel Pipes, principal intellectual architect of the neocon lens on the Middle East.

12 Seymour Hersh, "Last Stand," and "Watching Lebanon." (See notes 5 and 7.)

13 Uzi Mahnaimi, "Revealed: Israel Plans Strike on Iranian Nuclear Plant," *Times* (London) 13 March 2005.

14 "Let no one make the mistake of thinking that the people of Israel might be swayed by inequitable pronouncements. ... not Security Council resolutions, but the attitude and actions of the governments in the area will determine the destiny of the Middle East." Mr. Tekoah, reacting to Security Council Resolution 262 (1968), which denounced Israel for an attack on Beirut in reprisal for a PFLP attack on its planes. Cited in Richard Falk, "The Beirut Raid and International Law of Retaliation," in Jean Allain, ed., *Unlocking the Middle East: The Writings of Richard Falk* (Northampton, MA: Olive Branch Press, 2003) 286n20.

15 "All members of this Council must be aware that its inability to act sooner has badly shaken the world's faith in its authority and integrity. ... Delays will mean only more lost lives, more shattered hopes, and a further decline in the standing and authority of this Council and the Organization." Address by Secretary-General Kofi Annan to the UN Security Council, 11 August 2006, following passage of SC Resolution 262.

16 For example, "Halutz says Lebanon Conflict a 'Definite Victory,'" *Jerusalem Post* 20 August 2006).

23. A JEWISH PLEA

Sara Roy

We have nothing to lose except everything.
—Albert Camus

During the summer my husband and I had a conversion ceremony for our adopted daughter, Jess. We took her to the mikvah, a Jewish ritual bath, where she was totally submerged in a pool of living water—living because it is fed in part by heavenly rain—and momentarily suspended as we are in the womb, emerging the same yet transformed. This ritual of purification, transformation, and rebirth is central to Judaism and it signifies renewal and possibility.

The day of Jess's conversion was also the day that Israel began its pitiless bombing of Lebanon and nearly three weeks into Israel's violent assault on Gaza, a place that has been my second home for the last two decades. This painful juxtaposition of rebirth and destruction remains with me, weighing heavily, without respite. Yet, the link deeply forged in our construction of self as Jews, between my daughter's acceptance into Judaism and Israel's actions—between Judaism and Zionism—a link that I never accepted uncritically but understood as historically inevitable and understandable, is one that for me, at least, has now been broken.

For unlike past conflicts involving Israel and the Palestinian and Arab peoples this one feels qualitatively different—a turning point—not only with regard to the nature of Israel's horrific response—its willingness to destroy and to do so utterly—but also with regard to the virtually unqualified support of organized American Jewry for Israel's brutal actions, something that is not new but is now no longer tolerable to me.

I grew up in a home where Judaism was defined and practiced not so much as a religion but as a system of ethics and culture. God was present but not central. Israel and the notion of a Jewish homeland were very important to my parents, who survived Auschwitz, Chelmno, and Buchenwald. But unlike many of their friends, my parents were not uncritical of Israel. Obedience to a state was not a primary Jewish value, especially after the Holocaust. Judaism provided the context for Jewish life, for values and beliefs that were not dependent upon national or territorial boundaries, but transcended them to include the other, always the other. For my mother and father Judaism meant bearing witness, raging against injustice, and refusing silence. It meant compassion, tolerance, and rescue. In the absence of these imperatives, they taught me, we cease to be Jews.

Many of the people—both Jewish and others—who write about Palestinians and Arabs fail to accept the fundamental humanity of the people they are writing about, a failing born of ignorance, fear, and racism. Within the organized Jewish community especially, it has always been unacceptable to claim that Arabs, Palestinians especially, are like us, that they, too, possess an essential humanity and must be included within our moral boundaries, ceasing to be "a kind of solution," a useful, hostile "other," to borrow from Edward Said.[1] That any attempt at separation is artificial, an abstraction.

By refusing to seek proximity over distance, we calmly, even gratefully refuse to see what is right before our eyes. We are no longer compelled—if we ever were—to understand our behavior from positions outside our own, to enter, as Jacqueline Rose has written, into each other's predicaments and make what is one of the hardest journeys of the mind.[2] Hence, there is no need to maintain a living connection with the people we are oppressing, to humanize them, taking into account the experience of subordination itself, as Said would say. We are not preoccupied by our cruelty nor are we haunted by it. The task, ultimately, is to tribalize pain, narrowing the scope of human suffering to ourselves alone. Such willful blindness leads to the destruction of principle and the destruction of people, eliminating all possibility of embrace, but it gives us solace.

Why is it so difficult, even impossible to incorporate Palestinians and other Arab peoples into the Jewish understanding of history? Why is there so little perceived need to question our own narrative (for want of a better word) and the one we have given others, preferring instead to cherish beliefs and sentiments that remain impenetrable? Why is it virtually mandatory among Jewish intellectuals to oppose racism, repression, and injustice almost anywhere in the world and unacceptable—indeed, for some, an act of heresy—to oppose it when Israel is the oppressor, choosing concealment over exposure? For many among us history and memory adhere to preclude reflection and tolerance, where, in the words of Northrop Frye, "the enemy become, not people to be defeated, but embodiments of an idea to be exterminated."

What happens to the other as we, a broken and weary people, continually abuse him, turning him into the enemy we now want and need, secure in a prophecy that is thankfully self-fulfilling?

What happens to a people when renewal and injustice are rapturously joined?

A New Discourse of the Unconscious

We speak without mercy, numb to the pain of others, incapable of being reached—unconscious. Our words are these:

—" . . . [W]e must not forget," wrote Ze'ev Schiff, the senior political and military analyst for the Israeli newspaper *Ha'aretz*, "the most important aspect of this war: Hizballah and what this terrorist organization symbolizes must be destroyed at any price. . . . What matters is not the future of the Shiite town of Bint Jbail or the Hizballah positions in Maroun Ras, but the future and safety of the State of Israel." "If Israel doesn't improve its military cards in the fighting, we will feel the results in the political solution" (26 and 30 July 2006).

—"We must reduce to dust the villages of the south . . ." stated Haim Ramon, Israel's minister of justice, and long known as a political dove. "I don't understand why there is still electricity there." "Everyone in southern Lebanon is a terrorist and is connected to Hizballah. . . What we should do in southern Lebanon is employ huge firepower before a ground force goes in." Israel's largest-selling newspaper, *Yedioth Ahronoth,* put it this way: "A village from which rockets are fired at Israel will simply be destroyed by fire. This decision should have been made and executed after the first Katyusha. But better late than never."[3]

—"[F]or every katyusha barrage on Haifa, 10 Dahiyeh buildings will be bombed," said the IDF Chief of Staff Dan Halutz. Eli Yishai, Israel's deputy prime minister, proposed turning south Lebanon into a "sandbox," while Knesset member Moshe Sharoni called for the obliteration of Gaza, and Yoav Limor, a Channel 1 military correspondent, suggested an exhibition of Hizballah corpses followed by a parade of prisoners in their underwear in order "to strengthen the home front's morale."[4]

—"Remember: distorted philosophical sensitivity [*sic*] to human lives will make us pay the real price of the lives of many, and the blood of our sons," read an advertisement placed by Israeli neocons in *Ha'aretz* (30 July 2006).

—"[A]ccording to Jewish law," announced the Yesha Rabbinical Council, "during a time of battle and war, there is no such term as 'innocents of the enemy'" (30 July 2006).[5]

—"But speaking from our own Judaic faith and legal legacy," argued the Rabbinical Council of America, "we believe that Judaism would neither require nor permit a Jewish soldier to sacrifice himself in order to save deliberately endangered enemy civilians. This is especially true when confronting a barbaric enemy who would by such illicit, consistent, and systematic means seek to destroy not only the Jewish soldier, but defeat and destroy the Jewish homeland. New realities do indeed require new responses."[6]

—The Israeli author Naomi Ragan, after learning that many of the war dead in Lebanon were children, wrote, "Save your sympathy for the mothers and sisters and girlfriends of our young soldiers who would rather be sitting in study halls learning Torah, but have no choice but to risk their precious lives full of hope, goodness and endless potential, to wipe out the cancerous terrorist cells that threaten their people and all mankind. Make your choice, and save your tears."[7]

Many of us, perhaps most, have declared that all Palestinians and Lebanese are the enemy, threatening our—Israel and the Jewish people's—existence. Everyone we kill and every house we demolish is therefore a military target, legitimate and deserving. Terrorism is part of their culture and we must strengthen our ability to deter. Negotiation, to paraphrase the Israeli scholar Yehoshua Porat, writing during the 1982 Lebanon war, is a "veritable catastrophe for Israel." The battlefield will preserve us.

The French critic and historian Hippolyte Taine observed: "Imagine a man who sets out on a voyage equipped with a pair of spectacles that magnify things to an extraordinary degree. A hair on his hand, a spot on the tablecloth, the shifting fold of a coat, all will attract his attention; at this rate, he will not go far, he will spend his day taking six steps and will never get out of his room."[8]

We are content in our room and seek no exit.

In our room, compassion and conscience are dismissed as weakness, where pinpoint surgical strikes constitute restraint and civility and momentary cease-fires, acts of humanity and kindness. "Leave your home, we are going to destroy it." Several minutes later another home in

Gaza, another history, is taken, crushed. The warning, though, is not for them but for us—it makes us good and clean. What better illustration of our morality: when a call to leave one's home minutes before it is bombed is considered a humane gesture.

Our warnings have another purpose: they make our actions legitimate and our desire for legitimacy is unbounded, voracious. This is perhaps the only thing Palestinians (and now the Lebanese) have withheld from us, this object of our desire. If legitimacy will not be bestowed then it must be created. This explains Israel's obsession with laws and legalities to ensure in our own eyes that we do not transgress, making evil allowable by widening the parameters of license and transgression. In this way we ensure our goodness and morality, through a piece of paper, which is enough for us.

What are Jews now capable of resisting: Tyranny? Oppression? Occupation? Injustice? We resist none of these things, no more. For too many among us they are no longer evil but necessary and good—we cannot live, survive without them. What does that make us? We look at ourselves and what do we see: a non-Jew, a child, whose pain we inflict effortlessly, whose death is demanded and unquestioned, bearing validity and purpose.

What do we see: a people who now take pleasure in hating others. Hatred is familiar to us if nothing else. We understand it and it is safe. It is what we know. We do not fear our own distortion—do we even see it?— but the loss of our power to deter, and we shake with a violent palsy at a solution that shuns the suffering of others. Our pathology is this: it lies in our struggle to embrace a morality we no longer possess and in our need for persecution of a kind we can no longer claim but can only inflict.

We are remote from the conscious world—brilliantly ignorant, blindly visionary, unable to resist from within. We live in an unchanging place, absent of season and reflection, devoid of normality and growth, and most important of all, emptied—or so we aim—of the other. A ghetto still but now, unlike before, a ghetto of our own making.

What is our narrative of victory and defeat? What does it mean to win? Bombed cars with white civilian flags still attached to their windows? More dead and dismembered bodies of old people and children littered throughout villages that have been ravaged? An entire country disabled and broken? Non-ending war? This is our victory, our achievement, something we seek and applaud. And how do we measure defeat? Losing the will to continue the devastation? Admitting to our persecution of others, something we have never done?

We can easily ignore their suffering, cut them from their food, water, electricity, and medicine, confiscate their land, demolish their crops and deny them egress—suffocate them, our voices stilled. Racism does not allow us to see Arabs as we see ourselves; that is why we rage when they do not fail from weakness but instead we find ourselves failing from strength. Yet, in our view it is we who are the only victims, vulnerable and scarred. All we have is the unnaturalness of our condition.

As an unconscious people, we have perhaps reached our nadir with many among us now calling for a redefinition of our ethics—the core of who we are—to incorporate the need to kill women and children if Jewish security required it. "New realities do indeed require new responses," says the Rabbinical Council of America. Now, for us, violence is creation and peace is destruction.

Ending the Process of Creation and Rebirth after the Holocaust

Can we be ordinary, an essential part of our rebirth after the Holocaust? Is it possible to be normal when we seek refuge in the margin, and remedy in the dispossession and destruction of another people? How can we create when we acquiesce so willingly to the demolition of homes, construction of barriers, denial of sustenance, and ruin of innocents? How can we be merciful when, to use Rose's words, we seek "omnipotence as the answer to historical pain"?[9] We refuse to hear their pleading, to see those chased from their homes, children incinerated in their mother's arms. Instead we tell our children to inscribe the bombs that will burn Arab babies.

We argue that we must eliminate terrorism. What do we really know of their terrorism, and of ours? What do we care? Rather, with language that is denuded and infested—give them more time to bomb so that Israel's borders can be natural—we engage repeatedly in a war of desire, a war not thrust upon us but of our own choosing, ingratiating ourselves with the power to destroy others and insensate to the death of our own children. What happens to a nation, asks the Israeli writer David Grossman, that cannot save its own child, words written before his own son was killed in Lebanon?

There are among Israelis real feelings of vulnerability and fear, never resolved but used, intensified. Seeing one's child injured or killed is the most horrible vision—Israelis are vulnerable, far more than other Jews. Yet, we as a people have become a force of extremism, of chaos and disorder, trying to plow an unruly sea—addicted to death and cruelty, intoxicated, with one ambition: to mock the pauper.

Judaism has always prided itself on reflection, critical examination, and philosophical inquiry. The Talmudic mind examines a sentence, a word, in a multitude of ways, seeking all possible interpretations and searching constantly for the one left unsaid. Through such scrutiny it is believed comes the awareness needed to protect the innocent, prevent injury or harm, and be closer to God.

Now, these are abhorred, eviscerated from our ethical system. Rather the imperative is to see through eyes that are closed, unfettered by investigation. We conceal our guilt by remaining the abused, despite our power, creating situations where our victimization is assured and our innocence affirmed. We prefer this abyss to peace, which would hurl us unacceptably inward toward awareness and acknowledgment.

Jews do not feel shame over what they have created: an inventory of inhumanity. Rather we remain oddly appeased, even calmed by the desolation. Our detachment allows us to bear such excess (and commit it), to sit in Jewish cafés while Palestinian mothers are murdered in front of their children in Gaza. I can now better understand how horror occurs— how people, not evil themselves, can allow evil to happen. We salve our wounds with our incapacity for remorse, which will be our undoing.

Instead the Jewish community demands unity and conformity: "Stand with Israel" read the banners on synagogues throughout Boston last summer. Unity around what? There is enormous pressure—indeed coercion—within organized American Jewry to present an image of "wall to wall unity" as a local Jewish leader put it. But this unity is an illusion— at its edges a smoldering flame rapidly engulfing its core—for mainstream Jewry does not speak for me or for many other Jews. And where such unity exists, it is hollow, built around fear not humanity, on the need to understand reality as it has long been constructed for us—with the Jew as the righteous victim, the innocent incapable of harm. It is as if our unbending support for Israel's militarism requires, as a friend put it in a letter to me in July, "putting our minds as it were into Auschwitz where being a Jew puts your existence on the line. To be Jewish means to be threatened, nothing more. Hence, the only morality we can acknowledge is saving Israel and by extension, ourselves." Within this paradigm, it is dissent, not conformity, that will diminish and destroy us. We hoard our victimization as we hoard our identity—they are one—incapable of change, a failing that will one day result in our own eviction. Is this what Zionism has done to Judaism?

Israel's actions not only demonstrate the limits of Israeli power but our own limitations as a people: our inability to live a life without barriers, to free ourselves from an ethnic loyalty that binds and contorts, to emerge, finally, from our spectral chamber.

Ending the (Filial) Link between Israel and the Holocaust

How can the children of the Holocaust do such things, they ask? But are we really their rightful offspring?

As the Holocaust survivor dies, the horror of that period and its attendant lessons withdraw further into abstraction and for some Jews, many of them in Israel, alienation. The Holocaust stands not as a lesson but as an internal act of purification where tribal attachment rather than ethical responsibility is demanded and used to define collective action. Perhaps this was an inevitable outcome of Jewish nationalism, of applying holiness to politics, but whatever its source, it has weakened us terribly and cost us greatly.

Silvia Tennenbaum, a survivor and activist, writes:

> No matter what great accomplishments were ours in the diaspora, no matter that we produced Maimonides and Spinoza, Moses Mendelssohn and hundreds of others of mankind's benefactors—not a warrior among them!—we look at the world of our long exile always in the dark light of the Shoah. But this, in itself, is an obscene distortion: would the author . . . Primo Levi, or the poet Paul Celan demand that we slaughter the innocents in a land far from the snow-clad forests of Poland? Is it a heroic act to murder a child, even the child of an enemy? Are my brethren glad and proud? . . . And, it goes without saying, loyal Jews must talk about the Holocaust. Ignore the images of today's dead and dying and focus on the grainy black and white pictures showing the death of Jews in the villages of Poland, at Auschwitz and Sobibor and Bergen-Belsen. We are the first, the only true victims, the champions of helplessness for all eternity.[10]

What did my family perish for in the ghettos and concentration camps of Poland? Is their role to be exploited and, in the momentary absence of violence, to be forgotten and abandoned?

Holocaust survivors stood between the past and the present, bearing witness, sometimes silently, and even in word, often unheard. Yet, they stood as a moral challenge among us and also as living embodiments of a history, way of life, and culture that long predated the Holocaust and Zionism (and that Zionism has long denigrated), refusing, in their own way, to let us look past them. Yet, this generation is nearing its end and as they leave us, I wonder what is truly left to take their place, to fill the moral void created by their absence?

Is it, in the words of a friend, himself a Jew, a

> memory manufactory, with statues, museums and platoons of "scholars" designed to preserve, indeed ratchet up Jewish feelings of persecution and victimhood, a Hitler behind every Katyusha or border skirmish, which must be met with some of the same crude slaughterhouse tools the Nazis employed against the Jews six decades ago: ghettos, mass arrests, and the denigration of their enemy's humanity?

Do we now measure success in human bodies and in carnage, arguing that our dead bodies are worth more than theirs, our children more vulnerable and holy, more in need of protection and love, their corpses more deserving of shrouds and burial? Is meaning for us to be derived from martyrdom or from children born with a knife in their hearts? Is this how my grandmother and grandfather are to be remembered?

Our tortured past and its images trespass upon our present not only in Israel but in Gaza and Lebanon as well. "They were temporarily buried in an empty lot with dozens of others," writes a *New York Times* reporter in Lebanon. "They were assigned numbers, his wife and daughter. Alia is No. 35 and Sally is No. 67. 'They are numbers now,' said the father. There are no names anymore" (8 August 2006).

"They were shrunken figures, dehydrated and hungry," observes Anthony Shadid in the *Washington Post*. "Some had lived on candy bars, others on pieces of dry bread. Some were shell-shocked, their faces blank... One never made it. He was carried out on a stretcher, flies landing on lifeless eyes that were still open" (1 August 2006).

As the rightful claimants to our past we should ask, How much damage can be done to a soul? But we do not ask. We do not question the destruction but only our inability to complete it, to create more slaughter sites.

Can we ever emerge from our torpor, able to mourn the devastation?

Our Ultimate Eviction?

Where do Jews belong? Where is our place? Is it in the ghetto of a Jewish state whose shrinking boundaries threaten, one day, to evict us? We are powerful but not strong. Our power is our weakness, not our strength, because it is used to instill fear rather than trust, and because of that, it will one day destroy us if we do not change. More and more we find ourselves detached from our past, suspended and abandoned, alone, without anchor, aching—if not now, eventually—for connection and succor. Grossman has written that as a dream fades it does not become a weaker force but a more potent one, desperately clung to, even as it ravages and devours.

We consume the land and the water behind walls and steel gates, forcing out all others. What kind of place are we creating? Are we fated to be an intruder in the dust (to borrow from Faulkner) whose presence shall evaporate with the shifting sands? Are these the boundaries of our rebirth after the Holocaust?

I have come to accept that Jewish power and sovereignty and Jewish ethics and spiritual integrity are, in the absence of reform, incompatible, unable to coexist or be reconciled. For if speaking out against the wanton murder of children is considered an act of disloyalty and betrayal rather than a legitimate act of dissent, and where dissent is so ineffective and reviled, a choice is ultimately forced upon us between Zionism and Judaism.

Rabbi Hillel the Elder long ago emphasized ethics as the center of Jewish life. Ethical principles or their absence will contribute to the survival or destruction of our people. Yet today what we face is something different and possibly more perverse: it is not the disappearance of our ethical system but its rewriting into something disfigured and execrable.

As Jews in a post-Holocaust world empowered by a Jewish state, how do we as a people emerge from atrocity and abjection, empowered and also humane, something that still eludes us? How do we move beyond fear and omnipotence, beyond innocence and militarism, to envision something different, even if uncertain? "How," asks Ahad Haam, the founding father of cultural Zionism, "do you make a nation pause for thought?"[11]

For many Jews (and Christians), the answer lies in a strong and militarized Jewish state. For others, it is found in the very act of survival. For my parents, defeating Hitler meant living a moral life. They sought a world where "affirmation is possible and... dissent is mandatory," where our capacity to witness is restored and sanctioned, where we as a people refuse to be overcome by the darkness.[12]

Can We Ever Turn Away from Our Power to Destroy?

It is here that I want to share a story from my family, to describe a moment that has inspired all of my work and writing.

My mother and her sister had just been liberated from concentration camp by the Russian army. After having captured all the Nazi officials and guards who ran the camp, the Russian soldiers told the Jewish survivors that they could do whatever they wanted to their German persecutors. Many survivors, themselves emaciated and barely alive, immediately fell on the Germans, ravaging them. My mother and my aunt, standing just yards from the terrible scene unfolding in front of them, fell into each other's arms weeping. My mother, who was the physically stronger of the two, embraced my aunt, holding her close and my aunt, who had difficulty standing, grabbed my mother as if she would never let go. She said to my mother, "We cannot do this. Our father and mother would say this is wrong. Even now, even after everything we have endured, we must seek justice, not revenge. There is no other way." My mother, still crying, kissed her sister and the two of them, still one, turned and walked away.

What then is the source of our redemption, our salvation? It lies ultimately in our willingness to acknowledge the other—the victims we have created—Palestinian, Lebanese, and also Jewish—and the injustice we have perpetrated as a grieving people. Perhaps then we can pursue a more just solution in which we seek to be ordinary rather then absolute, where we finally come to understand that our only hope is not to die peacefully in our homes, as one Zionist official put it long ago, but to live peacefully in those homes.

When my daughter Jess was submerged under the waters of the mikvah for the third and final time, she told me she saw rainbows under the water. I shall take this beautiful image as a sign of her rebirth and plead desperately for ours.

NOTES

1 Edward Said's favorite poem by Constantine Cavafy, "Waiting for the Barbarians," says, "they were, those people, a kind of solution." See Aliki Barnstone (trans.), *The Collected Poems of C.P. Cavafy: A New Translation* (New York: W.W. Norton, 2006).

2 Jacqueline Rose, *Suffering and Injustice Enough for Everyone—On Empathy and the Complexity of Political Life, Essay in Honor of Edward Said*, draft, May 2004.

3 Harry de Quetteville, "You're All Targets, Israel Tells Lebanese in South," Telegraph.co.uk, 28 July 2006.

4 Gideon Levy, "Days of Darkness," *Ha'aretz* 30 July 2006.

5 Yesha Rabbinical Council, "During Time of War, Enemy Has No Innocents," 30 July 2006.

6 Rabbical Council of America, "RCA Solidarity MIssion to Israel Expresses Views of 'Tohar Hanashek'..." 17 August 2006, www.rabbis.org.

7 Leonard Fein, "Was There Really No Other Way?" Forward.com, 11 August 2006.

8 Cited in Maxwell Taylor Kennedy, *Make Gentle the Life of This World: The Vision of Robert F. Kennedy* (New York: Harcourt Brace, 1998) 74–75.

9 Jacqueline Rose, *The Last Resistance*, pre-publication manuscript, Verso, forthcoming, May 2007.

10 Silvia Tennenbaum, "Why Doesn't Israel Work for Peace?" Newsday.com, 4 August 2006.

11 See Jacqueline Rose, *The Question of Zion* (Princeton: Princeton University Press, 2005).

12 Marc H. Ellis, *O, Jerusalem! The Contested Future of the Jewish Covenant* (Minneapolis: Fortress Press, 1999).

Part Six

THE REPERCUSSIONS OF WAR

24. THE ECONOMIC AND HUMAN COSTS OF THE WAR

Haneen Sayed and Zafiris Tzannatos

The views and findings in this paper are derived from publicly available information in November 2006 and are those of the authors and do not necessarily represent those of the World Bank, its member governments, its executive directors, or the countries they represent.

The first half of 2006 had many signs of what might have been a bumper year for Lebanon. During those six months the country enjoyed its strongest period of economic growth since 1995 and expected to reach 6 percent by the end of the year. More than 630,000 tourists entered Lebanon in the first six months of 2006, representing a 24-percent increase from the same period in 2004 and an 81-percent rise compared to the first six months of 2003 and suggesting that the total number of tourist arrivals would reach 1.6 million by the end of the year. The country's construction sector was enjoying a strong first half of the year, up by 61 percent from the same period in 2005. The value of cleared checks, an indicator of healthy demand, was up by 12 percent. Also during the first half of 2006, revenues from Lebanon's exports reached US$1.6 billion, representing a substantial 18-percent increase compared to the same period of 2005 while, on the public finance front, the primary surplus (government revenues minus government expenditures) more than quadrupled.

The expectations were not fulfilled. On July 12, Hizballah crossed the border into northern Israel and captured two Israeli soldiers. What happened next has been well documented throughout this book. The hostilities ended on August 14, 2006, though the Israeli–imposed embargo was lifted later, on September 9, 2006. As a direct result of the war, nearly 1,200 Lebanese and 160 Israelis were killed, though the losses on both sides are still being counted.[1] The expected 6 percent rate of economic growth for 2006 is now estimated to turn negative—though estimates vary from −3 percent (International Monetary Fund [IMF]) to −8 percent (Economist Intelligence Unit [EIU]). Local currency deposits have fallen and confidence in the Lebanese economy has decreased. Already high public debt increased further.

This chapter focuses on the costs of the war for Lebanon. The next section explains the methodology of compiling various estimates of direct and indirect, short- and long-term, tangible and less visible damage from the war, and costs of reconstruction. The following section presents a nationwide assessment as well as separate estimates for some key economic and social sectors. Next, we look forward, arguing that the task of reconstruction and recovery is probably less of a challenge than that of the design and implementation of an agreed development agenda. The chapter concludes by offering suggestions for universal policies and programs that, if adopted, could contribute in a systematic way to poverty reduction (e.g., through increasing the coverage of pensions), social development (e.g., through more and better education for the less fortunate), decrease in vulnerability (e.g., through worker social insurance), and increased social coherence (e.g., through objective selection of beneficiaries independently of religion, location, or other characteristics that have been proven to be divisive and perpetuate differences in Lebanese society). These four highly desirable ingredients of social policies are currently largely absent from Lebanon but are required for nationwide outreach, minimal fiscal outlays, and high impact. If implemented as proposed, they could lay the foundation for modern nation-building in this economically, regionally, confessionally, socially, and politically divided country.

Methodology

Many assessments of damage and the cost of reconstruction and recovery have been or are currently being carried out by the Lebanese government, international donors, bilaterals or their representatives, international and local research agencies and think tanks, and local and international independent organizations.[2]

The estimates from these sources vary, at times significantly, as they focus on different aspects of the war and employ different approaches. For example, some estimates relate to relief/humanitarian needs while others refer to the value of damage that could be different from the value of a repair, that could in turn be different from the value of rehabilitation or replacement or more broadly reconstruction, which may in turn focus on narrow preexisting needs or broader redevelopment. In some cases, the focus is only on public assets and infrastructure while in others it includes the private sector. The estimates can also be based on different methodologies (e.g., surveys versus field visits), different groups, different areas, or simply refer to different periods in time.

Given the proliferation and diversity of the available estimates, this chapter makes no attempt to assess the credibility of individual figures and aims to provide a broad summary of them, indicating also the range of their respective values. For reasons of brevity, the chapter does not always cite the relevant sources relating to specific estimates unless this is deemed to be necessary.[3] But even the rather uncritical exposition of facts presented here is probably adequate to provide an answer as to whether the costs of the war were localized, significant at the national level, or simply enormous.

Caution must be applied to self-reported individual damages because of the incentive of affected groups to exaggerate in hope of receiving more generous compensation by the government. In turn, some estimates by the government may be on the upper end in hope of attracting greater donor support. And as mentioned earlier, donor estimates vary in terms of methodology, scope, and timing. The information collated below is therefore based on work-in-progress as of the time of writing this chapter (November 2006). It remains tentative until formally validated.

The Cost of the War

According to Prime Minister Fouad Seniora, at the end of the war 1,100 civilians were killed, a third of whom were children; 4,000 more were wounded; one million were displaced; tens of thousands of homes as well as hospitals, schools, factories, roads, airports, power stations, fuel depots, warehouses, and most of the bridges were destroyed. By the end of August 2006, the direct damage of the war was estimated to be $3.6 billion (Table 1).

Table 1: Council of Development & Reconstruction (CDR): Damage Assessment

Figures by Field	Total Damage (US$millions)
Housing & commercial spaces	2,406
Transportation	484
Electricity	244
Industry	220
Telecommunications	116
Water	80
Health and Education*	34
Military	16
Fuel Distribution Stations	12
TOTAL	3,612

Environmental damage (e.g., due to the oil spill from the bombarded Jiyyeh power plant, the use of heavy bombs that have left toxin residues in the air, unexploded ordnance, etc.) is not included.

* Probable underestimation   *Source: Government of Lebanon* (August 2006)

The table focuses mainly on public infrastructure and does not, for example, include losses from the bombardments that stopped production in many areas, the paralysis of trade resulting from the blockade, or employment losses that peaked during the war at 120,000 among the one-million-strong labor force. Table 1 may still underreport the narrow direct losses during the war as, for example, later estimates bring the damage to schools alone to more than $80 million, while additional medical expenditures during the war may have reached nearly $50 million (see sectoral estimates for Health and Education later). This brings the combined effect on the education and health sectors to more like $130 million.

Another underreported cost is that associated with cleaning up the rubble generated from the bombings. It is estimated to have been up to 3.5 million cubic meters (with 1 million cubic meters in the Haret Hreik quarter alone).[4] This amount of rubble is more than three times the total amount of municipal waste typically generated by the whole population of Lebanon in the normal course of one year. Finally, the table does not include private losses (for example, in agriculture or industry or the many smaller businesses, some housed in apartments and houses that were damaged or destroyed). Some of these additional costs are presented in the sections below, which focus on selective productive and social sectors and also present more recent estimates than those reported in Table 1.

Residential and commercial property

By far, most of the direct damage of the war was concentrated more on residential than on commercial property. The bombardment was particularly extensive in south Lebanon, the Beqaa, and in the southern suburbs of Beirut where housing was mainly privately owned. A preliminary housing damage assessment prepared for the government calculated that to rebuild the identified 106,914 damaged units (Table 2) would require about $1.8 billion—and probably closer to $2 billion, if some of the damaged buildings are later deemed impossible to repair economically and are subsequently delegated to the totally destroyed category.[5] In terms of forgone flow of services from these houses, using a typical rent-to-value ratio, the damage to the housing sector represents an annual reduction of available services of about $100 million. Households that can no longer live in their units may need approximately $50 million per year for rent until their housing is replaced, a process that can take on average at least two years.

Table 2: Number of Housing Units Destroyed or Damaged

	Damaged		Destroyed		TOTAL
	Lightly	*Severely*	*Partially*	*Totally*	
Mt. Lebanon/ southern suburbs of Beirut	24,985	16,013	711	4,620	46,329
Nabatiyeh	20,657	8,874	5,148	4,764	39,443
South	10,078	4,420	1,401	1,775	17,674
Beqaa	1,972	697	294	299	3,262
North	114	68	20	4	206
Total	57,806	30,072	7,574	11,462	106,914

Source: War Damage Assessment and Restoration Program, Khatib & Alami (31 August 2006)

Education

The war had a significant impact on the education sector. At least 76 private schools and more than 209 public school buildings were directly affected (though some claim the latter number may be closer to 250, equivalent to 15 percent of public schools). Most (84 percent) of the damaged public schools were located in the south and Nabatieh regions. In addition to direct damage, approximately 700 public schools were used as temporary shelters by internally displaced people during the war with consequential losses in some cases of furniture, laboratory equipment, computers, audiovisuals, library books, instructional supplies, and other learning resource materials. The rehabilitation and recovery of the education sector over the next two years may require more than US$83 million. This is a low estimate, as information on additional schools needing rehabilitation is still coming in as of the time of this writing.

Health and Social Services

The war, mainly through bombardment, had the predictable impact on life and health services. The month-long war resulted in an estimated 1,200 deaths and 5,500 injuries—though both numbers are approximate. Equally predictable was the distribution of human suffering by region: the greatest number of injuries were in the south (estimated at about 2,500) followed by Mount Lebanon/suburbs of Beirut (nearly 1,000), and the Beqaa region and Nabatiyeh, each with about 700 injuries. The cost for treating the injured alone was estimated by the Ministry of Public Health in September 2006 to be about $10 million; damage to 16 hospitals and 65 outpatient facilities in the governorates of the south, Nabatiyeh, and the Beqaa was estimated to be over $2 million. The United Nations system played a critical role in supporting the Ministry of Public Health in its coordination of emergency relief and humanitarian efforts during the crisis. The funding requirements during the war were largely met by the large inflow of humanitarian assistance (see Table 3).[6]

Table 3: Health-Related United Nation System Clusters
Funding and Expenditures (US$ million)

Cluster	Original Requirements (24 July)	Revised Req. (30 August)	Funding Received	Expenditure
Health and Nutrition	32	12	12	3
Food Security	18	13	13	11
Water and Sanitation	14	6	6	4
Shelter	28	12	12	10
Protection	17	23	23	22
Total	109	66	66	49

Social Services

As a result of the war, six Social Development Centers of the Ministry of Social Affairs (MOSA) were fully destroyed and five partially destroyed. In addition, eight welfare institutions were destroyed and thirteen were damaged. These institutions provide various forms of support and assistance to the needy, including health services. As most of the centers directly affected by the war were in regions with higher than average poverty rates (such as in southern Lebanon, Beqaa, and Nabatiyeh: see Table 5) the disruption of social services is likely to have accentuated regional differences in transient, if not permanent, poverty and vulnerability.

Agriculture

The war interrupted crop and animal husbandry, damaged land and other assets of farmers, and dislocated agricultural markets. The bombing prevented the harvesting of crops, including tobacco, which is concentrated in the south and largely supports 14,000 families. In all, nationwide 40,000 families of farmers are estimated to have been adversely affected. Even when harvested, crops could not be distributed nationally (for example, due to damages to roads and bridges as well as to the broader transportation and distribution network) or exported (due to the Israeli blockade). Fishing also suffered a significant and highly localized setback due to Israeli restrictions on sailing, the destruction of boats, and the oil slick (more to follow on that). Damage to tubewell pumps in the fruit-growing coastal plains around Tyre was significant; an estimated quarter to third of the pumps in this area were destroyed. Lack of irrigation, consuming about 64 percent of the total water supply, affected particularly high-value crops. Crop damage and livestock losses are estimated between 8 percent and 15 percent. Oxfam reports a loss of over a million chickens, 25,000 goats and sheep, and 4,000 cows. Overall, according to the Ministry of Agriculture, direct damages to the agricultural sector arising from losses of physical assets such as trees, irrigation systems, livestock, bee hives, and fishing boats, came to $212 million by the end of August 2006. Subsequent estimates suggest that forgone revenues (indirect losses) from agriculture may reach nearly half a billion dollars ($450 million) by the end of 2006, peaking at 70 percent in southern Lebanon.

Industry and Business

The industrial sector was also hit badly, as Israeli targets included all sorts of factories. Early estimates based on 10 completely or partially destroyed large factories and 700 small and medium industrial units indicated the cost of the damages to be $190 million. But more recent estimates suggest that up to 30 large industries and about 900 smaller businesses suffered direct physical damage from the conflict. By another estimate, the direct damage and destruction to larger industrial firms alone amounts to $170 million. And some forecast that repairing the physical damage to industrial ventures (without taking into account loss of stocks, production, or trade) would cost US$220 million (EIU 2006). This amounts to some agreement that direct damage is about $200 million, but to this additional losses must be added, because businesses were cut off from supplies and markets and saw demand for their products plummet. For example, agro-industries preparing to process seasonal fruits and vegetables in the summer could not get their goods from the farmers, some of whose crops and livestock died from neglect. Though a relatively small number of businesses suffered direct or complete damage, most (over 90 percent) suffered sales losses averaging two-thirds during the war. This problem was compounded by the fact reported in some surveys that for three-quarters of firms, their overhead and related expenses either stayed the same (36 percent) or even increased (40 percent) during the war. Overall, the most severe impact of the war on the private sector, industry, and business evolved around loss of customers, interruption of transport and loss of suppliers, the interruption of electric power supply, loss of key personnel and more broadly the negative image and bad publicity the conflict created for Lebanon.

Tourism

Tourism, estimated to account for about 12 percent of the GDP, was set for a record year. The war came in the middle of the crucial June–August period, which typically accounts for more than half of the annual tourism activity. It therefore gave a devastating blow to tourism, both because of the early termination of the 2006 season and the long-term impact on Lebanon's image abroad. Hotels were filled to over 90 percent of capacity on July 12 but, according to the Hotel Association, occupancy subsequently went down to 5 percent. By late September, occupancy rates recovered slightly (to only 25–30 percent) and the Ramadan and Eid seasons elevated this to 40 percent, still below the break-even level of 45 percent. The Ministry of Tourim estimates the losses in the sector to reach $3 billion.

Electricity

The Ministry of Energy and Water estimated the physical damage on electricity infrastructure to be US$115–125 million. The most significant damage was to the Jiyyeh power plant, whose five units accounted for close to 20 percent of available capacity before the war. Other estimates bring the losses to about $208 million—$128 million in power transmission and $80 million in power generation. More recent estimates of damages to infrastructure affecting the electricity network system come to $244 million, with repairs to fuel-distribution facilities, including the rebuilding of 26 destroyed service stations, expected to add another $12 million (EIU 2006).

Transportation

Losses to the transportation sector are estimated at US$484 million, arising from damages to 137 roads and 107 to 140 bridges, including the recently completed Mdayrej Bridge on the Beirut–Damascus highway, for which repair costs alone have been put at US$65 million. The damage to the airport, including bombed runways and fuel storage facilities, was estimated at around US$55 million.[7]

Though smaller in relative terms, the main impact in the ports sector was the destruction of the vessel traffic systems and related radar at the ports of Beirut and Tripoli; they will cost over $2 million to replace. These estimates do not include the destruction of many cars and trucks on the road. In addition, the daily cost of additional congestion in and around Beirut's central business district and other areas is estimated to be more than US$500,000 per day. Assuming that the bridges along the principal corridors are not repaired until the end of December 2006, the indirect impact to the economy could exceed US$75 million. The direct losses on Middle East Airlines (MEA) are estimated at $16 million, arising from the expense of relocating its fleet to Damascus and Larnaca (Cyprus) during the conflict. The indirect loss is even greater, as an additional $29 million in revenues were lost in the period between July 13 and September.[8] This brings the costs to MEA alone at $45 million.

Water and Sewage

Estimates for damage to the water and wastewater infrastructure vary from $65 to $80 million. Most of the damage was to networks lying along roads, houses, and the bridges that were bombed during the conflict. Damage was heavily concentrated in Nabatiyeh (US$15 million), Bint Jbeil (US$14 million), Marjeyoun (US$16 million), Sour (US$9 million), Baalbek (US$4 million), and the southern suburbs of Beirut (US$7 million).

Environment

The massive destruction of infrastructure left enormous piles of debris and rubble, placing strong demands on waste disposal, particularly on the coast. Quarries will also come under pressure to provide construction material in the fastest possible, but not necessarily environmentally prudent, way. The bombing of fuel storage tanks in Jiyyeh's power plant, whose total capacity is 75,000 tons, led to the escape of 60,000 tons of fuel, of which up to half was discharged into the Mediterranean Sea, creating a 3-cm layer of oil, which kills birds, fish and other wildlife.[9] The oil slick affected particularly the areas around Beirut, Tabarja, the historic town of Byblos, and the Palm Islands Nature Reserve off Tripoli, before it drifted 150 km north, eventually reaching the Syrian coastline. It caused multiple losses related to the natural resources and economic activities on the coast in what is said to be the Mediterranean's worst-ever environmental disaster. Oil from the Jiyyeh fuel tanks burned for 20 days, releasing noxious clouds that blew over Beirut and a third of the country. Tests showed that the cloud contained high levels of toxic lead, mercury, and dioxin. Some short-term respiratory symptoms were reported among people living in the vicinity of Jiyyeh.[10] Moreover, reports that depleted uranium ordnances were used during the conflict are raising concerns of long-term effects on health. According to the Lebanese environment minister Yacoub Sarraf, "Lebanon's coastline could take up to ten years to recover from a massive oil spill." The cost of cleaning up this environmental damage was originally estimated at $50 to 100 million but the government's figure comes closer to $200 million.[11]

Unexploded Ordnance (UXO)

The Israeli army dropped a large number of cluster bomblets on rural areas of southern Lebanon mainly, according to some sources, in the final days of the war. UN officials estimate that as many as one million of them may remain unexploded.[12] Although aid organizations and the government are engaged in intensive mine-clearing operations, their initial focus has been on populated villages rather than fields. It is estimated that only 40,000 cluster bombs had been cleared by September 26, 2006. The MACC-SL (UN Mine Action Coordination Center for Southern Lebanon) expects clearance of most of the UXO and cluster submunitions will take between 12 and 15 months.[13] As of November 7, 2006 there had been at least 22 deaths and 133 injuries.[14] Meanwhile, the presence of such vast quantities of unexploded ordnance is likely to delay any large-scale revival of the agricultural sector, especially in southern Lebanon.[15] Unexploded ordnance can have regional poverty implications, as south Lebanon is one of the country's poorest regions and half of the population relies entirely on agriculture.[16]

Labor

According to government sources, employment losses peaked at about 120,000 during the war, particularly hitting workers in tourism and agriculture. Information International reports that 40,000 farmers have been affected by the war, 10 percent of permanent employees were laid off, and most of the 30,000 seasonal workers in the tourist sector discharged. Overall the tourism and hotel sectors may have accounted for more than a third of those who lost their jobs. In other sectors, estimates vary widely. For example, the industrial sector employs about 130,000 workers and reports employment losses between 2,000 and 4,200 (according to the Lebanese Association of Industrialists) and 6,000 (Ministry of Industry survey).[17] Others predict that the number of jobs lost in the industrial sector could reach 10,000.[18] According to the Ministry of Labor, direct employment losses in industrial plants and institutions that were either destroyed or damaged may have resulted in 11,000 workers seeking recourse to their termination benefits (End-of-Service Indemnity, or EOSI) by the end of October 2006. Many employers, suffering financial duress but seeking to retain employees, put employees on partial payments or temporary leave without pay. Though little is known about how many of those who left the country during the war will return, some estimates suggest that about 250,000 Lebanese left the country during July and August 2006, and

100,000 of them have not come yet back.[19] A postwar survey found that 48 percent of the Lebanese now plan to emigrate for professional reasons.[20] Overall, in relative terms, the effect of the war on direct employment may have been relatively small for the private non-agricultural sector and some sectors perhaps incurred only a few employment losses. For example, the banking sector employs over 15,000 workers but laid off 200 to 300 workers. But the impact of the war on earnings or employment in the longer run is unknown, and estimates of unemployment vary. Minister of Labor Trad Hamade reports that the unemployment rate increased from 14 percent before the war to 20 percent after; a report by the Ministry of Finance suggests an increase from 10 to 25 percent. A 10 percentage-point increase in unemployment may be likely also because an end of October survey indicated that full time employment was only at 92 percent of its prewar level, and part-time employment has been slower to recover. Thus, unemployment may well be stabilized at a high level (about 20 percent or so) unless there is a relatively quick rebound of the economy.[21]

Pensions and Social Insurance

The war increased the government's liabilities to civil service and military pension plans both in the short- and medium-term. The increase in the war alert stage to level 3, during which pension entitlements accrue at the rate of 3 years for each year in service, will add considerably to the pension expenditures for the military. These additional fiscal costs are yet to be estimated but could be in the order of 0.2 percent of GDP over the short-term, and more, if the government recruits retired military personnel and includes this post-retirement service as additional years for pension accumulation. The war will also increase the outlays related to the End-of-Service Indemnity (EOSI) scheme administered by the National Social Security Fund (NSSF) as the number of employers who closed businesses or had to cut personnel as a result of the war will increase. These are precisely the employers who are likely to be facing liquidity constraints and therefore not be able to pay their share of the EOSI—if the laid-off employee immediately applies for one. The consequence is an increase in the outlays of the EOSI and a reduction in reserves. Preliminary estimates vary significantly and put these losses between 0.2 and 3.8 percent of GDP—with a likely amount closer to 1 percent if the number of claimants reaches about 15,000 workers.

Indirect Effects on the Economy and Livelihood

As reported in Table 1, the direct damage from the war on public infrastructure may be $3.6 billion, but the previous discussion on the sectoral estimates of direct and indirect costs (such as forgone production in key sectors such as agriculture, construction, industry, tourism, and other services, loss of foreign investment flows and the cost of stabilizing the currency) suggests that total costs will be much higher. Some estimate total direct and indirect losses at US$11.4 billion (US$3.6 billion in damage to infrastructure, US$3 billion in tofrism losses, US$2 billion in lost current and future investment, an increase in public debt of US$1.5 billion, and US$1.1billion forgone GDP growth). Others, such as the United Nations Development Program (UNDP), estimate the overall costs may reach at least $15 billion.[22] Tourism, industry, agriculture, and banking provide illustrative examples of the magnitude of direct and indirect effects as well as the linkages between various sectors. As an illustration, the direct losses to the hotel sector through the end of September 2006 came to $228 million for payments of existing debts, overheads, and labor costs. In addition to these costs, the Ministry of Tourism estimated the total losses within the sector from the non-arrival of 1.6 million tourists for the summer season could be $3 billion. Yet this figure excludes the effect of the war on other sectors and the economy as a whole.

For example, the decline in tourism impacted domestic food producers who were caught with large inventories (often financed by high-interest loans) anticipating the high season demand. The loss in demand for food directly impacted farmers who could carry on with their activities during the war but faced limited access to both local markets (due to the unavailability of local distribution networks rising from damage to roads, bridges, and trucks) as well as foreign markets (due to the blockade). This could in turn lead to a loan crisis among affected businesses, if they are no longer able to meet their debt repayments. This problem could be further compounded by the fact that many of the indebted businesses have also lost their collateral, which is now destroyed property. In fact, a recent survey estimated that nearly two-thirds of firms are facing cash-flow problems and a large majority of them would like their payments rescheduled, their debts refinanced, and their tax relieved or deferred. Given that 30 percent of Lebanese commercial banks' outstanding loans are to the private sector, this is likely to affect the health of the banking sector unless significant help is provided soon.

Though the Lebanese banking sector is the biggest and the most developed in the region, the war affected commercial banks both from the assets and liabilities sides. On the asset side, the quality of the business loans portfolio has deteriorated due to direct damage inflicted on businesses and to the interruption of business cycle that affected the whole economy. It may deteriorate further due to the increase in government financing needs that may put pressure on bank resources and compromise the quality of their public portfolio. From the liability side, the inflow of capital has been interrupted, thus weakening the ability of banks to finance Lebanon's chronic current account deficit. The war halted a strong upward trend in deposits[23] while the dollarization rate of deposits rose to 75 percent in August from 68 percent in June (EIU 2006). Thus, though the banking sector estimated that the direct losses from the war amounted to less than 2 percent of their commercial portfolio and less than 1 percent of their housing portfolio, the longer-term effects on bank portfolios (arising from the economic duress and slowdown at the macro level as well as the deterioration of public finance at the fiscal level) could be of concern. For example, debt-to-GDP ratio is expected to grow to 190 percent of GDP by the end of the current year, against 175 percent at end 2005, due to a negative GDP growth and increased public deficit (to 13 percent compared to 9 percent at end 2005). The increase in the deficit would raise demand for bank financing, which would in turn increase the pressures on interest rates. Indeed, banks would need higher remuneration on their assets to be able to attract resources to such a risky country at a time when international rates are increasing.

Another significant adverse effect of the war is on trade. Though the war stopped on August 14, the blockade was lifted on September 9. The cost of lost trade is hard to gauge because of the absence of accurate statistics on transshipment and transit business. But it is likely to reach hundreds of millions of US dollars (according to the EIU) as Lebanon is one of the most open economies in the region, with its annual trade routinely equal to as much as half of the country's GDP.[24] Speaking at an IMF meeting in September, Minister of Finance Jihad Azour estimated the daily cost to business and trade activity of the blockade alone at US$50 million. In addition, though the blockade is now over, following UN Security Resolution 1701 businesses are facing longer delays for their consignments at the seaports, airports, and border crossings due to the enhancement of security measures at Lebanese seaports and border crossings. Though these are important attempts at restoring investor confidence and increasing security, they have inevitably increased trade costs in the form of lost time in trade transactions: Consignments are now systematically inspected, leading to long waiting times at the ports of entry. Such additional "frictional" trade costs (imputed by lost time in trade transactions and assuming a trade volume of $9 billion) are estimated to be at least $3 million a day.

In addition to these tangible losses in the productive sector, there are many invisible ones. The previously mentioned damage excludes in most instances much that is unrecorded, such as losses incurred by many small businesses, some housed in apartments and houses that were damaged or destroyed. Similarly, damage in the transportation sector does not include the destruction of numerous cars and trucks on the road. Also, estimates for the housing sector do not take into account the invisible private costs to about 60 to 70 percent of families who ended up with inhabitable houses. More generally, while most of those who moved during the war have returned to their original residences, UNHCR estimates that 200,000 people remain displaced[25] because of the level of destruction of key civilian infrastructure (water, electricity, roads, and hospitals), damages to private housing, and as a consequence of the presence of UXO and cluster bombs.[26] Also, estimating the incidence of the loss of labor earnings and family incomes remains elusive. For example, though the agricultural sector accounts for less than 10 percent to GDP, it contributes to the incomes of about 20 percent of the population. And though the estimated value of marine capture fisheries production is only about 1 percent of agricultural value-added (US$20 million annually), the losses are very significant in specific areas and, according to UNDP, have affected the livelihoods of 3,500 of the 6,500 professional fishermen. In the formal labor market, unemployment is only in part responsible for lost incomes as many workers have been placed on some kind of unpaid leave by the employer (underemployment) or were forced to switch to whatever alternative employment they could find (with associated costs of change and adjustment).

The war may have long-term repercussions on the Lebanese economy that go beyond the damages mentioned in this chapter. These are likely to affect both human capital and investment. There is likely to be a general loss of the educated and the skilled through emigration, including the quasi-permanent departure of private investors. This kind of emigration may be difficult to reverse as it is based on lifetime considerations and at times significant sunk costs in the form of transportation, settlement, and liquidation or purchase of lump assets. The extent of the brain drain during and following the war has so far not been counted. In more direct terms, the academic year started with one month's delay in October 2006. Though this may not sound like a lot, the trauma of children—some of whom attend classes in the same place where they found refuge during the war—has so far been excluded from any formal valuation of losses.

Looking Forward

Lebanon faces the following three challenging tasks with increasing difficulty.

War Reconstruction

In terms of reconstruction, as the earlier discussion of direct damages suggests, the affected areas have been identified and if donor promises translate into actual funding, this is more or less a technical issue with an important double-sided caveat. The first one is whether donors will transfer the funds in a way that will not exacerbate existing divisions in Lebanon. For example, there have been cases where donors have bypassed the government and transferred funds directly to local or regional organizations. This has been justified on the grounds that this can reduce red tape, increase the speed of implementation, and directly reach the beneficiaries. But it can also lead to reinforcement of regional or confessional divisions and can be adversely affected by lack of overall coordination. The second caveat is whether the government has the technical ability to provide such coordination and the political power to come up with a credible national plan that would take advantage of the donor funding. Both caveats are self-evident and existed before the war. It is beyond the scope of this chapter to dwell in these political economy areas.

Economic Recovery

The earlier discussion suggests that the enduring impact of the war would come less from the direct physical damage and more from the indirect effects on the economy, including its changing prospects. Recovery will depend on micro/private and macro/public considerations compounded by development problems Lebanon faced even before the war and managed to address then only to a limited extent.

Despite the euphoria of the first half of 2006, Lebanon had problems and policy challenges across a wide range of sectoral and economic issues. For example, the war accentuated the environment degradation, but the problem was not new to Lebanon: Annual environmental costs were already estimated to be about US$565 million (or 3.4 percent of GDP).[27] In the electricity sector, the direct effect of the war is estimated at about US$150 million but, even in the absence of this additional burden, the overall cash shortfall of the Électricité du Liban had already been estimated by the Ministry of Finance to reach more than five times as much by the end of 2006. The war damage on the water sector compounded an already dire situation that was plagued even before the war by poorly maintained infrastructure, inefficient management, water losses that currently create over 40 percent intermittent water supply in many areas (particularly during the summer months), contaminated surface and ground water resources, inadequate sanitation services, leaking or overflowing wastewater collection systems that cause severe sanitary conditions, and overall low-quality service and poor cost recovery. Just these three issues alone (environment, electricity, and water) indicate that the war has aggravated an already critical situation and the development challenge for Lebanon is huge, even before social issues (to follow) are taken into account.

At the micro and private-sector levels, tentative forecasts indicate that agriculture may largely recover in 2007 (except in southern Lebanon, where losses are expected to carry over for longer). Recovery in the tourism sector could prove more problematic as it may take longer to restore tourists' confidence about safety in Lebanon than even the ten years that the clean-up of the coastline from the oil spill is expected to take.[28] The fortunes of the construction sector could be more mixed. For example, without the prospect of a guaranteed tourist season in 2007, companies may diversify in the development of prestigious residential projects aimed at Gulf visitors who could continue to benefit from the increasing liquidity resulting from the high price of oil. With respect to other private-sector areas, a survey in October 2006 indicated that the average business is producing at about 60 percent its prewar level, with the majority of firms expecting that they will get back to pre-conflict sales levels by the middle of 2007. Still a significant minority believe it will take them between one and two years to recover to their prior level of sales.[29]

The biggest challenge in the area of economic recovery relates to the macro and fiscal imbalances. Surely, by the end of 2006 the war decreased government revenues by $920 million, at the same time that public spending may need to increase by $800 million to finance higher military spending, relief operations, reconstruction activities, and support measures to the deficit-ridden electricity company. Even if this additional burden is somehow fully absorbed and the existing public debt of $40 billion (200 percent of GDP) does not increase further, the government still faces the Herculean task of reducing its historical debt to manageable levels.

Setting the macro-fiscal framework in order is long overdue. The need for reforms is now more critical than ever, but what is required are systemic and deep-cutting reforms (often with sectarian and geographical dimensions), not quick or easy fixes. Two key sectors that are candidates for reform and the ones with the most severe budgetary implications at the macro-fiscal level are electricity and pensions (especially for the military). For example, due to significant operational inefficiencies in the electricity sector, including years of operating losses and bill collection problems, government subsidies reached $570 million (nearly 3 percent of GDP) in 2005 and, according to the Ministry of Finance, the deficit for 2006 might reach US$1 billion. Similarly, annual pension payments for civil servants and military personnel have already reached 2.7 percent of the GDP (of which 2.2 percentage points are for military pensions), while implicit (unfunded future) liabilities are estimated at more than 50 percent of GDP.[30] Reforms in these two sectors have been debated for years and if they could be implemented relatively swiftly, they could reduce the fiscal drag significantly.

Social Development

The aforementioned tasks of reconstruction and recovery can be largely thought of as being subject to technical and political economy considerations. Though the technical part is known and good professional advice abounds, the political (and confessional) part constitutes a formidable constraint. Since the end of the civil war in 1990, reforms have been not just sporadic and spasmodic but simply too few. Their impact has made no major dent in the social fabric and divisions in Lebanon. One symptom of Lebanon's divided nature is that many social services are privately financed. Thus, the social sectors can possibly become the entry point for policies in a new Lebanon. This last section deals with an assessment and some proposals for increasing the impact of government in the social sector.

Private spending on social sectors (such as education and health) comes to 15 percent of GDP. This figure alone exceeds the combined private and public spending on these sectors in many other developing and OECD countries. And if one adds to this the government expenditure on the social sectors (including pensions and social programs for the poor), the proportion of total national spending on the social sectors comes to a staggering 24 percent of GDP. Putting these numbers together, and assuming that private money is spent more efficiently than public money, it is tempting to conclude that social services and social protection in Lebanon must be on par with the most socially advanced European countries. Unfortunately, Lebanon's social-sector performance is in many respects inferior even to other regional economies. The issue that therefore requires more attention and ingenuity (to complement the existing provisions but contain any side effects of sectarian-based social services) is the area of social development, so far largely neglected in practice, if not always in intent.[31]

Despite its smallness—in land and population—Lebanon is a divided and inequitable country. In the education sector, untouched by Lebanon's premier institutions from kindergarten to universities, 55,000 children are not in school. In the health sector, half of the Lebanese are uninsured and therefore uncovered by modern state-of-the-art facilities in modern hospitals. And against the multimillion-dollar residences of Beirut stand social welfare recipients appreciative of a monthly $15 cash transfer provided by the Ministry of Social Affairs. Despite being the richest non-oil Arab economy, claiming a prestigious upper-middle income status ranked 79th country in the world in terms of nominal per capita GDP, in real (purchasing power parity) terms Lebanon loses a staggering 44 places and slips to the 123rd position (Table 4). This brings Lebanon practically on par with Jordan and the Philippines and far behind Malaysia, Algeria, Tunisia, and Turkey as, for example, one dollar is worth more than three dollars in Tunisia but only an extra 20 cents in Lebanon.

Table 4: GNI Per Capita in Nominal US Dollars and in Purchasing Power Parity (PPP)

	Nominal $ Income	$Index		PPP income	PPP index
Lebanon	3,990	100	Malaysia	8,500	185
Malaysia	3,540	89	Iran	6,690	145
Turkey	2,490	62	Tunisia	6,440	140
Tunisia	1,990	50	Turkey	6,300	137
Jordan	1,760	44	Algeria	5,530	120
Iran	1,720	43	**Lebanon**	4,600	100
Algeria	1,720	43	Philippines	4,450	97
Egypt	1,470	37	Jordan	4,180	91
Morocco	1,170	29	Egypt	3,810	83
Syria	1,130	28	Morocco	3,730	81
Philippines	1,030	26	Syria	3,470	75

Source: Tzannatos (2006) based on World Bank "World Development Indicators," 2004

The combination of low incomes and a divided society is exacerbated by the relative absence of the government in the area of social services in terms of both policies and oversight. This encourages individuals and communities to seek support from local benefactors, who often grant it but may also require forms of reciprocity and allegiance. This compartmentalization of social services is associated with historical divisions that are also manifested in persistent and substantial demands for the formation of a government of national unity that would be different than the one that was in charge during the war and the postwar period thus far. Whatever view one holds on this matter is immaterial for the purposes of the present chapter, whose aim is by far too humble to offer solutions to the historical legacies of Lebanon and the geopolitical forces operating in the Arab region.

An area that can, however, be more promising to start building a more coherent social capital in Lebanon is the creation of national mechanisms for social protection that are visibly associated with the state and do not depend on, for example, location or confession. A basis for starting the creation of national mechanisms that can reach all Lebanese is illustrated in Table 5. With hostilities having taken place primarily in poor areas, anti-poverty programs are even more critical today.

Table 5: Poverty within and between Governorates, 1996–2004*

Area	Poverty Rate within Governorate			Share in National Poverty		
	1996	2004	percent change	1996	2004	percent change
Beirut	19	9	−53	13	4	−69
Mt. Lebanon	26	16	−38	37	28	−24
North	49	31	−37	22	23	5
South	39	37	−5	9	15	67
Beqaa	44	38	−14	13	18	38
Nabatiyeh	51	46	−10	7	11	57
All Lebanon	**35**	**25**		**100**	**100**	

* Constructed from "Evolution of Living Conditions Indicators between 1995 and 2004," UNDP/MOSA unpublished study

Without downplaying the need for deep and systemic reforms in education and health sectors and broader social sectors, this chapter proposes three simple but potentially promising policies to be introduced in the short-term as part of the recovery measures. These measures will result in widespread coverage of social protection, will be provided visibly by the government on the basis of objective targeting and will require very low fiscal requirements—the latter being a critical constraint in the debt-ridden economy of Lebanon. These three proposals are presented in Table 6.

Table 6: Proposed Measures for Providing Universal Social Protection with Maximum Impact and Minimum Fiscal Implications

Promote human development especially for the poor
• Implement a cash-transfer (scholarship) program to the families of the 55,000 out-of-school children conditional on these children being enrolled and progressing to the next grade.

- This group constitutes of the most marginalized Lebanese today and in the future, and addressing their needs can have high payoffs for them and the regions in which they live.

Old age security and poverty reduction
- Offer a small social (non-contributory) pension to all those above the age of 70.
- Though there are 180,000 people in this age range, not all will claim it (negative self-selection), but for those who do so this should be a welcome income addition most likely to be spent by the families the elderly live with.

Social Insurance
- Increase worker protection without increasing labor costs.
- Introduce an unemployment insurance scheme and temporary layoff regulations in combination with amendments of the labor law in areas governing contract termination and severance payments.
- At present, expensive unemployment insurance is de facto provided to only a few workers in the formal sector by requiring employers to pay substantial benefits in case of worker separation.

Notes

1. Monitoring and evaluation measures should be introduced at the same time as the policies themselves for subsequent fine-tuning of the policies with respect to adequacy of benefits and impact upon beneficiaries.

2. Any expansion of social services at the national level would require an inter-ministerial committee focusing on cross-cutting social policy issues, which would oversee progress of implementation and regularly reform service delivery provisions and mechanisms.

3. Good information systems are currently lacking and urgently need to be introduced. In the meantime, the proposed measures can be introduced on a pilot basis with sunset clauses (for example, initial duration of programs for one year or so).

4. Other things being equal, the government should target its transfers directly to beneficiaries (without intermediaries) to increase transparency, avoid delays, and maximize impact.

These three measures—which include 55,000 out-of-school children, 400,000 workers, and 200,000 elderly—would expand the coverage of beneficiaries from government-sponsored schemes dramatically. There will be no fiscal implications for the biggest of these groups (workers) as the financing of unemployment insurance can come from low but mutually agreed payroll deductions among workers and employers. The $20 million required for a social pension is a trivial amount compared to what it can accomplish for all older Lebanese living in poverty and compared to the more than half a billion dollars currently spent on pensions for retired civil servants and military personnel. The case of bringing out-of-school children into the education system needs no justification: these children, if left uneducated, will drag down the Lebanese economy and put a much higher future burden on the society for many decades ahead compared to the current cost of scholarships.

Summary and Conclusions

The costs of the July–August 2006 war are still being counted while this chapter is being written. The estimates vary a lot with respect to total costs and whether they refer to the short- or the long-run. They also vary by sector no matter whether they relate to direct measurable costs (such as loss of life, damage to infrastructure, or forgone revenues from the non-arrival of tourists during the critical summer season) or indirect costs in terms of broader economic, social, and political losses. Either way, the estimates tend to be incomplete as, so far, there is little information on invisible private monetary or non-pecuniary costs—such as private housing costs or health costs for the injured, lower wages and higher unemployment, longer travel time, informal social support, psychological shock and trauma, or eventual emigration.

Though this article shows that the precise figures for the damage are and may stay uncertain, some have characterized the costs of the war to Lebanon as "enormous" (EIU 2006). The government gave an initial $3.6 billion estimate of the costs of the war in late August 2006, but the war is now said to have culminated in such damage that "the last 15 years of work on reconstruction and rehabilitation, following the previous problems that Lebanon experienced, are now annihilated" (Jean Fabre of the UN Development Program, who subsequently put a $15 billion figure on the damage).[32]

Any country would have been under stress under such conditions, but for Lebanon the situation is worse. Countries can cope better with crises when they have systems, especially social safety nets, in place before a crisis strikes. They can also cope better when their population is homogenous. Neither precondition is present in Lebanon. In addition, the already stretched government's budget deficit will increase further for reasons of lost revenues and increased expenditures due to additional war-induced needs.

Lebanon is therefore ill-equipped to deal alone with the additional financial and technical challenges added by the war. As Prime Minister Fouad Seniora stated, "the losses that were inflicted on Lebanon are something we cannot shoulder alone." He went on to say that "Lebanon is not a house without any doormen," and went on to insist that donor funding should be channeled through the government. This constitutes effectively an admission of the apparent low integration of the reconstruction effort between the government and international organizations—in addition to the historical but nevertheless still intense internal divisions among the Lebanese.

It remains to be seen whether the Lebanese state itself will become this war's next major casualty or will reemerge strengthened by a better reconstruction performance than it offered in the past. The issue is not just money. For example, the government pledged $33,000 in aid to each family whose home was completely destroyed during the war, and an additional $10,000 to families with a deceased person, $13,000 for an injured person 10 years or older, and $6,600 for a child below the age of 10. Similarly, Hizballah offered homeowners who lost their houses $12,000 and tenants $8,000, and it already gave 5,000 families handouts to cope with their situations. The issue is more whether resources are spent in a way that contributes to nation-building.

No matter what the precise cost estimates of the war are, Lebanon remains a fractured country. Its government cannot be seen as the representative of all Lebanese unless it is able to act like one. This chapter put forward proposals that would assist the government to reach the population through needy children, vulnerable workers, and the elderly. This broad outreach can increase the coherence of the Lebanese society by targeting all citizens according to an objective characteristic rather than specific groups distinguished by other criteria. It will reduce the dependence on sub-national coalitions, increase the role and transparency of the government and thus accelerate economic and social development. The underlying assumption here is derived from historical experience: countries with inclusive social policies are in a better position to reduce inequalities, attain faster economic growth, avoid conflict, and accentuate social development.

Lebanon's weaknesses have multiplied since the war. Its impact on the social sectors is perhaps the most devastating of all. Though social sectors are at times scorned by hard-core economists (who may focus more on critical fundamentals such as the size of the debt or the rate of economic growth), this chapter proposes that the social sectors are the door leading to Lebanon's future. If it is opened, then the war's costs might serve as an opportunity to set the foundation for a new Lebanon, whose internal cohesion could act as a deterrent to future incidents like those that took place in the summer of 2006.

NOTES

1 The quoted numbers in this chapter are those available in November 2006 and may be subject to revision.

2 Among others, the following produced various estimates of the costs and implications of the war: FAO, ILO, IMF, UNICEF, WHO, the World Bank, various UN agencies such as UNEP (United Nations Environment Program), OCHA (Office for the Coordination of Humanitarian Affairs) and High Relief Commission (HRC), as well as the European Union and its constituent governments, the Arab League, individual Arab states and others countries, the Economist Intelligence Unit (EIU), and Oxfam.

3 An earlier detailed version of this chapter ended up with more than 100 footnotes. The resulting amount of additional text could not be accommodated in the present book. Nor was it perhaps worth it given that any detailed estimates at this point are bound to be reconsidered as the history of the war is still being written. The authors can provide specific sources to references made in this chapter upon request.

4 UNEP/OCHA United Nations Environment Program/United Nations Office for the Coordination of Humanitarian Affairs, *Environmental Update: Lebanon Crisis* 24 August 2006

5 Other assessments estimate that a total of more than 70,000 housing units have been affected: HRC "Communication from the Presidency of the Council of Ministers," 18 October 2006.

6 This assistance emanated from over 28 foreign country governments, 25 United Nations agencies and international organizations, 20 foreign NGOs, and many local Lebanese NGOs including the Lebanese Red Cross, the YMCA, Caritas, and the Imam Sadr Foundation.

7 "Al-Moustaqbal Tanshur Taqreer Markaz al-Da'm al-Iqtisadi," *Al-Moustaqbal* 22 August 2006.

8 Mohammad Hout, chairman of Middle East Airlines (MEA) in *Daily Star* 2 November 2006: 8.

9 Others estimate the bombing of a power utility in Jiyyeh caused the burning of about 20,000 tons of heavy fuel oil and the spilling of another 15,000 tons in the Mediterranean (see Oxford Business Group, "Lebanon: Change in Energy," 6 November 2006).

10 The information about the oil spill presented here is drawn from IUCN/Green Line (2006) Lebanon Oil Spill Rapid Assessment/Response Mission, final report, prepared by Richard Steiner.

11 IMO/REMPEC/UNEP-MAP. International Assistance Action Plan, 15 August 2006.

12 A report by the London-based Landmine Action cited in Reuters, 1 November 2006.

13 "Unexploded Bomblets Hinder Southern Lebanon Recovery," Reuters, 26 September 2006.

14 Lucy Fielder, "Injuries in Lebanon Revive Bid to Ban Cluster Bombs," ABC News Internet Ventures, 7 November 2006. She also notes "According to the UN, Israel dropped 90 percent of the cluster bombs in the last 72 hours of the war when all parties knew a cease-fire was imminent… [E]xperts say Israel dropped about 4 million submunitions on Lebanon. More than a quarter failed to explode on impact and have effectively become a multitude of landmines… [S]outh Lebanon's fallout has fueled campaigns for a ban on cluster bombs, akin to the prohibition of antipersonnel mines adopted in 1997. Civilians, many of them children, make up 98 percent of those killed and injured by the munitions across the globe, campaign group Handicap International found in a report of unprecedented scope released last week."

15 According to local reports, some farmers are paying approximately US$6.50 per bomblet for "artisanal" bomb disposal in order to resume farming. Though this strengthens the belief in the power of "the market," it may also indicate lack of confidence that the Lebanese army will clear fields rapidly.

16 "In Lebanon, a War's Lethal Harvest," *Washington Post* 26 September 2006.

17 According to the *Daily Star* 21 October 2006, the president of the Lebanese Association of Industrialists estimated that 4,200 laborers lost their jobs following the destruction of 142 industrial plants, an increase from the estimate of 2,000 provided by the president in the October 2006 *Executive* magazine.

18 According to Marwan Iskandar, a prominent Lebanese economist.

19 Of those who left, 30 percent are said to be young and educated. For example, in the IT and computer sector, which was only marginally affected by direct damage during the war, layoffs were estimated at 15 percent of staff, with an additional 5 percent of staff leaving the country. Of these, most were highly qualified personnel—managers and technical experts.

20 Published in the magazine *Le Commerce de Liban*, quoted in the *Daily Star* 2 October 2006: 3.

21 Kamal Hamdan, *Daily Star* 2 October 2006.

22 Marwan Iskandar, *Daily Star* 2 October 2006.

23 Deposits rose by 6.5 percent (nearly $4 billion) in the first half of 2006 but declined by 5.6 percent (US$3.5 billion) during July and August. The decline in these two months is almost double the decline in total deposits following Prime Minister Rafiq Hariri's assassination, which did not exceed $1.8 billion.

24 Damage to trade infrastructure *per se,* however, was relatively small (about $9 million), as was the loss of business for ports during July and August ($10 million).

25 According to the Lebanese Economy and Trade Ministry's announcement, "a quarter of Lebanon's population has been forced out of their homes, and as many as 200,000 of the estimated 1,000,000 evacuees may have no home to return to when the war is over" (Kim Murphy, "Lebanon's Renewal is Dashed in Weeks," *Los Angeles Times* 13 August 2006).

26 OCHA Situation Report 39, Lebanon Response, 20–27 September 2006.

27 The figures apply to the year 2000 as estimated in a study was prepared by the World Bank and the METAP program in collaboration with the Ministry of Environment. *World Bank Environment Department Paper 97*.

28 "Lebanon's Coast is Drowning in Oil," *Los Angeles Times* 4 September 2006. A spill caused by an Israeli strike has blackened popular beaches and threatens the economy and delicate ecosystems.

29 A critical question is how long the economic impact of the war and blockade will endure. Key factors will be the kind of expectations and rates of investments that would ensue, and both depend on the prospects for political stability. For example, before the war 74 percent of firms had planned new investments, but only 19 percent of them planned to carry out those investments by the end of the year, and 25 percent expected their investments to be realized after one year or so. This means 30 percent of firms are not going ahead with their prewar plans for the next year and more. This can in turn put a strain on the labor market, increased emigration, loss of human capital, and so on.

30 This significant fiscal outlay for pensions covers only 6 percent of the labor force.

31 A 2005 World Bank study covering 166 countries found that Lebanon uses at least 25 percent more public spending on health and 13 percent more spending on education to produce the same outcomes observed in Oman, Kuwait, the UAE, and Trinidad and Tobago. Though private education and health services have created a few "centers of excellence" and some of these shortcomings in the provision of public services are addressed by strong informal safety nets, both are largely irrelevant for a sizable part of the population.

32 Though this estimate may be proven to be too high, it does not diverge in essence from a statement attributed to Israel's chief of staff, Lt. Gen. Dan Halutz: "If the soldiers are not returned, we will turn Lebanon's clock back 20 years" (www.cnn.com/2006/WORLD/meast/07/12/mideast).

25. LESSONS FROM THE WAR

Elias Khoury

This chapter combines two articles by Elias Khoury. The first was titled "Two Lessons from the War," and was published on September 10, 2006 in Al-Nahar *Literary Supplement. The second article, "The Pierced Basket," was published in the same forum on December 17, 2006. In the first piece, Khoury extracts immediate lessons from the war, then addresses the charged postwar Lebanese political predicament. He published the second essay as the anti-government demonstrations and mass strikes, which started on December 1, 2006, persisted. These demonstrations were led by Hizballah and their allies, including the Amal movement led by Nabih Berri (speaker of the Lebanese parliament), and General Michel Aoun's (Maronite) Free Patriotic Movement, and others. The protesters established a tent city in downtown Beirut. They sought to increase opposition posts in the governing cabinet, and demanded the resignation of Prime Minister Fouad Seniora. The standoff between the Hizballah coalition and the government and its allies (including Saad Hariri and the Sunnis, and Walid Jumblatt and the Druze) was punctured by an outbreak of violence on January 25, 2007. Many people fear the return of civil war, a painful chapter in Lebanon's modern history. Both pieces are translated by Sinan Antoon.*

Two Lessons from the War

The Lebanese political clamor around the war and the blockade seems fragile and gratuitous and hence the need for offering a rational reading of the lessons of the destructive war launched by Israel against Lebanon. The war's lessons are more subtle than the media's hysteria around the government, which has no meaning.

Let us exit the political melodrama to read the war's lessons in their local and regional aspects and to discover that they have the potential to cause a turn in the Lebanese and Arab state of affairs, provided that we read well.

First: On the Lebanese level, the war brought a number of major political changes, the most important of which is the redeployment of the Lebanese army in the south. But the strategic substance of the war remained outside the discussion. Through their bravery, sacrifice, and organization, the fighters of the Islamic Resistance [Hizballah], proved that one fighting brigade is enough to break the Arab circle of weakness and submission vis-à-vis Israeli occupation. The resistance proved a legendary ability to remain steadfast and gave the enemy a clear message that aggression against Lebanon is not a picnic and that the aggressor's fate will not be less than failure. The missile response, in addition to persevering in the trenches, forced the Israeli military to change its plans more than once and confused it, which led to the failure of the entire military operation. It is true that the Lebanese price was high and perhaps beyond Lebanese capabilities, but so was the Israeli price, which may force the Israeli army to think a great deal before committing any new foolishness in Lebanon.

This strategic dimension, which was produced by the sacrifices and steadfastness of the fighters and citizens must be the first brick in constructing a Lebanese defense strategy. One that will make Israel understand that Lebanon's borders are fenced with blood and sacrifice and that there are no limits to a small country's ability to defend itself, and that it is not made by weapons, but springs from national will.

Those who think that UN Resolution 1701 was a gift from the UN are mistaken [see the chapters by Bennis, Falk, and Zunes for a detailed analysis of this]. This resolution would not have been issued in its current form were it not for the heroic steadfastness in the south. Everyone remembers that Lebanon fought a fierce diplomatic battle against the US and forced the Americans to withdraw their old draft resolution.

Reaching this international resolution was the product of the balance of power created by the resistance. Without this steadfastness, Lebanon would have fallen into the American orbit and would have succumbed to the New Middle East that Condoleezza Rice wants as a gate to Iraqize the region and destroy it.

From this point, then, one must search for a way to make this steadfastness part of our Lebanese reality—an approach to build the fighting capability of the army in terms of infrastructure, but also its fighting creed. The fear is that the government may sleep on the silk of the international troops and UN guarantees.

The national dialogue about a defense strategy must continue, starting from this point, and must benefit from the great lesson of the war. It must be remembered that taking Lebanon into the national project does not only assume leaving the logic of Syrian patronage, but also American patronage. This must also mean declaring a Lebanese strategy with Arab depth against Israeli military hegemony over the Arab east.

Does this mean incorporating the Islamic Resistance into the army or establishing a border guard in which the resistance fighters play an essential role? Or do things have to start with genuine coordination to reach an acceptable formula? These questions are left to the national dialogue, but they are today pressing questions in order to complete all dimensions of Lebanese independence.

Second: A major achievement of the war is the reinforcing of UN troops with European and Islamic forces. With American support, Israel had demanded multinational forces, that is, NATO forces that are but another form of American occupation. Everyone knows the Israeli sensitivity to the presence of UN forces. But the Israeli government was forced to swallow its own objections due to the steadfastness of Lebanese and French diplomacy. This steadfastness would not have been possible without the steadfastness of the fighters in the south.

What is perhaps even more important than the arrival of UN troops in Lebanon is the possibility of sending UN troops to Palestine. The Arab initiative is still useless, because it was unable to take Palestine out of the whirlwind of the American administration's war on terror. Consequently, it was unable to present a tangible suggestion to separate the Israeli occupation army and the Palestinian resistance.

The Lebanese achievement offers the only window out of the bloodbath in Palestine. The success of UN troops and European diplomacy in defusing the situation in Lebanon will open the path for an Arab–international resolution to the Palestinian question based on applying UN resolutions, establishing a Palestinian state over all territories occupied in 1967, by forcing Israeli society to swallow the bitter pill of international forces in Palestine.

In this sense the Lebanon war opened the door of the battle to its Arab horizon. This assumes the existence of a Palestinian consciousness to reach a national unity agreement. The battle with Israeli occupation is long and complex and necessitates using all forms of struggle. It also assumes a general Arab awakening from the lethal slumber that makes Iran the sole regional player and threatens to strip Arabs of the Palestinian question which, for them, is a question of life or death.

These two strategic lessons must correct the current debate in

Lebanon and the Arab world so that the Lebanon war can exit the circle of absolute glorification or risk. The blood and destruction that has been shed in the south, the southern suburbs, and the Beqaa Valley and other Lebanese areas must open a new, rational page in the context of resisting the Zionist project.

The Pierced Basket

We may say now that the introductions [between the opposition and the pro-government forces] in downtown Beirut are over. The celebrations and the camps have fulfilled their role. The freedom camp, which was erected following the assassination of Hariri [the late prime minister was assassinated on February 14, 2005] broke the sectarian barriers between Christians, Sunni Muslims, and the Druze. The tents of the Hizballah coalition [since December 1, 2006] broke the barriers between Shiite Muslims and some Christians. The freedom camp ejected the Syrian army from Lebanon and the "Inactive Third" camp [Hizballah coalition] will not bring it back. The party is over, voices are hoarse, and the escalation reached its zenith following the speeches by Hassan Nasrallah, Fouad Seniora [Prime Minister], and Michel Aoun. It is time for the test, and the main political forces have nowhere to escape to. One question confronts everyone and these forces must answer either "Yes" or "No" and then we will see.

The question consists of seven short questions:

First: Are you for the international tribunal? There is no justification for expressing reservations. There is almost a national consensus that the killers of Rafiq Hariri, Basil Flayhan, Samir Qassir, George Hawi, Jubran Twayni, and Pierre Gemayel must be brought to justice. Without justice there is no hope for a sound national structure. Why is the tribunal being turned into a barter, unless there are reasons unknown to us, or services being rendered to this or that regional party?

Two: Are you for electing a new president of the republic? It is true that General Lahoud [current president] has constitutional legitimacy, but all parliament members know that he was elected by force, oppression, and threats. His political and ethical legitimacy is gone and there is no hope in a new beginning without bidding farewell to the "extension" [Lahoud's presidency was extended due to Syrian pressure] saga, which has bequeathed all this destruction to the country.

Three: Are you for a new election law to bid farewell to the laws of Ghazi Kanan [Syrian intelligence chief in Lebanon for decades] and Jamil al-Sayyid [Lebanon's security chief under Syrian tutelage] and establish proper parliamentary representation according to the bill presented by the Fouad Butrus committee [parliamentary committee]?

Four: Are you for changing the cabinet in order to prepare for early elections to break the intensity of sectarian and confessional polarization?

Five: Are you against liquidating the Resistance? The Resistance has proven that it is not a militia, but rather a means to defend Lebanon. Instead of fear and distrust, why not have the Resistance be the nucleus of a national guard, one that not only brings the Lebanese together in supporting it, but one which they can also join?

Six: Are you in favor of establishing neighborly relations with Syria while rejecting its patronage and regional domination? Are you against being drawn into the Iranian expansion game or the new Middle East that the American president has turned into a tool to destroy the region?

Seven: Are you against Israeli occupation and do you believe that Lebanon can play a role in reestablishing an Arab consciousness and praxis in order to end the Israeli occupation and reach a just resolution to the Palestinian question?

Seven questions that must be answered all at once, or in one basket as it is usually said, so you may prove to yourselves that you are not tools for external powers that want to turn Lebanon into an arena for regional conflicts. And so that you may prove to yourselves that you learned from—death, war, occupation, and resistance—the lesson of being Lebanese patriots, and want to stop playing the role of war merchants and engaging in bloody mediation in a region filled with tragedies.

Seven answers can be summed up into one answer that privileges the national interest over any other, and privileges national alliance unity over any other alliance. Grand slogans are meaningless if Lebanon is turned into an arena for death. There is no meaning to anything if the land we stand on is gone and we become the dead who dig our own graves.

These answers cannot be postponed. The atmosphere of sectarian escalation is truly suffocating, and muscle flexing has gotten us where we are. There is no way out except in going back to reality and not using words for obfuscation. We are in need of clear and candid words. We must all fully accept the solution in one basket that ends fear and does not allow hot heads to pretend that they can resolve the issue of power with threats or by committing bloody foolishness.

This time we demand to know who stands behind the war that threatens us. If the fate of Lebanon does not interest you, be clear so that we may know who is fighting whom. This time we will not allow anyone to laugh because of our death. They can kill us and they can very well kill Lebanon, but we will not allow them to lie and hide behind false slogans.

It is the moment of truth. Let Hizballah declare that it supports the tribunal and let the "Future" movement [led by Saad Hariri, the son of the assassinated PM] say that it does not want to monopolize [political power], and let's force the General [President Lahoud] to resign and form an expanded government. The issue is that all must declare their intentions. If we cannot save Lebanon because some, or all, perhaps wish to privilege their regional and international bonds over their national ones, then we have to save the truth, expose the game and force the masks to fall.

The basket they are trying to pierce is not the solution. The solution must either be simultaneous, or not at all.

But there are those who pierce the basket, play smart and hide behind the lost confidence and hidden intentions in order to hide their unwillingness to exit the status quo. In doing so they not only pierce the basket, but the entire social fabric, and in doing so expose Lebanon to a sectarian war from which no one will emerge a winner.

This party must stop. Things must be said as they are. Then the great majority of the Lebanese people will discover that what unifies them is much more than what divides them and that they can stop the crime that wants to kill the spirit of this tiny country.

26. LEBANON ON THE BRINK

Fawwaz Traboulsi and Assaf Kfoury

Assaf Kfoury introduces and translates two columns by Fawwaz Traboulsi, which first appeared in Arabic in the Lebanese daily Al-Safir *on November 24 and December 7, 2006.*

In this chapter, historian and long-time political commentator Fawwaz Traboulsi explains that the dangers faced by Lebanon today, when this little country is exposed more than ever to the political storms east of the Mediterranean, are in part the result of its confessional system. This system did not always exist and the Lebanese were not ordained to live in it. In fact, when a majority of the Lebanese unite, as when they overwhelmingly embraced resistance to the Israeli onslaught in July–August 2006, they do so at a spontaneous popular level and across confessional lines, largely ignoring confessional parties and their external sponsors who claim to represent their interests; that is, they do so despite the confessional system and against it.

Lebanese and other communities of the Levant existed for hundreds of years before this peculiarly factious power-sharing formula based on religious denominations was first introduced in the second half of the 19th century, partly dictated by the contest between the declining Ottoman Empire and encroaching European colonial powers. The latter sought out local partners (commercial agents, political allies, consular officers) among co-religionists or members of religious minorities, in exchange for special privileges and protection against Ottoman authorities. This arrangement has been adjusted and readjusted—but never abandoned—after every political upheaval ever since, always at the prodding if not behest of external actors. By tying the fate of the country to external interests, and different ones for different confessional parties, the confessional system belies lofty proclamations by Lebanese politicians about "national independence" and voids that term of its meaning, as pointed out by Traboulsi.

The most recent version of the confessional setup, in place since the Taif Accord of October 1989, which ended the civil war, is a variation of a formula adopted in 1943 when France was forced to grant Lebanon its formal independence: the president of the republic must be a Maronite

Christian, the speaker of the parliament a Shia Muslim, the prime minister a Sunni Muslim, and parliament seats are equally divided between Christians and Muslims, with each of the two blocks divided among various Christian denominations and Muslim denominations in predetermined proportions. Even on the rare occasions when parliamentary candidates representing non-confessional interests are elected, they must fill seats that are allotted to the religious sects to which they belong. This effectively excludes all political parties that are organized on platforms other than the confessional. Thus, for example, the Communist Party has never been represented as such in government in any capacity, even though it is the oldest political party in Lebanon (founded in 1924) and has had a strong presence in labor unions throughout its history.

The first of the newspaper columns by Fawwaz Traboulsi appeared three days after the minister of industry, Pierre Amin Gemayel, was assassinated in broad daylight in Beirut. Gemayel belonged to the Christian Phalangist Party and was part of the March 14 coalition, which supports the current government of Fouad Seniora. The traditional parades on Lebanese Independence Day, which falls on November 22, were canceled and a state funeral was held for Gemayel the next day instead. It turned into a massive anti-Syrian demonstration by several hundreds of thousands in downtown Beirut.

Who killed Gemayel? Walid Jumblatt, a leader of the pro-government March 14 coalition, accuses the Syrian secret services. Hassan Nasrallah, head of Hizballah and a main party in the anti-government March 8 coalition, points his finger in the opposite direction, observing that the main beneficiaries this time are Israel and the US, not Syria. Political assassinations have been far too common in Lebanon in recent years and usually carried out on orders from the outside. Jumblatt and Nasrallah may be short on the whole truth, but both have valid reasons to suspect their external enemies. Jumblatt is publicly reported to be on the assassination list of the Syrian government, and his own father, Kamal Jumblatt, was murdered on Syrian orders. Nasrallah is openly declared to be an assassination target by Israeli Prime Minister Ehud Olmert; his predecessor as the head of Hizballah, Abbas Musawi, was murdered in a raid by Israeli helicopter gunships. In these two cases, as with all other assassinations, the local victim came to represent an obstacle or the "fall guy" for the interests of powerful regional and international state actors. And the Lebanese body politic, instead of rallying to unite and defend itself in times of increased external dangers, is made to expose all the cleavages of the confessional system.

Traboulsi's second column appeared one week after the beginning of an open-ended sit-in in downtown Beirut by the March 8 coalition, including Hizballah, the predominantly Christian Free Patriotic Movement led by former general Michel Aoun, and several extra-parliamentary parties.

The two columns complement each other and can be merged seamlessly, as they explain the many connections between the current crisis and the confessional system, in its external (the first column) and internal dimension (the second). The first column is rendered here as "The Woes of Confessionalism," and the second, with some minor omissions, as "The Internal Crisis."

The Woes of Confessionalism

In 1867, at another time of civil strife in Lebanon, a prominent Lebanese leader regretfully observed about the state of his own society that "tribes that are engaged in killing their own members for sectarian reasons deserve to be subjugated by foreign powers that come to the rescue of one faction against another." This was Yousef Bey Karam, addressing the Algerian Emir Abdel Kader, then in exile in Damascus after his defeat by colonial France.

Today, as we watch confessional leaders in Lebanon holding forth on the meaning of national independence, we cannot but smile with sadness and hope for mercy, for ourselves and for those who believe these leaders and vote for them. They hold forth as if there is no connection between independence, or the lack thereof, and the confessional system, the latter remaining the main factor in creating conditions of subservience to external rulers in Lebanese political life.

From the time that Yousef Bey Karam took notice of the golden rule connecting internal sectarian divisions and external domination, the Lebanese have yet to come to their senses and desist from this odious practice. Confessional leaders keep looking to the outside for protection against impending marginalization, for maintaining a dominant position, or for keeping a monopoly of wealth and power against other confessional leaders. Seeking external support usually results in blunting internal dialogues and concessions to domestic opponents, which often exacerbates civil conflicts and in turn facilitates further external interference.

We must recognize that Lebanese parties have sought arms or external help, or both, in order to impose themselves on a rigid and factious political (and socioeconomic) system that treats citizens differently, with different rights and privileges. In recent decades, major components of Lebanese society have thus achieved political and socioeconomic ascendancy by force of arms and reliance on outside powers. In this way, for example, we can view the bloody events of 1958, pitting the Christian-dominated government of the Lebanese president Camille Chamoun against a coalition of parties representing mostly Sunni (and, to a certain extent, Druze) elites, which resulted in the empowerment of the latter within the confessional power-sharing system. Similarly, we can view the civil war of 1975–1990 as the means by which Shia elites acquired greater participation in the system, leading to a more equitable overall balance between Christians and Muslims in government institutions.

The question of Lebanese independence can never be separated from the three-way interaction of regional and international forces in which Lebanon has been caught since the colonial fragmentation of the Levant in 1920. Time and again in this history, two main regional actors reach an understanding of sorts, usually facilitated by a third international actor, which in turn imposes a settlement on the Lebanese. An accord between two major regional parties, coupled with international sanction, then allows for finalizing a new local arrangement and providing it with guarantees.

Thus, in 1943, Egypt under Prime Minister Mustafa Nahas Pasha, supported by a Britain eager to evict France from the region, reached an understanding with the Syrian national movement, which had sought independence from France and union with Lebanon. In this context, an agreement was reached between Lebanon and Syria (and also between Bechara al-Khoury and Riad al-Solh, soon to be the president and the prime minister of Lebanon, respectively) that came to be known as the Lebanese National Pact. And again, in 1958, an understanding between the United States and the United Arab Republic under Gamal Abdel Nasser permitted an end to the civil war in Lebanon and the selection of General Fouad Chehab as president in succession to Camille Chamoun, together with a renewal of the National Pact and an adjusted confessional setup.

So long as the logic of the confessional system prevails, when conditions are lacking for an agreement between regional and international actors, as was the case after the October 1973 war, the Lebanese proxies fail to reach a settlement among themselves and then resort to armed confrontation. Such was the explosion of 1975–1990. They then failed because some of their leaders continued to rely on the outside to extricate their parties from the internal stalemate or because they were under the illusion that the external party to which they were connected would likely prevail in the regional or international balance of forces.

There is no need to dwell at length on the different discourses on national independence emanating from different Lebanese parties, all couched in absolutes and expressing inflexible ultimate goals. In an increasingly interdependent world where larger countries, such as Russia, for example, with its enormous natural resources and industrial potential, still struggle to achieve a margin of independence via-à-vis the American empire, there are politicians in tiny Lebanon who will not accept anything short of an absolute notion of independence. They talk about complete independence in a country whose economy is almost entirely dependent on the outside, engaged as it is in exporting most of its labor force and importing virtually all material goods, whose national debt is nearly three times its annual GDP (the highest ratio for any country in the world), and where confessional parties are increasingly made to rely on, and do the bidding of, their respective external allies.

Let us, more concretely, consider the question of Lebanon's independence in the context of current regional circumstances. The United States, now bogged down in a bloody occupation in Iraq, is scrambling for new options to realign its policies in the region and cut its losses, especially after the Republican Party setbacks in the most recent midterm elections. American policies are now less predictable and will continue to shift in coming months. Some in Washington still suggest a more aggressive approach to Iran, including bombing its nuclear installations, but others counsel engaging Iran and prodding it to play a special regional role that will help extricate US troops from the Iraqi quagmire. Simultaneously, we are witnessing a complex diplomatic dance between Washington and Damascus, at times aiming at distancing Syria from Iran and encouraging it to play a "positive" role in Iraq, but at other times accusing Syria of terrorism and threatening to bring it to accounts in an international tribunal set up to pursue Rafiq Hariri's killers.

In such circumstances, which are bound to affect the entire region in ways that are difficult to foresee, should Lebanese parties not call for a truce in their internal show of force and take note of the surrounding storms? Should they not take pause and stop betting on illusory victories against each other? Should the little wounded country that is Lebanon not be navigated cautiously through these regional storms? Is it not utter foolishness on the part of some Lebanese players to presume there are two sides—one American-Israeli and one Iranian-Syrian—and that one of the two must be joined? Should they not recognize that in order to prepare themselves for external dangers, there is only one thing that they can truly control: their own internal affairs?

Until now we have lost the battle for independence twice, or more precisely, we have lost two battles for independence in little more than a year. On the one hand, the leaders of the 2005 independence movement against Syrian domination have forgotten the continuing Israeli threat and decided to put their trust in what appears to them to be the juggernaut of the American empire after September 11. On the other hand, the leaders of the May 2000 liberation of southern Lebanon from Israeli occupation and the July 2006 resistance to Israeli aggression have failed to convince the rest of the Lebanese that they can act independently of Syrian priorities. The negotiations for a government of national unity broke down because each of the two camps sought to block the dictates of the other camp's external ally. The two camps thus acted as if Lebanese policy and decision are fated to follow external dictates. And both camps demonstrated that their "independence" is a total sham.

The Internal Crisis

The current polarization in Lebanon cannot be limited to the proclaimed political disagreements—be they on the international tribunal pursuing the Hariri assassination, or on the makeup of a national unity government, or on the extent to which local parties are goaded by external and regional forces. These should all be read as a cipher, for us to decode the underlying socioeconomic conflicts in relation to the various confessional communities. Not only because politics in Lebanon has become inextricably tied to the confessional system, but also because the two opposite camps have markedly different confessional compositions.

Whereas the weight of the Maronite community is about equal in both camps, the vast majority of the Shia community (represented by Hizballah and Amal) support the March 8 coalition, and the vast majority of the Sunni and Druze communities support the March 14 coalition.

The March 8 coalition wants changes in government and national policies; the March 14 coalition is opposed. The side demanding changes include two mass movements that are relative newcomers to the fray of Lebanese politics: Hizballah and the Free Patriotic Movement (FPM), led by former Army General Michel Aoun. Both of these movements were marginalized or kept away from politics during the time of Syrian domination in Lebanon, in the years following the 1989 Taif Accord. During that time, while the FPM was excluded from politics by the forced exile of its leaders or by internal repression, Hizballah was almost entirely engaged in resisting the Israeli occupation in southern Lebanon. This marginalization had similar implications for the social makeup of both movements, as they both drew their support from segments of an emerging middle class and from inhabitants of disfavored suburbs surrounding the capital. Both parties drew closer as their constituencies had both been largely kept away from government institutions and the civil service, and both had mostly drawn their livelihood from the private sector.

This has been the foundation of the alliance between Hizballah and the FPM, which are now united in their demand for a bigger role in national affairs, as they both call for a national unity government in which they together control a blocking third of the ministerial seats. This demand from the FPM for a larger share in power responds to a profound desire among many Christian sectors to reverse the marginalization they have endured since the years of Syrian domination. The same demand from Hizballah is a means to shield itself from various political plans to disarm it and diminish it after Israel's massive military onslaught in July August 2006 failed to achieve the same goals. Both the FPM and Hizballah now insist on their right to be at the center of the executive branch and to help determine the conditions under which a new electoral law will be enacted and a new president of the republic elected.

The Taif Accord of 1989 redistributed power among the three top positions in the confessional setup, namely, those of the president of the republic (Maronite), the prime minister (Sunni), and the speaker of parliament (Shiite). While restoring some of what the presidency lost after the Taif Accord, and with it a sense of Christian empowerment, will have to await a new electoral law and the next presidential elections in November 2007, the current contest on the distribution of ministerial posts between the two opposite camps will affect immediately the balance between the three centers of power in the confessional setup. The issue of the "blocking third" did not raise much of a debate before the May 2005 parliamentary elections; consisting of ministers allied to the presidency, the "blocking third" was considered a measure accorded to the president to compensate for his curtailed power after the Taif Accord, as the council of ministers practically became the main framework within which he could exercise his prerogatives. In the current crisis, however, granting a "blocking third" to Hizballah and its allies may introduce a new element in the confessional power-sharing formula—namely, it will give more weight to the Shia community within the council of ministers, hitherto considered a preserve for Sunni political influence.

Regardless of how much the preceding is a factor in causing it, the current political crisis cannot be resolved by simply inviting ministers affiliated with the March 8 coalition to rejoin their posts—and then insisting that it will be "business as usual" in government affairs. While the two sides raise the stakes in their declarations and denunciations of each other, they naturally compete in repudiating any hint of civil strife and inviting everyone to bury the idea, as if it is merely a contest of slogans and public pronouncements.

What is particularly worrisome in all of this is that the confessional system has reasserted itself anew as a regime of obstruction and gridlock. It has frustrated the different confessional groups partaking in it, thus encouraging them to finagle ways around the Taif Accord and the constitution, while they all proclaim their commitment to both and compete in denying the need for any changes in either.

The confessional system has shown once more the extent to which it is divorced from ordinary people's concerns. It forces people to squeeze out their rights—if it accords them such rights at all—through the pinholes of their confessional affiliations. It is a system in which confessional leaders, whose function in times past was to distribute benefits and services to their respective communities, are now in effect left to distribute the debts of a stagnant and heavily indebted national economy.

Something has to give. The deadlock has to be broken. In the past, the Lebanese polity solved its crises by removing people through internal killing or forced emigration, or else by having besieged internal parties impose themselves through force of arms and recourse to their external allies. Will the current crisis be resolved in the same way? Do we change the system of government or do we change the people it governs? This is the fundamental question. And only by addressing it squarely can a dialogue between Lebanese parties prevent the catastrophe.

27. THE NEW SECTARIAN WARS OF LEBANON

As'ad Abukhalil

Lebanon after the Israeli war of the summer of 2006 is not what it was before. The repercussions of that war will be felt for years to come. It has changed the perceptions of the various groups and sects in Lebanon, and it has added distrust among the groups in conflict. Hizballah accused its rivals in Lebanon of either wishing for an Israeli victory or of actually working for it (in the case of Walid Jumblatt). And those who were relying on the US/France/Saudi Arabia had to figure out a way to use the war to undermine support for Hizballah.

There was hope in Israel and the US that Hizballah would be eliminated after a few days of war, and then there was hope, nurtured by the propaganda of the Hariri camp in Lebanon and the deliberate delays in relief and reconstruction by the government, that the Shiite population of southern Lebanon would turn against Hizballah. When all that failed, the March 14 camp resorted to blatant sectarian agitation and mobilization, after giving up all hope of delivering Shiite support for the ruling coalition.

Of course, the very nature of Hizballah lends itself to sectarian accusation. The party adheres to an ideology that comes out of Khomeini's Vilayet al-faqih concept, rooted in Twelver Shiite tradition. The Shiite sectarian composition of Hizballah is thus not coincidental. Furthermore, Hizballah could not, and maybe did not want to, extricate itself from the sectarian alliances of the Iranian regime. Many Sunni Arab and Arab nationalist critics of Hizballah wonder why the party has not been critical of the Shiite parties in power in Iraq, since they serve as enforcers of the American occupation. In that regard, Hizballah facilitated the endeavors of the sectarian ruling coalition.

For the first time in the history of the Arab–Israeli conflict, Arab regimes came out publicly—albeit timidly—if not actually in support of Israel, at least in opposition to Hizballah. The Saudi, Egyptian, and Jordanian governments expressed criticisms of Hizballah, although they later had to distance themselves from their own statements or reverse positions altogether. In the case of Saudi Arabia, the government announced sudden gestures of charity in the hope of erasing the bad traces of its earlier statement in which a "Saudi source" criticized the "blameworthy consequences" of Hizballah capture of the Israeli soldiers. The Lebanese allies of Saudi Arabia, especially Saad Hariri, who spent the month of the war touring foreign capitals, ostensibly to secure a cease-fire for Lebanon, relied on the Saudi position to put more pressure on Hizballah.

The war broke taboos in Lebanese politics: it allowed the allies of the US and Saudi Arabia to begin a campaign not only against Hizballah but also against the very notion of resistance to Israeli occupation and aggression. The rhetoric of the Phalange Party and of the clients of Israel during the years of the Lebanese civil war was adopted by the March 14 movement, and also—just like Bashir Gemayel—in the name of sovereignty and independence. But as much as Hizballah tried to argue that the line of demarcation in Lebanese politics is politics, the more the March 14 movement argued that the lines are sectarian, and that the Lebanese are basically united against the Shiites, who are aligned with Iran and Syria.

But the Israeli war on Lebanon did not create a two-front confrontation in Lebanon; it merely reinforced the nature of the external links of the local combatants. There has always been a debate in Lebanon (and by experts on Lebanon) whether any of the Lebanese wars is due to indigenous, local factors or to outside conspiracy—be it American or Iranian. Lebanese sectarian factions have never hesitated to invite outside powers into the fray in order to bolster their own positions. The Israeli war on Lebanon did not start the Lebanese conflict; it merely capitalized on it, and compounded it. Likewise, Israel was never a bystander to the Lebanese wars—not having financed and armed a variety of right-wing factions, all the way from the 1950s and the parliamentary campaigns of Phalange.

The Sectarian Wars of 2007

Lebanon in 2007 seems more on the verge of civil war than in any year since 1991, when the civil war ostensibly ended. At times of intense conflict in Lebanon, a variety of internal and external factors seem to converge to paint a bleak picture for Lebanon's future. But the eruption of civil strife is not inevitable; Lebanon has exhibited an ability to stay on the verge of civil war for years. For much of the 1960s and 1970s, social and political conflict was so intense that predictions were frequently made about the inevitability of civil war, which officially started only in 1975—although there were earlier "rehearsals" (as Lenin called the 1905 revolt in Russia).

The US has a big stake in Lebanon. The failures of US policies in Iraq put a direct emphasis on Palestine and Lebanon, in the hope of achieving for Bush a victory that has eluded him in Iraq. The Bush doctrine needs a new arena. The noisy and massive demonstrations that followed the assassination of Hariri created a deep split in the country's social and political landscape. No more is the classic Christian–Muslim divide relevant; nor the narrow Sunni–Maronite divide, which dominated the squabbles of Lebanese political elite in pre-1975 Lebanon. The two new camps have crystallized along lines that are rather new to the history of Lebanese conflict.

Origins of Sunni–Shiite Conflict in Lebanon

The conflict between the Maronites and the Druze is the major fissure of 19th- and 20th-century Lebanese history. The Maronite–Druze mountain war of 1983 was one of the bloodiest and most savage chapters of the Lebanese civil war. But new forms of sectarian conflict seem to be shaping up. Not that the old conflict has subsided or evaporated: Lebanon lends itself to dramatic and sharp changes in alliances and stances, but sectarian leaders and warlords often resume their past sectarian positions. Revenge and counter-revenge have been part of the play book of Lebanese sectarian leaders.

But in 2007, especially with the December birth of the opposition movement, a new discourse spread in Lebanon. The beleaguered Seniora government was facing strong pressures from an opposition movement that—while dominated by Hizballah—included various sectarian groups, though Sunni representation was weak. Under that pressure, and when the opposition was considering storming the official headquarters of the prime minister, the Hariri camp resorted to what had been perfected under Rafiq Hariri: When in a position of weakness, the best comeback is narrow sectarian agitation and mobilization. Rafiq Hariri mastered that trick back in 1998, when the new president Emile Lahoud selected Salim al-Hoss as prime minister. But Hariri began much earlier when he worked with the Syrian *mukhabarat* in Lebanon to marginalize and exclude rival Sunni politicians. In all his battles with the Maronite presidents (from Elias Hrawi to Emile Lahoud), Rafiq Hariri portrayed the conflict in sectarian terms: he accused the president of trying to weaken the office of the prime minister. In the Lebanese political climate, this language is easily deciphered. Though to be sure, Rafiq Hariri never resorted to the blatantly sectarian language that is being used in Lebanon today by his successors and inheritors.

This particular crisis in the relationship between the Sunnis and Shiites, or their representatives, began in the last election of 2005. It was Saad Hariri's first hands-on experience with the nitty-gritty of Lebanese political life. Hariri grew up in Saudi Arabia for much of his life and later managed his father's businesses from Saudi Arabia. He did not know much about Lebanese politics, and had to be tutored in the Beirut accent. After all, like his Sidon-born father, he had to emerge as a leader of Beirut. But Hariri had three advantages that his father had also used in his political ascendancy: 1) the unlimited use of cash not only for campaign expenses, but also for bribing voters and political leaders; 2) the reliance on foreign powers—his father had the Syrian regime to rely on, in addition to Saudi Arabia and others, while Saad Hariri has France, Saudi Arabia, and the US, primarily; 3) the resort to narrow and acute sectarian agitation and mobilization in order to ensure the needed majority control in the parliament. Hariri cultivated support among some of the most extreme bin Ladenite Sunni fundamentalist groups, especially in the north and the Beqaa regions.

But the Hariri family alone cannot be blamed entirely for the sectarian conflict. The Lebanese political system as set up by the French in 1926, even after the so-called Taif reform of 1989, reinforces the sectarian affiliations of the citizens. A citizen is only dealt with by the state according to his or her sectarian affiliation, through their sectarian representatives. The Taif reforms did not alter or change these fundamentals; they merely changed the terms of the formula according to which political powers (and benefits) are distributed among the various sects to reflect the changing demographic realities of society.

Saad Hariri inherited not a national leadership but a very blatantly formed sectarian camp that had been gradually built and cultivated by his father. But lacking the political skills of his father, and lacking the support of the Syrian troops in Lebanon (which had installed Rafiq Hariri back in 1992), Saad Hariri needed sectarian agitation and mobilization more than his father. Furthermore, just like the Saudi king, he needed legitimization from Sunni clerics in order to build a bridge between a dynasty not known for piety or religious dedication and a popular base that cares about religio-political legitimization of political actions and alliances. Hariri spent millions in the campaign and had the assistance of the Sunni Mufti (who had been handpicked by his father) to ensure the political loyalty and subservience of Sunni clerics around the country. Those who did not toe the line would be dismissed, as was the case in December when a Sunni cleric was suspended by the Mufti for deviating from the Hariri family line.

And in tracing the origins of the Sunni–Shiite political conflict in Lebanon, one has to take into consideration the long legacy of anti-Shiite Wahhabi doctrine, which in principle treats Shiism as infidelity. The anti-Shiite literature of Wahhabism was always around, thanks to the lavish propaganda budget of the House of Saud (especially during the reign of King Fahd, who had more than one reason to give the kingdom's clerical establishment extravagant funding for propaganda, especially during the cold-war years when such expenditure was regarded approvingly by the US).

The Recent Crisis and the Decline of the Cedar Revolution

The events of December 2006 ran counter to the US media coverage of the cedar revolution that was dear to the heart of George W. Bush. Images of a united Lebanese people were replaced with images of divisions and demonstrations and counter-demonstrations. The Bush administration could not celebrate the victory of its doctrine in Lebanon: as in Iraq, early reports were quite misleading. The ability of America's allies to prevail was thwarted by the deep political and sectarian divisions in Lebanese society. The defection of Michel Aoun from the ranks of the March 14 movement also dashed the hopes of those who wanted to isolate the Shiites and portray them as less Lebanese than other Lebanese (although such articles continue to run in Hariri's newspaper, *Al-Moustaqbal*, especially those of Nasir al-Asad, a former leader of the Communist Action Organization who joined Rafiq Hariri's cause in the 1990s).

The US wanted to push its agenda in Lebanon, taking advantage of a new reality: No longer did it have to rely on the Maronite political establishment; here was a golden opportunity to act more realistically in a country with a Muslim majority. The Hariri family moved Sunni public opinion (or some 80 percent of it, according to public opinion surveys) toward the right-wing agenda of the traditional Maronite political movement in Lebanon. Even the slogans about "sovereignty" and "independence" of Lebanon—consistently used not so much to achieve real independence or sovereignty for Lebanon but to align Lebanon with Western countries, and to distance the country from either Nasser's Egypt or, more recently, from Syria. In Lebanon, all sides object to the violation of sovereignty but only when perpetrated by outside powers who sponsor and support their rivals. Thus, the March 14 movement objects to interventions by Iran and Syria, but not by Saudi Arabia, Egypt, the US, France, and (behind the scenes) Israel. Conversely, Hizballah and its allies don't object to interventions by Iran and Syria, but to interventions by the US-led coalition that sponsors and supports the March 14 movement.

How does one explain the conflict in 2007? It is not easy to borrow the terms of civil war. We can't talk about left vs. right. The Aoun movement, for example, judging by its economic program, is to the right of all factions and political parties in Lebanon. Furthermore, the so-called Socialist Progressive Party and the Democratic Left Movement are aligned with the Hariri dynasty's right-wing movement. And Hizballah can't be said to be leftist when the party has disregarded the cause of socioeconomic justice in Lebanon. And the Muslim–Christian label of the Lebanese conflict does not apply either, because both sides of the political divide in Lebanon have a share of the Christian community and its political representatives.

But it would not be inaccurate if we underline the political salience of the Sunni–Shiite political conflict in Lebanon. According to various public opinion surveys in Lebanon, Hizballah and Amal command the loyalty of no less than 95 percent of all Shiites. Similarly, the Hariri-led Future Current commands the loyalty of somewhere between 80 to 85 percent of all Sunnis. Furthermore, the political role of the Christians has declined sharply over the years, especially after Taif and after the consolidation of the Hariri rule in cooperation with the Syrian regime. (This, of course, is also related to the demographic decline of the Christians in Lebanon; they now constitute no more than 25–30 percent of the population, though the Lebanese republic was founded on the assumption of a Christian majority.)

In the two opposing camps in Lebanon today, one group has more weight than the others: the Hariri faction in the March 14 movement, and Hizballah in the opposition. But the narrow sectarian divide does not shape and determine the entire course and orientations of the conflict. To be sure, outside powers are fueling and aggravating the Sunni–Shiite conflict because it is effective in undermining non-Shiite support for Hizballah. The Hariri camp wants to stress the sectarian nature of the conflict partly to serve the regional US–Saudi agenda to split Arab public opinion, and partly to drive a wedge between Sunnis and Shiites within Lebanon, in order to portray Hizballah as a mere tool of Iranian foreign policy. On the other side, Hizballah wants to belittle the sectarian nature of the conflict, partly to serve the Iranian agenda of avoiding that conflict at all cost, and partly because Hizballah wants the support of (Sunni) Arab public opinion. The fear of this conflict has tied Hizballah's hands: some allies of Hizballah wanted to push things, for instance, by storming into the headquarters of the prime minister to force him out of government altogether. At the same time, the momentum of Sunni sectarian agitation by the Hariri camp strengthened the position of the government because it succeeded in providing the prime minister—a man who never had popular support, since as minister of finance he had presided over unpopular measures affecting the lives of working people and the poor—with a sectarian cover of protection.

The Hariri family relied in its sectarian endeavor on the clerical Sunni establishment in Lebanon, especially the Mufti, who publicly expressed his support of Seniora through sectarian demonstrations. Saudi Arabia was also glad to be spreading its Wahhabite warning against Shiism, on religious and political grounds. It also pleased Saudi Arabia that its sectarian agenda was fitting into US foreign policy in terms of countering what is seen as Iranian regional influence. If the Saudi royal family was very close to the Saudi citizen Rafiq Hariri, it has gotten even closer to Saad Hariri, who closely coordinates his actions and policies with the royal family. (It was they who decided that Saad, and not his older brother Bahaa, should inherit Rafiq's political position.)

But Saudi and US designs in Lebanon have not gone smoothly; there was little success in installing a government loyal to the Hariri family without dissent from the Shiite and Christian communities. The cedar revolution did not work as planned; the Lebanese people did not rally around their flag, and the cracks within the ruling group appeared before long, especially when the influential Aoun movement defected and later aligned itself with Hizballah. American and Saudi policies insisted on keeping Fouad Seniora in his position, even as Hizballah and its allies lost confidence in Seniora, especially as his closeness to the US and even Israel became all too clear after the Israeli war.

But the opposition's attempt to topple the government with the massive demonstrations in December 2006 did not work according to plan either. The demonstrations succeeded in turning out an unprecedented number of people, never seen before in Lebanese history (even if estimates of the crowd are never accurate, since all sides exaggerate the number of their followers in those events). And while General Aoun remains the most influential Maronite leader in Lebanon, there is some evidence in public opinion surveys that he may have suffered due to his alliance with Hizballah, even after the Israeli war on Lebanon, which the ruling group in Lebanon wanted to blame on Hizballah's miscalculations. Hizballah and their allies did not anticipate how much the regional and international backers of Seniora rely on his leadership to pass their own policies and measures, and how far Seniora and his allies in the Hariri family would go to engage in sectarian agitation and mobilization to bolster his political support and standing. By early 2007, the confrontation between the two sides seemed to reach a standstill, although Hizballah continued to threaten further protests.

Those who expected a new Lebanon to emerge out of the withdrawal of the Syrian troops from Lebanon were mistaken. The new Lebanon resembles—in features and in details—the old Lebanon, especially in the extreme, narrow sectarian calculations of the political leaders of all its sects. The major difference that emerged from the conditions that predated the withdrawal of Syrian troops is simply that Syrian political domination has been replaced by US–Saudi domination. The speaker of parliament told me that the French ambassador in Lebanon told him back in 2005 that France was opposed to his election as speaker of the Lebanese parliament. The US interfered in that same year with the electoral law, and it pressured the Hariri family and its allies to reject all attempts to postpone the parliamentary elections in order to capitalize on the tides of public sympathy for the March 14 movement following the assassination of Rafiq Hariri. The UN used its office in Lebanon to treat the country as one not fully independent, and instead as in need of a "mandate"—akin to the arrangements once sanctioned by the League of Nations. The representative of the UN secretary-general in Lebanon, who appears more than willing to serve US interests in Lebanon and beyond, regularly discusses in great detail domestic issues with all Lebanese political leaders.

The investigation of the assassination of Rafiq Hariri has dragged on, but continues to serve the US interest as leverage against the Syrian government. Leaks and unprofessional practices have characterized the investigation so far, especially in the phase under Detliv Mehlis, who publicly accused the Syrian government of responsibility even before completing the investigation. As of early 2007, there were no signs of progress in the investigation, and the new UN investigator was rumored to be leaving his post.

A Rehearsal for Civil War

The month of January 2007 brought matters into focus. The fears of many Lebanese were confirmed when acute sectarian tensions came to the surface as the opposition escalated its protests in Beirut and around the country. But the government of Seniora had become part of Bush's vision for the Middle East and could not be brought down by protests in the street. So when the Paris III Conference was hastily rearranged to be held in France rather than Beirut, it was a signal from the Bush administration (along with the various government and world organizations that take such signals from the administration) that the so-called international community stood behind the Seniora government, against its enemies and critics. With all the failures in Iraq, the Bush administration was adamant about keeping Abu Mazen and Seniora in place; their removal would signal failures beyond Iraq, and that might have domestic consequences in the US.

The atmosphere in early 2007 also showed that the external dimensions of the Lebanese civil conflict are strong and deep: an end to the Lebanese crisis was being negotiated in meetings at the highest levels between Saudi and Iranian officials. The meetings confirm what many Lebanese suspect: that Lebanese factions owe allegiance to governments outside of Lebanon, slogans about sovereignty and independence notwithstanding. The Saudis (on behalf of the US—and Israel is never far behind) control the Hariri camp, while the Iranians are very closely aligned with Hizballah. The Syrian government may have become far less relevant after the withdrawal of Syrian troops from Lebanon in 2005.

But the events of January also confirm that the fundamental axis of conflict in Lebanon is the Sunni–Shia divide: this raging conflict now supersedes all others. So much so, that *Al-Diyar* ran a headline suggesting that the country's Christians are now themselves split into Sunni Christians and Shiite Christians (which underlines the marginal political role of the Christians in present-day Lebanon). The Sunni–Shiite divide is very likely to remain the most important determinant of conflict (and of politics in general) in Lebanon. Immigration, demographic changes, and the rearrangement of political power after Taif have all contributed to the marginalization of Christians in Lebanon.

And the Bush administration, for reasons that have little to do with Lebanon and much to do with Iraq, is showing tremendous interest in Lebanon. The US has been working to tip the balance in favor of its allies. But Lebanon has always frustrated US plans: the grandiose designs of the US and Israel themselves hit the rocks and barriers of sectarian divisions. Furthermore, the rival of US allies in Lebanon, Hizballah, is one of the largest and best-organized political parties in the region; it is also the best armed and financed.

US plans don't seem to work for Lebanon, and it is likely that the failures of 1958 and 1984 will be repeated. Lebanon, despite its ostensible Western orientation, has not proven to be an easy target for US plans for the Middle East. It is not clear that the civil war will resume, and it is less clear whether outside intervention will calm things down. US designs in the Middle East and the rush by Arab governments to appease the US will only compound Lebanon's troubles. The Lebanese people have rarely succeeded before in confronting foreign intervention with national unity. Sadly, national unity is as elusive a goal as it has ever been.

28. PEACE OR PERPETUAL WAR

Azmi Bishara

This article was originally titled "Precarious Clarity" and published in Al-Ahram Weekly *online (28 September–4 October 2006).*

Israel's invasion of Lebanon ushered in a new regional situation that has made the choice between war and peace extremely clear. This clarity is troublesome for Israel, which is unwilling to pay the price of either choice. As a result, the US, Israel, and a number of Arab governments are feverishly trying to cloud that clarity, and their instrument for doing so, at least at the PR level, is the Palestinian settlement industry: that inexhaustible source of quasi-initiatives, pseudo-dialogues, confidence-building "processes," and efforts to find a way back to the roadmap. Meanwhile Palestinians wake up every morning to find that they need a new map just to get to work, so frequently does the terrain change with all the additions to the separation wall and the barricades and checkpoints that appear from one day to the next.

It was no coincidence that Olmert shelved his agenda for unilateral disengagement from the West Bank as soon as the war in Lebanon ended. I say "agenda" because this scheme for dictating a permanent border intended to annex the whole of Jerusalem and large chunks of the West Bank to Israel hardly merits being ranked as a political platform, there being no others in sight as far as the Palestinians are concerned. Why was it no coincidence? Because to the Israeli mind, the withdrawal from Lebanon in 2000 was a unilateral action: it was then that it first occurred to the Israelis that unilateralism was a feasible alternative to diplomatic settlements. Coming in the wake of the collapse of negotiations with Syria, the withdrawal is—rightfully—regarded by Arabs as a retreat forced upon Israel by the liberation struggle. The Israelis, however, look back on it as a voluntary action undertaken independently of any settlement or peace agreement, even though they could have just as well withdrawn from Lebanon within the framework of a settlement with Syria that resolved the question of the Golan Heights. In this sense, Barak rather than Sharon was the father of unilateral withdrawal.

The unilateral disengagement from Gaza was Israel's response to the collapse of Camp David II, which took place under Barak, and the subsequent desire, under Sharon, to block all avenues to any new initiatives, such as the Arab peace initiative or even the roadmap that Likudist Israel wanted to wriggle out of in spite of how damaging it was for the Arabs.

Israel had staged a complete withdrawal from Sinai as the price it had to pay for eliminating one of the key Arab states from the equation of the Arab–Israeli conflict. Since then, Israel's negotiating behavior can be summed up as follows: If any of the remaining Arab negotiating parties reject Israel's conditions for a settlement and for the amount of occupied territory to be returned in exchange for peace, Israel declares that there is no "Arab negotiating partner." Then it proceeds to execute plans of its own, withdrawing from those portions of occupied territory that it regards as too much hassle because of resistance operations or too burdensome demographically.

But it's not just the unilateralism that those no-longer-existent negotiating partners find so irksome. It is the fact that Israel invariably leaves in its wake some nasty and intolerable problems, such as keeping one last piece of territory under occupation or transforming the territory it withdrew from into a huge ghetto-cum-concentration camp, the ports of entry of which it controls entirely and which it raids or invades with routine regularity since, after all, there was no agreement and there is no peace. In other words, Israel does exactly what it wants.

As differently as the Arabs view the situations in Gaza and in Lebanon, to Israel the reasons its unilateral policy backfired can all be reduced to the same source: the growing impetus of the resistance. If this phenomenon manifested itself in Palestine in Hamas's electoral victory, it drove itself more powerfully home through the bravery and efficacy of resistance forces in Lebanon. Add to this the fact that the Olmert government cannot afford another confrontation with the Israeli right over even the smallest withdrawal from the West Bank when the domestic atmosphere is already charged by the heated controversy over the causes of Israeli failure in Lebanon, and it becomes obvious why the unilateral withdrawal plan from the West Bank has been called off.

Long before this, in Camp David II, Barak overrode the Oslo Accords concluded with Rabin and the Wye River understanding made with Netanyahu. It took only the unilateral disengagement plan to effectively dismantle all previous agreements. At Camp David, Barak declared that he did not want partial, phased agreements, but a once-and-for-all settlement. Yet when those talks collapsed, all previous agreements remained frozen, after which unilateral disengagement came along to effectively bury them. Now, unilateral solutions have fallen by the wayside after having put paid to partial solutions.

But that is not all that is evident in the wake of war against Lebanon. It is also obvious that the politics of brute force has collapsed. One reason that Israel fought an American war in Lebanon was to revive that deterrent power it had depended upon on as long as the Arabs refused to accept its dictates. Yet Israel emerged from that war with the mystique of its deterrent power more shattered than ever. No one in Israel is disputing that Israel failed in the war on Lebanon. Rather the contention revolves around why it failed and whom to hold responsible. The Arabs would do well to bear this in mind, because the very fact that everyone from the far left to the far right in Israel is debating the consequences of failure implies that the war is ongoing, if by other means. Meanwhile, in the Arab world the question of Israeli failure appears not to have been settled, suggesting a strong reluctance on the part of some to give the Lebanese resistance the credit it so fully merits.

A big question mark now hovers over the efficacy of the air force, which has not only been a major component of the Israeli deterrent principle but also a long-fabled instrument of offensive battle against a resistance that enjoys such a broad base of popular support. Israel's air force may be effective against national armies of unpopular governments, but in this short war against Lebanon (albeit long from the Israeli perspective), Israeli air power, in spite of the enormous destruction it wrought, failed to crush the will of the people.

But there's more. The resistance put paid to that fundamental corollary of the Israeli deterrent policy, which is "to export the war to enemy territory and keep it out of Israeli territory." That Israel's air force could do nothing to halt the increasingly heavier missile bombardment of northern Israeli towns and cities eventually compelled Israel to send in land forces, which only exacerbated Israel's military predicament.

Simultaneously, the war put paid to another corollary of Israeli military philosophy: the blitzkrieg principle. Before Lebanon, Israel had always been able to resort to massive tactical bombardment, the immediate destruction of the enemy's line of command, rapid incursion into enemy territory to occupy a strip of territory, and whatever other tactics it took to resolve the battle quickly so as to avoid getting bogged down in an extended war of attrition. The resistance proved true to its definition; by its very nature it is the antibody to blitzkriegs. This should serve as a reminder to those who maintain that the resistance deterrent collapsed upon the Israeli attack of Lebanon.

One after the other, Israel's alternatives collapsed. The politics of force fell to the wayside in Israel's recently botched attempt to resurrect its deterrent strategy and, before this, partial solutions were shunted aside by the unilateral disengagement policy, which, too, now, has been taken off the drawing board. What choices does it have left? Only two: either a just, lasting, and comprehensive peace, or political and diplomatic stagnation that can only degenerate into war and, most likely, a protracted one if its adversaries adopt the strategy of resistance. The very clarity of this choice presents Israel with its foremost strategic dilemma.

If the Arabs are to capitalize on this situation, they should, at the very least, not budge one inch from their initiative for a just and lasting peace. The ball is now in the Israeli court. Any new initiatives or adjustments will merely offer Israel and others an opening to lead everyone down that garden path of diplomatic maneuvers, dialogues over nothing, and visits intended to build up hopes, sow new illusions, and obfuscate self-evident facts. These are the tactics not of dispelling illusions but of dispelling clarity.

This is not to deny that the Arab initiative was ill timed. Coming, as it did, in the post-9/11 furor, it was a sign of weakness. Originating with Saudi Arabia, in deference to a hint from Washington following the wave of anti-Arab and anti-Muslim provocations in the US at the time, it was an image-enhancing initiative, as though it fell upon the Arabs to prove how peace-loving they were. It was a caving-in to blackmail. No wonder it offered the opening for extracting new concessions from the Arabs, starting from their first visits to Washington after adopting this initiative, which ultimately was reduced to little more than a footnote in the roadmap.

This said, it is simultaneously important to recall that Israel issued no positive response whatsoever to the Arab initiative. But, rather than emphasizing this fact, and rather than sticking to the initiative so long as it was out there and, indeed, rather than making Israel's predicament so crystal clear that Israel can't help but face it, we find Arab governments helping to disseminate new illusions.

Meanwhile, there is another fog machine operating in the region: "the Palestinian cause routine." The most obvious examples are Blair's visits to Palestine after the war against Iraq and, again, after the war against Lebanon. Whenever there is a lull between Western military campaigns in this region you know it's Palestinian cause time again. It is a fleeting season, for after a brief flurry of activity and displays of earnest concern, the cause is again put on hold until the next crisis.

These PR routines serve multiple functions. Above all, they work as a kind of antiseptic that cleanses the image of the aggressor as he rallies support for the next round, and they smooth the way for Arab governments, which cannot take part in coalitions or boycotts or sanction campaigns unless some movement is being made on the Palestinian cause. The operative word, here, is movement, as opposed to solution. Movement is better than stagnation. It's all in the "process," they say. Just keep it going, and all will be fine.

According to *Ha'aretz* of September 19, the US advised Israel to stick to goodwill initiatives toward the Palestinian president. Olmert should agree to meet Abu Mazen and, perhaps, release a few Palestinian prisoners, for example. That should be enough right now to enable Arab governments to continue to pitch into the drive to isolate and topple the elected Palestinian government. Instead of making the choices explicit to Israel, Arab governments are helping to make the choices explicit to Palestinian officials who Israel and the US have decided should not have been popularly elected. Those choices are either to recognize Israel and agreements that Israel itself no longer recognizes or to remain under economic blockade.

By playing along with the Palestinian cause routine, the Arabs are helping the US and other powers rescue Israel from the wall it has run up against. This could be a historical watershed, because if Israel were made to choose it would not opt for comprehensive war over comprehensive peace. Major developments in the region have palpably demonstrated that overturning or dismantling an Arab status quo by force produces more dangerous types of enemies for the American and Israeli projects. These types of enemies, moreover, do not offer, nor are they in a position to offer, constructive alternatives for their societies, unlike

Hizballah or Hamas and its allies. These resistance movements are working on the ground in and with their societies and, therefore, are in a position, if they summon the appropriate will and ingenuity, to promote socio-political visions that can take their societies beyond the logic and tactics of resistance to new horizons of peaceful coexistence among diverse political trends committed to national sovereignty and opposed to foreign intervention.

I am unable to recall an occasion in which Israel was so bereft of a political alternative as it is now. This has come at a time when Israel has come face to face with the most crucial decisions ever. Until now, the Israeli leadership has never asked its citizens to choose between a just and lasting peace or lasting warfare. If it were to put the choice before them so succinctly, I have no doubt that the government would be surprised by the numbers of people who would vote in favor of peace and would be willing to pay the necessary price. Sadly, there is no leadership in Israel capable of rising to such a historic moment. Sadder yet are the many Arabs who are denying the results of the war against Lebanon, calling for the resurrection of a dead roadmap and doing whatever else they can to extricate Israel from one of the toughest spots it has ever been in.

29. ALL WARS ARE DIFFERENT: LEBANON, ISRAEL, AND THE MATURING OF THE "GREATER WEST ASIAN CRISIS"
Fred Halliday

The background and development of the "Greater West Asian Crisis" are discussed in Chapter 5 of Halliday's The Middle East in International Relations *(Cambridge University Press, 2005). An earlier version of this article was published by Open Democracy in August 2006.*

All wars are different, but some are more different than others, or so it would seem in the aftermath of the most recent war between Israel and its neighbors. For all that this war, unexpected, but long brewing, and explosive in its consequences, immediate and long-term, bears similarities to other conflicts in the recent history of the region, it is in some very important respects different from, and more than, any of these: it is more than an Arab–Israeli war of the kind seen on five previous occasions since 1948; it is more than another chapter in the wars of Lebanon, which began in 1975–1976 and lasted to 1990; it is more than, but most certainly linked to, the wars that have in different parts of the region ensued from the Iranian Revolution of 1979, in Lebanon, as in Iraq. It is part of a pattern of separate regional conflicts that have come to form over the past decade or so a more integrated pattern, what I have, for want of a better phrase, come to term the "Greater West Asian Crisis."

Although its roots lie in the late 1970s, this latest war, because of its original relation to the conflicts of the rest of the region, marks the beginning of a new phase of uncertainty in the Middle East, not the continuation, let alone the end, of the decades of wars and upheaval that have preceded it. For this reason it is meaningless to ask who has won and who has lost: neither side has gained its maximal goals, but this new phase of conflict has only begun. All the indications are that Israel is preparing for a much-sustained and costly war against Hizballah, under the illusion that it can "finish the job" left undone in 2006, while Iran, Syria, and their allies in the region show no sign of relenting in their hostility to the Jewish state. The conflict is not just one between Israel and an armed group in Lebanon. It is, in one phrase, a war for supremacy and survival in the region as a whole, a war in the newly emerged political and strategic space of Greater West Asia. Its causes, and effects, will be felt throughout this region, from Beirut to Kabul to Mumbai. Perhaps, for all the obvious differences, and certainly on a smaller scale, it resembles more the European war that began in 1914, another regional conflict long planned if suddenly, almost casually, detonated, but which, once started, drew all the major states of the area into its wake, with, in the longer run, dire consequences for many.

The first problem this war poses is that of evaluating how far the distinct conflicts of the region are interrelated. "In the Middle East people always mix everything up with everything else." This familiar complaint, heard as much in the region as outside it, has been often heard in recent decades as politicians and commentators in the Middle East seek to put events of individual countries or sub-regions into some broader regional, if not global, context. The Israelis do it with the references to the Iranian role; President Assad of Syria did so in his speech in Damascus on August 15 [2006], linking the Lebanon war to Iraq.

Such arguments have long been part of the rhetoric of the region: thus the different phases of the Arab–Israeli conflict, the Iran–Iraq wars, revolution in Yemen, civil war in Sudan or Algeria, not to mention oil prices, sundry assassinations, and the rise of Islamist parties and guerrilla groups are all seen as part of some broader pattern, if not "plot," "conspiracy," or agenda. When he invaded Kuwait in 1990, Saddam Hussein talked of "linkage" between this event and the Palestinian intifada that had broken out three years before, while the late King Fahd of Saudi Arabia saw the Iraqi occupation of his neighbor as part of a "Hashemite encirclement" that included Iraq, Jordan, the PLO, and Yemen.

All this assimilation of what are local or national events in a region of 25 distinct states into one single regional pattern is of course itself absorbed, when not compounded, by the immediate relation of what is happening in any part of the Middle East to global or international processes: in earlier decades the cold war; the allegedly global "Zionist" conspiracy; the ever active machinations of the old imperial powers, Britain and France; in more recent years "globalization," seen as just another chapter in the colonial-imperial project; the "Peres Plan" of the early 1990s; the mischievous if not destructive US "democracy promotion" of the early 2000s and much else besides.

Until the 1990s most talk of linkage and of a single, interrelated region was exaggerated. For much of the past half century and more, roughly since the accession of Arab states to independence after World War II, and the first, formative Arab–Israeli war of 1948–1949, the skeptical, disaggregating note has been in large measure correct. The Israelis liked to claim, in their self-serving account of that war, that their new state was "invaded by the armies of eight countries," as if the whole region descended on them. In fact, only three countries, those bordering Palestine, sent forces of any significance—Egypt, Syria, and Jordan. On the other hand, Arab apologists have for decades blamed all the problems of the region, from corruption, unemployment, Islamism, and the lack of democracy on "Zionism," when, in fact, Israel, and the Arab conflict with Israel, have had little or nothing to do with these problems. Major regional events, such as the Turkish–Kurdish war, the Iranian Revolution or the rise and fall of violence in Algeria had little to do with the overall regional context.

The problem is that this time "it"—the assimilation of individual countries and events into a broader and determinant regional pattern—is to a considerable measure true: it is not possible to understand what is happening today, let alone what will happen, between Lebanon and Israel, or in Iraq or Afghanistan, or indeed in Turkey and Libya, without seeing these events in the broader regional and, to a considerable degree, global context, understanding the latter to include US policy on the one hand, and the shifting interests and power of the newer powers, Russia, India and China, on the other. The linkage of the Persian Gulf to the Arab–Israeli conflict, of hitherto almost insulated Turkish politics to those of the Arab world, of long remote Afghanistan to the politics of Iran and the Arab states, and of Pakistan to the Middle East as a whole has, in recent years, become much more of a reality. It is the reality for states who look at each others' nuclear and other programs and react accordingly; it is the reality for opposition and military groups, be they based in Palestine, Lebanon, or Iraq, who operate in different states of the region; it is the reality, very importantly in the age of satellite TV, for public opinion; and it is the reality for the outside world, particularly the US and Europe, who are trying to contain and manage, with almost no success, the tensions in the region. The result is what can be seen on the wide, necessarily very wide, screen on which individual wars and crises can be set, that of the new Greater West Asia.

This time around, therefore, things most certainly are different: most things (if not everything) are linked, in a manner not seen before. It is now possible to talk in a way that is not distorted by regional oversimplification of a crisis and a war that encompasses the region as a whole—the Arab states, Iran and Israel—and indeed of a region that has, over the past decades, changed and increased, so that the events of hitherto remote areas, such as Afghanistan and Pakistan, and hence Kashmir, have for the first time come to be connected to the interstate relations of the Arab world and Israel. Few have noticed how, in some respects, the region has shrunk in recent decades: the affairs of Ethiopia and Eritrea, once seen as part of the Middle East, and involving as they did the Arabs and Israel, are no longer so connected; ditto those of Western Sahara. But the contrary process, of expansion, has been stronger: in effect, since the mid-1990s, a new region, not just a Middle East but a Greater West Asia, has emerged, with the result that what appear as individual conflicts—the US invasion of Iraq in 2003, the crisis in Afghanistan, the Israeli–Lebanese war—are connected and feed off each other.

This change is evident in the new pan-Islamic consciousness that ties Arab with non-Arab causes, and is also evident, at times with dramatic effect, among young Muslims living in Europe. But it is also reflected in the language of US policy: in yet another example of the inanity that Washington seeks to package as grand strategy, Bush has talked of a "greater Middle East initiative." However, his "Greater Middle East," while it includes Afghanistan, as for the purposes of his "war on terror" it must, symptomatically excludes the country more responsible than any for spreading terrorism, Islamic fundamentalism, nuclear proliferation, and base, greedy corruption across the region: the "rogue state" par excellence, Pakistan. If future historians want to know why Iran decided to go ahead with its nuclear program, it is in considerable measure because of the Pakistani decision to explode nuclear weapons in 1998; if they want to know who organized, promoted, funded, and, indeed, still protects the Taliban and al-Qaeda, the answer is the same.

Herein lies the significance of, and longer-term prognosis for, the latest war between Israel and Hizballah. Naturally enough, many in the Arab world and in Israel have set this war in the context of the not less than five earlier Arab–Israeli wars (1948–1949, 1956, 1967, 1973, 1982). There are points of comparison: this war is, in the insecurity it has bred in Israeli cities, and in the connection between external, in this case Hizballahi, intervention and Palestinian resistance, in Gaza, comparable to 1948; insofar as it involves a large-scale Israeli intervention in Lebanon, it is comparable to 1982; insofar as the war has been taken to the Security Council and has been halted in the framework of a UN Security Council resolution, it is comparable to 1956, 1967, and 1973. Many older Israelis and Arabs, not to mention aging Western observers of the region, can be forgiven for feeling they have been here before, as if an alcoholic relative, apparently resigned to staying on the wagon, has decided once again to go back to the bottle: the stomach wrenches, but you certainly know where you are.

But the war of 2006 was not just the sixth Arab–Israeli war, a revival of the Lebanese civil war, or an internationalization of the second Palestinian intifada, let alone another outbreak of the "global war on terrorism," although it was all of the above: rather it was an episode, by far the least bloody, of another, broader and more protracted conflict, one that has multiple centers—Afghanistan, Iraq, now Lebanon, that involves a rapidly shifting coalition of regional states with political and social movements, and which has, we can now see with the hindsight of over two decades, been in the works since the late 1970s, and in particular since the two strategic detonations of 1979, the Iranian Revolution of February and the Soviet intervention in Afghanistan in December.

The shape of this Greater West Asia and the laying down of linkages that were years later to have such lethal effect was already evident more than two decades ago. The Israeli intervention in Lebanon in 1978, first, let it be remembered, intended just to secure territory "up to the Litani," and then encompassed almost all of Lebanon and lasted 22 years, made its contribution, but it was the Iranian Revolution and the subsequent state support provided to the Lebanese Shiites that turned the contained Israeli–Lebanese confrontation of 1978 into the protracted conflict that was to follow, out of which the Hizballah of today has emerged. And it was in that Lebanese war of the 1980s that Iran and its Lebanese allies first engaged, to considerable military and political effect, with both Israel and the US. Meanwhile, to the east of the region, the new Iranian state was being tested and greatly hardened in its eight-year war with Iraq, even as the US and its conservative Arab allies, with a little help, let us now recall, from both Iran and Israel, were brewing the guerrillas and killers of the Afghan mujahideen out of which bin Laden and his associates were to emerge.

The originality of this current conflict is, in several respects, evident enough. First, the major protagonists on the Arab side are not states, but an armed political group, Hizballah, an organization that will prove much more difficult to negotiate with and to reach any binding cease-fire or other agreement with than was the case in earlier wars: in the one earlier Arab–Israeli war in which significant non-state forces were involved, that of 1948–1949, these latter were simply smashed, and dispersed, in the overrunning of Palestinian society by the newly established Israeli state, and only emerged two decades later as an independent force. Secondly, insofar as states are involved on the side of Hizballah, as they most certainly are, in the case of Syria and Iran, they will pursue their involvement in a way quite different from the Arab states in earlier conflicts.

As is evident from the postwar triumphalist declarations of Presidents Assad in Damascus and Ahmadinejad in Tehran, these states are not primarily interested in armistices, frontier delimitation or peace negotiations, but in using the Lebanon conflict to bargain with the US on other issues, and to enhance their nationalist and radical legitimacy at home and regionally. There is no direct or immediate causal relation between the Iranian role inside Iraq, where its influence is far greater than that of the US, the question of Iranian nuclear enrichment, and its support for Hizballah (about which Israelis and Americans are, if anything, rather reserved), but all form part of a broader Iranian drive for regional influence and for confrontation with the US and its major allies—Egypt, Saudi Arabia, and Israel.

Here, however, there arises yet another dimension, at once regional and autonomous, of the current crises, namely the visible tendency in several countries for this enhanced confrontation with the US, Israel, and their allies to be accompanied by conflict between different factions within the Middle East itself. This is evident in both Palestine, where a conflict between Hamas and Fatah has been looming since the elections of early 2006, and in Lebanon itself, where the war of the summer was preceded, and followed, by confrontation when not outright conflict, between the pro-Syrian bloc of Hizballah and its allies on one side, and the anti-Syrian alliance of Maronites, Sunnis, and their allies on the other. In both cases, regional wars and external pressures, as well as encouragement from the US to one party in the conflict, have contributed to the tension.

But the most important and ominous intra-popular conflict accompanying the Greater West Asian crisis has little to do with the machinations of Washington or Israel, and is less likely to be contained by political compromise: namely the radically new spread of direct conflict between Sunni and Shia Muslims. This is evident most of all in Iraq, where what began in 2003 as a largely Sunni and former Ba'athist rising against the American forces and their Iraqi allies developed by mid-2006 into a multisided conflict in which Sunni and Shia forces were in conflict with the Americans but also increasingly with each other. By early 2007 it was estimated that up to two million people had been displaced by the intercommunal war, one million inside Iraq and another million forced into exile, and dozens were being killed each day in sectarian violence.

This Iraqi sectarian war had, moreover, echoes elsewhere in the region: in the Gulf states, notably Kuwait and Bahrain, relations between the Shia and Sunni populations, respectively a quarter and a half of the total population, worsened. In Lebanon the forward advance of Hizballah during and after the summer 2006 war led to sharper relations with the Sunni population, although not initially direct conflict. In Palestine, where there are no Shiites, supporters of Fatah nonetheless took to denouncing the supporters of Hamas as Shia, because of their links to Iran.

In Syria matters were less overt, but it was no secret that for decades the Sunni majority of the population had resented rule by an Alawite elite, represented in the Ba'ath Party, who had controlled the country since 1963. The one direct challenge to the Ba'athists by the Sunnis, in the form of a Muslim Brotherhood insurrection, was crushed with great brutality in 1982, but two decades later, the Muslim Brotherhood had, once again, gained considerable influence in the country, especially among the Sunni middle classes, and would be the main beneficiary of any fatal crisis of the regime itself. Against this background it was not surprising that some Arab leaders, notably those of Egypt, Jordan, and Saudi Arabia began to warn of the dangers of the advance of Iranian and Shiite power and to present themselves as a "moderate" Muslim bulwark against the advance of the revolutionary Shiite alliance.

At the level at which it was developing in 2006 and early 2007, it was possible to envisage this conflict between Sunni and Shia as becoming the dominant regional fracture in the ensuing period, amidst a withdrawal, at whatever pace, of the American forces from Iraq, the militancy of the Shiites provoked a Sunni response. The form it would take would combine popular, intercommunal conflict, as in Iraq, with interstate rivalry, above all between Iran and Saudi Arabia. Obviously, Iran's nuclear program, and the prospect of Tehran acquiring nuclear weapons, served to fuel the suspicion of many Arab states and raise the possibility that they too would go down the nuclear road.

Here, of course, there were many who, in analysis or rhetoric, sought to argue that this sectarianism had long underlain the politics of the region and that the overt violence of 2006–2007 was a product of deep, atavistic hatreds coming to the surface. Similar arguments were, for sure, heard in regard to the emergence of other sectarianisms in modern times, notably in the former Yugoslavia and in Northern Ireland. Another analysis is possible, which sees the Sunni–Shiite conflict as essentially a recent development, a product of the politics of the past few decades and, indeed, of the growth of the Greater West Asian Crisis itself. Within this perspective, the origins of the conflict, and of Arab–Persian conflict more generally, lie not in ancient hostility and grievance, but in the modern history of the region, in particular the ways in which the twin revolutions of Iraq in 1958 and Iran in 1979 set in motion rivalry and insecurity that were to explode in the Iran–Iraq War of 1980–1988, and again, this time within Iraq, from 2003.

In support of this position, two observations may be in order. First, the actual religious and theological distinctions between Sunni and Shiite are small, far less than those between Catholics and Protestants within Christianity and revolving not so much around questions of belief or even interpretation of holy texts, but around two rival claims to legitimacy and succession in the aftermath of the Prophet Mohammad's death in 632, with Sunnis favoring the Successors or Caliphs, and Shiites seeing succession in the Prophet's son-in-law Ali, the latter's son Hussein, and those who come after them. The death of Hussein at the Battle of Karbala in 661 AD, at the hands of the Umayyad Caliph Yazid, is taken as the founding moment of Shiism, to which all later historical legitimation, and annual mourning ceremonies, refer. One of the major complaints of Sunnis against Shiites is that in their mosques the preachers curse the early successors of the Prophet, the Caliphs revered by Sunnis. But the division in the 7th century did not account for the major conflicts of the

Islamic world over following centuries, as wars between Catholics and Protestants did in early modern Europe.

There were, moreover, forms of coexistence and interaction between the two that find little parallel in Europe: In addition to widespread intermarriage in Iraq and elsewhere, even places of worship associated with one confession were used for religious purposes by followers of the other group. The Sayyidna al-Hussein mosque in Cairo, built by the Fatimids, the Shiite dynasty that ruled Egypt in medieval times, is also revered by Sunnis. On some occasions, the president of the country goes there to pray. The Umayyad mosque in Damascus, the most historically important in the Sunni world, has a section devoted to the commemoration of Hussein, to which Shiite pilgrims from Iran regularly make pilgrimage.

Despite clear communal and religious divisions within Muslim countries, and with Shiites representing about 10 percent of all Muslims, actual and direct conflict between Sunnis and Shiites has, until recently, been remarkable in its absence. What certainly has been observed is differential support by one community or another for, among other things, Arab nationalism, secularism, and the Iranian Revolution: communal loyalty correlates with political position. It has, moreover, been possible to identify particular Muslim ruling elites as either Sunni or Shiite: Sunni in most cases and Shiite in Iran, Yemen, Syria. Yet even here, where a sectarian element clearly entered into the distribution of power, it did not spark a revolt based on sectarianism itself. Thus, in Iran the Kurds are mainly Sunnis, and this no doubt contributed to their resistance to the Shiite state created by Khomeini after 1979. In Iraq, the Shiites rose up in 1991 against Saddam, but this was in conjunction with the Kurds, on a mainly national political basis, even as Saddam replied by crushing the uprising under the slogan *La Shia baad al yaum* [no Shia from now on]. In the case of Iraq, the Sunni monopoly was partly broken once before 2003, in the person of the first president after the revolution of 1958, Abd al-Karim Qasim, who was half Sunni and half Shiite, but seen as favoring the latter.

In recent times, overt conflict and sectarian violence between Sunni and Shia originated first not in the Arab world or in Iran, but further east, in Pakistan and Afghanistan. In the former, it became in the 1970s part of the ideology of militant Sunni groups associated with guerrilla action in Kashmir, and later in Afghanistan, to promote hostility to Shiites, and from the 1980s on there were regular attacks on Shiite mosques in different parts of Pakistan. Later, in the Afghan wars of the 1980s and 1990s, the militant Sunni groups who dominated the mujahideen came to attack the Shiites of Afghanistan as enemies of their cause. Two decades later, however, this conflict of Sunni and Shia has been much more widely distributed across the Middle East, so that while it has no immediate impact on the Arab–Israeli question, it affects Lebanon, Syria, and Jordan and has some consequences, at least in rhetorical form, for the Palestinians themselves.

It is not that "everything"—all conflicts—have been fused into one single axis of violence and rivalry, but rather that the forms of interaction between different conflicts have become closer and more complex. This is above all clear in regard to the implications for the region of the Iraqi civil war, and, perhaps most importantly, in the multiple implications of the Iranian nuclear program. While the latter is seen by Israel as an existential threat to its survival as a state, a perception which the demagoguery of President Ahmadinejad encourages, the Iranian nuclear program is seen in the Arab world, and especially in the Gulf, as directed at them. Individual policies or actions by a single state, or a political and/or armed group have in such a context multiple consequences and may evoke multiple responses. It is as if each state or actor is playing on several chessboards at the same time.

This Greater West Asian crisis is thus more complex, multilayered, and long-lasting than any of the individual crises, revolutions, or wars that have since World War II characterized the Middle East. The current West Asian wars involve a triangular conflict, between Iran and its radical allies on one side (Syria, Iraqi Shiite parties, Hizballah, Hamas), the forces of radical Sunni insurgency, in Iraq and in al-Qaeda, on the second side, and the US and its regional allies on the third. In some cases it is the Iran–US conflict that predominates, as in Lebanon; in others, as in Afghanistan or Saudi Arabia, it is the Sunni–US dimension that has primacy, while in Iraq the triangular conflict is taking every day clearer and more bloody shape, with the US pitted against both Shiites and Sunnis, even as these two communities kill and terrorize each other. It is in this multidimensional context, in some ways like that of Europe in 1914, rather than in the memory of earlier bilateral, Arab–Israeli, wars, that the current Israeli–Hizballah conflict must be seen.

Given the passions and interests involved, and the new complexity of events, it is hardly surprising that few ready solutions are available. Whatever partial solutions or even stopgap measures are available, this one looks destined to run and run. It is a new and indeed more interactive Middle East, but not the one many had hoped to see. Pointless now to ask who has won and who has lost: this game is much longer than four weeks in 2006 in southern Lebanon.

30. WORLD ORDER AFTER THE LEBANON WAR

Richard Falk

There has been much commentary on the significance of the Lebanon war. There is an unresolved debate about whether there was a victorious side in the war, and even about what the idea of victory means. There are various suggestions about how to prevent a new war between Israel and Hizballah, whether by relying mainly on the UN stabilization force or by reviving diplomacy between Israel and its various adversaries. Is it time for Israel and the United States to talk with Hizballah and Hamas? What does the inconclusiveness of the war tell us about the benefits and limitations of military superiority, conventionally understood, in such a conflict? Are questions raised about the nature of power in the setting of conflicts between non-state political movements and a foreign state? Could Israel have used its military capabilities more effectively, or were deeper structural restraints operative? These are all important issues, deserving of reflection and dialogue, and could, one hopes, encourage a turn away from violence by all sides in the search for peace and security.

Beyond these immediate concerns lies the question of world order, and the extent to which some gaps and weaknesses were disclosed by the Lebanon war and its outcome. In a deep sense this question of the shape of world order has been present at least since the collapse of the Soviet Union in the early 1990s. It was given a temporary spin by the first Bush president, George H.W. Bush, who in 1990 introduced the phrase "a new world order" to describe the possibility of using the UN Security Council as an effective instrument of collective security in the aftermath of the cold war. The Security Council was no longer gridlocked by the pervasive antagonism between East and West, as was shown by the success in obtaining a UNSC mandate to reverse Iraqi aggression against Kuwait in the first Gulf war.

It seemed for the first time since the establishment of the United Nations in 1945 that it might be possible to implement with some consistency the Charter promise to protect victims of aggression and conquest by enlisting the world community as a whole in an undertaking of collective self-defense. Of course, the 1991 Gulf War raised doubts as well as hopes. It was far from definite that force was really needed to remove Iraq from Kuwait. There seemed a reluctance in the months prior to the initiation of the war to pursue diplomatic channels or to allow sanctions to operate long enough to achieve an Iraqi withdrawal. Once the Security Council gave its authorization, the conduct of the war, as well as its goals, was shaped by the American-led coalition. This limited UN role was not in keeping with the spirit of the Charter, or with the general expectations about how collective security would operate. Even more questionable, Iraq was made to accept cease-fire conditions that were onerous and included the maintenance of comprehensive sanctions that caused great suffering for the civilian population of the country over the next twelve years. In effect, a punitive peace was imposed under UN auspices, in the context of a society already devastated by war, with its major water purification facilities destroyed.

There were many criticisms of the manner in which the UNSC gave unrestricted discretion to the American-led coalition to take over the conduct of the war, determine its goals, and control the dynamics of post-conflict diplomacy. But the undertaking did effectively restore Kuwaiti sovereignty, and in that sense could in a limited sense properly proclaim "mission accomplished." But no sooner were the guns silent in Iraq than the idea of a new world order was quietly abandoned by Washington, put back "on the shelf," as one senior American diplomat described the new mood. On reflection, the US government seemed reluctant to affirm UN authority to such an extent as the phrase implied, or to find itself assigned unwelcome and costly undertakings (by a more confident Security Council), on behalf of the world community in the future. The American approach to global policy in the 1990s was firmly in a mainstream pragmatic mode, and while the role of the UNSC in legitimating the response to Iraq was useful, there was no disposition among American leaders to embark upon a more idealist statecraft that was built around the implementation of Charter norms and international law, rather than the pursuit of national interests. Kuwait was the special case where the idealistic argument overlapped the realist position, but after the Gulf war it became evident that the rhetoric of a "new world order" might easily take the United States where it had no interest in going. Recalling the 1990s, the more liberal Clinton presidency did a shameless diplomatic dance in 1994 to avoid the word "genocide" since it was feared that would push the US government toward taking protective action in Rwanda.

In any event, subsequent developments during the 1990s moved the United States away from reliance on the UN to address world order challenges. The failure of peacekeeping in Somalia (1993), the non-response to genocide in Rwanda (1994), and the apparent ineptitude of the UN in Bosnia, especially the dismal spectacle of UN peacekeepers standing by as virtual spectators during a series of events culminating in what most of the world regards as the massacre of some 6,000 Muslim males at Srebrenica in 1995. To blame the UN for these world order setbacks is to miss the central point that the UN can only do as much as it is authorized to do by its major members, above all the United States. These developments that did so much to undermine the UN took place during the presidency of Bill Clinton, a moderate, supposedly internationally minded American leader. This new trend reached its climax in 1999 when an alleged imminent threat of ethnic cleansing in Kosovo led to a war under NATO auspices, a "coalition of the willing" led from Washington, engaging in a controversial instance of "humanitarian intervention," undertaken unlawfully without seeking a mandate from the UNSC, which would not have been forthcoming, given the prospect of a Russian, and possibly a Chinese, veto.

In Kosovo, unlike the sub-Saharan African conflicts, there was, as earlier in relation to Kuwait, a convergence of strategic interests and humanitarian goals on the part of the United States and its allies, but unlike Kuwait, there was no strategic consensus supportive of the use of force. The strategic interest had to do with a demonstration of the continued usefulness of NATO, as it approached its 50th anniversary, despite the collapse of the Soviet Union and the disappearance of an external threat directed at Europe that had led to the formation of the alliance in 1949. Russia has strong sentimental and ethnic ties with Serbia, and was not willing to endorse force against the former Yugoslavia, while China, especially after the Gulf war, was sensitive about encroachments on the sovereign rights and territorial integrity of states. In some respects, the Kosovo war, despite the reality of the humanitarian mission of preventing a new cycle of ethnic cleansing, established a dangerous precedent for the use of non-defensive force by states without prior authorization by the Security Council.

This precedent weakened opposition to the more extreme geopolitics pursued by the neoconservative presidency of George W. Bush. This became all too clear in 2003, when the Iraq war went ahead despite the failure of the US and Britain to persuade the Security Council to authorize the use of force and without imminent humanitarian catastrophe as an impetus to action, as in Kosovo. In both these instances, there seemed to be a renewed reliance on traditional alliance diplomacy to pursue a mixture of humanitarian and geopolitical objectives. Rather than a new world order, there was a reversion to an older idea of a world order managed by dominant sovereign states to serve their interests and promote their values. Embarking on the Iraq war was a much more menacing move than the Kosovo war. For one thing, there was no regional support for attacking Iraq in 2003. Even America's strongest regional allies, with the exception of Israel, were opposed to the war. Turkey, generally a follower of American policy in the region, actually withheld its consent from a request by Washington to mount part of the invasion from Turkish territory. Beyond this, there was no convincing reason to make war at that moment against the Saddam Hussein regime, although it was recognized throughout the world to rule in an oppressive manner. In this setting, unprecedented mass antiwar demonstrations occurred in more than 600 cities, 80 countries, involving as many as 11 million people.

At the same time, outside the security domain, there were other ideas being discussed about the changing nature of world order. Some observers expressed the view that the rise of market forces combined with the compression of time and space as a result of information technology and the mobility of international capital was producing a borderless world, leading many to adopt the label of "globalization." Others speculated that the internet was an extraordinary instrument of empowerment that was making the peoples of the world a potential "second superpower" based on the leverage that could be generated by a networked world civil society acting in unison. And still others emphasized the revolutionary relevance of climate change, with its extreme weather in the form of tsunamis, hurricanes, polar melting, droughts, and disease, threatening human catastrophe that could be averted only if effective global governance were established as a matter of urgency.

All of these developments have greatly complicated our understanding of the nature of world order in the 21st century, but we have yet to absorb the implications of the 9/11 attacks on the United States, and the American decision to declare a "global war on terror" in response. The

Lebanon war (as well as that in Iraq) reinforces what I would call the unlearned lessons of 9/11. The particular extremism of the Bush presidency, with its visionary commitment to managing global security and dominating the Middle East, is particularly resistant to an appreciation of the limited usefulness of a traditional state war machine. Such an ideological outlook has led the United States to an unprecedented over-investment in military capabilities, spending more than the rest of the world combined. The irony present here is that despite this dominance as measured by relative state power, the United States has never felt more vulnerable and less secure throughout its history.

The most important of these unlearned lessons relates to changes in the nature of power and security: even the most traditionally powerful state is now vulnerable to a devastating attack by a determined and skilled non-state actor with minimal resources at its disposal. Unlike an enemy state, this adversary is itself basically invulnerable to a debilitating counterattack by military means. Such an actor occupies no territory, and offers no targets, cannot be contained or deterred, and has no leadership that can be persuaded to compromise or surrender. The failure to heed the lesson of 9/11 resulted in relying on a war strategy to address the adversary instead of adapting the response to the distinctive non-state and non-territorial nature of the threat. What was appropriate after 9/11 was not a generalized war, but a set of particularized responses associated with greatly improved international criminal law enforcement, possibly supplemented in exceptional situations by special-forces operations undertaken with the consent of either the territorial government or the UN. Such a police and intelligence approach, to be successful, would need to be combined with concerted efforts to address whatever legitimate grievances had played some part in motivating such extreme violence. Without addressing the just causes of such extremism it is not possible to restore normalcy.

What did the Lebanon war add to this picture? It reinforces in a more vivid fashion and extends to a quasi-territorial domain this new ratio of power with respect to combat between state power and an entrenched non-state adversary with a strong base of popular support. The military might of the state can inflict virtually unlimited destruction and cause great suffering to civilian society, and yet it cannot consistently destroy the capacity of its non-state adversary to strike back, nor can it reliably weaken such an adversary.

Israel over the entire course of its existence had repeatedly defeated and deterred Arab states that had challenged its security in a number of wars. Its military might and skill had been successfully used in the past to achieve a series of political victories in a sequence of wars that expanded its territory, raised its prestige, and intimidated and humiliated its neighbors, while creating a reputation of invincibility. But in this different world order, relying on military muscle against a seemingly weakly armed opponent will not yield a victory, even for Israel. Instead, militarism now exposes the acute political and psychological vulnerability of supposed military powerhouses to the increasingly effective tactics of non-state political adversaries. Of course, both sides learn within their respective paradigms, and strain to adapt. Israel adapts future war plans to overcome failure in Lebanon, while Hizballah tries to anticipate these adjustments in planning to mount an even more devastating resistance in the course of the next flare-up.

In the face of experiences in Iraq and Lebanon, the frustrated states, addicted as they seem to be to military solutions for political problems, are likely to go back to their drawing boards, devising new weapons, doctrines, and tactics, still convinced that in the future it will be possible to restore the relevance of superior military power as measured by wealth and technological capacity. This will be a costly mistake. It overlooks the extent to which war is becoming dysfunctional in the 21st century, wasting incredible amounts of resources that could be put to much better uses in raising living standards and creating a more stable, cooperative world, and thereby undercutting the appeal of extremism and restoring security for the peoples of the world.

If military power is not the answer, or at least less and less of an answer, what is?

It has never been more important to find sustainable solutions to the deep, unresolved conflicts of the Middle East. The problems of Israel could be most reliably addressed by a fair political compromise that acknowledges Palestinian rights, restores Syrian territory, and produces a full withdrawal from Lebanese territory.

The United States could similarly gain security and confidence by disengaging from wars that have no foundation in law or morality, and joining with other countries to protect the societies of the world from extremist violence, constructing arrangements for improved international cooperation and for global governance. It is instructive to take account of the greatest achievement of Europe since 1945, which is not, as generally believed, the high level of economic integration, but rather the truly remarkable establishment of a culture of peace that has made the outbreak of war within the boundaries of the EU virtually unthinkable, relieving the countries of the continent of the burden of heavy defense budgets and overcoming public anxieties about the recurrence of war.

An appreciation of the Lebanon war from the perspective of world order may encourage this perception that the viability of the war system was based on being able to limit the playing field of international conflict to sovereign states exercising governmental control within recognized international boundaries. Even this role for war has been earlier deeply challenged by the advent of weaponry of mass destruction, especially nuclear weapons, the existence of which continues to threaten humanity in a variety of ways.

But with the rise of non-state actors as international players, modalities of war are more and more likely to lead to the persistence of deadly conflict rather than to victory. Doctrines of preemption and preventive war are efforts to pretend that the old pattern of warfare among states can resolve fundamental conflicts. It overlooks the stark reality that a small group of extremists with no weapons were able on 9/11 to inflict more symbolic and substantive harm on the most powerful state in the world than had ever been done by a foreign state. It is this potency of non-state extremism combined with the relative political impotence of state war-making that describes truly the "new world order" of the 21st century. It can become the occasion for peace and prosperity, or it can, if present trends persist, produce a slide toward perpetual warfare and an enveloping sense of chaos.

All in all, the Lebanon war is likely to be remembered not for the "birth pangs of a new Middle East" (as Condoleezza Rice put it), but as one of the early indications of death tremors for a system of world order that had long grown accustomed to accepting the institution of war as the inevitable basis of stability and change in relations among sovereign states. We need to awaken to the reality that we are no longer living in a world where territorial states and their governments can gain their ends by relying on military prowess. Political approaches, ethical realism, and a diplomacy of compassion and compromise are the only imaginable building blocks for security in the 21st century.

31. REMEMBER, PALESTINE IS THE REGION'S FESTERING SORE

Rami G. Khouri

This article was originally published in the Lebanese English-language daily newspaper the Daily Star *(21 August 2006).*

We have a very simple choice before us in the Middle East: we can get serious about working together to give the people of this region a chance to live normal lives in peace and security; or we can all act silly in the ways of provincial chieftains, as many public figures in Lebanon, Syria, Iran, Israel, and the United States have done in recent days.

The chances of achieving a regionwide peace in the Middle East are slim to nonexistent right now, because the key non-Arab players are focusing on the wrong issues. They are trying to manage or eliminate the symptoms of our region's tensions instead of addressing the root causes. Hizballah and Iran are among the best examples of this.

Israel and the US are obsessed with disarming Hizballah and confronting Iran. But a quarter of a century ago neither of these issues existed. How Hizballah and Iran became so problematic is worth recalling. Until 1979, Iran under the Shah was a close ally and friend of the US and Israel, and Hizballah was not even born. What happened in the three decades from the mid-1970s to today? Many things. The most consistent one was that we all allowed the Arab–Israeli conflict to fester unresolved. Its bitterness kept seeping out from its Palestine–Israel core to corrode many other dimensions of the region.

The constant clashes between Israel and Lebanon since the late 1960s derived heavily from the unresolved Palestinian–Israeli conflict that started with the 1948 war. Since Iran's 1979 revolution, Islamist revolutionary zeal has found effective expression in its close association with Hizballah, which Iranian Revolutionary Guards were instrumental in establishing and training. Tehran's assistance to Hamas today follows a similar pattern. A non-Arab power such as Iran exploits the resentment against Israel and the US throughout the Arab world to make political inroads into Arab regions. If the Arab–Israeli conflict had been resolved decades ago, Iran would not have this opportunity.

Hizballah has many people working backwards. While the American–Israeli effort to disarm Hizballah aims mainly to protect Israel, the fact is that Hizballah has developed its military capability primarily in response to a need to protect Lebanon from repeated Israeli attacks over the past four decades. (Lebanese calls to disarm Hizballah are motivated more by a desire to prevent the party from bringing more ruin from Israeli attacks, or to prevent it from taking over the country's political system and aligning it with Syria and Iran.)

The way to end Hizballah's status as the only non-state armed group in Lebanon is to rewind the reel, and go to the heart of the problem that caused Hizballah to develop its formidable military capabilities in the first place. If we solve the Arab–Israeli conflict in a fair manner, according to UN resolutions, we would eliminate two critical political forces that now nourish Hizballah's armed defiance: the Israeli threat to Lebanon, and the ability of Syria and Iran to exploit the ongoing conflict with Israel by working through Lebanon.

Iran has its own reasons, including some valid ones, for developing a full nuclear fuel cycle, though the potential atomic weapons capability that derives from this is more problematic. Iran's political meddling in Lebanon and other Arab lands is another issue. Yet it is linked umbilically to the assertion of Islamist identity, Shia empowerment, anti-Western defiance, and domestic challenges to autocratic Arab regimes—four dynamics that have often been associated with, and exacerbated by, the ongoing Arab–Israeli conflict.

Israel's persistent attempts to secure its place in this region by military force have always generated a greater Arab will to fight it, now also supported by Iran. Local attempts to secure its borders—occupations, surrogate armies, cross-border attacks, separation walls, massive punishment and humiliation of civilian populations—have not worked for Israel, and only generate more determined and capable resistance, as with Hizballah. Israel will also fail in its desire to subcontract its security to foreign or regional states, as it is attempting to do through the international force in southern Lebanon, or by having Turkey prevent arms shipments to Hizballah from Iran.

Every tough issue in this region—Lebanon, Iraq, Syria, Iran, terrorism, radicalism, armed resistance groups—is somehow linked to the consequences of the festering Israeli–Palestinian conflict. The politicians and government leaders who dominate this region, or engage it from Western capitals, all look like rank amateurs or intemperate brutes as they flail at symptoms instead of grappling with the core issue that has seen this region spin off into ever greater circles of violence since the 1970s.

A comprehensive Arab–Israeli peace agreement is achievable from the Arab side, to judge by the repeated offering of the 2002 Arab summit peace proposal. Israel and the US must quickly decide if they too can become sensible and work for a comprehensive peace as the most effective way to reduce and then reverse the cycles of resentment, radicalism, and resistance that now define much of the Arab-Islamic Middle East.

AFTERWORD
Nubar Hovsepian

Parts of this text appeared in "The Palestinian Refugee Camps in Lebanon: More Than a Lebanese Problem," ZNet, 24 June 2007.

This book offers historical and political context to explain the complexities of Lebanon's local, regional, and international predicaments. Most of the chapters in this book were completed in early 2007. Despite the fact that some details have changed, I contend that the framework of the analysis remains intact.[1]

More than a year has elapsed since the start of the 34-day war of 2006. No one emerged victorious; instead, each party to the conflict has paid a price. The Israeli government has been weakened. Hizballah has lost some of its luster, and the Lebanese government remains unable to govern effectively. The Seniora government failed to oversee a national reconstruction effort that could, as Sayed and Tzannatos argue in this book, lay the foundation for modern nation building in a divided polity.[2] Furthermore, the Lebanese political class has so far been incapable of reaching agreement on a power-sharing formula to guide Lebanon out of the ruins of the devastating war. In effect, as noted in the introduction above, Lebanon is faced with a predicament that requires alignment with one of its regional neighbors: Syria or Israel (and its international allies, namely the US). The absence of alternatives suggests that the reconstitution and reform of the Lebanese political system along more secular lines is a deferred dream.

Lebanon's geographical location has forced it into the vortex of the festering Arab–Israeli conflict, so Lebanon continues to serve as a theater for regional conflict. Despite Syria's formal withdrawal from Lebanon in 2005, Syria's ability to interfere in Lebanese politics has not waned. The Syrian government wants to undermine the UN-mandated international tribunal charged with investigating the assassination of the late Prime Minister Rafiq Hariri. It is quite likely that the Syrian regime is heavily implicated in the assassination, and the Lebanese political landscape remains deeply divided over this issue. The March 14 Hariri-led opposition favors the tribunal, and Hizballah and its allies reject it as an infringement on Lebanese sovereignty. It is this context that may explain the timing of the flare-up between the Lebanese military and Fatah al-Islam that began on May 19, 2007. Though the Syrian regime is opposed to Salafi Islamic movements, it has facilitated the entry of this gang in northern Lebanon to divert attention from the tribunal.

One of the outcomes of the perpetual "war on terror" is the emergence of many mini bin Ladens, whose perspectives are essentially nihilistic and murderous. Such gangs, such as Fatah al-Islam, are vehemently opposed by the overwhelming majority of Palestinians in Lebanon. But the fighting in northern Lebanon cannot be explained by this alone. Rather, we need to explore the context of Palestinian life in Lebanon. Almost 400,000 Palestinians live in Lebanon, and a large percentage of this population lives in twelve formal refugee camps scattered throughout the Lebanese landscape.

The Palestinian population did not come to Lebanon gratuitously; they are the original victims of the 1948 war, which caused their diaspora. Thus, since the establishment of Israel, Lebanon has been in the vortex of the Arab–Israeli conflict. Upon their arrival in Lebanon they were herded into temporary refugee camps, which over time were transformed into permanent slums and shantytowns. Before the reemergence of the modern Palestinian national movement, Palestinians were under the control of the Lebanese *deuxieme bureau* [internal security]. But with the growth of the PLO and the Lebanese secular forces (Lebanese National Movement), Palestinians secured some freedoms and rights. By 1969 the relations between the Lebanese government and the PLO were governed by the "Cairo Agreement," brokered by President Nasser of Egypt on November 3, 1969. This agreement served to legitimate and control the Palestinian commando presence in Lebanon. After the 1970–1971 civil war in Jordan, the PLO transferred its center of activities to Lebanon.

The presence of the PLO in the 1970s contributed to the growth of the Palestinian and Lebanese national movements, with Israeli raids contributing to their mutual ascendance. For example, in April 1973 the Israeli Mossad assassinated three top Fatah leaders in Beirut (less than 200 meters from my apartment). A major demonstration ensued that pitted the Lebanese national movement against its soon-to-be Phalangist enemies in the civil war. Also in 1973, a clash between the Lebanese army and the PLO broke out. My apartment was destroyed in the crossfire;

this same neighborhood of Harat Hreik would be pulverized by the Israelis during the summer of 2006.

The escalations in 1973 led to the renegotiation of Lebanese–PLO relations through the adoption of the "Melkart Understanding" in May of that year, which partly reaffirmed and partly circumscribed the Cairo Agreement. These revisions did not prevent the obliteration of the Tel Zaatar Palestinian refugee camp in 1976 by the combined forces of Syria and the Phalangists. After the forced evacuation of PLO forces in 1982 from Lebanon, these agreements remained in place, but the realities on the ground changed dramatically, and with chilling effect on the dwellers of Palestinian refugee camps.

From 1969 to 1982 the camps were mostly governed by various PLO factions. The United Nations Relief and Works Agency (UNRWA) provided a modicum of social, educational, and employment services. But after 1982, the PLO, for all practical purposes, abandoned its responsibilities to its people in the camps. Left unprotected, the unimaginable took place in Sabra and Shatila— massacres conducted by Lebanese militiamen under the supervision of Israeli forces (General Sharon lost his job because of this tragedy, but his Lebanese counterparts were later honored by postwar ministerial portfolios). With no one to protect them, Palestinians have lived fearful of mass expulsions, a refrain that enters Lebanese political discourse periodically.

The camp dwellers have, for the most part, been relatively quiescent since 1982. Their life conditions are even more precarious and tragic than those of their beleaguered compatriots in Gaza. For example, the World Bank issues a quarterly publication, *The West Bank and Gaza Update*, the IMF and UNESCO issue frequent reports on Palestinian conditions, but no agency seems determined to shed light on the conditions of Palestinian refugees in Lebanon. They are truly the forgotten of the earth. According to Lebanese laws, Palestinians are denied work opportunities in most domains of economic activity. If they manage to get out of the country, it is likely that they will be unable to return. Social disintegration has led to rising problems: severe unemployment, insecurity, prostitution, and drug addiction. The Palestinian experience in Lebanon has been aptly captured by Rosemary Sayigh in the title of her book: "Too Many Enemies." Who is responsible for these refugees? At present, no one. The absence of central authority (as in Yugoslavia, Iraq, and Lebanon of yesteryear) is a perfect incubator for the emergence of nihilistic groupings, civil war, and disorder.

The solution to the current fighting cannot be undertaken by the Lebanese alone. Since 1948 and the creation of the Palestinian diaspora, the general wisdom has been that the refugee problem in Lebanon and elsewhere cannot be resolved until a formal Israeli–Palestinian peace is negotiated. This approach is evasive and callous—it reduces Palestinian refugees to perpetual vulnerability. They are constantly threatened with expulsion. But to where? Where is their homeland?

Once the fighting stops, serious talks between the Lebanese government and Palestinian organizations in camp Nahr al-Bared and across Lebanon must start in earnest. But agreement between these parties is impossible without international guarantees and funding. Palestinian camps should be placed under an international UN trusteeship, to guarantee their safety from within and without. Palestinian civic organizations will have to step up to create viable systems of governance, under temporary UN supervision. The Lebanese state will demand the respect of its sovereignty, but such respect should not be predicated on the continued oppression of the Palestinian refugees. The international community, which contributed to the creation of the modern Palestinian diaspora, as well as wealthy Arab states must step up with serious funding.

Given the implosion of the Palestine national movement, the Palestinians of Lebanon are in the unfortunate position of being manipulated by exogenous forces like Fatah al-Islam, or other Syrian-controlled organizations (such as the PFLP-General Command). The latter might stir troubles in Lebanon to foil international attempts to implicate it in the 1988 Lockerbie bombing of Pan Am 103.[3] To prevent and to curtail Lebanese–Palestinian fissures, the UN must immediately issue a report on the misery of Palestinian refugees in Lebanon. This must be followed by a UN resolution to establish a trusteeship over the camps. Failure to do so will result in further tragedy and will produce more mini bin Ladens, and could provide cause for widening conflict in Lebanon.

The 34-day war of 2006 did not resolve any of the sources of tension that afflict Lebanon and the Middle East region. Instead, the region has been pushed to the brink of more conflict and violence. Indeed, the US and Israel are expected to train jointly at Israel's new National Training

Center to prepare for further military campaigns in Gaza, Lebanon, the West Bank, and Syria.[4]

NOTES

1 Data on casualties (both deaths and injuries) and on physical damage and cost estimates of the war is difficult to ascertain with exactitude. Full accounting needs more time.

2 See Jim Quilty and Lysandra Ohrstrom, "The Second Time as Farce: Stories of Another Lebanese Reconstruction." *Middle East Report* 243 (Summer 2007).

3 See Hugh Miles, "Inconvenient Truths," *London Review of Books* 21 June 2007.

4 Barbara Opall, "Marines to Train at New Israeli Center," *Marine Corps Times* 25 June 2007.

CONTRIBUTORS

Asᶜad Abukhalil is professor of political science at California State University at Stanislaus and visiting professor at the University of California at Berkeley. His blog is at angryarab.blogspot.com.

Asli U. Bali serves as the Irving S. Ribicoff Fellow at the Yale Law School, where her research focuses on the politics of enforcing international law. She also has a private law practice in New York, where she has worked pro bono representing immigrants detained in connection with the post–September 11 sweep of arrests of men of Arab, South Asian, and Muslim descent.

Phyllis Bennis is a fellow of the Institute for Policy Studies in Washington, DC and the Transnational Institute in Amsterdam. Her most recent books are *Challenging Empire: How People, Governments, and the UN Defy US Power* (Olive Branch Press, 2006) and *Understanding the Palestinian–Israeli Conflict: A Primer* (Olive Branch Press, 2007).

Frida Berrigan is a senior research associate at the World Policy Institute's Arms Trade Resource Center. A contributing editor to *In These Times* and a columnist with *Foreign Policy in Focus*, Berrigan writes on arms export policy and military spending, and has recently been focusing on US weapons sales to Israel, including cluster bombs. She is the primary author of *US Weapons at War 2005: Promoting Freedom or Fueling Conflict?* (World Policy Institute).

Azmi Bishara is a leading Palestinian political activist and former member of the Israeli Knesset. Bishara is former head of the philosophy department at Bir Zeit University, and writes a column online in *Al-Ahram Weekly*.

Noam Chomsky, professor of linguistics at the Massachusetts Institute of Technology, is the author recently of *9-11* (Open Media, 2001), a national bestseller, and *Failed States* (Metropolitan, 2006). His articles and books revolutionized the contemporary study of linguisitics, and his political essays are widely read and translated throughout the world. In 2003 a profile of Chomsky in the *New Yorker* described him as one of the most widely cited scholars in history.

Georges Corm is former Lebanese minister of finance and author of *Le Proche-Orient éclaté 1956–2006* (Gallimard, 2006) and *Orient-Occident, la fracture imaginaire* (La Découverte, 2005).

Lara Deeb, a cultural anthropologist, is assistant professor of women's studies at the University of California at Irvine. She is also an academy scholar at Harvard University's Academy for International and Area Studies. She is the author of *An Enchanted Modern: Gender and Public Piety in Shi'i Lebanon* (Princeton University Press, 2006), as well as of a number of articles on the transformation of Shiite religious ritual, Islamic women's participation in the public sphere, and Hizballah in Lebanon.

Richard Falk is Milbank Professor of International Law emeritus at Princeton University, and since 2002, visiting distinguished professor in global studies at the University of California at Santa Barbara. He is chair of the Nuclear Age Peace Foundation. His most recent books are *Crimes of War: Iraq* (co-edited with Irene Gendzier and Robert Jay Lifton, Nation Books, 2006), *The Declining World Order* (Routledge, 2004), and with Howard Friel, *The Record of the Paper: How the* New York Times *Misreports American Foreign Policy* (Verso, 2004).

Irene L. Gendzier is professor of political science at Boston University. Among her recent publications are "Democracy, Deception, and the Arms Trade: The US, Iraq, and Weapons of Mass Destruction," *Middle East Report 234*; *Crimes of War*, co-editor (Nation Books, 2006); and a new and updated edition of *Notes from the Minefield: United States Intervention in Lebanon and the Middle East* (Columbia University Press, 2007). She is currently working on a study entitled "Dying to Forget: Aspects of US Foreign Policy in the Middle East."

Fred Halliday is professor of international relations at the London School of Economics. His publications include *The Middle East in International Relations* (Cambridge, 2005) and *100 Myths about the Middle East* (University of California, 2005).

William D. Hartung is the president's fellow at the World Policy Institute at the New School. He is an expert on the arms trade and military spending, and author of *And Weapons For All* (HarperCollins, 1995). His most recent book is *How Much Are You Making on the War, Daddy?—A Quick and Dirty Guide to War Profiteering in the Bush Administration* (Nation Books, 2004). His articles and interviews have been featured in many places, including *Foreign Policy*, the *New York Times*, and the *Washington Post*.

Nubar Hovsepian is associate professor of political science and international studies at Chapman University and the author of the forthcoming *The Politics of Palestinian Education: State vs. Nation-Building*. He has written and edited four books (in Arabic) and has published numerous articles—on the Arab–Israeli conflict, the crises in the Gulf, and on the competing ideological currents in the Arab world—in professional journals and the international press. In 1982–1984 he served as a political affairs officer for the United Nations International Conference on the Question of Palestine.

Assaf Kfoury is a mathematician, computer scientist, and longtime political activist. An Arab American who grew up in Beirut and Cairo, he is currently professor of computer science at Boston University.

Rashid Khalidi is the author of *Resurrecting Empire* (Beacon, 2004), *Palestinian Identity* (Columbia University Press, 1997), and most recently *The Iron Cage* (Beacon, 2006). He holds the Edward Said Chair in Arab Studies at Columbia University, where he heads the Middle East Institute.

Rami Khouri is an internationally syndicated columnist, the director of the Issam Fares Institute at the American University of Beirut, and editor-at-large of the Beirut-based *Daily Star*.

Elias Khoury is director and editor-in-chief of the literary supplement of the Beirut daily *Al-Nahar*. He is a novelist, playwright, and journalist. The English translation of his novel *Bab al-Shams* [*Gate of the Sun*] (Archipelago Books, 2006) was a 2006 *New York Times* Notable Book. Khoury is also Global Distinguished Professor in the department of Middle Eastern and Islamic studies at New York University.

Yitzhak Laor writes in Hebrew, is editor of *Mita'am: A Review of Radical Literature and Thought*, lives in Tel Aviv, and is looking for a job in the United States.

Ziad Majed is a researcher and political writer in Beirut. He is one of the founders of the Democratic Left Movement, and his latest book (in Arabic) is the *Lebanese Spring and the Missing State* (Al-Nahar, 2006).

Ussama Makdisi teaches Middle Eastern history at Rice University and is the first Arab-American Educational Foundation Chair of Arab Studies. He is the author of *The Culture of Sectarianism: Community, History, and Violence in Nineteenth-Century Ottoman Lebanon* (University of California Press, 2000) and co-editor with Paul Silverstein of *Memory and Violence in the Middle East and North Africa* (Indiana University Press, 2006).

Yoav Peled teaches political science at Tel Aviv University. He is co-author, with Gershon Shafir, of *Being Israeli: The Dynamics of Multiple Citizenship* (Cambridge University Press, 2002).

Gabriel Piterberg teaches history at UCLA. He is the author of *An Ottoman Tragedy: History and Historiography* (University of California, 2003), and he is completing a book called *Myths, Politics, and Scholarship in Israel* (Verso, forthcoming).

Sara Roy is the author of *The Gaza Strip: The Political Economy of De-development* (Institute for Palestine Studies 1995, 2001), now in its second edition with a third edition forthcoming; and editor of *The Economics of Middle East Peace: A Reassessment* (JAI Press, 1999). Her most recent book is *Failing Peace: Gaza and the Palestinian–Israeli Conflict* (Pluto Press, 2007) and she is completing *Between Extremism and Civism: Political Islam in Palestine* (Princeton University Press, forthcoming).

Hanady Salman is managing editor of *Al-Safir* newspaper in Beirut. She earned a master's degree in Arab studies from Georgetown University and her bachelor's in political science at the American University in Beirut. She is in charge of human interest and local news at the newspaper.

Rasha Salti, a curator and freelance writer, lives in New York and Beirut. She is the director of CinemaEast Film Festival. She edited *Insights into Syrian Cinema: Essays and Conversations with Contemporary Filmmakers* (Rattapallax, 2007).

Haneen Sayed is lead operations officer in the MENA region of the World Bank and is currently stationed in Beirut, working on social development issues for Lebanon, Jordan, and Syria. Earlier she was country manager for Korea and Myanmar and senior advisor on the Middle East to the executive director. She has written about the economic impact of the financial crisis in East Asia on human capital development, the relationship between public spending and outcomes in the social sectors, and sex segregation in the labor force.

Kirsten Scheid is assistant professor of anthropology at the American University of Beirut. She defended her dissertation on contemporary art production in the Arab world at Princeton University in 2005. With her husband, the writer Samah Idriss, she has produced a series of Arabic children's books and co-founded Nadi al-Saaha cultural facility center. Their children are Sariya and Naye.

Virginia Tilley is presently serving as a chief research specialist at the Human Sciences Research Council in Pretoria, South Africa. She is author of *The One-State Solution: A Breakthrough for Peace in the Israeli–Palestinian Deadlock* (University of Michigan Press, 2005).

Fawwaz Traboulsi teaches history and political science at the American University of Beirut and is visiting professor at Columbia University. Before becoming an academic he was a journalist. He continues to write on a breadth of topics, ranging from democracy in the Arab world to Orientalism. His most recent publication is *A Modern History of Lebanon* (Pluto Press, 2007).

Hiam Turfe-Brinjikji emigrated from Lebanon when she was seven. She works as a high-school counselor. She dedicates her story to her husband, Abdul Hamid Brinjikji, and their children, Waleed, Sarra, and Lena.

Zafiris Tzannatos is advisor to the World Bank Institute, having previously served as advisor to the bank's managing director, sector manager for social protection in the MENA region, and leader of the bank's child labor program. He has more than 150 publications, including 14 books on labor economics and broader social policy. He has held many senior academic positions in Europe and elsewhere, including the chair of economics at the American University of Beirut.

Stephen Zunes is professor of politics and international studies at the University of San Francisco. He is the author of *Tinderbox: US Middle East Policy and the Roots of Terrorism* (Common Courage Press, 2003), *Western Sahara: War, Nationalism and Conflict Irresolution in Northwest Africa* (Syracuse University Press, forthcoming), and scores of journal articles and chapters in edited volumes on US Middle East policy and related issues. He serves as Middle East editor for *Foreign Policy in Focus* (www.fpif.org) and as a consultant and board member for a number of peace and human rights organizations.

Translators

Sinan Antoon is an Iraqi poet, novelist, and literary critic. He is also assistant professor at the Gallatin School of individualized study, New York University. For this volume he translated two articles by Elias Khoury (Chapter 25).

Michael K. Scott earned a degree in Arabic literature from the University of California at Berkeley. He teaches Arabic at McDaniel College in Westminster, Maryland, and in his spare time translates newspaper commentaries by major journalists and writers. For this volume he translated Elias Khoury's essay "Meditations upon Destruction."

INDEX